CALMIRE

Man and Nature

BY

HENRY HOLT

AUTHOR OF "STURMSEE: MAN AND MAN"

SIXTH EDITION, REVISED

WILDSIDE PRESS

Sixth Edition, Revised
March, 1906

COPYRIGHT, 1906, BY HOUGHTON, MIFFLIN & CO.

―――――

First edition published May 1892; Second (with considerable alterations), August 1892; Third, in 2 vols. for England (with slight modifications), October 1892; Fourth, 2 vols. in one (with some restatements and minor alterations), January 1893; Fifth, 1 vol. (revised and enlarged), May 1905.

CONTENTS.

PART I.

CHAPTER		PAGE
I.	A Real Ghost, ...	3
II.	A Youth of the Period, ...	14
III.	A Girl not of the Period, ...	19
IV.	A Man of Several Periods, ...	24
V.	The First Bout, ...	28
VI.	An Afternoon Drive, ...	32
VII.	A Town out of the Beaten Path, ...	40
VIII.	The Unjust and the Just, ...	53
IX.	The Band begins to Play, ...	68
X.	Sympathy?	77
XI.	The New Genesis, ...	84
XII.	Wilful Woman, ...	100
XIII.	New Foreshadowings from Old Questions, . .	110
XIV.	The Granzines, ...	124
XV.	Another Bout, ...	139
XVI.	A Tough Subject though not a New One, . .	144
XVII.	Mr. Courtenay Experiences some Sentiments and a Visit, ...	153
XVIII.	Faith and Fact, ...	160
XIX.	Courtenay and his Sister, ...	176
XX.	The All-including, ... ,	183

Contents.

CHAPTER		PAGE
XXI.	At a Tennis Match,	201
XXII.	Muriel takes a Short Innings,	216
XXIII.	Aids to Matrimony,	230
XXIV.	Gentle Magic and Hard Philosophy,	244
XXV.	A Bit of Knight-errantry,	258
XXVI.	In the Same Boat,	267
XXVII.	Dependence,	287
XXVIII.	Absence Omits to Conquer,	302
XXIX.	In Another Boat,	305
XXX.	Going Wooing,	316
XXXI.	Banished,	329
XXXII.	"Du sollst entbehren,"	335
XXXIII.	A Little Diplomacy,	340
XXXIV.	The Encounter,	345
XXXV.	Another Encounter,	354
XXXVI.	A Soulless Universe,	360
XXXVII.	Muriel Calmire to Legrand Calmire,	365

PART II.

XXXVIII.	Legrand Calmire to Muriel Caimire,	373
XXXIX.	Revelation,	382
XL.	The Natural and the Supernatural,	395
XLI.	An Outside Argument,	405
XLII.	The Essential Religion,	412
XLIII.	Mary's Story,	432
XLIV.	Courtenay's Faith,	444
XLV.	The Moral Order,	454
XLVI.	Misery makes Strange Bedfellows,	470
XLVII.	The Unknown God,	480

Contents.

CHAPTER		PAGE
XLVIII.	God and Man,	496
XLIX.	More Correspondence,	504
L.	Cain,	513
LI.	Tantalus,	522
LII.	Our only Glimpse of Town,	527
LIII.	Where Man may Go,	538
LIV.	Man's Range Enough for Man,	555
LV.	Making the Best of a Bad Case,	566
LVI.	Some Travel and Some Letters,	576
LVII.	Extracts arranged from the Diary of a Penitent,	588
LVIII.	De Profundis,	606
LIX.	Facing It,	624
LX.	Where All Roads Meet,	635
LXI.	Noblesse Oblige,	668
LXII.	A Hunter's Find,	684
LXIII.	The Finder's Hunt,	693
LXIV.	The Beginning,	702

PART I
CHAOS

CALMIRE.

CHAPTER I.

A REAL GHOST.

"THIS is outrageous! She has rung four times already!" exclaimed Nina.

"The door is open," answered her mother beside her in the carriage. "Send the coachman in."

"No! He had better stay with his horses. I'll go and see what it means myself. Let me out, please."

"Let Marie go in."

"No; I'll go myself."

And she got out. It was one Summer evening not far from 1880, when the two ladies and their maid reached Fleuvemont. Till within a few weeks, the house had been closed for two years—since Mr. Calmire had gone abroad immediately after his wife's death. Now he was back in New York, where he had found his cousin (by marriage) and life-long friend, Mrs. Hugh Wahring, in town later than her wont, and in a predicament. She had not settled for Nina and herself that most harassing of standard questions, where to spend the Summer. She had supposed it settled, and satisfactorily, a month before, when Mr. Wahring had seen them comfortably fixed in their house at Newport. All of them were vastly pleased with the new addition to it, and he had started off to visit his firm's office in China, to determine the question of yielding to the then recent revolution in trade, and closing the office up. A week after the arrival at Newport, a fog set in, which led Mrs. Wahring to order fires. The flues in the new addition had been built as usual, though the usual conflagration which they occasioned had not been subdued with the usual success, but had burned the house down, and sent the ladies back to their town house without their natural guide—the husband and father—to determine their course for the season.

Mr. Calmire determined it, however, by saying: " Now, Cousin Hilda, the judicious gods evidently burned down that well-insured house to reward my virtues. I need you and Nina this Summer. For one reason and another, my children are all away, though I had to make some of them go. You know how lonely I am. I have ordered Fleuvemont opened. Pierre has been up there, and reports everything ready. But it will be a dreary place with no woman in it, and I cannot count on even Muriel to stick by me long at a time. I must have you and Nina there. Go up with me Wednesday evening, and lay me under a lasting obligation."

After some demur, a few inquiries, and unmistakable indications that Calmire meant what he said, as he always did when he spoke seriously, Mrs. Wahring, without consulting Nina, said that they would accept the invitation.

"You will grant the favor, you mean. Wednesday, then, we leave Forty-second Street at eight. I'm sorry that I have a special appointment which prevents my going earlier in the day."

Wednesday turned out an oppressively hot day. At three o'clock, this note was put in Mrs. Wahring's hands:

"35 WALL STREET, Wednesday, 2.10 P.M.

"DEAR COUSIN HILDA : The person whom I was to see to-day has been delayed some hours by a railway breakdown. The business is very important and cannot be postponed. I must stay in town overnight. It's too hot for you and Nina to stay, and you are all packed for going. Your staying would add to the discomfort I must suffer. Pray go. Take the six train. As you're alone, it will be pleasanter to get in early. I have telegraphed the servants to expect you. I will join you to-morrow.

"Ever yours, L. C."

So here they were, at Fleuvemont, in the dark, and of the servants they knew to be inside, not one paying any attention to the hackman's ringing. Much less had any of them taken the pains to meet the guests at the station. And Miss Nina Wahring, among whose many undisciplined powers at eighteen was a temper, had that power in a very pretty state of excitation.

She rushed into the house.

She had heard the place described as impressive, and so it was. The hall was of noble proportions. The doors on the sides were large and dark, and framed in heavy carvings. The walls were paneled with dark oak to within a yard of the ceiling, which also was paneled. Between the ceiling and the wall-panels, was a frieze of dark leather, covered with antlers, antique weapons, and bits of armor. At the remote end of the hall, on high pedestals, were the effigies of two knights in full mail. The lamps were placed where they could not distract attention from the whole effect, so the light was subdued, and over all was silence.

Nina's impetuous steps grew slower almost upon the threshold. Her irritation was forgotten, and she felt as if she had come suddenly into some land of dreams. She walked lightly, as if afraid of breaking a spell. Soon, at the left of the mailed figures and at the foot of the broad niched staircase, appeared the light, softened through great globes, which rose from a mass of weapons stacked amid a base of shields. Passing to the farther side of these, she rested her left hand on one of them, and gazed up to where, beyond the gloomy curves of the stairs, shining through the roof-light, she saw two stars.

She made a lovely picture as she stood there—her slight figure, in its diaphanous Summer drapery, thrown in bold relief against the dark panels behind her—her fair, upturned face and careless red-gold hair against the great dark-lined hat, almost aureoled by the soft lights at whose pedestal she half supported herself.

For some moments she had forgotten her purpose, when it was brought back by the noise of a door closing upstairs. She called:

"I say, there!"

No answer, the silence gaining in impressiveness by the contrast with her echoed voice. A feeling came over her that she did not half like, but she imperiously smothered it, and waited for some repetition of the noise. Soon another door closed and footsteps began descending the stairs.

"No need of calling now!" she thought wearily, for she was very tired.

A flight or two above, there emerged from the shadows, a tall figure in dark dress. As it came down, she slowly realized, with a feeling almost uncanny, that the brown costume was not a livery, but a doublet with wide lace collar, trunks, and jack-boots with great spurs, and slung over one arm was a heavy sword. The face, though she could not see it very clearly, was plainly young, but serious, with a square brow, deep eyes, and a straight nose. The hair was cut close, and there was a dark mustache. The young Roundhead advanced slowly, lost in thought, unobservant of the graceful addition that had been made to the massive objects below him.

She was rapt in contemplation of the noble presence, until it reached the last platform of the staircase, stopped, gazed at her a few seconds, and then said slowly, in a rich, sweet voice:

"If you're a vision, pray don't vanish before I have a closer view."

"If you're a ghost, you take a very mundane tone for one."

"I am a ghost, but you needn't be afraid of me."

"Thank you, I won't. But why do you take the trouble to be a ghost? Is it your own sins or other people's that disturb your rest?"

"A good deal of both, sometimes. I'm only one of Carlyle's ghosts, though, just as you are, if you're really not a dream. He says we're all ghosts."

"Ghosts get pretty tired and hungry, then, sometimes. Didn't you expect us? I didn't come to vanish."

"I'm very glad of that," he said, descending the stairs. "But I didn't expect anybody. I came myself only half an hour ago, to go to a ball. I'm Mr. Muriel Calmire, very much at your service, and I have the pleasure of addressing—?"

"Miss Wahring;" and she added, holding out her hand: "Perhaps we'd better test each other's substantiality, especially as you're one of the family, and I'm going to stay here ever so long."

They shook hands very substantially for a first meeting, and he said: "Oh yes! I've heard the name in the family. I think I met your father once. General, isn't he?"

"Yes, was,—of volunteers. But it's odd your father didn't let you know we were coming."

"Uncle Grand isn't my father," he said; "but he's nearer a father than anybody else. He lets me come and go as I please. He didn't know I was coming now. When did you come?"

"Why, we've just got here, and mamma's waiting in the carriage while we're discussing family history."

"Oh!" he exclaimed, and, flinging down the big sword, started for the carriage without a word of apology.

When he emerged from the door, and ran down in the dim light to the first landing, whence two flights of steps wound down to the right and left, Mrs. Wahring, whose annoyance had been increased by the delay inside, hailed him with:

"Come, help the maid with these things. You people seem very careless. Didn't you get your master's telegram?"

"You mean Mr. Calmire's?" he said.

"Certainly. Who else employs you?"

"Nobody else!" and he reached the carriage-door and offered his hand.

Mrs. Wahring, not stopping to reflect that the Calmire servants were not apt to wear mustaches, ignored the proffered hand, as she got out, and said:

"There are two dressing-bags in there, two parasols, and two umbrellas tied together. One trunk, that you may help the man with, is behind. The rest will be up in the morning."

Then she started up the steps. Muriel took some of the things, leaving the rest for the maid, and followed Mrs. Wahring. His quicker steps brought him beside her on the landing, and after two or three paces more, he dropped a parasol, and it broke.

"Stupid!" she exclaimed, not quite intending him to hear. But he did hear, and turning to her, half angry and half amused, said:

"I've not been very long at this work;" but he explained no farther, and was too angry to express any regret.

Nina was at the door, waiting for them. When he stopped to pick up the pieces of the parasol, Mrs. Wahring got ahead of him, and when he appeared, with the things, in the half light, she exclaimed to her daughter:

"Well! that's the strangest livery I ever saw!"

The two young people broke into a laugh. Muriel's little irritation was soothed by it; and as soon as Nina could, she said:

"Mamma, this is Mr. Muriel Calmire."

Mrs. Wahring flushed at first, but soon joined in the laugh, shook hands with him, and said:

"How could you let me speak to you in that manner? It wasn't fair."

"You're probably entitled to choose your own manner of speech," he answered, still a little unamiable.

"But you deceived me."

"You deceived yourself."

"Mr. Calmire told me," she continued, "that you weren't expected for some time. Of course I was out of patience with the servants. I couldn't see in the dark that you were a gentleman, and" (after a little pause) "perhaps you'll excuse my saying that I don't think it was quite the act of one not to let me know who you were."

He flushed, and said bluntly: "Your tone of voice irritated me, and when I saw the joke, it seemed too good to let go all at once."

"I *was* out of temper," said Mrs. Wahring, "and I had no right to go as far as I did. I beg your pardon."

"Pray don't mention it. Consider me *always*

your servant, Madam." He accompanied his words with a bow and a smile, but apparently he did not realize that he had anything to apologize for.

"But what in the world are you doing in that costume?" asked Mrs. Wahring. "There's nothing going on here to-night, is there?"

"No; but I'm going off as soon as I see you taken care of. I wonder what ails those confounded servants. Didn't *anybody* know you were coming?"

"Yes; at least Mr. Calmire telegraphed, and we rang and rang."

"The bell must be out of order," he said. "Uncle Grand has been away so long that pretty much everything is. I'll ring again. Pray be seated," and he motioned them toward one of the great Italian carved benches. Then he opened the drawing-room door next them, put his hand inside, and pulled a heavy old-fashioned bell-cord. In a moment a maid appeared, and he said:

"Where are the men?"

"Down at the village, sir. Didn't know they'd be needed before ten."

"Didn't you get a telegram about these ladies?"

"No, sir. We only expected Mr. Calmire in the eleven-o'clock train."

"Country telegraph offices!" exclaimed Muriel. "Is the library lit?" he asked the maid, who said yes, and then he explained to the ladies, as he led them to the room: "Evidently the lost telegram contained Uncle Grand's instructions about you, and so the drawing-room is not lit. He always has them light the library for him, though."

The great room they entered was two stories high, with two galleries, and on the floor, alcoved shelves out to the edge of the lower gallery. The room had been built by Calmire's father, who was a collector of vast quantities of books that he seldom read. Calmire, on the other hand, was quite a student.

The tired ladies were put between a huge study-table and the great fireplace, in two big, comfortable Turkish chairs—comfortable at least in Muriel's eyes, though the backs were not straight enough for a woman's ideal; and Mr. Muriel disposed himself in an old Canterbury chair, before the logs which, though unlit in the Summer night, still looked comfortably suggestive: and he, with the big fireplace, the old chair, and his Cromwellian dress, made a picture that the ladies never forgot. For a large room, the one they were in was amazingly cosy, partly because it had been much lived in by a cheerful spirit fond of light and color.

"Now, Mary, have you anything to eat?" said Mr. Muriel to the maid, in a characteristically direct way, indifferent to the minor conventionalities that would have led to domestic discussions aside, or to an apology for entering upon them before his stranger guests.

"Oh yes, sir; I can order dinner at once," she answered.

"No, no!" protested Mrs. Wahring. "We had something substantial before we started."

"But Miss Wahring has already plead guilty to an appetite," said Muriel.

"Yes," said the young lady. "It was too hot to

eat in town, except as a precautionary measure. I'm ready to do it seriously now, though."

"Good Lord!" thought Muriel to himself, "there goes my vision!" He was very young and very imaginative, and therefore, of course, a good deal of a fool. This shade of "disillusion," as he saw fit to consider it, made it easier for him, after a few more explanations and the necessary orders for the ladies' comfort, to say to them:

"And now I must bid you good-night. I have an appointment and a six-mile drive before me. I trust you will find yourselves entirely at home, and that to-morrow I can hear you say you have been."

He bowed and was off. Somehow the almost cordial beginning that the various *contretemps* had given to their acquaintance, did not seem quite sustained. So much spontaneity seldom is, in our self-conscious and sophisticated age; though the relations with each other that we sometimes build when there is time enough, are probably as enduring as they are deliberate.

CHAPTER II.

A YOUTH OF THE PERIOD.

This Mr. Muriel Calmire was rather a chaotic young person, in both ancestry and education. His family was of French extraction and pronounced its name in the French way. His great-grandfather, Honoré Calmire, a Louisiana planter, had, while studying abroad, married a daughter of Nina's great-grandfather, General Freiherr von Wahring; their son Legrand was educated in New England, and while in college met his wife, who was an unmixed descendant of the Puritans. Their sons, including Muriel's father, were all educated North and settled there, marrying again into the Puritan stock, which had now, in spite of the family's French name, become the dominant strain in the branch of it with which we have to do.

Muriel's parents died early, from some local zymotic disease, while they were visiting one of his aunts at the South, and that threw the child in his early years principally among his Southern relatives. As he grew older, he drifted more toward his mother's sister Amelia, who had married his father's brother John, and later toward his uncle Legrand.

But Legrand was much away from home during Muriel's formative years, at least during such of them as had passed before this narrative opens, and the boy had felt only enough of his influence to counteract much of that of his aunts' husbands at the South. These gentlemen had led him to enter a Southern "University," where Muriel, being very precocious, had graduated at nineteen. He had meanwhile picked up some ideas during his visits to his aunt Amelia and uncle Legrand, which determined him to enter the junior year at a leading Northern university. There he had done brilliantly just what he liked, including many things he would better not have done at all, had failed deliberately in such enforced studies as he did not like, and had finished his complex career a few weeks before this story opens.

His Southern college had been almost virgin to the revolution in thought of the preceding twenty years. By nature, Muriel was made to accept the new light, but he had caught only faint glimpses of it from his uncle Legrand, and when he came into full view of it at his Northern university, it of course developed in him a very pretty radical iconoclasm. As so many of the ideas in which he had been brought up, were now proved absurd, of course he jumped to the conclusion that most all were, and he seldom had eyes or ears for that portion of his new teachings which simply adds support to the most important features of his old ones. Moreover, he was too fond of amusing himself, to thoroughly study the new philosophy and incorporate it into the working fibre of his being. Yet despite his spasmodic and superficial interest in those strong thoughts, he was, by virtue of the

German strain in him, something of a dreamer, and even capable of pumping up tolerable verses.

In college, he had been greatly loved and greatly hated. He was bright, accomplished, and genial, save for occasional moods; full of initiative and energy, and liberal enough with what it cost him no inconvenience to spare. He had even been known, a few times, not to stop at inconvenience. But as he was rough and hearty and strong, he demanded that everybody else should be rough and hearty and strong. He was brutally candid: give and take was his game, though he entirely overestimated his own readiness to "take," as such youngsters are apt to.

He was by nature moral and kindly. But he was impetuous, and had not had that steady home influence which curbs selfishness and passion. His very strength made him weak before some temptations, and he had never known his mother.

His powerful constitution had, so far, carried his body, at least, safely through the wildest follies of youth, and the centuries of sturdy puritanism in his veins had got him through without his deceiving anybody or taking anything that he did not pay for. But his arm was long and his grasp was strong. To his fervid impulses, woman was a toy when she presented herself as such, yet in his equally fervid imagination, when she was not a toy, there was always room for her as a goddess.

After he had left Mrs. Wahring and her daughter, he was bothered once or twice by a faint question whether he ought to have left them at all, or at least whether he ought not to have waited until they should have left him, for their rooms. He felt that this question had already contributed to the slight shadow over the evening's cordiality. Even the idea of turning back presented itself to his imagination. But the same momentum of character which had impelled him, in spite of the ladies, in the direction he had started, of course carried him past the notion of turning back. He had made an "appointment," whose nature may be inferred later, and that momentum of his was always strong in the direction of a promise, even if it were one that might perhaps better be honored in the breach than in the observance. But where amusement was waiting, he was not apt to trouble himself long over questions that involved anything less than his good faith; so he soon drove the present ones away with a "*Vive la bagatelle!*", and gave his powerful stepper an extra touch that jerked the groom behind him out of his nap, and nearly out of the dog-cart.

This "ball" to which he betook himself, was one that it is very doubtful whether he had any business to go to. It was given by a fire company in a neighboring village where his uncles, and he himself by inheritance, were owners of large factories. He did not by any means, however, go in the character of "lord of the manor," to give the entertainment the lustre of his patronage, but he went because he wanted to have a good time, and because, of late, one side of his nature was more apt to find a good time in the excitements of such free and easy assemblages, than amid the conventional proprieties to which he was born. Had the entertainment been a symphony concert, he would have been equally apt to go; but had it been a concert of commonplace music, he would have cared as little for it as for a ball characterized by the commonplace proprieties. He would have cared for the latter, however, if he had been sure of meeting any women who would, as he would have been apt to phrase it, "stir him up." But, young as he was, excitement of some kind was growing to be a craving with him, and he was nearing that dangerous point where one disregards the cost of it.

To do him justice, however, amid the excitements of this company, he did think more than once, with little self-approbation, of the widely different company he had forsaken.

After tearing several skirts with his big spurs, until, partly at the recommendation of a friend, he took them off; after also disarranging two or three quadrilles with his long sword, emptying a plate of salad over the hired pink satin court-dress worn by one of his partners; fascinating the reigning and two vice-regnant belles of that circle; and loading himself with the mysterious but effective punch to be found at such assemblies, Mr. Muriel Calmire had returned home with a clear head at five o'clock in the morning; and when Miss Nina Wahring bloomed upon the piazza at eight, was still intensely engrossed in sleeping the sleep of the just.

CHAPTER III.

A GIRL NOT OF THE PERIOD.

THAT circumstance, or rather the non-appearance which, for some hours, it entailed, was on the whole rather congenial with the young lady's taste. Muriel was a creature new to her experience, and not yet satisfactorily classified. He was handsome, she did not recall anybody handsomer, and bright enough, but he was not altogether agreeable. True, he had been passably peaceable under her mother's assault, and shown a certain dignified courtesy at first; but he had not displayed much tact in managing the situation, and on the whole had lacked deference. When it was plain that he was mainly in the wrong, he had not squarely owned up, but had tried to make courtesy take the place of confession. No! He was handsome, intelligent, vivacious, thoughtful, perhaps truthful; but he was subject to fits of awkwardness; he was not very chivalrous, not given to owning himself in the wrong, was possibly selfish, and probably conceited. She experienced something like a sense of relief at not finding him on the piazza.

After breakfast, the ladies busied themselves in supervising the unpacking and getting their belongings suitably bestowed. One of the several respects in which Nina was like heaven, was that order was her first law. Neatness she inherited from her mother; the good taste would have had to be sought in some other ancestor.

I have looked for Nina's face in most of the great galleries of the world, but in vain. The nearest to it is an angel at the left in a round Botticelli in the Uffizi, in the last room north-east of the Tribune. Nina's face had the same general character and the same sympathetic earnestness, but with more impression of thoughtfulness. Her hair was more the color of red bronze, and covered a broader brow. But, after all, what is there worth describing about a woman, that can be described? Her beauty, if supreme, cannot be described; her sympathies can be felt, but they can be described only by describing that which she sympathizes with, and that is not what she feels, and makes you feel, regarding it. If you go into her ancestry, you cannot indicate those best things there, any better than you can in herself. If you go into her education, if she happens to have a little, you cannot convey the quick and subtle uses she makes of it, and you might as well be talking about a boy. The bold facts that go to make up a man can be told about; but try to give the make-up of a woman in corresponding details, and you produce but a weak image of a man. Ask a woman for a definition and ten to one she will give you an illustration; and if she is a very great woman, and you don't stop to force logic out of her, her illustration will help you to make for yourself a definition better than any man is apt to give you. So a woman, if she is very woman, would better be indicated by illustrations. She cannot be narrowed within terminologies, any more than poetry can, and her subtleties can be caught only through watching her and listening to her. I have tried to give some set notion of Muriel, and shall try to give some of Calmire; but Nina?—she was beyond it. It might be done for a lesser woman; but for her, I had best only attempt a little of what she said and did. Yet in cold print, how like what all other women say and do, must it appear!

The faint sense of relief to Nina occasioned by Mr. Muriel's absence from breakfast, was clouded a little at luncheon by a shadow of unsatisfied curiosity and, it must be admitted, by a womanly fear that the young gentleman might have a headache. Reminiscences of the conversation of other young gentlemen, even awakened in her a solicitude as to whether the resources of Fleuvemont, so early in its occupancy, could be depended upon to the extent of soda-water.

Dismissing these cares, however, she announced: "Mamma, while you are taking your nap, I shall take a book and lounge around the grounds." It was a peculiarity in Nina's diction never to say, "I am going to" do anything; it was always the succinct "I shall," or "I will."

The day was delightful. Here and there some belated roses filled the soft air with sweetness. Away from the river, she saw to the East, a gentle descent dotted with trees, among them an orchard, and, perhaps a mile away, a second roll of hills, wild, with boulders and, she knew, mullens. "This world ends there!" she said to herself.

Turning South, where the ground sloped gently downward, she wandered along from one point of view, or one attractive plant or wild flower, to another, and at length deposited herself on the turf beneath a great oak whose branches shaded her, but were too high to obstruct the view which offered itself for miles in many directions. She gazed at the beautiful scene for a few minutes, and then began to read a story in the magazine she carried.

She was pleasantly interested, when she realized that strains of distant music had for some time been contending for her attention. She distinguished the notes of a cornet, well played and with intense, almost exaggerated, feeling. The artist scattered scraps of jerky dance-music among passionate cavatinas and even majestic sacred melodies; and despite his skill and feeling, he seemed indifferent to accuracy, though occasionally he would repeat an unsuccessful passage, and once, though once only, struggled with a phrase of enormous difficulty until he had conquered it.

Nina enjoyed many of the player's gentler strains, and felt moved as she had seldom been by some of his bursts of passion, but she was annoyed by a carelessness that his evident power showed to be almost contemptuous.

"A very unusual player to be practicing for one of these country bands," thought Nina. After perhaps fifteen minutes of the music, it ceased. She vainly waited some time for it to be renewed, and then betook herself again to her book.

Lingering mental echoes of the intense music made her story seem very flat, but she struggled through to the final orthodox distribution of rewards and punishments, and then took up her wrap and proceeded toward the house.

On the piazza toward her, she saw her mother, Mr. Calmire, and, sitting a little apart with a meerschaum and, apparently, a French novel, a gentleman in a rather loud plaid knickerbocker suit in the height of the fashion then prevalent, and a red tie (which she felt that no man of taste would have been apt to wear on a bright day), and in the wearer she recognized to her astonishment, her grave Roundhead of the night before Certainly the removal of the jack-boots had not affected his appearance unfavorably, for the rough Scotch stockings were extremely becoming to him, or he to them, and he knew it.

The people did not see her until she passed a clump of flowering shrubs near the piazza. Then Calmire ran down the steps, laughing, and said: "Lucky you came up without me, wasn't it? If I'd come, you'd have missed your unique reception."

"Yet we missed you," she answered.

"I half regretted sending you out," said he, "for you had hardly gone, when there sprang up one of those sea-breezes which so often save us in New York, and we had a delightfully cool evening, and pleasant morning."

"You show it, and I'm very glad of it," said Nina, both her hands still in his.

CHAPTER IV.

A MAN OF SEVERAL PERIODS.

He did show it. His face was very strong and buoyant, despite the traces of much thought, and much suffering and the overcoming of it. He was a little over fifty, and simply Muriel thirty years older. There were a few gray streaks at the chin in the short parted beard, and in the mustache, hardly any noticeable in the hair. He was perhaps a fourth heavier than Muriel, but was well proportioned, and light and graceful in his movements. What he wore, nobody ever noticed, though in the evening, when he was dressed exactly like other men, he seemed most distinguished from them.

The Calmire face does not appear in any of the world's great pictures, probably because it is too modern. It is suggested, though, by that directness which Velasquez got into most of his portraits through his unique power of feeling the qualities in a man which, if anything, the man must express.

Even had I not described Calmire's ancestry with Muriel's, it would be rather superfluous to do so: for men of his character usually conquer their antecedents by the time they reach his age. For the same reason I need not detail his education. M. Thomas has said: " You can educate the average man, but you cannot educate the genius. He will educate himself, and his first step will be to tear away the education provided for him." Calmire had enough genius to make this apply in no small degree to him.

Other countries than America may perhaps produce better men than he, but only America can produce exactly such a man. He was an "American business man," but with most of the associations which in other countries are reserved to men outside of business. He had succeeded his father in large manufacturing interests, but had also served his country in the Cabinet and at foreign courts. His diverse experiences, acting on a comprehensive character, had made him that rare creature—a man with wide sympathies and no little knowledge from books and the arts, who at the same time knew men and life—was systematic and practical, and abundantly able to take care of himself and the many dependent upon him. He had accepted his business as a matter of course: for without it, he would have had to limit the habits of living which were natural from his birth. But while he was entirely adequate to his affairs, they could not touch the greater part of his faculties, much less absorb them, and he had been able to allow himself leisure to yield to his spirit's insatiate demand that it should keep pace with all the important advances of thought.

He had done well as a politician and diplomatist, but he was neither politic nor diplomatic enough to become more absorbed in either pursuit than he had been in business. He was tempted, in fact, to class all three with "details," and for details he had no fancy. He sought principles and generalizations, the rest he declared to be some form or other of "shop." Yet he had no contempt for shop. only his individual preferences did not lead him into it. Though he very seldom said disagreeable things, some people professed themselves "afraid of him." Only people at the two extremes of culture and opportunity were apt to be attached to him. His servants and the poor worshipped him.

An exception to the indifference to him of commonplace people, was his attractiveness to all good women: though this exception is but provisional, for he declared that no good woman is commonplace.

As this story is apt to be a long one, and must deal with many of the faults of other people, there will not be much room in it for his. He had outgrown many of them, but he still had his human share. I do not think he can be the hero of the tale, because, despite his faults, he had grown too deliberate, too consistent, too calm.

Miss Wahring, fortunately, was not kept waiting for this description. He said to her:

"I fear Muriel was not so much impressed by the fact that two ladies were on his hands, as that he wanted to appear in costume, a few miles off. I trust, however, that you were eventually made comfortable?"

"Perfectly! Luxurious, indeed. Hasn't mamma told you how pleasantly we were cared for?"

"Yes; but I wanted to be told that *you* were pleased, too."

"We were delighted! *Such* a place! Why, last night" (and she had a little feeling as if she were giving him a confidence, but she liked to)—"last night I felt as if I were transported out of our commonplace century altogether."

"Our commonplace century is good enough for me—to work in," he added with a smile. "And as to the place, perhaps in the way you speak of, it's a little too good. A French château with a French name would be well enough if we had stayed in France, but I'm an American. Yet my father built it—and there are associations." And his smile faded, but into something more beautiful.

CHAPTER V.

THE FIRST BOUT.

On turning toward the porch, Nina found Muriel by her. He reached for her shawl, parasol, and book, saying:

"Let me carry them up. I think I can do better when not in disguise."

"Good *morning*," said the girl (it was three in the afternoon), and yielded up the things. "Does your head ache?"

"I never get up while it does," said Muriel.

"You deserve that it should, for your double masquerade last night."

"I can't see any connection between the part I played with you and your mother" (he was too unconventional to say "Mrs. Wahring") "and headache."

"Don't you think that the part deserved a headache?"

"Things deserve their natural consequences, I suppose," said the young man. "If I deserve any punishment, your displeasure and hers would be the natural one. I hope I have not incurred that."

"Not very seriously, at least not for letting her remain deceived."

"Well, for what then?"

"She begged your pardon; you did not beg hers."

He disregarded the point, and said:

"Aren't your notions of punishment a little primitive? You want to sentence me to a headache for *lèse majesté.*"

"What does that outlandish expression mean?"

"Why, don't you know?" and his habitual feeling of superiority came up, comforting him.

"If I had, I wouldn't have asked you," she said simply, and he had a dim notion that confessed ignorance was, in some vague way that he did not stop to examine, not so terribly inferior to vaunted knowledge. He answered:

"Why, *lèse-majesté* means, I suppose, lack of respect for the powers that be."

"So I'm one of the powers that be, am I?"

"Every young and pretty woman is."

"Thank you. How about my mother?"

"Well, she is too, I suppose, though as you claimed part of the injury, I didn't think of that."

"Didn't you? Well, it's worth thinking of."

She made the boy feel uncomfortable and a bit revengeful. The girl was very pretty, though, and not stupid; and he was glad enough to keep on fencing with her. He did not always realize when he was hit, and when he did, if he could get in a passable stroke in return, he lost all consciousness of his weak spot. Hoping to win yet, he began:

"Why did you want to give me a headache for what you seem to consider a failure in manners?"

"To punish you, of course."

"Upon my soul! Why, I believe you would whip a child for stealing."

"Of course I would. Do you think I'd spare the rod and spoil the child?"

"Solomon was an old fool!"

"I'd be obliged if you wouldn't speak disrespectfully of Bible characters to me. As you are so much wiser than Solomon, what would you do?"

"I should be sorry if a few thousand years' more experience hadn't made me wiser than Solomon. Why, I'd make the child replace the stolen article from his pocket-money, of course, and for a time I'd treat the child as coldly as I would an older criminal."

"Suppose the child didn't care for your punishment?"

"Suppose the moon to be made of green cheese! But even if the child were such a *lusus naturæ* as you're making out, do you suppose a whipping would make any difference to such a creature?"

"It might. But I wish you'd stop talking outlandish tongues at me."

He stared at her a second, wondering what sort of woman this could be, on whom his profound learning produced no effect. Yet he did not find the lack of appreciation altogether disagreeable, especially as she seemed interested in his matter, if not in his manner. Then he answered her, and after a few similar passages, in which he got the better of her, and she was surprised to find him interested in children and not unintelligently, Nina pondered a few moments and then asked suddenly:

"Where did you get all these notions?"

"Well, I have thought of these subjects a good deal."

"Where did you get all these notions?"

"Why? Do you think they're good?"

"I think they're admirable. I never thought of them before. Where did you get them?"

"From Spencer and Helen Hunt, I suppose. I'm rather fond of that sort of reading."

"So, after all, you've been drawing on your reading rather than your wit, to overwhelm me?"

"You don't seem to overwhelm worth a cent."

"No, I'm not apt to. Now let me tell you that I've found what you have been pleased to say to me, very sensible; and no matter where you got it, you have it. Nobody ever talked to me in that way before. Perhaps I shall think about it. Only I don't believe I think much. I'm very much obliged to you."

Muriel colored to the roots of his hair and bowed low. He had never felt cheaper in his life. And it would have puzzled him, philosopher as he held himself, to exactly define the reason why.

CHAPTER VI.

AN AFTERNOON DRIVE.

CALMIRE turned from the chat he had been having with Mrs. Wahring, and said:

"You two young people will have to suspend quarreling for a few minutes. The band plays on Calmire Green to-night, and we're going to start over in half an hour. I haven't yet been there since I came from abroad. We'll dine with my brother. All this, of course, subject to your good pleasure, as far as you two are concerned. Mrs. Wahring and I have agreed upon it for ourselves already."

"Yes, the elders always decide and ask our wishes afterward," said Muriel.

"I, for one, shall be delighted," said Nina.

"You'll go, Muriel?" asked Calmire.

"Certainly. You've telegraphed Aunt Amelia, or shall I?"

(There was a time, dear Madam, when there were really no telephones in the world.)

"It's done already," Muriel answered.

And they separated to arrange their preliminaries.

When Mrs. Wahring and Nina were secure behind their doors, the former turned half confidentially to her daughter and said :

"Oh, Nina dear, I've almost got a headache.

That dreadful young man spoiled my nap by blowing on some sort of a horn."

"Why, it wasn't he who was playing the cornet so beautifully, was it?"

"Perhaps he was; but I didn't find it so beautiful. I wanted to get to sleep. It's no proper instrument to play in the house. I think he's dreadful. Isn't he, dear?"

"Well, yes, mamma, in some ways. He does seem sometimes to think of nobody but himself. Yet last night, despite his letting you remain deceived, he seemed to care to make us comfortable."

And a moment after, she pondered: "It's very odd that he should have thought so much about children."

Muriel reciprocated these unheard compliments by observing to his uncle as they wandered off together:

"That girl you've brought here is the sharpest-tongued piece I ever saw!"

"Yes?" answered Calmire. "Is that the best you can say for her?"

"Well, she's about like the rest of them, she doesn't seem to know anything."

"Probably she doesn't, and yet there appear to me to be one or two particulars in which she's not quite 'like the rest of them.'"

"She's certainly prettier than most of them."

"Is that all?"

"Well, I don't know her much yet. What are you driving at?"

"She's honest," said Calmire.

"Any fool can be that," answered his nephew.

"You'll find your definition of 'fool' varying a good deal as you pass through life," observed the elder.

This was the first time that Calmire had known his nephew to say so much that was uncomplimentary to an attractive woman. But it was the first time that one had made Muriel feel so uncomfortable: yet he by no means wished that the conversation had not taken place.

At half-past four, the T-cart with a pair of sturdy roans was at the door.

"Well, shall we risk our necks with you? I suppose you like to drive?" said Calmire to Muriel.

"I don't care much for it, thank you," answered Muriel.

"I can," said Nina.

"I dare say you both can," said Mrs. Wahring, "but I think I would feel just as much at ease if Mr. Calmire were to do it."

"Then, dear madam!" said he, helping her to the front seat.

"Ah, Mr. Calmire, I hoped you were going to take me!" exclaimed Nina.

"And leave your poor old mother," bowing to that blooming and beautiful matron, "to be talked to death by that young chatterbox? No, you're young and strong. Help her in, Muriel!"

When they were seated and off, Nina said to Muriel:

"How far are we going?"

"Six miles."

"Tell me about the place."

"Historically, geographically, economically, or socially?"

"All of them; begin at the beginning."

"Well, it's the village where our mills are—about three miles up a branch. There's a big water-power there. What with the war and tariff-tinkering, it has had all sorts of ups and downs. In my grandfather's time it was all iron. Some twenty years ago, my father and my uncles began on wool. They've branched out, and added several things since. My father died soon after they began. My mother too. So I've been kicking around ever since, always tying up to Uncle Grand when I can get a chance, which isn't often: for he's been abroad most of my vacations. But I forgot that you didn't ask for my biography. Well, when father died, Uncle Grand—"

"Why do you call him Grand? Isn't his name Legrand?" asked Nina.

"Oh, I got into it when I was a baby, and nobody knowing him as I do, would ever stop it."

"I can understand that; but go on about Calmire."

"Well, when my father died, John Calmire told Uncle Grand that he'd got to manage the people: for John himself could manage only the business."

"But Mr. Legrand is away a great deal."

"Yes, John couldn't be, and doesn't care to be; Uncle Grand wasn't either, at first. But now, whenever he's around here, he's with the people a great deal. They worship him. He has made the town what it is. It's got everything—library, brass band, singing clubs, gymnastic clubs—you'll see."

"Yes, and John's treasurer of pretty much the whole of them," said Calmire, turning round. "Be a little cautious regarding what that young gentleman tells you about my doings, Miss Nina. I've overheard him taking my name in vain there."

"I flatter myself you've taught me to tell the truth, sir," retorted Muriel. Then he resumed to Nina in a low tone:

"He likes to be appreciated just as well as anybody."

"What sort of a man is your uncle John?" asked Nina.

"Well, he and I never pulled together much; yet he's a good sort of fellow—a great business man, perfect gentleman—too confoundedly perfect for my taste. Honors the ground that one treads on" (in a low tone and pointing to Calmire), "but never said so to a living being, unless to his quiet little wife who never tells anything. To his brother's face, he keeps making fun of his moonshiny notions. Yet he runs the factories and the town on them, at least on those he keeps. He brushes half aside, and very properly, I suppose."

Muriel's little disquisitions had not proceeded uninterruptedly, but were interspersed with many an interjection of "Hello, Jimmy!" "Howdy, Old Man?" "Mornin', Granny," and other equally graceful and conventional greetings, scattered among all the younger and poorer people met by the roadside. Calmire raised his hat to all the women whom he knew, while to the poorer ones Muriel was more apt to call out and wave his hand. The children invariably grinned as he went by.

At the town where the tributary joined the great river, they passed a beautiful new church, and Calmire said :

"Why, I didn't expect to see this finished already! There's some salvation in such architecture."

"Fearful waste of money!" said Muriel. "Why didn't they put it into an Art Museum or a Lecture Hall?"

"Because the people would not use them as much, as they have proved by putting their money here," said Calmire. "You people who are impatient with the churches are some generations before your time."

When, after a short hour, they got into Calmire, they created quite a sensation. It was the first time the town's sponsor had been there for two years, and many a hat was waved with a flourish, and even an occasional handkerchief was fluttered from a window.

Twice Calmire pulled up, as some special friends were on the sidewalk. But as a knot of people gathered each time, he said, "We won't stop any more," and contented himself with an occasional extra wave of the hand. Once or twice, with sportive gallantry, he kissed his hand to ladies who were evidently old friends.

"Why, it's a regular triumph!" said Nina, as they went bowling along amid these salutations.

"You bet the dear old boy enjoys it!" said Muriel, in a tone for her alone, his eyes sparkling.

Yet despite these sparkling eyes, Nina had for a moment one of those strange feelings which women know, that there was some uneasiness or anxiety in Muriel. The impression soon passed. She was at the careless age, and so was he.

A few minutes later Nina exclaimed:

"Who was that lovely woman?"

"Where?" asked Muriel. "I didn't see any."

"At that brown house on my side just back there. She came running to the door as we passed. She's the loveliest woman I ever saw."

"That's John Baldwin's house," said Muriel. "They don't keep any lovely women there."

"Perhaps she was a visitor," said Nina. "She had her hat and things on."

"What did she look like?" asked Muriel.

"A queen! Not an empress, because empresses are cold and hard. This one—"

But a burst of laughter from Muriel interrupted her, and after a moment she joined in it.

"Well, you know," she said after they had quieted down, "that's the way I always think of them. An empress is a great selfish, masculine thing like Catharine or Irene; but a queen now—well, a queen is tall too, but she is sweet and gracious and lovely, just like that one back there."

"Guess it must have been Mary," said Muriel.

"Who's Mary?"

"Oh, she's just Mary. Had she dark hair and a low forehead over which it rippled a little, and oh! *such* a nose and mouth?"

"How could I see all that?" answered Nina. "Her hair was dark, and, yes, I think her forehead must have been rather low, and she was so graceful although she ran to the door."

"It must have been Mary," said Muriel; "she must have been calling there."

"Well, tell me about her," exclaimed Nina. "She doesn't live in this little town?"

"Yes, she does," said Muriel; and after a moment he added, in a tone that was almost reverential: "She pervades it like music. But," and his tones grew hard, "it's music in a minor key. She's religion's perfect work here."

Nina turned her head and looked at him puzzled, and then said, with a genial little laugh: "Well, the town contains at least two rather unusual people."

"Who, besides her?"

"You. I can't make you out at all. Sometimes you make me think you're a— Well, I won't tell you what. And then you make me think you're a— Well, I won't tell you that either."

"That describes me exactly," said Muriel. "You're a marvel of penetration. But here we are at John's."

And they drew up toward the sidewalk.

"Why, is that the way you always speak of your uncle?" asked Nina.

"Yes, of this one."

CHAPTER VII.

A TOWN OUT OF THE BEATEN PATH.

John Calmire's house was the typical square stone residence of the northern village magnate, ample in its proportions and surroundings, a little peculiar, perhaps, in the absence of bizarre ornamentation, without and within, though everything was cheerful and in good taste.

When they drew up before it, Muriel jumped into the middle of the sidewalk without thinking of resting his foot on step or wheel. Half a dozen children bobbed up, shouting, from the high grass beside the lawn, and soon got themselves tangled up among Muriel's arms and legs. The master and mistress of the house came down the steps, he a little sandy-colored man, gentleman all over, leading out the little dark woman, despite their cordial haste, as if she were an empress.

Mrs. John, meeting Muriel first, did not reflect upon the ladies waiting, but put both arms around his neck and kissed him twice. His mother had been her elder sister, so he was her own nephew as well as John's, and she loved him dearly. Naturally she was alive to all his good qualities, and attributed his bad ones to the fate which had early deprived him of his mother, and her of her idolized sister. This sister she was constantly seeing and worshiping in Muriel. Her adoration had developed not a little his native blindness to his own mistakes and shortcomings. The boy loved her in a boy's ungrateful way, realizing more her lack of intellectual pyrotechnics than her wealth of sympathy and (except regarding him) good sense.

"Calmire, I'm glad to see you," said John, wringing his brother's hand, even before he noticed the ladies—a trifling oversight that in John Calmire indicated more feeling than shouts of welcome and lusty embraces would have done in most men.

"Are you all right, old man?" queried Calmire, taking his brother's hand in both his own. Then he flung his arm around his sister-in-law's neck and kissed her as if he liked it, which showed excellent taste and was cordially reciprocated.

"Ah, Mrs. Wahring," said John. "Pardon my leaving you till the second: it's a good while since I saw Calmire." He always called his older brother by the family name, and people intimate with them sometimes followed his fashion.

"Why, young lady," John continued, turning to Nina, "it's hardly fair to take me so by surprise. You surely ought to be a little girl yet."

"I hope you won't think so when we know each other better," she answered, shaking hands cordially.

The ladies being helped out, satisfactorily kissed by Mrs. Calmire, and ushered into the house, all amid the usual pleasant little confusions, John turned to Muriel, who was last but himself on the piazza, pretended to raise his hat, though he had none on, motioned with the other hand toward the door, and said with mock ceremony:

"Pray honor my poor house."

Muriel retorted: "Sir, to precede a gentleman of your age and distinguished merits—"

"Go in, you cub!" commanded John with a push. The two did not like each other and they did like each other. So, for safety's sake, they always began with their weapons covered with a double thickness of burlesque conventionality.

"Where's the baby?" was Muriel's prompt question, and the nurse, appearing in a few minutes, delivered it over to him as a matter of course, while Mrs. Wahring and her daughter laughed at seeing the impetuous young man handle it as tenderly and skilfully as a woman.

"Why," said Mrs. John, "he actually said he wanted to take the last one to college with him."

And the Wahrings found the young man more perplexing than ever.

Mrs. Calmire took her old friend Mrs. Wahring, to her own room, and her oldest girl, Genevieve, captured Nina. After a little talk about the children and some elder friends, Mrs. John asked:

"And how do you find Calmire?"

"Beautiful, so far as I've seen it. Everything looks so trim."

"Oh no: I mean brother Legrand?"

"He seems very well."

"Yet he has suffered terribly. He's a philosopher, though, and John believes he'll marry again in time, if he finds the right woman, and that will be easy, because he would probably prefer that she should be poor. John is always making fun of his contempt for policy in such matters."

"I know a girl who's not poor," said Mrs. Wahring, "whom I'd like to see safe in his hands."

Mrs. Calmire looked at her hard, and then burst out: "What, Hilda Wahring! You old Lady Kew! Make her the second wife of a man old enough to be her grandfather!"

"Such men are never old. When they get ready, they die, but that's all. Calmire is the strongest man in this house to-day. And I've seen enough of young husbands."

"You ungrateful thing! Hadn't you a young husband? Hadn't I? And aren't we both happy women—and healthy ones too?"

"You've lived in the country, and the Lord sent me but one child, and we're of an earlier generation. In this day of nervous strain, the younger women require more care than any boy will give them."

"Nina is not one of that kind. She can take care of herself. And she has had more air and exercise than either of us ever had. Lawn-tennis was not of our day; neither were the Adirondacks and Mount Desert."

"Well, dear, with Calmire I know she would have twenty years of happiness, and probably ten years more of peace. After him, she would have her grown children and her grandchildren. With a boy, it's all chance whether she has more than a year of anything."

"Well, I'd rather love and bully a man as I love and bully my John, and run all the chances, than be safe as half wife, half daughter, with the next best man in the world."

"John is an unusual man, my dear; he was always careful and patient."

"I'd have loved him the same if he'd been careless and impetuous."

"That's to say, you could have loved somebody else. Do you believe any woman could love him more than she could love his brother, other things even?"

"I believe that a girl like Nina, to whom a man like Calmire is an entire novelty, and whose mind would be first awakened by him, could love him madly; but it would be madness all the same, as a few years would show."

"No, it wouldn't. He could hold her always."

"Yes, because she's a good and brave girl," said deep little Mrs. John; "but that's no reason her goodness and bravery should be abused. But tell me, have you opened up your horrid scheme to Calmire?"

"No, I have no scheme."

"Tell *me!* As soon as a woman like you has a wish, she has a scheme. But as you've been foolish enough to have such a wish, I'm surprised you had sense enough to keep it to yourself."

"I'm too old a fox, my dear."

"Well, I must confess you don't look it. You make me hate you," and she rose and kissed the blooming cheek.

Of course Mrs. John had a double reason for disapproving Mrs. Wahring's idea: for she never saw a girl whom she approved (and she saw very few such) without thinking: "She'd make a good wife for Muriel, and the poor boy must have one as soon as possible."

As the party were seated at table, Mrs. Wahring opened the conversation with:

"Well! you're very civilized country-folks. How long has dressing for dinner been the fashion in American manufacturing towns? I should think the people would stone you."

"Well," answered John, laughingly, "it really did arise to the dignity of a serious question when we concluded to swarm over here from Fleuvemont. I didn't think of doing it. But Calmire said that if we were going to live here the whole year, and not relapse into barbarism and bring our children up in it, we'd got to stick to all the conventionalities we could."

"But it did stir up a little democratic ire at first, didn't it?" asked Muriel. "Seems to me I heard something said about it when I was a youngster."

"*When* you were a youngster!" observed John. "No, even at that remote period, people at least kept quiet about it."

"Don't some of them ape it?" asked Nina.

"Well, it's odd," said Calmire. "The first time Courtenay's singing club gave a concert, they all appeared in white ties. There was a variety of patterns in the coats, not an evening coat among them, I think, but all were dark."

"And you can't imagine that a set of factory hands would look so well," said Mrs. John.

"Do you have any trouble here with drunkenness?" inquired Nina, peering into her glasses.

"I'm told that it's apt to be the great curse of such places."

"Oh, we run opposition to the rum-shops," said Mrs. John. "All sorts of refreshments can be had in the library and gymnasium buildings. There's only one rum-shop left now, besides ours."

"Do you supply the same things the rum-shops do?"

"The people supply themselves," Calmire interrupted. "It's just like any other club."

"But," persisted Mrs. Wahring, "do they have what gentlemen's clubs do?"

"Certainly—the less expensive things. But most of our people use only the lighter drinks: they are cheaper, and the women set public opinion that way."

"Well, I'm in favor of laws to keep the dram-shops out anyhow."

"I'm in favor of limiting them," said Calmire, "but I doubt the justice of cutting off all my chance to get a drink because my neighbor abuses his. And anyhow Nature is killing off the drunkards wherever she's not interfered with."

"Oh, that's too terrible!" cried Nina. "You don't believe in letting such things be?"

"Do I believe in letting lightning-strokes and war and pestilence be? Certainly not, if we can find any remedy that's not worse than the trouble. But paternal government destroys the people's capacity to take care of themselves, and that's of more value than all the drunkards in the community."

"And water's such poor stuff," interrupted

Muriel,—"will nourish nothing but the lowest forms of life."

"The lowest creatures only absorb it by external contact," quietly observed Calmire. "Do you object to that relation to it?"

Muriel felt disposed to change the subject. The accidental shoving aside of the screen before the pantry-door gave him a chance:

"Uncle Grand, there's one argument for total abstinence that you've not mentioned."

"What is it?"

"The horrible faces people make when they draw corks."

"Ah, Miss Nina," said Calmire, "there's something apt to happen among us, you see, which you're more in danger of getting tired of than of talk about nature's hard remedies."

Nina, who was ready for a change in the tone of the conversation, laughed with both speakers and said:

"I'm not afraid. Let's have a little frivolity."

"Many a good fellow has died from the want of it," remarked Calmire.

"I hate flippancy," said Muriel with burlesque gravity.

"Yes, youth hates competition," observed John.

"Please don't anybody say anything about Shakspere's and Hardy's clowns," interposed Muriel.

"I knew *you* would," said John.

"I'm always safe for a compliment from you. Did you ever know a fellow who couldn't make a fool of himself, to amount to anything?" continued Muriel.

"I never knew a fellow to amount to anything

unless he knew *when* to make a fool of himself," answered John.

The little ripple of nonsense had spent itself, and one of those silences of which all are conscious, followed. Nina ended it with:

"A queer time for an angel to pass!"

This led Mrs. Wahring to say to John:

"I hope you are more religious here than you used to be."

"More churchy, you mean?" asked John.

"I mean more given to religious observances. You were no better than heathen savages," exclaimed Mrs. Wahring, forgetting in her enthusiasm, her interest in Nina's favorable opinion of Calmire. "Mr. Calmire never went to church, and Mr. John didn't go half the time. Do you still go, Amelia?"

"Oh, don't let's talk about that," said Calmire, "we'll get to quarreling."

"I wish you *would* talk about it," said Nina. "This seems the queerest place I ever heard of, and you are certainly the queerest lot of people I ever saw, and—" here she became conscious that her candor had led her a little farther than, girl as she was, she liked. She blushed and hesitated a moment, then smiled and continued: "And I'm not sure I hate you as much as I ought, so I want to know the worst about you."

"All the stupid folks in town go," broke in Muriel.

"I wonder," quietly observed John, "if some people are not as intolerant about other people going to church, as other people are about some people staying at home."

"I'm not quite so absurd as you're trying to make out," said Muriel. "Intolerance never forced anybody to stay away, and it has forced many to go. As to the stupidity—there's Genevieve, for instance" (who still took her evening meal apart with the children, when company dined at the house): "I'll admit (not merely for the sake of argument either) that she's the loveliest child that ever lived; but she's always the last to see through a thing, and can't take a joke to save her. She's the churchiest of the lot."

"And you know perfectly well," Calmire broke in, "that she's a born artist, musician, and actress—even of parts with jokes in them, and the most affectionate child of them all. In sympathies, and tastes too, she's head and shoulders above any of them, though her analytical powers may not be as quick. But you're simply mad over analytical power. All the boys are nowadays. I may as well own, though, that I was, myself, once." Then he added in a lower tone: "It cost me something to get over it, and it'll cost you something, too, before you get through."

Mrs. John felt moved to say: "Don't think our men are out of sympathy with the church. They do their share for it."

"But I don't know that we deserve any credit for that," said Calmire. "You know that, as Emerson said, if the good people were to fail in running it, the capitalists would have to, to keep thievery down." Then he added: "But don't let's argue, Cousin Hilda. A great many of our people go to church in the morning, and when they are out of church I think they spend the day more as Christ and his disciples did, than any American people I know. I never heard that Christ was very rigorous in his attendance at the temple. In fact, I have the impression that, as a rule, he was rather hard on the priests. I suspect he was regarded as a good deal of an infidel in his day."

"Do you keep the library open on Sundays?" asked Mrs. Wahring.

"Most certainly! And the club too. That's the only chance the people have at them by daylight. There Courtenay had to yield."

"Who's Courtenay?" asked Nina.

"A saint!" burst in Muriel. "But I don't half like saints."

This later ejaculation seemed to divert Muriel's intention of enlightening her, if he had had any. After a moment John said:

"I beg pardon, Muriel, but I didn't understand Miss Wahring to ask our opinion of saints, but to inquire who Mr. Courtenay is. He's the rector."

"That means Episcopal, doesn't it?" asked Nina.

"Yes, my little Presbyterian," interrupted Calmire.

"Oh, I generally go to the Episcopal church."

"Music, and painting, and lights?" asked Calmire.

"Yes, and great deep shadows too," she said.

Muriel's face flashed, and he turned and looked at her. She did not notice him, but went on:

"Tell me about Mr. Courtenay."

"He's a noble fellow," said Calmire.

"Then why in the world don't you go to hear him preach?" asked Mrs. Wahring.

"He'd a mighty sight better come and hear Uncle Grand preach!" broke in Muriel again.

"Well, boy, you *are* irrepressible," exclaimed Calmire. "It's not a great many years since your Aunt Amelia would have sent you to bed for that."

"Well, if she'll let me sit up a little longer now, I'll try to be good. Go ahead; I won't interrupt till the next time."

"Why don't you go to hear Mr. Courtenay preach?" Mrs. Wahring again asked Calmire.

"It wouldn't be honest," he answered. "I should be held to indorse too much that I do not. Besides, I don't get any too much time at books, to absorb the wisdom of even greater men than my friend Courtenay."

"But how can you work together if you don't agree?" asked Mrs. Wahring.

"Well, in the first place," said Calmire, "you know Courtenay is very tolerant."

"His sister made him that," again interjected Muriel.

"And then," continued Calmire, "we don't attempt working together in things where he has been trained to believe that his office gives him the right of control. We do very well in others —in the library, the club, the hospital, or 'home' as we call it, and such of his private charities as he allows us the honor of helping in."

"But," persisted Mrs. Wahring, "I don't see but what you run the church 'opposition' (as Amelia puts it) with the club and the library, as much as you do the rum-shops."

"We have no distinct desire to," said Calmire. "But if the church can't stand that sort of opposition, so much the worse for the church. I think it can, as long as it needs to."

"Well, I hate to see anything interfering with it at all," said Nina.

"But the best men are not paying any attention to it," said Muriel. "Hardly any of those intellectual swells I used to see over at Fleuvemont ever went—unless to keep the peace with their wives," he added as he watched Nina's astonished face.

"But this is all new to me," said Nina, flushing slightly; "I can hardly suppose it to be correct. But if it is, what's the reason?"

"One is," answered Calmire, "that the ministry doesn't begin to absorb the talent it used to, partly because so many other things are made more attractive, but mainly because fewer able young men subscribe to the views of Christianity put forward by the churches."

"That they don't!" exclaimed Muriel.

"But some of them do. There's Mr. ——, who laid down his college professorship to preach," said Mrs. Wahring.

"And there's Mr. ——, certainly as able a man, who laid down his pastorate to teach, and —— too, now a professor in the same university, did the same thing," answered Muriel.

CHAPTER VIII.

THE UNJUST AND THE JUST.

"But all this doesn't prove anything against the truth of Christianity," said Mrs. Wahring.

"There's no danger that anything true in Christianity is going to be disproved," observed Calmire.

"But don't shirk the question, Uncle Grand," said Muriel. "To these ladies, Christianity and the church mean precisely the same thing."

"Well. They needn't have their dinner spoiled by anybody trying to convince them otherwise."

"But I want to know about it," said Nina, turning a face of bright expectancy to Calmire and then to Muriel. "This is all very strange to me, and I'm interested."

"Oh well, then," said Calmire, smiling on her, "to put it in an extreme way, are you willing to accept as Christianity, the indulgences, masses for the dead, Mariolatry, prayer to saints, worship of relics, Bambino miracles and all the other observances that sadden one in Rome?"

"No, of course I don't accept it," answered Nina.

"Yet," said Calmire, "all of that was held to be Christianity by everybody five hundred years ago. Now have you any reason to suppose that if you were living five hundred years hence, you would fully endorse the Christianity of the present?"

"But—I never thought of it that way before."

"You don't seem to realize," said Muriel, "that the Church preaches a lot of stuff that's not true, and stands in the way of others preaching what is."

"And *you* don't seem to realize," broke in his uncle John, "that it preaches a lot more that *is* true, and stands in the way of many others preaching what is not."

"As how?" asked Muriel.

"Well, you believe in the morality of Christianity, don't you?"

"Yes, in a general way, though it's rather milk and water; and if anybody can make the parable of the unjust steward anything but approval of conspiracy to defraud, he can do more than I can."

"This is getting a little too far," said Mrs. Wahring, and made a move as if to rise from the table.

Calmire laid a restraining hand on hers, and said:

"It looks a little, Muriel, as if it were impracticable to carry on this discussion without hurting somebody's feelings."

"Oh, Mrs. Wahring," said Muriel, "I beg ten thousand pardons. I really didn't think. I—" and the fellow evidently was confused and sorry.

"No, I don't suppose you intended to pain us," said Mrs. Wahring; "but as the subject is such a dangerous one, hadn't we better change it?"

"Not yet, please," said Nina; "I didn't enjoy Mr. Muriel's last remarks either, but what the men are saying is so strange that I'd like to understand more about it."

"Well, if you ladies will forgive me," said Muriel, "I'll try to put my idea in a less disagreeable way. Now, Mrs. Wahring, it seems to me that I've heard something about a heroic young lady in New York who, some twenty years ago, sent her young husband off to the civil war as a private, and by virtue of the blood of his grandfather, he rose to be General Wahring."

"Yes," she answered; "but, Mr. Muriel, the other side drew the sword first, and you certainly would not make light of such a virtue as patriotism —or such a wrong as the slavery our side fought?"

"And therefore, dear madam, I have all the more hope of your pardon for speaking lightly of a system whose founder didn't happen to mention the one, or condemn the other."

"Why!" she exclaimed, turning toward Calmire.

"He's right," quietly remarked that gentleman.

"And yet," said Muriel, "among the good things which I suppose Uncle Grand urges that the churches do sometimes teach, is that same virtue of patriotism, although Christ didn't give any encouragement for their doing so."

There was a few moments' pause—a thing Muriel never could endure. He broke it with:

"And while we're about it, Uncle Grand, we may just as well note the historic facts that the growth of that non-resistent creed rotted out the valor of Rome, and made the barbarians' destruction of that civilization possible. Next, Christianity's exaltation of shiftlessness into a virtue filled Europe with beggary for a thousand years, and shut up in the convents the men who ought to have redeemed their countries."

"You got most of that," said Calmire, "from Heine—a Jew who hated Christianity, a profligate who hated restraint, and, as it happened, probably the greatest satirist that ever lived, who naturally made the most of every chance to satirize. But you and Heine ignore the facts that most of the barbarians who overran Rome claimed to be Christians, and that many Christians in Rome desired the destruction of the empire, to bring on the 'kingdom of Christ' that they had been expecting ever since his day."

"Well," rejoined Muriel, "either way, Christianity destroyed Rome, and made Europe a beggar's hospital and a pandemonium for nearly a thousand years."

"I don't deny," said Calmire, "that Christianity had a share in all that, but you exaggerate. Rome would have fallen without Christianity; but for Christianity, the dark ages would have been vastly darker; and (if I càn enlarge a little without boring anybody) the Crusades, terrible waste as they were, brought back with them Arabian mathematics, medicine, and decoration; later, even at the time of the massacre of St. Bartholomew and the religious wars on the Continent, England was giving mankind the Elizabethan age; and cotemporaneous with the Spanish Inquisition and the worst corruptions of the Romish Church, blossomed the Italian Renaissance."

"Yes," retorted Muriel, "and much Christianity there was in Arabian civilization and, for that matter, in Elizabeth's England and in the Italian Renaissance!"

"Well," said Calmire, "there seems to have

been a little of it hanging around Sir Philip
Sidney and Sir Thomas Browne, as well as Fra
Angelico and Savonarola, not to speak of Petrarch
and Dante. Do try to see both sides."

"You admit that there are two?" asked Muriel.

"Unquestionably," answered Calmire. "Two
dozen, if you please!"

"And I," exclaimed Nina, "never had wit enough
to reflect that there was more than one!"

Muriel turned to her with great interest, and said:
"I don't object to seeing all the sides there are."

"Then I suspect you'll admit," observed Calmire, very deliberately, "as to Christ not having
preached the pugnacious virtues, that it doesn't
seem to have been much needed in his day. And
if his preaching of peacefulness was corrupted by
some into advocating cowardice, his followers generally haven't lacked pluck—even the pluck to
keep peaceful; and that if his preaching against
covetous competition was corrupted into advocating laziness, his followers have nevertheless done
more than their share of the world's work."

"But why claim that all the faults are corruptions?" asked Muriel. "Why pick out all that is
good and venerable from the records, and give the
credit of that to Christ; and why lay up all that is
absurd against the makers of the records?"

"I attribute much that is good," answered Calmire, "to some of the writers themselves. Paul said
on his own account many of the best things that have
ever been said. And as to the absurdities, it hardly
seems fair to attribute them to a person of Christ's
transcendent genius. But whatever he may have

left out, you'll admit that now the churches preach every virtue which the best judges approve."

"Yes, whether Christ ever preached it or not," answered Muriel. "But the churches preach such an awful lot of rot besides. Oh Lord! There I go again! Do forgive me, ladies! I'll try not to do it any more."

This set them laughing in spite of themselves, and his forgiveness was, at least ostensibly, secure.

"Well," asked Calmire, after a moment, "are you finding fault with the churches because they preach virtues which Christ did not, or simply because in your opinion they are not perfect?"

"No, they're not!"

"On that basis," responded Calmire, "you'd have to destroy every human institution, for nothing we know is perfect, except young ladies, and"—to Mrs. Wahring—"all ladies are young."

"I don't believe," answered Muriel, "in destroying any useful thing that has growth in it, but (Be patient with me, ladies) the church has culminated and is going downhill and is doing more harm than good."

"Well," answered Calmire, "*you* will have to be patient with *me* this time, for I think that view of the churches an excessively superficial one."

Mrs. Wahring and Nina brightened up, as if the fight were going for their side.

"Well, Uncle Grand," said Muriel, "there's not a university in this land where a man abreast of the age can teach all the truth that is in him, for fear of hurting the religious prejudice; and in the most intellectual city of the land, they can't use a history in the public schools that has not lots of the truth cut out of it by the Catholic Church. Matthew Arnold said that the church is the only organization of our time for the promotion of goodness. But that fellow Sill, whose name is getting frequent in the magazines, upset that by answering that it is the only organization for the suppression of truth. It has fought discovery in every age; it imprisoned Galileo, burnt Giordano Bruno, and persecuted Priestley, and to-day it is turning professors out of colleges for preaching evolution."

"Yes," said Calmire, "every syllable of that is true, but so is every syllable of this true, and you knew it all and ignore it: (Young people always leave so much out!) The church saved the literature of Greece and Rome; in the dark ages, it was the only conservator of knowledge: between the fall of Rome and the accession of Charles the Great, there was very little else to prevent men degenerating into simianism. The church has built most of the hospitals and schools in Europe and, till very lately, most of those in America—certainly most of the best schools; and, to get above the roots of civilization to its fruits, the church was the mother of Gothic architecture, of the great Italian painting and sculpture, and of modern music. Whenever I go into a fine cathedral during a full service, I seem to be more in the current of the world's past achievement than anywhere else—if I can stop thinking and give myself up to the art side."

"Yes," said Muriel, "if you 'can stop thinking' or think only of 'the world's past achievement.' But that's just the point. The church is obstructing present achievement; it has survived its usefulness, and I think we'd be better off without it."

(Remember, wondering reader, this was in the eighties of the last century.)

"You're too fast," said Calmire. "I admit that its contributions to schools and hospitals are not relatively as great as they used to be; but take things right here in America, where we know something of what we are talking about—the church's work for education and charity is still enormous. Admit that Harvard is no longer a church institution, and that Johns Hopkins and Cornell and the Universities of Michigan and Virginia never were: nevertheless Yale and Princeton and Columbia and Amherst and Williams and most of the others of any consequence still are."

"Yes," said Muriel; "but some of them are eager to deny it with one breath while they assert it with the next, and your very phraseology admits that the tendency of the colleges is to grow away from the churches."

"Oh, the discussion is not about tendencies," answered Calmire, "it's about the facts to-day. Now the fact is, that if the church contributions—I mean the contributions of people inspired by the church—were taken from those institutions, they would be in a bad way. That's *the fact:* to pull them away from the church, would be to break off their principal roots. What it would be in that 'five hundred years hence' that Miss Nina and I were just talking about, is another question; but you propose to pull them away from the church, or the church away from them, *now*."

"But—" interrupted Muriel.

"Wait a moment," said Calmire. "What I have to say is commonplace enough, so is what I *have* said, for that matter, and obvious enough when you come to think about it; but when you talk as you do, it shows that some people of a good deal of sense *don't* think about it. If Christianity has done something to develop shiftlessness, it has done more to develop charity. Turn away from the schools, and look at the hospitals and asylums. What are St. Luke's Hospital, and the Catholic Orphan Asylum just below it,—both right under your eye every day" (neither had been moved then), "and the great Presbyterian Hospital, and the Mount Sinai and innumerable others? Even the most of those which are technically secular, outside of those provided by government, are mainly run by societies in the churches. Consider Hospital Sunday! Go to any meeting for charitable administration: most of the men you meet there will be church members. Agnostics may have their uses, but the fact is that they're a precious small minority in that sort of work!"

"What does that queer word mean?" asked Nina.

"What? Agnostics?" asked Muriel. (The word was not then as much in vogue as it has become since.)

"Yes," assented Nina.

"Why, it means a fellow who has sense enough to know what he doesn't know, and pluck enough to say so."

"Well, that's the most puzzling explanation I ever heard," said Nina. "'A fellow who knows what he doesn't know'! How can one do that?"

"Why," rejoined Muriel, "in your sense, it's just what orthodox people are professing to do all the time—to know what they don't know, and what nobody can know."

"Then 'agnostic' is another name for orthodox Christian, I suppose," said Nina, and turned toward Calmire. "You used the word, Mr. Calmire; please tell me what you meant by it."

"You took Muriel's words in the wrong sense," answered Calmire. "He meant a man who says he does not know anything unless he has the same evidence for it that is required in ordinary matters. That involves the doctrine that knowledge comes to us only through investigation and discovery: in consequence of this doctrine, such people necessarily hold, too, that there has never been any 'revelation' in the usual sense, and therefore they are bound to hold that Christ's teachings were not different in their essential nature from those of other moralists."

"If you'd only write a dictionary, Uncle Grand!" exclaimed Muriel.

"It might be a little stiff in the joints!" said Calmire.

"Are you an agnostic, Mr. Calmire?" asked Nina.

"Oh, I'm accused of a great deal," laughed Calmire, evasively.

"Why don't you tell me?" said the girl. "I'm not ashamed to tell that I'm a Christian."

"When you tell that," said Calmire, "everybody knows pretty well what you mean. But I've heard many people say that an agnostic must be an atheist and a disbeliever in all moral law, and as I don't happen to be quite that, by calling myself an agnostic I should appear to many people to take ground that I think foolish and dangerous."

After a moment's pause, Muriel went back to the main subject. "You said, Uncle Grand, that there were mighty few agnostics doing any charitable work; but there are mighty few of us anyhow. Don't we do our share?"

"Well, I hardly expected you to be tripped up by so slight a fallacy as that," said his uncle. "Of course we're a small minority, and even if we do many times our share, the church still does vastly more than we, and that's precisely what I've been trying to demonstrate."

"But the State," Uncle Grand, "isn't it doing more of the hospital business now than the church?"

"Very likely, and more of the education too, perhaps; I'm not trying to demonstrate that the usefulness of the church is not being absorbed by other agencies. And I confess I don't want the contract of proving that, in time, other agencies can't do the whole thing. But what I'm driving at, is the enormous amount that the church is doing *now*. Not only through her did charity and education come among us, whether you like the way of their coming or not; but it's largely through her that they stay. If you fight the church, you're fighting *them*, except as you furnish other agencies to do the work; and that's slow business. And here's another very important thing—the enormous circulation of the religious weekly papers, which are pretty near the only education beyond commerce and politics that a vast portion of the people get."

"So much the worse," said Muriel. "They're poor stuff."

"That doesn't touch my argument, even if it's correct, which it's not, entirely. The religious weeklies are the best stuff that most of those who take them can assimilate, and vastly better than none. Then, too, look at the educational influence of these Summer schools—that whole Chautauqua business, for instance, is from the church."

"Great heavens! Uncle Grand, what are you giving us? Have I lived to hear you commend such rot as that?"

"Easy, Muriel, easy! It isn't as bad as it used to be, and they're making it better. By the way," he said, laughing, "a number of their journal which I happened to see the other day, would perhaps commend itself to your approval; for it contained a paper by one of the most uncompromising infidels of my acquaintance, and papers by two or three other men who I believe belong in the same category. But they are trying now to get the best things that their people can take, even if they have to get them from the opposing camp. But why should I say 'opposing'? In many respects both sides plainly want the same thing. And now— Bless you, ladies, am I tiring you to death? I don't care about Muriel: he's tough, and he's better used to my garrulous moods than you are. Nina, are bonnets to be high or low this Fall?"

"Oh stop, Mr. Calmire!"

"That's precisely what I was proposing to do."

"You know perfectly well that I meant: 'Go on!'"

"You mean that I apply to your words the meanings that tradition ascribes to those of your sex. I don't generally."

"Oh, stop teasing me! I was interested in what you were saying."

"Then I've been shamefully ungrateful, haven't I? But how can I tell that you will be interested in what I was *going* to say?"

"Well, stop chaffing, and try me and see."

"At your own peril, then. I merely wanted to say a little about the social side of the church."

"Why the new people take pews in Grace, I suppose," said Mrs. Wahring.

"No, that's plain enough. But I didn't mean that, though something ridiculously near it. What I meant is that the lower down you go socially, the more and more the church becomes a sort of social club. It's about the only society that vast numbers of people have; it gives them company for their pleasures and in their sorrows, and follows them to their graves: there's a world of meaning in the undertakers' signs on the churches. Then, too, there's another article, sometimes of value and sometimes not, which the church supplies—namely, a talkative old gentleman to harangue at the people's tables about a good many things beyond daily toils and cares."

"Seldom one, however," observed Mrs. Wahring, "troubled by as much modesty as some gentlemen I've known to defend the church at table."

"Modest or not," said Calmire, very earnestly, "the clergymen are generally extremely useful outside of the church as well as in it. It's often remarked in England, that a clergyman is always a gentleman and, in many out-of-the-way places, the only civilizing influence his flock comes in contact with. The same is true to a great extent here, though we have the schoolmaster also; and to a degree not dreamed of in England. But you people in society, to whom the church, as a social institution, is but one in many, don't begin to realize what a social help it is to the vast mass of people who have no other. Courtenay could tell a thing or two about that, if he were not too modest."

"You haven't spoken of the church yet as a police institution—for servant-girls," said Muriel.

"Yes, and you won't sneer at it so much, even in that function, when you come to keep house," said Mrs. Wahring. "I thank my Heavenly Father that he has given me the light to despise the Catholic Church—"

"'Even as this publican,'" interjected Calmire, *sotto voce*.

"—but I send my servants to it," continued the lady, and then joined in the laugh which she had almost deliberately raised at her own expense.

"So do I mine," said Calmire, "unless they happen to be Protestants."

"My Protestants don't go nearly as regularly as my Catholics," said Mrs. Wahring.

"Nor mine," said Calmire. "Are yours any worse servants?"

"No," the lady admitted.

"The less church, the less need of it, then," said Muriel.

"Can't you say: the more need, the more church?" asked Calmire.

"Well, perhaps," admitted Muriel, candidly. "I hadn't thought over all you've been saying."

"But bless you, boy, I haven't been saying anything new. Everybody here knew it all before, just as well as I did."

"Yes; but I've been bored and pestered so about the church—forced at college to go to a lot of services that I didn't care about, and all that, that I've done most of my thinking on the opposition side."

"Yes, that's one way the colleges are turning out the infidels. But you haven't been bored by it as much as I was. You had (Let me see) eight services a week. In my time they had sixteen—seven of them before daylight in winter."

"What blasted fools!" muttered Muriel.

"Well," said his uncle, who was not the only one who heard him, "I don't know that I've any particular objection to offer to that sentiment—whatever I may think of your way of expressing it," he added in a good-natured way.

Mrs. John here broke in with: "The conversation of you wise people has spun my poor dinner out very late for village folks. The band must be gathering. Let's have coffee on the front piazza."

CHAPTER IX.

THE BAND BEGINS TO PLAY.

It was a pretty sight as they came upon the piazza. The square was ample and well cared for, with serpentine walks, beds of flowers here and there, and two large but simple fountains scattering diamonds under the great electric lights. These latter were a much-admired novelty then. In the centre of the square was the band-stand, where the bright uniforms of the band had already begun to appear. The evening was perfect. People were on the piazzas of the houses around, others were scattered thickly on the walks, and children were running freely over the turf.

"I never saw a scene of greater happiness," exclaimed Nina.

"Or for less money," said John. "It cost Calmire about fifty dollars, with the help of our machinists, in off-hours, to get those fountain-jets there, and to connect the electric lights with the dynamos at the mill. Thursday is as nearly an off-night as we can make it, so we can spare the power. We don't run these lights every night yet, but shall soon. The members of the Village Improvement Society, which includes most of our people, keep the green in order in their off-hours, and as new flowers are needed, my gardener supplies them. Calmire bluffed me into that by putting up the fountains and lights himself. But what's the matter with the band? They seem to be breaking up."

Truly enough, the band were getting up and leaving the platform, and running toward them was a youth lugging a ponderous bearskin cap and a drum-major's staff. These portentous paraphernalia were assumed by one of the men, who placed himself in front of the others, marshaled them into rank, raised his staff and set them marching to the tap of the drums, and followed by the crowd, over to where our friends were sitting. After they had gone a few steps, the drum-major raised his staff again, and the band struck up, "Hail to the Chief." When they were in the street before the house, the leader signaled a halt, pulled off his big cap and cried, "Now, three cheers for Mr. Calmire."

That meant Legrand. His brother was "Mr. John."

The cheers were given with a will by the whole crowd, hats and handkerchiefs waving all around the square, for even the people on the piazzas at a distance saw what was going on and participated.

Calmire moved, uncovered, to the head of the front steps, his brother and Muriel behind him, when the crowd, true to its American instincts, began to clamor: "Speech! Speech!" He waited, smiling, for the noise to subside, and then said, so that all within long ear-shot could hear: "I don't believe we want any speechifying to-night. We're all here to listen to the band. You know I'm glad to get back among you, or else you wouldn't be glad to see me, and your being glad to see me makes me doubly glad to get back. I've seen a great many beautiful and wonderful places since I've been away from you, and a great many kinds of people, but I've seen no place and no people that can make life worth as much to me as it is just here. How d'ye do, Billy?" With the last few words he had walked down the steps and grasped the hand of the drum-major, who with the rest of the band had moved up to the steps to hear him: "Are you all well? You seem to stand it pretty well, Mr. Bissell," to a gray-haired, fierce-mustached, kind-eyed little man behind the bass drum, who had performed with acceptance on that instrument in the Mexican War, and been for the last twenty-eight years chief engineer in the Calmire Mills. "Well, Clint, old boy, I suppose the high notes come in tune by this time," to a gigantic fellow, with the bass tuba, whose hand he shook with special heartiness.

The big fellow's expression of joy was a tremendous oath, to which he added, almost weeping, "But *ain't* I glad to see you back, Mr. Calmire!"

"What's the news from Africa?" Calmire asked.

"Ah, Jim's a damned big man out there, sir," was the answer.

"Well, Johnny," continued Calmire, as he laid a hand affectionately on the shoulder of a slight, great-eyed boy of twenty, "I'm glad to see you've got the horn. How goes it, my son?" So, with a word for nearly every man, he shook hands with each of the players. Then he turned to go back to the porch, saying, "Now, the music, please. You know one or two things that I've wanted to hear you play, ever since I left you."

By the time the Calmires and their guests were reassembled around the tables on the piazza and the cigars lit, a single strain, clear and sweet, arose from a French horn on the band-stand. It was supported in the first few bars by little more than a hint of accompaniment, but gradually the instruments dropped in until there swelled up what Calmire felt to be the greatest surge of harmony that man has yet known—the Pilgrim Chorus from *Tannhäuser*. It kept rising, rising, stirring sympathetic listeners to feel: "Ah! there is a height commanding all things. We are nearing it!" And then it fell back, as all human experiences do, and, more happy than most, lost itself in sweetness and silence.

For some moments our friends said nothing. Mrs. Wahring was the first to speak: "Mr. Calmire" (turning to John), "that band has been under an artist; who was he?"

Legrand took it upon himself to answer. "That boy with the French horn is a genius. I suppose he's kept that band in shape since I heard it last. His name is John Granzine. His father is employed in our offices."

"He didn't find his way to the *Tannhäuser* overture alone," said Mrs. Wahring. (It was less known then than now.) "It's still more certain that he didn't find his own way to leaving out all of it that is unsuited for a brass band. It's equally certain that no boy was able to drill all those clods to keep their places under him as they did. Who was the master?"

"What's the use of fooling, Uncle Grand?" burst in Muriel. "Mrs. Wahring can't help learning sooner or later that you taught the band."

"No mortal man taught them to do that," said Calmire. "They caught some of the inspiration which the Universe itself throbbed through Wagner. They never played it so under me. I do believe the kind souls were lifted to it by their feeling at seeing me home again," and Calmire's lips gave a hardly perceptible twitch. "That was why Johnny had the French horn instead of his regular instrument. I must go over and thank them by and by."

Soon they trooped down the steps, John and Nina in front. Nina had trusted John at once, and, without any thought of reticence, began to pour out to him what was first in her mind. "What queer talk we had at table!"

"Yes, Legrand will talk you deaf, dumb, and blind."

"Now, Mr. Calmire, what makes you go on in that way? You know you admire your brother more than you do any human being but that quiet little lady with him now. Haven't I seen you with them for two whole hours?"

"Well, I do admit that Legrand has a good point or two. He's certainly a relief from Muriel's jabber."

"Is Mr. Muriel really a trial to you?"

"Well, he's a kind-hearted cub. He wants everybody to be happy, provided they'll be happy in his way. He always takes that way himself, without troubling himself about other people. He doesn't seem to care to do anything, though, but blow his cornet, and flirt with the girls. But I mustn't be prejudicing you against the boy. You put one in a confidential mood, somehow, and I've talked beyond bounds."

"Isn't Mr. Muriel enormously influenced by the people he is with? He seems to care for Mr. Calmire's society, and Mr. Calmire is not exactly a girl. Does he avoid you?"

"No, he hangs around and talks, and sometimes gets me to talking: for I do rather like the fellow, though I don't like his ways."

"I've had some specimens of them!"

The object of John's misgivings was now visible, in conference with the leader of the band, who seemed to have come down to speak with him, and they heard Muriel say: "Yes, after a while." Then Calmire said to the leader: "It was very kind in you, George, to give me the *Tannhäuser* to welcome me home. No other music could have given me as much happiness."

"I'm very glad, indeed, Mr. Calmire, but Johnny Granzine deserves the credit."

"Yes, Johnny knows; but you're all very kind. Does Johnny stick to his work, or does he want to be at his music all the while?"

"His father has taken him out of the mill altogether, and Mr. Courtenay is getting him ready to go to college this Fall."

"Well, I don't know but that is best. I had a

talk with his father about it before I went away."

Nina strolled through and around the square on the arm of John, who was greeted by most of the people with kindly respect, he invariably touching his hat to the men and taking it off to the women. In the throng were a good many gentle people, some of them owners of factories in the vicinity, a few living at economical ease in Calmire because it was a place of exceptional prettiness, orderliness and peace, and a few "Summer boarders" who were there for the same reason. Moreover, the Thursday evenings on the Calmire Green, with its fine band and electric lights, had come to be talked about in the neighborhood so that people came to them from even farther than our party had, in all sorts of vehicles, from the farmer's rockaway to the village blood's piano-box and the dog-cart of the Summer sojourner, and now and then a four-in-hand.

"Tell me some more about Mr. Courtenay," said Nina to John Calmire.

"Oh, he's a splendid fellow."

"What is he like?"

"Look like? Like the pictures of St. John. I call him St. John. It won't do to call him Jack any more, now that he's a parson."

"You used to call him Jack? He's a young man, then?"

"Yes, about twenty-five. But I tell you he has an old head on him when it comes to prudence and patience and kindness. You don't catch him bursting into things and people the way Muriel does."

Somehow Nina wished that John would not be

quite so hard on Muriel all the time: although she had been perfectly willing to be hard on him herself.

A little pause ensued, and while Nina was fairly reveling in the happiness around her, her ear was attacked by a most elaborate roulade on the cornet, which had been preceded by a few introductory chords by the band. Then came three or four pairs of notes, the first a high one sustained, increased, diminished with great delicacy and power; the next a gymnastic drop to a tone at the bottom of the instrument's compass which fairly made the air throb; after them a sustained trill, and then a dash off into a chromatic waltz that was a marvel of grace and execution. All motion among the crowd converged toward the bandstand, and there, the band lightly touching an accompaniment for him, stood Muriel, playing away at a second, madder strain with the fire of all the satyrs.

"Wasn't it delightful?" demanded Nina of Mr. John Calmire after the piece was over. It did not silence her as the *Tannhäuser* overture had done.

"I'd like it just as well if the beggar didn't show himself off before this crowd," sympathetically responded John.

Then Nina heard a girl behind her say to another: "Yes! He *is* a wonderful man. I know that better than anybody else."

"What do you mean?" asked the girl's companion.

"Oh, nothing. He's a great friend of Johnny's, and I play the piano while Johnny practices his parts in their music, and Johnny tells me all about him. So I feel that I understand all about him, you see."

None of these observations had been made in a confidential tone, and Nina unconsciously turned to look at the speaker. She was very pretty, a year or two over twenty, of medium height, full and not ungraceful figure, brown velvety eyes and brown hair. She was rather showily dressed, but not expensively, evidently not a menial, and yet not quite a lady.

"Who is that girl talking about Mr. Muriel?" asked Nina of John.

"Minerva Granzine, the sister of the boy who played the horn. She sings as well as he plays."

"I only half like her. She seems pretty, though."

"She professes to be, I believe."

"You odd man! Don't you ever *begin* by speaking well of people?"

"Get somebody to ask me about you!"

John's habits of speech, and Nina's uncertain feeling, were not far out about Minerva Granzine. In saying that Muriel was a great friend of Johnny's, she told a little lie. She would not have done it, though, if her somewhat vainglorious speech had not made it awkward for her to tell the truth: for lying was not her habit. Muriel had never been intimate with Johnny, though he liked and admired him, as everybody did; but Muriel could not act a part, and there were facts inconsistent with professions of friendship from him to Minerva's brother: so he made none.

CHAPTER X.

SYMPATHY?

THE T-cart was at the door at ten. It was clear starlight—so clear that Calmire had ordered the lamps put out "so that we can see the night," and until they were in sight of the great river, save for an occasional comment on something in the scenery, they enjoyed the beautiful silence that was only emphasized by the rhythmic trab-trab of the horses' feet.

Nina afterward said more than once, that in that meditation, she began to be a woman. Before then, life had not brought her any questions, nor had anybody in her world. It was the cut-and-dried world of a New York girl of easy circumstances, educated at home and seeing nobody but the usual run of society people—a society (at *that* time, let us say,) probably more moral, more intelligent, and less intellectual than that of any other great metropolis in the civilized world. During that day Nina had heard questioned, for the first time, several things which she had taken as matters of course, just as she had taken light and air. She had never heard the Calmires spoken of in any other tones than those of respect, yet here she had found them all professing opinions which, so far as she had thought anything about them, she had supposed to be held only by the depraved. What was stranger still, she had not found these opinions, as these people put them, too repulsive to interest her. Thinking was natural to her, but had not yet become habitual: she had known too little of either sadness or loneliness to be driven to it, and the books and friends that had been furnished her, had not tempted her to it. She had unquestioningly taken her peaceful life as it had come. And now as she was pondering these new and strange things, in spite of all her interest, she felt a sense of disturbance and unrest: the sense of insecurity was hardly developed; and she also experienced a shadow of resentment against the authors of the commotion, as if somebody were rocking a boat in which she had been smoothly gliding.

As her mind drifted back, it came to Muriel's incidental mention of his own life, as they had passed over the same road in the daylight. Somehow the darkness that had come over the scene seemed to have come over his allusions. She had not thought anything about them in the afternoon: she was so much interested in what he was telling her of the place they were going to, and the way it had come to be what it was; but now, she was struck almost suddenly by the consciousness that in his daylight story of activity and sympathy and prosperity, there had been a dark passage. She fell to musing over it. This young man by her side had never known a mother or father. She had heard one of the visitors whom her father's business-connection brought to the house, quote a Chinese saying, that the three greatest losses are, in youth, the father;

in middle life, the wife; in old age, a son. The young man by her side, had known the first; Calmire had known the second. To her, who had known none, it seemed unimaginably terrible. She recalled Muriel's words: "So I've been kicking around ever since, always tying up to Uncle Grand when I can." Why, he had been for months at a time, without anybody to love him! That was as vaguely terrible as the rest. Involuntarily she turned to him with:

"I'm so sorry for you, Mr. Muriel!"

The young man was never more astonished in his life. Sorry for *him?* For *him*, the envied of the envied—the handsomest, most talented, most accomplished, most free-handed, most princely, most courted young man at his college! Why, what in the name of all that was ridiculous could she be thinking about? He had never had more than two or three hard knocks in his life. These came out distinctly enough in the flash which her sentence cast over his reminiscences; but when they occurred, they had been speedily hidden by fresh successes and fresh laudations. The memory of them had an ugly habit, it was true, of obtruding itself, sometimes on the most inconvenient occasions. They did make a little drop of bitterness in his overflowing cup. But it was so little! It kept pretty well by itself, and did not spoil the wine of life; and who had had more of that than he? And whose merits entitled him to more? Consciousness of all this flashed through him too quickly to make any perceptible pause before he asked:

"Why, what do you mean, Miss Wahring?"

"I was thinking of what you told me about yourself this afternoon."

He had had it in mind very definitely that he would like her to spend some thought on him— on the way he had played the waltz, and on the elegant appearance he flattered himself he had made in the various costumes he had sported before her. These moderate ambitions were not based on any desire for her admiration more special than he felt for that of every approved member of her sex: unless, perhaps, there was a certain stimulus to such ambitions in the fact that she had made him feel a little more uncomfortable than any woman ever had before. And here, she had indeed been turning him over in her mind, and instead of being resistlessly impelled to burst out with some compliment to his unprecedented splendors, she was simply occupied in pitying him. And that, too, because of circumstances which, though he dutifully, and sometimes very sentimentally, recognized them as afflictions, did not really enter into his view of his life, as any very serious detraction from its joys or its successes. Of course, most of this had passed through his mind again and again before, and required only a glance of recognition to color his response to Nina.

"Why, is that the most interesting thing about me that you've found to think of?"

"Yes."

"Well!!!"

He was but a boy, and in his way a very candid boy. But perhaps if he had known how petty a thing his chagrin was, he would have held in his expression, or at least the long breath which followed it. He was conscious, however, of there being something awkward for him in the silence which ensued—conscious enough to break it, and in a conciliatory way:

"Well, it *is* kind in you to be sorry for my losses: but you know that I never knew my parents—they died when I was so young; so, though I wish I had them, it really has not made so much difference to me."

"Why, you have had no home!"

"Oh, I've got along pretty well!"

Now in Nina's opinion, he had not got along well at all, and, young as she was, she spontaneously traced to this very absence of a home, some of the particulars in which he had not got along well. She had been unable to hold back the blunt "Yes!" with which she had just given him his second fall for that day, but she was really, as she said, sorry for him, and perhaps was not as unconscious of the things which he considered most interesting about himself, as that blunt "Yes" had indicated. So, despite this new development of his interest in himself, her answer was:

"I'm glad you have not suffered as much as I thought. You know I have always had home and father and mother, and it seemed to me very horrible that anybody should be without them."

"Well, I try to console myself by seeing as much on the bright side as I can," he said. "I haven't had much care, but I've at least had free swing for my wits"—the gentle implication that she had not had free swing for *her* wits, being inspired by the fall she had given him.

"I believe you intimated, too, that you'd had more or less the run of Mr. Calmire's wits!" his courtesy prompted her to add.

"Well, not so very much, but I've learned more from him than from everybody else put together." Even Muriel's wounded vanity could be forgotten in his loyalty to Calmire. The girl felt it, and felt more amiable toward him for it. She said:

"But, Mr. Muriel, I'm not so sure that it's the best thing for us young people to have what you call free swing for our wits. Why, you don't seem to have anything to hold on by."

"Don't want to hold on by anything. I like free swing."

"But even a swing must be fastened to something."

"Well! I've got my seven senses and this big universe to swing 'em in, and Uncle Grand to talk to when I can get at him, and plenty of young ladies to give me good advice." He didn't know whether he meant to be sarcastic or gallant, and she knew that he meant both.

"I don't remember giving you any."

"That's so! You haven't! Yet, I feel as if you had. I suppose I ought to be grateful, oughtn't I?"

"Wait till you see if it does you any good."

"It tastes bad enough to!"

"Can't you young people manage to keep the peace back there?" called Calmire, who had caught the general tone of the conversation.

"We've just come to a stopping-place," said Muriel.

"Well, I'm glad of it," said Calmire. "Mrs. Wahring and I have been gradually brought to silence by all the beauty there," pointing to the river, which was calm and mirrored the hills, and the lights and stars in long quivering rays of fire and silver. "I'm sorry I didn't take you here, Miss Nina. That boy is a little too bumptious to talk to you, and your mother would have kept him in order."

"It's Miss Wahring keeping me in order that makes all the fuss, sir." Calmire was the only man whom Muriel ever addressed as "sir."

After his remark, they relapsed into silence.

Muriel loved nature. He had long given up imagining celestial visions, and such communion as he had with the Power behind our lives, was principally through its manifestation in broad expanses of natural beauty. He was soon lost in contemplation of the scene. Whatever he might feel regarding himself before men and women, before such surroundings as these, self was nothing. Yet they brought him a certain invigoration, and he seldom contemplated those high waving sky-lines without recalling: "I will look up unto the hills, from whence cometh my strength." In a few minutes he was lifted out of his pettiness, and, turning to Nina, said: "Look here, Miss Wahring. Upon my soul, I believe you and I must have a taste or two in common. Suppose we try not to quarrel so over everything under God's heaven."

"It's over things *in* God's heaven," she answered, "where I fear that our most serious differences are apt to arise."

CHAPTER XI.

THE NEW GENESIS.

"WELL, I'd like to know what you know about things in God's heaven?" said Muriel.

"We are told a great deal," she answered.

"Yes," he said, "by Milton and other poets, but less by the Bible than people generally suppose."

"Why!" she exclaimed, "I supposed that all we knew came from the Bible."

"A good deal more than we know," he replied, "comes from poets and Bible both."

"Mr. Calmire, I don't like to hear you talk in that way. When you spoke against the church, at dinner, it was one thing; but to speak against Christianity itself is another."

"The discrimination, at least, does you credit," he said; "but we're getting to quarreling again. Let's talk about the heavens we *can* see."

"Well," she said, "who made those stars?"

"I don't know. Do you?"

"Don't joke with me, I really want to know what you think about it," she said.

"Is that the reason," he asked, "you began with the question with which Napoleon is said to have posed certain of his unbelieving officers?"

"I didn't ask it with any desire to 'pose' you."

"Well, I answered you just as I would have answered Napoleon."

"Suppose, then, that Napoleon had replied 'God'?"

"I should have asked him what he meant."

"Why, *God!*" she said. "What can God mean but God?"

"It seems," he answered, "to mean very differently to different people—to Moses and Christ, for instance."

"Well," she said, "I can't understand that; but even if it's so, suppose I say the God of Moses, who made the world in six days and rested on the seventh?"

"I should have said that Moses evidently made his creation, and therefore presumably his God, out of the whole cloth. We *know* that this earth was not made in six days; we *know* that the other globes, the sun and stars visible to Moses, were not, as he supposed, mere lights for the benefit of this globe; and that even the most violent stretching of what we know, to make it fit Moses' statements, does no more than convince any candid mind that Moses didn't know what he was talking about."

"I've heard that his narrative was the best in all the religions," she said.

"It may be," he answered. "*Some* narrative had to be the best, and it's quite natural that we should now find that one in the possession of the most advanced nations."

"But I think I've heard, too," she continued, "that there is a correspondence between the order in which science says things were created, and the order in which Moses tells us they were."

"It would be very strange if there were not *some* correspondence," he rejoined, "and if the hosts of able men who have been trying to find what correspondence there is, had not succeeded. It would be utterly impossible to give any two coherent plans, even if one of them were the actual one, between which such vast ingenuity would not find some resemblance. But yet most of the resemblances found, are based on assumptions that Moses didn't quite say what he meant, or didn't quite mean what he said."

"Well, it may be an odd confession for a girl who is called 'educated'; but I have only the loosest ideas of what is said to have been discovered of the way things got to be as they are. And I suspect that, after all, at bottom I hate your cold science."

"Now, Miss Wahring!" the boy exclaimed, "you've too much sense to use a parrot phrase like that."

"Why," said the girl, "it's bugs, and stones, and weeds, and cutting people up," and she laughed.

"I thought," said the boy, "that you just spoke of it as concerning the start and the origin of all things."

"Forgive me!" she said seriously. "I'm afraid I have a little stubborn fit to-night. When I've been having a good time, I like to chaff."

"Yet," he answered, "you didn't like me to do it a few minutes ago, though I didn't really contradict anything true: I only exaggerated. But you girls are all alike," graciously observed the young gentleman. "Even when you know anything, you never think of what you know. You know perfectly well that there is a science of Light and a science of Thought and a science of Morals."

"Yes," said she, "and the books look awfully big and hard and stupid."

"But here you've been expressing an interest in what's in some of them!" he remonstrated.

She did not respond promptly, and Calmire, who in a lull in his talk with Mrs. Wahring had caught their last few sentences, said:

"You don't hate knowledge, Nina?"

"Of course not, only when it's stupid."

"That's the way they generally administer it to girls, I'm afraid," said Calmire; "but if you don't hate knowledge, you don't hate Science, for it's only knowledge classified—*all* knowledge, of everything—of beautiful things as well as homely ones, belongs in science as truly as the baldest equation or the coldest iceberg."

"Yes, I've sometimes really had a notion of that," she said, "but I didn't realize it just now because I've been quarreling with Mr. Muriel about Moses, and because I've always been hearing science spoken ill of, as an enemy to religion. What makes religious people hate science so, anyhow?"

"It's not the religious people, but the dogmatic people. Pretty much every religion has had to profess some account of the origin and destiny of things, to get its moral principles from. In early days it was all guesswork, and so the dogmatic notions are always coming into conflict with the new truths which *are* based on actual knowledge, as fast as Science brings them out: therefore those who love dogma, hate Science."

"But," she expostulated, "Moses didn't write the whole Bible. It can't all be dogma, even if his part is."

"Yes," answered Calmire, "but haven't the pope and the councils been making dogma, even in your time?"

"Yes, but only Catholics accept that."

"But don't you suppose," asked Calmire, "that before our branch of the church split off, they must have made a tremendous amount of that same sort of doctrine, which we necessarily inherit from the common stock? And haven't we different dogmas through all the Protestant sects?"

"Why, certainly. I never thought of that before."

"It's worth thinking of," said Muriel, *sotto voce*, remembering her comment of the morning. She recalled it too, and turning with a deprecating wave of the hand, which barely touched him, burst into candid laughter.

"Why! what are you laughing at?" asked Calmire.

"Oh, at myself!" explained Nina. "Mr. Muriel has got the joke on me."

After another silence, in which Calmire resumed conversation with Mrs. Wahring, Nina said to Muriel:

"I *would* like to know about what Science says of the origin of the stars up there and our earth down here."

"Why! didn't you learn all that at school?" he asked.

"No," she exclaimed, "I've had a suspicion to-day that there may be several things that girls don't learn at school."

He turned toward her with an expression of approval, tinged with surprise and perplexity, and went on:

"Well, probably you've heard that this earth and all the stars, and everything—even we ourselves, were once very fine dust, finer than we can imagine, diffused through space."

"But," she asked, "how did this dust get to be all these things, if not as the Bible says? God even made man out of it, didn't he?"

"Man was certainly made out of it, but not in the way the Bible says."

"Well, never mind that now. Tell me about the stars."

"Suppose," he resumed, "any quantity of the dust you please. That quantity must have a centre of gravity. You know what that is?"

"Yes, in a sort of a way."

"And you know that everything attracts everything else. You do me, for instance."

"But I didn't know that you did me."

"I do, little as you may be aware of it. Now, as each particle of this dust attracts each other particle, it must all be moving about, and no matter how various those motions are, they must all tend at length toward the centre of gravity, and as the dust rushes together, it must get to whirling around the centre, just as you've seen a lot of dust whirled together in a circle by puffs of wind meeting, haven't you?"

"I remember noticing it in drifting snow," she answered. "Oh, it was so beautiful!"

"Well," he resumed, "that always reminds me of the way the heavenly bodies were made. Those little eddies of snow or dust are circles, or rather cylinders, partly because they are made by only two opposing currents. But suppose there were no earth under the dust in one of those little whirlwinds, and currents were coming from all sides. Don't you see that they would make the dust a ball instead of a cylinder, and that it would whirl in the direction of the strongest current? That gives a notion how this star-dust rushing from all directions took round shapes and began turning."

"But how did it get solid?"

"Slap your hands together hard, or better, rub them. Don't you feel heat? Well, all bodies striking or rubbing each other, turn the force that brings them together, into heat. These masses of star-dust, jamming together with such force, and their particles rubbing so among themselves, got hotter than anything we know, and became great glowing masses. The biggest ones are not all cooled off yet. You see the sky full of them burning now. When the sun rises to-morrow you'll feel the heat of the only big one near enough to affect us. Our earth is so vastly smaller, that it has got pretty well cooled down in comparison, though not as cool as the moon has, which is much smaller still."

"How strange! But go on and give me the rest of your genesis."

"Am I as interesting as Moses?" asked the boy.

"Such questions mustn't be encouraged," she said. "Please go on. Why is the moon so much smaller than the earth?"

"The earth and the planets," he answered, "are only drops flung off from the sun in revolving, as drops fly off from a wet base-ball, and the moons are similar drops flung off from the planets. Very tantalizing things, those moons!"

"What do you mean?"

"Why, for instance, that's a pretty good sort of a moon up there, so far as I know, but they've got half a dozen or so out in Jupiter; and even poor little Mars, they've found out lately, has two or three. Now what jolly nights they must have there—lovers especially! A girl for each moon, I suppose."

"You're a very improper young man."

"Very! And those canals in Mars! Why don't the magazines publish illustrated articles of trips on them?"

"Ah," she laughed, "it's rather an out-of-the-way place to get particulars."

"I don't know about that; they send to New Jersey! And," he continued, "there's Saturn! I wonder if they use those rings for race-tracks! Just imagine—the whole planet for a grand stand, and the rings for courses."

"How far is it from the planet to the rings?" she asked.

"Blest if I know," he answered.

"Perhaps, then," she suggested, "the people couldn't see across, and they couldn't see all the way around anyhow."

"That's so. The real dodge would be to have the track on one ring and an observation train on the other, as they do at New London."

"How wide are the rings?" she asked.

"I don't know that either."

"Have you any guess?"

"Some thousands of miles."

"Then your race-course idea would appear a little extravagant."

"Yes, my ideas often are. Wouldn't give much for 'em if they were not."

"But as they are, I suppose they justify very large investment."

He was not used to this sort of thing, especially when he was condescending to try to make himself agreeable, and he did not like it. But he was too taken by surprise to assume the offensive without a moment's deliberation; and that deliberation ended with an indolent, good-natured, self-satisfied assumption that perhaps she did not mean it after all. She, too, was not ill-naturedly disposed, and had no wish whatever to be pert. So after a little she resumed amiably:

"I suppose, Mr. Muriel, that among so many ideas you are occasionally visited by a serious one?"

"Yes, I have been known to have spasms of that kind."

"Do they hurt you much?"

"Well, yes, sometimes they rather do."

"In my limited reading, I have encountered a few geniuses who seemed to like to consider their great thoughts a burden and a pain. Are you troubled in that way?"

As she had classed him with the geniuses, whether she meant it or not, he did not get angry, but took up a little of her own tone.

"Yes, my thoughts weigh on me almost as much

as your anxieties about them seem to weigh on you. But why do you want to chaff? Don't let's be restless. Let's enjoy the night."

"My homœopathic medicine seems to have done its work very well," observed Nina.

"Oh, that was it, was it?"

"Yes. I wanted to see if you really could keep serious."

"Well, I can. Wasn't I serious long enough at dinner?"

"Somehow, the sort of thing you said then always impresses me as the reverse of serious. The subject is serious; but you don't really seem to take it in a serious way."

"You don't understand me yet," said the boy.

"Are you sure *you* do?" she answered.

"Why, of course! I never thought about that."

"'It's worth thinking of'" she said in her turn, and despite their laughter, he he had a feeling that Miss Wahring was not as thoughtless, relatively to himself, as he had several times assumed.

"Well," he said, after a few moments, "whether I understand myself or not, I don't object to being serious awhile, if you want me to be; but if we talk seriously about the stars, I'm afraid we'll get to quarreling again."

"Why?"

"Because I can't say much about them without pitching into Moses, and you appear to be a friend of his."

"Oh, I don't feel about the Old Testament quite as I do about the New," she said. "Please go on and give me the rest of your Genesis."

"Am I as interesting as Moses?" the boy repeated.

"You give more reasons for things," she answered; "but you must not think so much about the effect you produce, but go on with your work. You've only got the universe filled with soft hot balls so far, and it's not comfortable."

"It does *not* seem very much as if they had been put there 'for a light by day' and for 'lights by night,' does it?" he asked.

"They seem to answer those purposes very well," she said quietly; "but aren't you ever going to tell me how the earth got as it is now?"

"Well," he resumed, "different parts of the matter were exposed to different conditions. All was bubbling and seething, but that at the poles being less exposed to the sun's influence than that at the equator, was cooler; and currents were therefore setting to and fro. As it all went on cooling at a variety of temperatures, it took on a variety of characters and shapes. Some became lava, some hard rock, some softer rock, some even water. Great cracks and ridges came —canyons and mountain ranges. In short, a crust came over the earth like the crust on a custard cooling in a dish, even to the puddles of water that you sometimes see on the surface of the custard, which will do for our oceans, and the ridges that it has cracked into, which will do for our mountains and water-sheds.

"Now," he continued, "if you were to leave that custard standing a few days, you'd find some mould coming over its surface. That mould is organic matter—matter with life."

"How strange!" she exclaimed. "But how did life come on the earth?"

"In some such fashion as mould comes over custard, I suppose, only much simpler than custard mould, which is quite a complex substance —probably in some such state as the substance we call protoplasm, out of which all plants and animals are made. From some such substance, we've reason to believe, all living beings have been evolved by slow changes from generation to generation. To put it very roughly, suppose that substance to become worms; the worms, tadpoles; the tadpoles, frogs; the frogs, as they're such good jumpers, we'll suppose to live more and more on land, until their descendants become little chaps like kangaroos; then suppose the little kangaroos to split into two families, one becoming, in time, the kangaroos we know, and the others, we'll say— well, for alliteration's sake, Calmires."

"Your uncle doesn't seem much like it," observed Nina, "whatever you may assert regarding other members of the family. I don't think I like it."

"I don't see that you need object unless he does," said Muriel. "He's rather proud of the way the family has got ahead."

"That's one way to look at it," said Nina.

"Yes," he assented, "but the theologians haven't taken that way, but have fought every step of discovery all the way up. They didn't wait for protoplasm though, but shut up Galileo, you know, for asserting that the earth itself moved."

"But, Mr. Calmire, those were bigoted Catholics

hundreds of years ago. There's nothing like that, now."

"Nothing so extreme, perhaps, but enough that's exactly like it. The clergy raised the mischief in the first half of this century over the discoveries of geology which proved the absurdity of the Mosaic record of this earth. But they've given up that fight now, as well as the astronomical one. They are fighting still, however, over the discovery that all living beings, but the lowest, were evolved from inferior ancestors. That's the fundamental proposition of the Darwinism that they dread and hate so much. But the evidence is too strong for them, and they are slowly and meanly, not manfully, giving up that fight. They make their stand now, on the question of whether living matter was evolved from dead matter. They make this fight despite the fact that their prophet, Moses, asserts that it was,—asserts it specifically regarding man and by implication regarding all other creatures— except woman, whom even he recognized as something superior. He doesn't assert an evolution, though, but a creation."

"What's the difference?"

"Why, one asserts the arbitrary making of something out of nothing, or at least the sudden change of something into something entirely different, like the sudden making of a man out of earth, as the ancients thought Prometheus made him, or as most Christian people think their God made him. Evolution asserts that, with the exception of occasional catastrophes, like volcanic eruptions and earthquakes and hurricanes, there are no sudden changes in nature; and that there are no arbitrary ones whatever—that everything occurs under the uniform and majestic control of law, even the earthquakes and hurricanes and death itself; and that life in all its forms, nay, even the colossal things which have no life—that river and those hills and the whole earth and the stars and all we see—and even all we know and think and feel, grew up by changes gradual, imperceptible, as those which turn the seed into the tree, or the dust into this beautiful and glowing universe."

As the boy spoke, the girl had gradually turned toward him, and when he moved upon her the eyes which had been dreamily peering over earth and sky, he half started at the gaze of surprised interest with which she was regarding him.

"Why, it's grand!" she exclaimed.

"If you believe it, you'll be damned," graciously observed the young gentleman.

"Oh, why will you talk so?" she exclaimed, disappointed and grieved. "Nobody believes that way now."

"You never lived South, did you?" asked Muriel.

"Or anywhere else twenty years ago," added Calmire, whose attention their raised voices had attracted.

"Not that I can remember," Nina replied.

"Well," Muriel resumed, "there's no telling *what* people believe nowadays; they've got a lot of creeds and confessions of faith that were made Lord knows how many years ago. And you, most of you, hang on to churches that profess to believe them all, and yet you yourselves profess not to.

I don't know what you call such inconsistent positions, but I don't call them honest!"

"Now you're getting polite again!" Nina remonstrated.

"Well, I declare such positions are not entitled to polite treatment!" he exclaimed.

"Suppose I'm honest, but stupid?" asked the girl.

"Miss Wahring!" and he turned toward her. "Well, I'll be hanged if I know what you are! But if begging your pardon is to admit that you're stupid, I won't do it."

"But aren't there two ways of saying disagreeable things?" she asked.

"You've just illustrated it very prettily," he answered. "But I never thought of it before."

"'It's worth thinking of,'" she said.

"Now you've got the joke back," he exclaimed. "That's the third time you've said that to-day."

"Was I right each time?" she asked. "Are you going to think of all those things?"

"Maybe. But I can't practice the mealy way of saying things to-night; for we're almost home."

Before eleven, their good horses had brought them to Fleuvemont. The ladies said good-night as soon as they were in the house. To Calmire's exhortation not to hurry off, Nina replied:

"I never was so tired in my life. I never in one day heard so many new things."

"Why, there's no particular novelty in anything that's been going on to-day," said Calmire.

"New to me. Very new. Aren't you people going to let me rest in any of my own ways? I'll have to run away from you."

"I should be sorry if our ways brought upon us any such result as that. You'll get used to them. They're not so bad."

"They're not unkind," said she as she gave him her hand in parting. "That is, not so very," as she turned toward Muriel.

Mrs. Wahring, although no more in sympathy than Nina, and by nature not as much, with most that had been said during the day, was old enough to have become somewhat used to hearing views not her own. Though not seriously fatigued, she followed her daughter, saying as she departed, "If you don't tire my child to death, I'm afraid you'll make a pagan of her."

"Do you so dislike pagans, dear madam?" asked Calmire.

"Not all of them. Good-night."

Nina spoke truly when she said that she was tired with new impressions. She was too tired to sleep, and as she lay awake pondering things of which some were very serious, one question in varying shapes, dominated all the rest—"Are that boy who used bad langage and was impolite; the man who told me so many deep things as we drove home; the vainglorious fellow who tooted his cornet so deftly before the villagers; the elegant young gentleman at dinner who said so many frivolous things and so many profound ones, even if they were bad; the young jack-a-dandy on the piazza this morning; the grand creature who stalked down the staircase last night,—are they all, can they all, be the same person? Which is he really? Well, I'm sorry for the one in the T-cart who grew up without a mother or a home!"

CHAPTER XII.

WILFUL WOMAN.

For the next morning, a sail on the river was arranged. The wagonette was at the door an hour after breakfast. After the ladies and certain lunch-baskets were handed in, Muriel said he would drive, and placed himself beside the coachman instead of in the seat next herself, which Miss Nina had always been used to consider a point of ambition to any young gentleman who might be in her society.

Muriel did not really care about driving, though he was very fond of riding; but somehow this morning he felt tired of enduring this young woman's habit of shying at observations of his that he thought were harmless and, he flattered himself, profound. Reaching the dock, he went around and helped the ladies out, and did his share of duty with the parasols and wraps.

"Now, Nina dear," said Mrs. Wahring, as soon as they had got aboard, "do take care of your complexion."

Nina turned toward Muriel and said *sotto voce:* "Mr. Muriel, do you think I might venture to observe, in the manner I've learned from you—'Bother my complexion!'?"

"Miss Wahring, I think such an observation would do you infinite credit. But don't quote my opinion to your mother." And he wondered what made her manner a little more intimate than it had been most of the day before.

They were under way almost immediately, sailing with a fair wind directly up the river.

Not long after they had started, while Calmire was forward in conference with the cook, Nina turned from Muriel, who was teasing her by persistent refusals to take seriously anything she might say, and said: "Captain, I want to steer. I've been watching you, and I can do it."

"Well, if we were at sea, Miss, I wouldn't mind letting you try. That's where you ought to learn. There's too many craft along here."

"Why, it's perfectly easy. You just turn the wheel in the direction you want the boat to go. I'm not such a baby as to be unable to do that. Tell the Captain I'm not, Mr. Muriel."

"Captain, Miss Wahring is not such a baby as to be unable to turn a wheel in the direction she wishes the boat to go."

"Oh, stop laughing at me, and make the Captain let me do it."

"It's not generally found expedient to make Captain Conroy do anything, unless his judgment approves, on a vessel where he commands," said Muriel, with a smile toward the Captain which awakened an answering smile, as Muriel's smiles almost always did. "I think you'd find it easier to coax him."

"Well, I don't like to be treated like a child. Captain, don't you think I can do that simple thing?"

"I don't know about the simple things, Miss. Whenever I hear of simple things I'm apt to think of our cruise down Florida-way three years ago. There was one of Mr. Calmire's friends on board, an artist—a very great man I knew he must be before anybody told me, though he never seemed to have very much to say, except once in a while at table. Well, the first few times I stood over him while he was at work, I felt as if I could do it too."

"Well, painting a picture and steering a boat are two very different things."

"Yes, Miss, it takes a great man to do one well, and a very common man can do the other well; but it doesn't follow that a young lady can do either without practice."

Muriel held up his right hand and said, "Please, ma'am, may I laugh out in school?"

"No! you—" But his eyes met hers with an expression that had already more than once stopped the utterance of such a sentence as she had begun. She turned again to the Captain.

"Captain, I flatter myself I've as much sense as 'a very common man.'"

"There's different kinds of sense, Miss. You have as much will as some uncommon men, if you'll let me say so. But it would be a good deal easier to oblige you than not to. I'll leave it to Mr. Calmire. Here he comes."

"Mr. Calmire," said Nina, "Captain Conroy doubts if I can turn that wheel to the left when I want the boat to go to the left, and to the right when I want it to go to the right. I hope you don't agree with him."

"Miss Nina, I've seen some of the strongest and bravest men that live, fail in doing that very simple thing under very simple circumstances. It's not a question of intelligence, but of habit: one who has to stop to think about it before doing it, may fail."

"Oh, well, there's no danger here, Mr. Calmire. The Captain says I may try it if you'll let me;" and she looked up at him in the confident though candid way that he had once or twice before failed to resist, and which, with one or two other considerations, made it such hard work for Muriel to hate her.

When Calmire was lazy, he was very lazy; and he began this day, determined to do his capable best in that direction. The resources of his nature which made him resolute and even imperious, on occasion, were off duty. He said:

"Oh, well, if the Captain says so," and seated himself on the low cabin deck in the shadow of the sail, on the other side of Mrs. Wahring.

"Confound that girl!" muttered Muriel, as he walked forward to speak to the sailors; "she'll be getting us into trouble yet."

Some time later, as he happened to be looking astern, he found himself almost spell-bound gazing at her graceful figure relieved against the beautiful blending of blue water and green hills, the harmony of color being filled by her red-gold hair, as some of its ends had been pulled down and blown outward by the breeze.

"What's the reason," he thought to himself, "that I love all beautiful things but beautiful women? I never met one yet who wasn't a discord when you came to strike all her tones."

"Hard aport!" yelled a sailor in the bow. But it was too late, or Nina made it so. They were nearing the end of a pier, where the man at the bow had seen, through the piles, a light wherry pulled by two men shooting like an arrow out into the river. Muriel saw it and rushed back for the wheel. Nina did not understand the cry, but involuntarily pulled the wheel toward her; but this threw the rudder just where the sailor did not mean it should go, and in six seconds the wherry was cut in two. Unluckily, the Captain had gone below for a moment, and Muriel reached the wheel.

"Go 'way!" he shouted almost angrily, seized the spokes, and brought the boat around into the wind.

The craft was now motionless, with canvas quivering. They could see a dark mass on the water about a hundred yards South of them.

Soon they could see one man with his right arm over what appeared to be nearly the whole of the wherry, and with his left supporting the other man, who was nearly submerged.

"Ah, he's gone!" exclaimed Calmire, as they approached the spot.

Calmire's lazy spell was over for that day. "We can't get there without a couple of short tacks. Give the Captain the wheel, Muriel, and bring the log-line here."

Calmire then threw off his outer clothing and boots and said:

"Muriel, now tie that line under my arms; let the men take care of it, and pull me up if I give three tugs. You stand by with your watch, and think of nothing but letting me stay under for half a minute, and no more, if go I must. There are two of them floating there now. No, boy!" he added peremptorily as he noticed something in Muriel's face. "You mustn't try it. It's my work. Lie to, Captain."

The boat's speed slackened, and the Captain brought them so close to the man still above water that the sailors hauled him on board too exhausted to speak. At the same moment, Calmire dived. The boat was virtually still, and the Captain had already ordered the sails lowered. Fortunately, it was slack tide, and they were well in shore out of the current. Calmire appeared at the surface, swimming easily. He said:

"Help me aboard. I'll get down better if I dive again."

As they pulled him up he said:

"Be careful not to let any tangle get in that rope; and if you find any slack, haul it up gently."

He was over again in less time than it takes to tell it, and they all watched the rope in breathless suspense. Several times the bystanders said to Muriel, "Isn't it time yet?" He held his watch and said, "No, he's still moving."

Twenty-two seconds elapsed, when all swaying of the rope ceased. Three regular tugs were given to it.

"Bring him up!" said Muriel. "Haul! Steady! Don't jerk."

Half a dozen regular hauls brought Calmire to the surface, and in his arms, insensible, a young man with light hair and beard, the latter partly concealing an ugly bruise on the right side of his face. As soon as Muriel saw his face, he said:

"Great God! It's Courtenay!"

As soon as both were on board, the spell that had held all tongues was relaxed.

"Silence!" said Calmire, panting, his voice faint, but so clear that they all heard it. "We can't have anything misunderstood here. Give me a glass of brandy."

Nina, uttering her first word since the accident, impulsively said to Calmire in awe-struck tones, "I did it. It's my fault. Why *wouldn't* I listen to you?"

Calmire merely responded, "I hope he's all right yet." And then, turning to Mrs. Wahring, added, "Take your daughter below."

"No! I did it, and I must stay here and see the end of it," expostulated Nina.

"Cousin Hilda," said Calmire, "take your daughter below. She'd find it embarrassing here. Please send Muriel to me with your smelling-salts."

And he set his men to stripping the upper part of the body.

"Sha'n't we roll him over a barrel, sir, and get the water out of him?" inquired the Captain.

"Not unless you want to finish him," said Calmire. "Here, boys," he continued, "dry him and lay him on the cabin deck, face downward. Keep away from his feet until you can put blankets on them. Put his right arm under his forehead. Give me a handkerchief."

He took it and turning the young man's head, gently wiped out his mouth. The brandy came—a small tumbler of it—and Calmire swallowed it at a gulp. It had not come any too soon: for he was very weak and had begun to shiver.

"Here, Sandy Campbell," he called, "Give me your snuff-box."

He applied a pinch to the patient's nostrils: but there was no inspiration to carry it to the sensitive spots. Muriel appeared with the smelling-salts. Calmire seized the vial, saying, "This is better." But they, too, produced no effect. "This is serious," he murmured; and set to work with them on the operations usual in such emergencies—rolling the body gently from side to side with intervening pressure between the shoulder-blades, and alternate dippers of hot and cold water on the chest.

After a few minutes, Muriel said: "Uncle Grand, there'll be two dead men here if you don't get those wet things off."

"Well, I hope he won't be one of them, and the exercise has set me fairly steaming. Still, I *am* tired. It's time to change our tactics, though. I guess we've rolled all the water out of him that we can."

Then he told them to dry the patient where the dippers of water had been dashed over him, and himself took hold of both arms a little above the elbow and began artificial respiration by slowly extending them above the head and alternately restoring them to the sides, while he set a couple of men chafing the body, under the blanket, but would not let them touch the chest, for fear of impeding breathing.

In a few minutes he let Muriel take his place and said: "Captain, we must make sail and get out of this, or we'll be overrun by these people from the shore. Don't let any of them come aboard. The mainsail will fill to the port: so we can go on without swinging the boom over our man. Keep on, Muriel. We may have a couple of hours of this before we can be sure."

Then he sent below for some clothes and changed himself on deck, refusing to quit his patient.

The Captain soon took Muriel's place at the artificial respiration, and said to Calmire:

"Guess this feller's time's about come."

"Why work on him, then, Captain?" asked Muriel. "If he has a time set, nothing you can do will change it."

"Well, mebbe he hasn't," said the Captain; and increased his vigor.

Toward the end of the half-hour, Calmire noticed something in the patient which, after a little close scrutiny, led him to say, "Stop, Captain; I think he's breathing! He is!"

Muriel had been in the cabin at intervals, to reassure the ladies. When he saw the patient, he exclaimed, "Why, he's alive! I must go right back and tell that poor girl. She's in torture!"

"It's too uncertain yet," said Calmire. "Keep on working over him!"

The breathing continued, and the face gradually assumed a natural color. At the end of a quarter of an hour, Calmire said to Muriel:

"He's saved. You may tell Miss Wahring."

Calmire poured a few drops of warm water into Courtenay's mouth. There seemed to be an effort to swallow.

"That's good!" said Calmire. "Bring some brandy."

Soon Nina, followed by her mother, rushed on deck and up to the spot.

"Ah, he is going to live!" she cried to Calmire, as she ran up with her hands clenched before her, while the men made way. She bent over the patient's face as if all her fate were in it.

After a minute or two, in which Calmire continued his ministrations, Courtenay moved a hand to the bruise on his face, and Nina, still bending over him, impulsively seized the hand. In another minute he half-opened his eyes, but after a moment more, closed them, as if dazzled and bewildered. But soon he opened them full upon the radiant face above him with its intense and anxious happiness and its halo of glowing hair, all standing out from the wondrous blue of the Summer sky. The sufferer's features gradually took expression, at first of surprise, and soon of sudden rapture, and he faintly murmured:

"At last, Heaven!"

CHAPTER XIII.

NEW FORESHADOWINGS FROM OLD QUESTIONS.

NINA's religious faith had been mainly an æsthetic ʽmatter. She had not paid much attention to the words of the chanted services in the church she had forsaken her mother's to attend; and what reading she had given her Bible, had been receptive rather than critical. The admirable things she had enjoyed, and those that some people have questioned, she let go among " the mysteries " which, she was informed, were essential to a religion,—mysteries that, with the dim light of the churches, and the deep, strange harmonies of some of the old chants, took their place in the poetic side. She had never felt any need for a strong faith, even of the every-day kind: for she had, so far, been spared those assaults of temptation, perplexity or sorrow, against which the support of such a faith is a defence.

But since the drive to Calmire, there had grown up in Nina a disturbing curiosity. She had been led to notice the distinction between Christ's religion and the Church's, but her curiosity was, at first, only regarding the historical vicissitudes of the latter. She had been made to realize not only that it was less powerful and influential than it had once been, but also less characterized by absurdities and—cruelties. Stranger than all, the longer it had been away from the direct presence of its founder, the less these absurdities and cruelties had become. Thought once having been directed to the subject, there was certainly, in a mind like hers, enough to think about.

It seemed astonishing, even to herself, that these facts, nearly all of which she had known before, had not before set her mind at work. But that might not have seemed so strange if she had realized how peculiarly sheltered a young girl's life often is from that leaven of thought which, at a parallel age, often sets a young man's in a ferment.

The ferment in Nina's, however, had at last, in a very mild way, begun. It was not diminished by the nervous shock of running down Courtenay's boat, and the terrible strain of anxiety that followed. While she had been in the cabin, she had prayed, for his resuscitation, the first really impassioned prayers she had ever had cause to make. To pray with that new intensity was to consider with a new intensity, whether her prayer would be answered. Sometimes, when a paroxysm of agonized entreaty had exhausted itself, her mind would not only dwell on this question, but would mingle with it some of the strong impressions which had haunted her since the preceding night; and they prevented her stopping merely at the question: "Will my prayers be answered?" and led her to some vague hint of a deeper question that she had never asked herself before: "Is prayer ever answered?" This doubt was so contrary to all her habits of mind—she had been so sheltered from even the second-hand presentations of it as one of the great problems agitating the world, that she hardly realized that it had crossed her mind at all. But it had, and a long and arduous mental revolution had begun.

The revolution was promoted, too, by a second influence. As they had looked back at the boat from the hill on their way home, she had said to Calmire, but loud enough for all to hear, "A very stubborn, wilful, foolish girl steered that boat to-day. I hope she learned something on it." The breach in her confidence in herself included a breach, though as yet unrecognized, in her confidence in her habitual convictions; *and*—it also did a good deal to soothe the antipathy that her wilfulness had aroused in Mr. Muriel Calmire.

As soon as they reached home, she went to her room. She lay there all the next day pondering many things, but her vigorous young constitution asserted itself, and she appeared at dinner the second night hardly the worse for wear.

As they sat on the piazza after dinner, the faint questions that Muriel had set working under her mind, were brought to the surface by one of those remarks which he was apt to touch off like a fuse ending in a blast.

"Uncle Grand, what was the sense in Captain Conroy saying, when we were standing around Courtenay there: 'Guess his time's come'?"

Nina shivered, and Calmire noticed it and said:

"I wonder if we hadn't better talk about something else? That was a pretty hard pull on some of us."

"Isn't that 'something else,' Mr. Calmire?" asked Nina, feeling that she, if anybody, had a right to deprecate Calmire's kind intentions. "Mr. Courtenay is safe" (Calmire had brought over word to that effect), "and I too would like to know what you think about everybody having a set 'time' to die."

"Ah, my dear young lady, that's one form of the old question of 'fate, free will, foreknowledge absolute,' and I think the same of it that I do of a great many other interesting questions—that I can't solve it, and that nobody can—not even Muriel." And he laid his hand on the boy's arm in a way that made the little irony affectionate.

"But, Mr. Calmire," said Nina, "aren't we taught that not a sparrow falls without the Divine knowledge?"

"We're taught a good many things," said Calmire.

"But that," said Muriel, "isn't teaching that the sparrow's time is fixed beforehand. I suspect the sparrow has something to do with it himself; and for my part, I'd like it better if he didn't fall at all. I don't see why an infinitely wise God wouldn't stop it, if he were infinitely good."

"He didn't stop my boat," said Nina.

"And you and Courtenay are of more consequence than many sparrows?" queried Calmire, smiling and finishing her argument.

"Of course," said Muriel. "So why didn't God stop her?"

Nina turned inquiringly toward Calmire.

"I suppose you're aware, my boy," said his uncle, "that you're talking nonsense?"

"No. Why?"

"Why, your terms don't mean anything. You speak about 'infinitely good' and 'infinitely wise,' when your word 'infinitely' is itself but a confession of ignorance. It simply means, as you know, without limit. Now the only way we can think at all, is within limits. We can't think of 'infinite goodness' and 'infinite power.'"

"But the words must have been made for something, Uncle Grand."

"Yes, to express that a thing is too big for our minds to compass: we often need to use them, reverently, for that. But what nonsense it is to say that if one thing we don't understand exists in conjunction with another thing we don't understand, something we do understand will be the result!"

"Give it up!" said Muriel, "and yet it seems to me that there must be something in what I said."

"There *is* something in what you *intended* to say, but your words were too big. Try it again."

"Well," answered Muriel after a moment's reflection, "apparently there's no God good enough to hate all pain, who has power enough to stop it."

"There may be," said Calmire.

"How?"

"There may be one who thinks it better in the long-run to permit it."

"Why, for instance?"

"Why, that's one of the commonplaces of theological teaching. He may think pain is good for us. Sometimes it unquestionably is."

"But," insisted Muriel, "he could do us the good without the pain, if his power were infinite."

"There you're talking nonsense again," said

Calmire. "What do we know about 'infinite'? All we know is that pain is here—that it sometimes does us good to endure it, and that it always does us good to study Nature's laws and follow them, so as to avoid it. I presume that's enough for practical purposes."

"Well, I suspect there's not much sense in thinking anything farther about it," admitted Muriel.

"That's the wisest thing you've said to-day: there's enough else to think about. But I don't see what you children ever went to Sunday-school for, if I have to tell you these old things over again."

"But somehow," said Nina, "they come up in different ways."

"Yes, in many," said Calmire, with a far-away look.

After a little pause, Muriel turned and said to Nina:

"I suppose you didn't like my pitching into Christianity the other night?"

"Of course I didn't; though, to be honest, I was interested in the talk."

"Of course," he continued, "you consider the church a divine institution—whatever that may mean?"

"I never happened to reflect before," she answered, "upon how intensely human it has been. But its shortcomings do not affect the divine authority of Christ himself. And, by the way, you were not just, the other night, when you said that he preached the gospel of shiftlessness. Didn't he tell the parable of the talents, and say: 'To him who hath shall be given, and from him who hath not, shall be taken away that which he hath'?"

"And that," said Calmire, "is as profound a sentence as was ever uttered."

"Well," said Muriel to Nina, "you've simply illustrated his inconsistency. You can't deny that he did say, in a thousand ways, 'Take no thought for the morrow,' as well as the sentence you quoted. The fact is, he kept contradicting himself in lots of things."

"Haven't you yet realized," said Calmire, "that proverbs are too terse to express more than one side of the truth? It's hardly fair to contrast them. Moreover, those natures burning with enthusiasm (and Christ could not have set the world on fire if he had not been) don't trouble themselves to be consistent. Their power is not in making systems. Christ's system, so far as there is a system, was made by his followers. The great moral geniuses simply supply the inspiration. Look at the greatest one that our country has had—Emerson. He contradicts himself all the time. Yet he probably has done more to set people thinking, and inspire them with a desire to think rightly, than any other American."

"Well," resumed Muriel to Nina, "admitting all Uncle Grand says, if there was any *supernatural* power about Christ, it ought to have kept him consistent, and kept his church straight. Isn't that so?"

"Ah, that's beyond me," said Nina. "Why didn't God keep Mr. Courtenay's boat out of my way?"

"Or yours out of his," said considerate Muriel.

"Yes," she said submissively—a new thing in her.

"Look here!" exclaimed the boy. "It wasn't decent in me to say that, and I beg your pardon."

This was a new thing in him, and her look and

smile made him think that it was a thing worthwhile. After a little deliberation she said:

"But now, my impetuous friend, what do you make out this great fact of Christianity to be?"

"Simply," he answered, "the best, and one of the latest, of dozens of great moral inspirations which have affected large portions of mankind."

"It might be just as well to add," said Calmire, "that those lessons in morality, wherever they started, have pretty generally reached us through Christianity, and been enormously developed and emphasized in the process."

"But were they all in some shape in the false religions?" asked Nina.

"There are no false religions, my child," answered Calmire.

"Just as there's no bad whiskey," Muriel broke in.

"What does that mean?" asked Nina.

"Well!" exclaimed Calmire, "it's certainly one of the great consolations of growing old, to find constant crops of you fresh young things to whom the old stories are new. It's yours, Muriel."

So Muriel told it, and went on to say:

"And it's about as true of religions as it is of whiskey. There *is* bad whiskey, and how about Baal and Juggernaut and the thugs?"

"Yes, and you might add indulgences and the inquisition and witch-burnings," said Calmire. "Yet they are only excrescences on the religions."

"Well, sometimes," said Muriel, "the excrescences are bigger than the thing itself, and have done more harm than the religions themselves ever did good."

"Possibly in a few cases," said Calmire, "but I doubt it."

"And," said Muriel, "when I think of Christianity having Alexander Borgia for chief priest, imprisoning Galileo, burning Bruno, and meddling with all the schools to-day, I'll be hanged if I'm not tempted to include Christianity in the number."

"Yes," said Calmire, "when you think of only that side. Galileo and Bruno seem to have taken very strong possession of your mind lately."

"Yes, they have," said Muriel, "and that side's big enough to make it high time the church were done away with."

"Of course you don't mean that you want its moral teachings to disappear, and its consolations to the lowly and afflicted?" said Calmire.

"Well, the shiftless side of the moral teachings has pretty well disappeared already, I suppose," answered Muriel, "and if they'd only keep their fingers off of knowledge, the rest may be good enough. But they're always interfering outside of morals, to keep up their confounded dogmas."

Nina looked inquiringly at Calmire.

"There are many dogmas that must go, my child," he said, "just as so many have gone already. But Christianity holds much that cannot go—some of it much older than Christ or Moses. The disappearance of the churches would not be the disappearance of that. Already its existence is far from dependent on the churches."

"Well, I should rather think it is 'far from dependent on the churches'!" exclaimed Muriel. "I don't believe the world was ever as good as it is to-day. Look at those people in the back towns of New

England: there's not a more honest set of people on earth; and yet the religious papers are full of complaints that they won't go to church, and of schemes to make them go—sociables, club-houses, cornets and chromos. The chromo has always been a favorite means of getting the children to Sunday-school: now they have to try it to get the parents to church. Fact is, the institution is playing out."

"You're simply the most dreadful young man I ever saw," said Nina. " *You* don't talk like this, Mr. Calmire; where did he learn it?"

Mrs. Wahring now appeared, and after some general chat, the ladies said good-night. Calmire then said to Muriel:

"You're doing that girl a doubtful service in disturbing her mind on these questions."

"Why, I don't know," answered Muriel; "I find them great fun. And I'm getting sicker and sicker of orthodoxy: the more I hear, the more absurdities I hear."

"Well," said Calmire, "there's no way to stop fools from preaching, but isn't it rather hard on a system to judge it from what any fool sees fit to say about it?"

"I never heard a man preach it who didn't talk nonsense," said Muriel.

"You mean *some* nonsense," replied his uncle. "I've heard Christian preachers talk a great deal of sense."

"Yes, so have I sometimes. But the nonsense predominates, so that at last I've broken with the whole thing."

"Well, that's more than I've done with even Buddhism or Mohammedanism," answered Calmire. "It's one thing to reason away a faith, and another thing to do without it when you need it. It's all very well when things are going so smoothly with you that the question of something to fall back upon, beyond yourself and your friends, is merely an abstract proposition. But a time comes to every young fellow of your complexity, especially if he happens to have a conscience, when some spark of circumstance blows his character from unstable equilibrium into chaos. He suffers the agonies of annihilation, and must perform the labors of creation to make himself anew. He generally ends in constructing creeds in some fashion, but he has to do it in the sweat of blood."

"Oh, I know all about that," exclaimed Muriel. "Do you think it has cost me nothing to give up the faiths of my childhood?"

"Has anything gone wrong with you while I have been away?"

"No."

"Then, you've not yet experienced what I speak of. You'll know it when it comes."

"But tell me more about it, to help me prepare for it."

"It would be useless: some diseases must be gone through with."

"But you don't want me to believe nonsense?"

"No; nor to be too eager to believe that anything *is* nonsense. The trouble nowadays is, that so much which the world has clung to has been proved nonsense, that people incline to think that *all* that it has clung to, is. Yet there's nothing more thoroughly ingrained in the system of things than these religions: you can't imagine the race being evolved to the present point without them, and no community has ever got very far without one."

"Yes," assented Muriel, "and there's nothing more thoroughly ingrained in the religions than their absurdities."

"Now Muriel, that isn't so! It's very superficial. You know perfectly well that the absurdities have been wearing off from Christianity for hundreds of years. Evolution gets rid of them, as it does of other primitive noxious things."

"Yes," said Muriel, "and it gets rid of the religion at the same time! Haven't they all got to go?"

"The underlying principles never go, but all forms change, and for the better. Already has come the difference between temples for human sacrifice and religious organizations for saving human life; between the barbaric relic-worship and idolatries of Rome and the comparatively rational observances of Protestantism: and the observances are certainly more religious than they have ever been. But of course all human things have their imperfections, religion with the rest: yet it has been just as much an agent in the world's progress as anything else in Nature, and it is as much *of* Nature as anything is."

"So are the snakes as much as the stars!" exclaimed the incorrigible youth.

"Another of your impetuous fallacies!" quietly

rejoined the elder man. "One could almost infer from it that lately you have seen more of snakes than of stars. Have you?"

"Not by any manner of means!" exclaimed the boy with a candid smile. "Not by any manner of means! No! the good things predominate—even in the religions, I suppose. No! I cave!"

"Well," said Calmire, "I don't hold to any anthropomorphic religion, as you know, but it has its uses. You'll find soon or later that every man who is a man, must have that or something to take its place."

"Yes, but he needn't have rot," said Muriel.

"If he has an inferior mind," answered Calmire, "it can hold only inferior ideas. Unless he has a soul capable of saturating itself with the conception of Law (and very few men have that yet, though many would claim to have), he'll have to land in some sort of anthropomorphism. But the religions hold all the best conceptions, not only of Law but of morality, that their adherents have been able to grasp; and to call them 'rot' because they don't hold better ones, is to despise the moon because it's not the sun. The religions shine with reflected light, it's true; but it's light all the same,—reflected from Nature Herself, and though there are many aberrations in it, it's the best that most people can get."

"Well," asked Muriel, "you don't expect to get all that into this girl's head, do you?"

"You act as if *you* did," said Calmire, "and a great deal that's much harder: for you're always attacking what's there already, and there's no knowing what she can take in place of it. You keep me busy soothing what you ruffle up, and trying to show her how the essentials of her old faiths can be looked at in the new way. I think it's the greatest mistake to disturb such people as you do."

"Well, what in thunder can be done about it?" asked Muriel. "Are people to be left to grovel in their blindness forever?"

"You're a pretty impatient soul," said Calmire, quietly, "for one who professes to believe in the slow processes of evolution. This world has got along a good while without your help, although that's the sort of fact which it's very difficult for youngsters of your make-up to realize. You're actually more of a revolutionist than an evolutionist. Have some of the patience of the faith you profess. Leave people's needs to develop as the people themselves develop; then do what you can to satisfy their needs. But don't try to stuff all the babies in the land with beef and burgundy. This is a serious matter, Muriel: how serious, you'll find out some day. Now take my advice and leave that girl in peace, if there's any peace left for her without a complete change, which I doubt. But on the chances, leave her all the peace you can, rather than give her more of this stimulation of unrest. Good-night."

"Good-night, Uncle Grand; I'd really prefer to be decent, if I could conveniently."

CHAPTER XIV.

THE GRANZINES.

WHEN Calmire talked with the band-master about Johnny Granzine going to college, he did not mention that he had told Mr. Granzine that Johnny was to be educated, if Calmire had to bear the expenses himself, which he was perfectly ready to do, but which Mr. Granzine had said he thought he could manage himself, if he was sure that "a hankering after books would do anything more than spoil the boy for anything good he may be fit for." Mr. Granzine's experience of profound culture, or what he considered such, in the mind of Mrs. Granzine, did not appear to have prejudiced him greatly in its favor.

That Granzine family had always had a sort of mysterious interest for Calmire. The name, though apparently corrupted, pointed to French Canadian extraction, yet the father was as blue-eyed and hay-haired and nasal-voiced a Saxon as ever drove a plow between New England stones. His wife, who had been a school-teacher of the name of Doolittle, was herself as unlike her name as her husband was unlike his—a slight poetic creature without any hips, with cold gray eyes, and unmanageable dark hair, ambitious, refined above her station, and intensely vulgar in her all-absorbing consciousness of that fact. Johnny got his genius from her, and Calmire, who loved the boy, forgave her a great deal because of that; but he hated her nevertheless, among other reasons because he was sorry for poor old Granzine, for whom the woman evidently cared nothing; and because, like the lower creatures, she cared less for her mate than for her offspring.

Calmire might well love Johnny, who was one of those rare instances where sometimes Nature selects only virtues from either parent, and intensifies them in the offspring. Whatever worthy aspirations made his mother restless, were in this boy easy powers, and from his father he had inherited gentleness, truthfulness, and industry.

Minerva, who was really Granzine's step-daughter, though she bore his name, Calmire half admired, but did not trust. Her impulses he felt to be kindly, and he thought her, as far as he thought about it, possessed of some sort of a conscience. But he had once said to himself: "She's a dangerously rich creature." Yet her faults were those of a careless and luxurious temperament: not, like her mother's, of a scheming and envious one. Calmire saw a good deal of her because she was the leading soprano in the choir, for which organization he had performed substantially the same services that he had for the band. His brother John had said to him once: "Oh, if the girl hadn't such a fool for a mother! Or if her mother would only rest satisfied with being a fool, and stop there!"

But John Calmire, at bottom as gentle a soul as lived, did pass a good many hard judgments. Most people, including herself, regarded Mrs. Granzine as very far from a fool.

The lady in question had greeted her daughter when she got home after listening to the band, with: " Well, my darling, did you derive pleasure from the performance?"

" Yes, mother dear."

" I hear Mr. Calmire has arrived. Did Mr. Muriel come over with him?"

" Yes."

" Of course you derived great pleasure from each other's society?"

Then Minerva told another little fib like the one she told when we had the honor of introducing her:

" Certainly."

She and Muriel had not seen each other at all, except to exchange salutations. She wondered why, and Muriel, despite the fact that he had been busy with his friends and his music, rather wondered why, too.

Yet it should be understood that Minerva sometimes had serious difficulty in lying. She *had* " derived great pleasure" from Muriel's playing at least, and the fib slipped out. It was flattering to her own vanity, and was apt to keep alive the appreciative tenderness of the maternal heart. This was a desideratum to a young woman who, after an evening spent, since an early tea, in walking around the green, desired perfect liberty among the pies, cakes, and other sources of gustatory satisfaction with which the pantries of that latitude abound. Minerva's roundness—a great contrast to her mother's proportions—was not sustained on thin air, and her "unlady-like appetite," as her mother called it, was one of the minor burdens of the elder woman's unsatisfied life. Sadly enough, the appetite had never seemed less affected than at present by the maternal aspersions. It was not even affected by any disappointment the young lady herself may have felt at not having been more fully honored during the evening by the attention of Mr. Muriel Calmire. In due time the appetite was satisfied, however, and, after the good-night kiss dutifully exchanged, mother and daughter sought their respective rooms. The father was always away at the factory until one o'clock, and Johnny had remained out on some devices of his own.

Free as Mrs. Granzine was to seek sleep, it did not readily come to her; and not before her husband's return, had she so withdrawn her mind from certain speculations to which it had lately become addicted, that she was able to calm it to rest.

Whatever may have been the state of that lady's account on the recording angel's ledger in heaven, nobody on earth (with the exception of Mr. John Calmire), had ever expressed a doubt that she was a superior woman. Taking that term in its vague general sense, even he had been known to concede it to her, but he hated her nevertheless. The one thing most likely to lead to qualifications in such exalted praise, was the amount of time which, instead of devoting to pursuits more natural to such a superior person, she spent in obtaining data for her philosophy of Man and Nature, from her little parlor window. Each morning, except Sunday, since the events just recorded, after she had, with Minerva's rather languid assistance, most energetically and systematically discharged her domestic duties, she was more prompt than usual in seating herself about eleven o'clock, with a book, in her accustomed perch.

The book did not seem to engross her during these three days even as much as usual. On the last of them she had, as usual, exchanged salutations with several passers-by, and had given more than one the benefit of a few courteous, not to say stilted, phrases, when who should come riding by on a light sorrel thoroughbred, but Mr. Muriel Calmire! It must be confessed that he did not sit a horse as well as he did some other things, but he did it well enough to make what appeared to Minerva, gazing through her chamber blinds, far from an unpleasing picture.

He was lost in meditation, and might have passed the house without knowing it (although his intention had been distinctly otherwise), had not Mrs. Granzine, whose expression on seeing him was wonderfully as if she had been waiting for him, called out: "Good morning, Mr. Muriel! Glad to see you back!" Apparently the woman could avoid polysyllables when there was not time for them.

The abstraction passed from his face like the shadow of a swift cloud from a lake, and he was all smiles when he stopped his horse before the window, saying, "I'm always glad to get back, too. How are you all?"

"Very well, I thank you. Minerva will be down in a minute."

Was this superior woman, in her prompt and inconsequent allusion to Minerva, just a little off her balance, with trepidation or anxiety or something of that sort? If she was, Muriel, though he might have felt it, was hardly worldly-wise enough to recognize it.

"Yes? I should be very glad to see her, but I can't stop now, I have a message to Mr. John Calmire."

"Well, you must stop to luncheon going back."

Muriel hesitated. He did not exactly want to, and consciousness of that fact, coupled with the necessity of concealing it, so upset his ingenuous nature as to incapacitate him from saying anything more than: "Thank you!"

"At what hour shall you return?" inquired the lady, not unconsciously naming an hour, as some different ladies would have done.

"Oh well, don't you dine at twelve?" inquired the gentleman, not ignoring that plebeian fact as some different gentlemen would have done.

"Oh no, we often lunch at one," lied the superior woman, intensely convinced that that was the proper thing to do.

"At one then, thanks," said Muriel, and the thoroughbred, feeling a slight pressure from the gorgeous boots, started briskly off.

The meditations in the rider's mind, if the privilege of quoting them exactly may be again accorded, were substantially: "Why the devil must that woman always be putting on airs? Often lunch at one, indeed! As if I didn't know, and as if she didn't know I know, that the *maison* Granzine wrestles its hash at twelve sharp." Then, after a brief interval: "Poor Minerva!"

And soon his thoughts wandered far from Minerva, his face fell into the same lines that Mrs. Granzine had pulled it out of, and his thoughts ran on Nina in strains something like: "Yes, she is an unusual girl. I certainly never did meet one like her. But why the devil must she be making herself disagreeable all the while? Ain't I as bright as she is? Don't I know more than she does? She hasn't a bad heart, though. And she's certainly nobody's fool. What? Why, of course she's a fool! If she isn't, it may cross my mind some of these days, to imagine that I may be a fool myself."

Such very inconsequent cogitations occupied him for the few minutes it took to trot to his uncle's office. The business there was soon dispatched, and he had time to run over to the house and get a little petting from his aunt, and caress and tease the children a little, before starting back to keep his appointment (which he took precious good care not to mention) at the Granzines'.

He met Mr. Granzine on the way to the mill, after the meal (he divined) which served that late worker as breakfast. But on nearing the house, he saw through the side window of the little dining-room, no indication of symposia past or to come.

At the gate (this was before the blessed destruction of so many fences in front of houses in small towns) he met Johnny coming out. The boy bowed with perfect respectfulness, and yet with the ease of a prince. But in place of the usual calm of his great gray eyes, as they looked into Muriel's, there was something not quite easy.

After bowing Muriel into the parlor, Mrs. Granzine excused herself for a few minutes, and, for the first time in his life, he was alone in the room.

On glancing around, he remarked to himself: "So they've got it here too, have they?" and picked up the illustration of the keramical craze then rampant, which stood nearest to him. He had been struck by the unexpected number and magnificence of similar objects displayed around the modest apartment. On examining the one in his hand, he found it cracked. Proceeding leisurely and unsuspiciously to the survey of another, his curiosity at finding it also cracked, drove him to a third. It, too, was cracked, and so was a fourth. He had barely ascertained this fact when he was struck by a consciousness of what he was doing, and with his usual intensity, elegance, and candor addressed himself: "Don't be a sneak! What business have you prying into Mrs. Granzine's splendor in this way?"

Close upon his remark, entered Minerva, followed by her mother. The girl looked extremely pretty. Her round cheeks were flushed, and her eyes were lowered as she advanced toward him with her hand outstretched. As soon as he took it, she looked up at him with a confident smile, and the confusion or whatever it had been, left her face and manner altogether.

"I thought you were never coming!" was her coquettish greeting.

"A queer thing for you to think!" said the young man, with less than half of his usual aplomb.

Then all seated themselves, before he, with his native incapacity to endure a pause, broke it with·

"I hoped to see you the other night." Perhaps he did, but his hope had not inspired him with much effort to realize it: in recognition of which fact, Miss Minerva responded:

"I was on the green. I heard you play."

"Yes? There were so many people to shake hands with, and my uncle had some company, so I was pulled here and there without being able to do anything merely because I wanted to."

"Is the beautiful young lady visiting at your house?" inquired Mrs. Granzine, who had noticed the inconsistency between his statements and Minerva's previous one.

"Miss Wahring is staying with us if you mean her."

"Why, do you not consider her beautiful?" asked Mrs. Granzine.

"Oh, I suppose she is. People generally think girls are."

Mrs. Granzine's scrutinizing glance took on a shade of perplexity. Was Muriel trying to make a fool of her? His insensibility to Miss Wahring's unquestionable charms was beyond her comprehension. Her only way of accounting for so strange a phenomenon was that Muriel was more attracted by the young lady than he cared to own. She determined to investigate this, and being entirely unable to understand his character, got herself, before he left, into a very pretty fog of self-deception.

Her first step, however, was to change the subject, which she did very naturally by saying:

"We will take luncheon in the garden, Mr. Muriel. Shall we proceed thither now?"

"Oh, that will be much pleasanter than here," said the candid youth, intending to compliment her selection, and blissfully unaware of any implication but a pleasant one. Mrs. Granzine's vanity was equal to the occasion, however, and saying, "I am glad you acquiesce in my preference," she took his arm and led him off as she had an impression that a hostess in a higher sphere would always lead a man when she was going to give him something to eat.

The garden, which was reached by a flight of a dozen steps from the back piazza, sloped to the river and had a view of the hills beyond. It was a pretty place, and, its owner's means not admitting of much care and elaboration, it was one of the most natural things about the establishment. Of course a path ran straight from the foot of the piazza steps to the water, and of course a whitewashed grape-arbor spread over this path halfway down, and, of course too, the path was liberally bordered by dahlias, hollyhocks, and poppies. All Mrs. Granzine's superiority was inadequate to a departure from the type of the region, in any of these fundamental particulars. It had been adequate, however, to the suppression of sunflowers around the veranda, as she considered them a coarse and vulgar plant, and had not yet reached that elevation of æstheticism which had already (though Mrs. Granzine did not know it) introduced a superb fringe of them along some of the walls at John Calmire's.

On the right of the straight path, was a fine peartree, and under this stood a table which had been taken from the house. Mrs. Granzine's researches into some of the lighter forms of European literature had convinced her that an informal meal *al fresco* was quite an elegant thing. She dimly confused the term with some horrible paintings on the walls of the edifice where she worshipped, which represented pillars and arches to give the illusion of porches, and open sky beyond. But even such reading had not so far corrupted her allegiance to the sad customs of her New England ancestry, as to lead to the establishment of a permanent table for occasional meals out of doors.

To her dining-room table, so wisely misplaced, she led Muriel, holding his arm all the way with heroic, even if mistaken, fidelity to high ideals. Depositing him on one of the chairs, she observed:

"You are aware, Mr. Muriel, of the distresses endured by American housewives with their domestic service. Mine have all left me" (only one topic did Mrs. Granzine ever permit to overcome her grammar, and that one was social elegance), "and I am reduced to preparing our meal myself.'

Muriel was sometimes a cynical dog (if the reader will pardon the tautology), but, having been so little under the influence of his family, and so much under inferior influences, he had become enough of a snob himself to feel some sympathy with poor Mrs. Granzine's sufferings; so, while through his mind flashed the sentence, "As if she hadn't cooked Granzine's dinners ever since she was married, and cooked them well too, I'll bet," his tongue, nevertheless, uttered the more courtly phrase, "I feel myself doubly honored, dear Madam." For at least once that day, it was his high privilege to make a fellow-creature happy. It may or may not have been gratitude that led her to say:

"While I am making my arrangements, I will leave my daughter to entertain you."

Minerva certainly *was* lazy, but somehow, to-day, she was not herself, even in laziness; and Muriel actually did not know whether he was glad or sorry when she bounced from the chair she had naturally dropped into, and said:

"No, Mother, I'm going to help you!"

"No; you remain here, my child. I am certainly adequate to the exertion myself."

But Minerva had already started.

"Mr. Muriel is never tired of looking at the river and the mountains," she called back. "He won't miss us."

She was generally ready to stay, and full of talk, spiced with a little good-natured chaff; but to-day, off she went, and help she did, with a will—with such energy and recklessness, indeed, that Mr. Muriel was more than once impressed by the fact that travelling up and down those piazza stairs, was a pair of little slippers surmounted by a pair of blue stockings with some little white figures worked on them, that were filled out with a degree of luxuriance which, to his young and omnivorous taste, was probably more impressive than would have been any symmetry that Pygmalion ever chiseled.

But something was out of gear in the boy. The quick coursing of the young blood was there, but, somehow, over it dominated a sense which had before been a stranger to him when such objects were visible. Though somewhat given to analysis, he was not at all given to self-analysis, and he hardly realized that the unaccustomed qualification to his feelings was distaste. Still less did he realize, in his mind contemplating the blue stockings, the presence of a suspicion of danger; and least of all did he realize a comparison of the feeling which the blue stockings inspired, with other emotions that he sometimes imagined and longed to feel. Yet back in his nature were all these complex elements, but the nearest approach to any definite thought that came into his mind, was a query: "Am I going to rush after those blue stockings wherever they see fit to run?"

So attractive, however, were the objects of his meditations, that he did not inquire very deeply into the unaccustomed turn the meditations had taken. The idea of his stopping in any such pursuit as he was picturing to himself, had never occurred to him before; and not till some time afterward, when it was brought up by even more unaccustomed thoughts, did he stop to ponder on the strangeness of such an idea occurring now.

The lunch was served, and a good lunch it was, though the young man could not escape his faculty of criticism far enough to enjoy it in free unconsciousness of its variations from certain conventions with which he was familiar. His biographer must even record, in faithfulness though in sorrow, that he did not entirely succeed in refraining from incidental allusions to fine houses where he had tasted viands inferior, as he declared, to certain ones set before him. These allusions, while impressing his companions with his social superiority, made them conscious, not without some twinges, of the shortcomings of the hospitality they were offering. He said nothing, however, with any intention of giving pain, and said so many things with the distinct intention of giving pleasure, and said them so effectively, that his hostesses were on the whole charmed with the success of their little *fête*, and he was quite charmed, as usual, with himself.

The mayonnaise, it must be admitted, was not a mayonnaise at all, but the lamb-chops were breaded to perfection, and the Spring-chicken was fried and bathed in white sauce in a way that did credit to the teaching of Mrs. Granzine's Virginia cousin. In the rolls which Mrs. Granzine had set before she took her station at the window that morning, there was no trace of the saleratus that then pervaded the cuisine of those latitudes; and there was a bottle of thin pinkish wine made of currants, or elderberries, or God knows what,—possibly grapes, but so well made and so well kept, and even so well iced (by some subtle divination of that superior woman: for if she had followed her literary lights, or those of her experience, she might have either served the stuff tepid and exhaling all its raw bouquet, or have iced Burgundy itself, if she had had it), that Muriel drank most of it (as perhaps he would have done if it had not been so good), with an effect on his eloquence and geniality that could not have been surpassed by his uncle's Clos de Vougeot.

Yet, under it all, somehow rumbled a negation, and after he had expressed with most graceful volubility his appreciation of the kindness of his entertainers, and turned his horse's head homeward, his strong face gradually fell into its meditative lines, and there floated through his mind in disjointed and inconsequent ways such sentences as: "So Miss Wahring pities me, does she? I wonder how she'd feel if she could see me worshipped and see what sort of a god I am!....Bounteous Nature! What a creature that Minerva is! How she did roll her gorgeousness up and down those steps!....Muriel, what ails you? Oh well! there must be an end to tomfoolery some time, and perhaps the sooner the better! Oh, if I could get but one clear and strong emotion to come and burn it away like the sun! But where? Where? I stretch out empty arms to the universe, and empty they fall!....Is my strong stomach turning against cakes and ale? Perhaps it isn't as strong a stomach as it was once. It certainly has had a good deal to do!...Well, it *is* a new sensation! I certainly never saw a woman before Miss Wahring, whom I couldn't master. But then I don't care to master her. I wonder if she's been glad to have me out of the way to-day! God knows I'm glad enough to escape *her*, with her ignorance and impudence!.... Does it occur to you, Mr. Muriel Calmire, that ignorance never was a bar to your seeking the society of Miss Minerva Granzine?" And after a little more meditation, the queer boy ejaculated aloud: "But God forgive me!" and actually took off his hat.

CHAPTER XV.

ANOTHER BOUT.

PROBABLY the last thing to be expected from a boy, unless he is a stupid boy, is consistency. So perhaps the reason Muriel raised his hat, was because he had uttered the name of God. Be that as it may, when he found Miss Wahring on the pizza at Fleuvemont, his manner could not have been more deferential if he had felt impelled to make her reparation for some wrong. Up to that time, he had treated her with the offhand ease of a young sultan, whose handkerchief had always been raised wherever it had happened to fall: not that he had consciously felt in that way toward her; but the boy *had* been spoiled, though he had sat too often at Mrs. John Calmire's feet, and, earlier, at Mrs. Legrand's, not to know what a true woman is, and, despite his aberrations, to long with more fervor than he bestowed on all other dreams, for the love of a true woman—that is, one made on an entirely new pattern which it would have been cruel suddenly to call upon him to describe, but one with a good deal more than either of his aunts had of rough commonplace intellect, though not with more of their transcendent genius for sympathy—which he felt, but failed to appreciate

His shade of compunction, or whatever it was,

toward Miss Nina Wahring, tempered the little conversation which they had in a stroll on the lawn before they went to dress for dinner. After they had chatted on indifferent things for a few minutes, Muriel said:

"See my uncle over by the grove. Did you ever notice his walk? He moves like the river."

"Yes. He is so calm and strong. He rests me." And then she added half to herself: "But it's a new thing for me to think of rest!"

"It's a very old thing to me."

"Yes, you *are* lazy," said the lady.

"No, I'm not. Give me any work I care for, and I work like a horse."

"Yes, you'll work at enjoying yourself."

"Well, how am I different from that beast whose cupola you see over the hill there? He works because he enjoys it. I heard him tell a man so, one day in the cars. Now what does his work amount to? He's a bank-president in New York. He goes down every morning in the six-twenty-four train, busies himself over purely material interests, and gets back in the evening about six. Then he dines, if that's what you'd call the sort of performance they have over there, and then he goes to sleep. As the days get a little shorter, he comes out too late for a drive. Then, after, he swallows his dinner, he goes to sleep too soon to open a book. In short, he leads the life of the beasts, and that's why I called him one. Now that man enjoys his laborious day as much as I enjoyed training my crew at college, and he lives such days *because* he enjoys them: just the same reason that I trained my crew or learned the cornet—two things that he couldn't do to save his life. Yet he's admired as a model of energy, while I am twitted for laziness by people whom—whose respect I believe, upon my soul, I'm really beginning to care for."

Her smile answered his, and her eyes met his as frankly as they had always done, but for the first time in their acquaintance, she lowered them before she began her reply.

"In regard to many people, what you have said, is just. In fact, our country is full of such. But do you know Mr. Plumfield?"

"No, I don't know him, and I don't want to. What I've heard about him is enough."

"Yet I must beg you to hear some more: for I do know him. In town, they live next door to us. Out here, he leaves, as you say, on the six-twenty-four train. He reaches New York not far from nine. He's not due at the bank until ten. How do you suppose he spends the interval?"

"Getting shaved and eating his breakfast, I suppose. He certainly can't do either before he starts."

"He does do both, and decently and in order too. No, he generally spends that time in personally visiting needy people who are recommended to him by the man he pays to investigate them."

"The Devil he does! Miss Nina, I beg your pardon!" he added as she turned her clear gaze upon him reprovingly.

"Isn't it rather childish to be making such a slip to beg pardon for? Understand, I'm not making the same sort of objection to the profanity, that I might have done even a week ago. It is more, perhaps, to what your uncle would call the disregard of convention. Though if you put your knife in your mouth before me, I should have no right to lecture you; but for saying such things before me, I have a right, and I intend to use it again if you do so again."

"Yes, do!" exclaimed the boy. "Go on. Make me feel like a baby some more. I'm getting to like it."

"Charmed to gratify you! Well, do you know what Mr. Plumfield does with his two hours after the bank closes in the afternoon?"

"Visits more poor folks, I suppose, as his genius runs in that line."

"No, he doesn't. His genius is capable of larger things. He goes to meetings of charitable committees. Yes, come to think of it, committees of literary and artistic things too. He's the prop and mainstay of three or four such concerns."

"I didn't suppose he could care for them at all. Well, I've done the man a wrong, and," as they turned and faced his house again, "I'd like to go and tell him so." (But he would not have gone.) "Yet you said I was right in the general drift of what I said—if he'd been like most of his style of men."

"No, I didn't say exactly that. But I feel as if you were to blame somehow. In short, I wanted to say to you what you have so often said to me: 'Try to be more catholic-minded.'"

"Me! More catholic-minded! Why, I'm not a narrow sort of a fellow. I haven't any of the stock prejudices."

"No, you have your own original prejudices.

You see how useful Mr. Plumfield is, but you still entertain a doubt whether, as a business man, he's of as much use in the world as an average fiddler."

"The world pays the fiddler three dollars a night," said Mr. Calmire, who had stopped to speak to a gardener, and was just passing to speak to a second, "and Mr. Plumfield, about three hundred dollars a day."

"The world's a fool, and you know it," Muriel called after him. "How much did it pay Archer, the jockey?" "Got the last word, for once," he added, turning to Nina. "So perhaps I can own up a little easier. Do you know I've lately had a faint suspicion of what you've just intimated to me. I *will* try to be more catholic-minded."

"And not to advise others to be so, so often?"

"Yes! Here's my hand on it."

She did not give him the opportunity he wanted to take hers, but, moving away, said: "I must get ready for dinner. You seem about to become quite interesting."

Her tone was merely playful, not sarcastic; and as they separated for their rooms, he went off, very conceited over his new virtue of humility.

CHAPTER XVI.

A TOUGH SUBJECT, THOUGH NOT A NEW ONE.

AFTER dinner the ladies started for their rooms rather early, and a few minutes later, Calmire made as if he were going too.

"Oh no," said Muriel, "let's have another cigar. Besides, I'm thirsty," and he rang the bell.

"Oh, I'm an old man, Muriel, I mustn't be keeping such hours. Do you know that there's a particular in which I'm like Sir Isaac Newton? I'm good for nothing without eight hours' sleep."

"Take it in the morning, sir. You're not going to the mills to-morrow, and there's nothing else to do, so you can afford to be good for nothing. Why, Uncle Grand, do you know I haven't had a square talk with you for over two years? And the Lord only knows when I'm going to have, with all these women chattering around here. Tell Pierre to give us something in the dining-room, and come ahead."

"You'll be the death of me yet. I tell you, I'm getting old."

"You're always charming when you talk nonsense, sir."

And they went off arm in arm.

Calmire put a match under the great logs in the

A Tough Subject, though not a New One. 145

dining-room fireplace: for the night had grown cool, and they drew up two of the great arm-chairs from the table. Their clay was duly moistened, biscuits nibbled and cigars lit, when Calmire asked:

"Well! What have you got to say for yourself?"

"I don't know. Of course, I want to talk about everything. Seems to me that nearly every time I've tried to get my mouth open lately, that girl has shut it. But somehow I can't talk commonplaces to her."

"She's rather too young to have learned or thought much," said Calmire. "But I've known you to talk commonplaces very volubly to ladies who knew nothing and thought nothing, and had not her sharpness either."

"Yes, that's just the trouble. One is not content to talk only nonsense with her, and yet if I try anything else, it only leads to disagreement."

"Invariably?"

"Well, no, not invariably; once she actually thanked me for some notions I gave her, but I'd rather she hadn't."

"Why?"

"Well, somehow, she made me feel cheap."

"Oh! I shouldn't think a stupid girl could do that. Not meaning to imply, of course, that you're the least stupid boy I ever saw."

"Thank you. Yet I don't more than half like her. Some things about her are awfully nice, but I'll bet she's stubborn as the devil."

"All of which sounds to me as if she had sat

down on you pretty hard. Has she been savage all the time?"

"Not exactly. Once she even was amiable enough to pity me."

"What for?"

"My orphaned state."

"I always gave her credit for a deal of penetration," said Calmire, "but that sounds as if she had more than I supposed."

"Why, Uncle Grand, you've never let me fee' that I had no father."

"Ah, my poor boy, I've loved you and scolded you when I got a chance. But the best I've done for you has been to bring you up at boarding-school and college. You've never had a home."

"What do you call this?"

"A place where you've been welcome to an occasional sojourn when I've not been away, but where it has not been possible for me to keep you so steadily that your character would grow into any shape the place might impose. You've grown up wild. You've not been obliged to care for women, and I suspect that Miss Wahring realizes it."

"Why, I care for women more than for anything else!"

"As an amusement," responded Calmire. "I meant that you had never been obliged to take care of them, to think of them before thinking of yourself. But as you care so much for them, and as you've got out of college now, I suppose you'll be wanting one all to yourself soon."

"Yes, if it were but possible to find the right one. There's nothing I so yearn for as a good woman whom I will think of before anything else —whom I can pour out my whole soul upon."

"You can't do that, my poor boy. Your habit is to think of yourself, and to pour out most of your soul upon yourself, and nothing but suffering can break that habit, and *it* can't break it in a day."

"Love can do anything."

"What do you know about love? You even make it a sort of boast that you've never been in love—an evidence, I suppose you like to regard it, of your superiority to every woman you ever met."

"Well," answered Muriel, "when I was a boy, I fancied myself in love two or three times, but I see plainly that it was mere fancy. The girls were in every way my inferiors, and there's no conceit in my saying it, although you seem to think I'm made of nothing but conceit."

"No, there's a good deal else in you, and you'll have the conceit ground out of you in time. But that love of yours was the kind of love that most of the poets rave about—the love that throws a glory over its object, as a sunset does over the most commonplace things—the love that does not study its object. You will study yours now, in spite of yourself."

"You don't mean that I can't love?"

"You can love in your way, but it won't be as the poets and old-fashioned novelists depict the passion. That's what I suppose you want to do?"

"Of course,—to have every faculty of my being merged in it."

"You can't do it. Your being is grown too complex. And you hardly need regret it: for that kind of love is based on illusions, and does not outlive them, as you say your boyish love did not."

"I'm not afraid," said Muriel. "I have it in me to love unqualifiedly. I shall yet meet some woman before whom I shall lay down everything."

"That's all very well, my boy, but there are several reasons why you won't, besides those I've already given. One is that you're not in the habit of 'laying down everything' or much of anything: you haven't had to often enough. Another is that a perfect woman doesn't exist, and you'll detect some of the particulars in which any one woman falls short. Another is that you're a worshipper of both beauty and brains, and you'll find it hard to get the two combined: the beauties don't generally think it worthwhile to train their minds: you may possibly grow old waiting for a delicate woman with a man's tough intellect."

"Well, why shouldn't one have it?"

"The reasons are far back in evolution. The differences in general structure and function involve differences in brain. Besides, woman hasn't yet had a fair chance: the world has been too much under the control of muscle; and her disadvantages have had their hereditary influences, along with the fact of sex. So, of course hardly any woman ever did any of the big things—at least the recorded ones. But one of these days you're going to find out that the best things are not the recorded ones. Way beyond literature, art, philosophy, politics, triumph if you will, the deepest and sweetest thing I've known or have seen any reason for supposing man can know, is human sympathy: and at that, women beat us all hollow."

"Maybe!" said Muriel with a skeptical drawl. "But I'm not such a worshipper of beauty as you suppose. I've fought shy of more than one pretty woman—in our own sphere, I mean ; of course with other women I'm no puritan."

"But at bottom you *are* a puritan, nevertheless," said Calmire; "and if your little strain of French blood ever gets the better of your puritan blood, there's going to be some queer trouble, and I don't like to anticipate trouble for you, Muriel."

"Why, I but follow Nature."

"So do you if you take what you like wherever you find it. Brute nature and human nature are two different things, though."

"The cases are not the same," Muriel objected. "I know that stealing is not right. But if I think anything else right, it's right for me."

"No! That blunder is frequent among the young. No one man's opinion is a test of right: the aggregate opinion is the only one. That's not always right, but it's apt to be right when it contradicts any one man's. But utterly independent of abstract ethics, I wish you could realize that any relation you may have with any woman but your wife, which the experience of mankind says should be reserved for the wife alone, you'll be sorry for. You may think that you can incur low reminiscences now, and still keep your soul's holy-of-holies uninvaded by them until you find a being that you care to place in it. But they will obtrude themselves at the loftiest moments, and you would have to lead your pure being to your holy-of-holies through memories of your own that you would wince to see her garments touch—things which, if you lay your whole nature open to her (and no woman is worth having as a wife unless she will welcome your laying it open), she will have to learn of with bitter pain."

"Oh well, what do other men do?" said Muriel, carelessly.

"Are you 'other men'? Would you be content with the half-arm's-length relation with your wife that satisfies 'other men'?"

"No. I'd rather have her know me and love me exactly as I am. I'd want her big enough to. But I'm not as bad as some fellows. I never deliberately wronged a woman, and I never will; and there are plenty of women as bad as I am."

"You've no right to help any of them continue bad, and you can't participate in the badness without harm to yourself; and I'm impertinent enough to have some feeling regarding harm to you. But I'm afraid preaching won't help: you'll have to undergo experience. Only let me tell you that as you're not apt to be drawn into love by illusions, there's double danger in your jading your susceptibility to the legitimate charms of sex, by 'not being a puritan.'"

"Oh pshaw! I can keep my soul virgin, no matter what my body does."

Calmire shook his head but did not speak.

After a moment's musing, Muriel asked: "Doesn't the man without illusions love more deeply and permanently than the man with them?"

"Yes, but not in the mad, poetical way. But he sticks to his love better than the poetical lovers do. You know the lovers Byron and Poe and their like depict. They're the kind all boys want to be. You know the kind of lovers such poets actually were: I suppose they too sometimes fancied that they 'kept their souls virgin.'"

"But I want to do the loving they depict, not that which they did."

"You've had your little turns at it. You're too old now. It's a babyish thing at best—as evanescent as all the emotions of childhood, as you found it yourself several times. But here it is past midnight. I'm going to bed. We'll have enough chance to talk during the Summer."

"Are you going to keep these women here?"

"I hope they'll stay. Why? Do they bore you?"

"No. Not exactly."

"But you usually like ladies' society. I can't understand your apparent indifference to these. Certainly they're as charming women as I know; and if the younger one ever has the chance, she's capable of something colossal."

"That's a big word," said Muriel.

"Yes," said Calmire, "but mind just that word: you *may* see it justified." After a moment's pause, he added musingly: "And she would be as faithful as Death!" Then he slowly shook his head, looking at Muriel, and added: "But you don't enjoy fighting her! Yet I've seen you enjoy it with other girls. Why not with her?"

"Oh well, she's not like any other girls."

"Well, perhaps a little of her castigation may do you good. Good-night, my boy. Oh! Muriel, by the way, wouldn't it be just as well while the ladies are here, to hold up a little on playing the cornet in the house? Ladies, and perhaps some old men, may be addicted to a little sleep between lunch and dinner!"

"Oh, bother sleep! Who cares for sleep?"

"Most people who are *obliged* to care for anything."

"Of whom, thank God, I'm not one," exclaimed Muriel. "Good-night."

"Yes, you are one," said Calmire, "but you don't know it yet. We all are."

"Oh well, Uncle Grand, I'm getting sick of this business—whatever a fellow wants to do, is always bumping up against some confounded Law of Nature. Nature is nothing but a dumb brute. I'm a man and I have a will of my own. She may blast me if she wants to, but she can't frighten me. Oh, I glory in old Ajax defying the lightning!"

"Of course! of course! Something big and sensational!" said Calmire. "Do you suppose that if you see fit to defy Nature, she's going to bother over you with her lightnings? She's more apt to send some petty filthy messenger so contemptible that even a microscope can't find it, and quietly and contemptuously rot you down as she does the oak: she does not often grant even the oak the honor of a lightning-stroke. Muriel, there are some things before which it does a man good to feel small!"

The boy first looked puzzled and then ashamed. He got up, held out his hand, and went off to bed without a word.

CHAPTER XVII.

MR. COURTENAY EXPERIENCES SOME SENTIMENTS AND
A VISIT.

COURTENAY had been put ashore at the scene of the accident, by the mouth of the tributary stream which, three miles up, passed the town of Calmire. He stood the drive home very well, but he was not fairly himself for more than a week.

During the long reflective hours of that week, even his impatient dreams over his beloved and noble work could not generally hold their place in his mind against a widely different image, equally noble in its way and—probable, though strange—equally beloved. Amid the faces—weak, yearning, cringing, grateful—with which the reminiscences of his ministry were crowded, now always obtruded itself that strong and beautiful one, his recent glimpse of which had seemed Heaven. It was the last face he had seen on quitting life, the first on returning to it. She had taken his life, she had given it back. She controlled it. It was hers. That sort of reasoning, under any inspiration of the good and beautiful, was easy to him. His whole system of things was made up of it; his life was passed in preaching it. On grounds about equally coherent, but with the loftiest motives, he had from the beginning given up his life to God; and now the second great inspiration, Love, had similarly taken possession of him. In common-sense matters, he was by no means devoid of common sense. But fond as he was of preaching common-sense sermons, religion was something higher than common sense, and so, he now felt, as he had often dreamed, was love. Was not religion, love; and love, therefore, religion? And was not faith in love therefore faith in religion? Any less view was a low view, a subjection to mere reason, of his highest impulses and his highest faiths. Reason he admitted to be a great thing—in law-courts, in laboratories, and on exchanges; but religion and love must be guided by something higher than reason: they were matters of inspiration—of faith. And so, as he was inspired by the faith that his life was Nina's, he was, of course, inspired with the, to him, logically correlative conviction that her life was his. A sense of his unworthiness suggested itself, as it often did: but he would have faith; and as soon as he should be well enough, he would go to her in his great faith, and it should be justified.

During his convalescence, this state of mind matured. It had been stimulated by his being told of Nina's bitter self-reproaches, not only for having so imperiled a human life, but a life so valuable as she knew his to be. All this had been recounted in various ways by the Calmires, who had all been to see him—Calmire himself twice, John on alternate days, and Mrs. John every day, once bringing a bunch of her children.

Even Muriel, after leaving his card the day he

lunched at the Granzines', concluded that he could manage to talk with the parson by Wednesday, and on that day presented himself in person.

As Courtenay walked forward to greet him, Muriel grasped his hand heartily. Unless he disliked a man, he could not take his hand in any other way, and he more than once had caught himself taking in that way, the hand of some one he did dislike.

"Well, Mr. Courtenay," he said, "I'm mighty glad to see you so well out of that scrape."

"Yes, it has indeed been a merciful deliverance," said Courtenay, "and I thank you for your sympathy."

Perfunctory as the words may read, there was nothing perfunctory in them. They came out in a perfectly hearty and manly way. So did Muriel's answer:

"Well, as regards the deliverance, it strikes me that a better time for that would have been before the boats struck."

"It's not for us to criticise the ways of the Lord, Mr. Calmire," Courtenay said, though not austerely.

"Perhaps not: though I believe in the liberty of determining which are the Lord's ways and which are the Devil's ways."

"Then," said Courtenay, laughing, "I suppose I should blame the Devil for getting me into the trouble, as I thank the Lord for getting me out."

"I thought Uncle Legrand got you out," said Muriel.

"He certainly was the Lord's instrument, and a very efficient one."

"Then Miss Wahring, who got you in, was the Devil's instrument, and equally efficient."

"Ah! I cannot be guilty of such double blasphemy as that," said Courtenay fervently.

Muriel turned his eyes from the flower-pots on the window-sill, where he had let them drift, and cast his strong glance full upon the speaker: though it was not to measure him for battle, but merely to determine, though not premeditately, whether Courtenay's fervor were gallantry or something less mundane. With all Muriel's vaunted slowness to love, he was entirely capable of being jealous of any man's regard for almost any woman. And as that universal jealousy existed for many generations in the remote ancestry of every man, probably the strongest traces of it exist still in the men who can love strongest. Such a feeling Muriel always crushed, or thought he did; but it came, and needed to be crushed. Without professing to love Nina Wahring, he felt that innate jealousy, or some other, when he turned toward Courtenay; and when he saw Courtenay's face, he realized that he felt it.

"What! This damned parson!" he said to himself. But he was much more in love with theological argument than with Nina Wahring, and so he returned to the charge.

"Where's the sense in thanking God for getting you out of a scrape, when he might as well have kept you out of it in the beginning?"

"Why, Mr. Calmire, our moral education comes from the scrapes we get into."

"Well, I prefer to get my moral education easier."

"But," said the clergyman, "we can't always have what we'd prefer. No man can understand the ways of God."

"I've found mighty few men," responded Muriel, "who are strong enough to profess not to, and stick to their profession through thick and thin. Men profess in one breath not to understand him; and in the breath before, they have thanked him in some fashion implying a better understanding than I, at least, can see my way to."

The rage of argument was upon the boy, and he would have gone on had his man been in the death-agony.

Courtenay changed the subject.

"Well, I'm not up to argument now, and I'm even afraid my people will have to put up with an old sermon Sunday."

"Fortunately they can't answer back," said Muriel with good humor, but not realizing the possible double meaning of his "fortunately."

Courtenay, however, took the remark as it was meant and went on:

"I've been able to read a little, but not to write."

"Why, I should think writing a sermon the easiest thing in the world," said Muriel.

"Not easy enough for me now. But why do you think it easy?"

"Well, as I've just said, the congregation generally endows sermons with a sanctity that puts them above criticism."

"That conception of a sermon would have been correct a hundred years ago," said Courtenay, "and perhaps later, but it's hardly correct now. Now, a minister is rather expected to discuss the questions of the day, and some have had to give up congregations, for preaching on the side of the minority."

"That's true!" exclaimed Muriel. "There has been some pluck there. But don't you think *anything* but religion a descent from religion?"

"There's theoretical religion and there's applied religion. I'm a practical man, Mr. Calmire, and I try to preach my religion applied."

"And I suspect there would have been a good deal less nonsense in this world if more people had taken your course," said Muriel, rising and holding out his hand to take leave.

"I'm afraid you're correct," said Courtenay with equal cordiality. And as they grasped hands he added: "I wish we could see more of each other, Mr. Calmire!"

From babyhood up, Muriel had been pestered by so many advances of this kind from people of religious professions desirous of making him what they saw fit to call "good," that he could not dissociate Courtenay's advances from the rest, and the situation embarrassed him. He did manage, however, to say, "We get along better than most," meaning most people who disagree, and vanished.

The minister had received Muriel in a little study upstairs in an humble boarding-house. More luxurious quarters were not within his means, as he saw fit to use his means: too much of his salary, respectable as it was, went home to the large family of which he was the eldest son, and to poorer people.

After Muriel had groped his way down the dark

and narrow stairway, the first clear thought he had was: "So the parson's in love with Nina Wahring!"

And then, but with no realization of rivalry, he fell to contrasting the parson with himself, and not altogether to the parson's advantage. The parson was a good fellow! What lots of good he did! But all sorts of namby-pamby people could do that. Muriel could, easily enough, if he cared to try. But, after all, the parson was not so namby-pamby: he could even, Muriel suspected, beat Muriel at tennis. But what was tennis? A mere game! fit for girls and parsons. Now for any real thing, say a pistol—Muriel had never seen a man who could handle one as well as he could, and that was a man's weapon. And as to pulling an oar or sailing a boat! Hadn't Muriel been a college stroke, and taken boats through all sorts of night and blow, while that near-sighted parson had let a girl run him down? And then his idiocy in thinking himself in heaven! "But, confound it!" Muriel thought, "I wish the girl hadn't run him down." The wish was not born of any tenderness for the parson, or for the girl either. And no one could have convinced him that it was born of any tenderness for himself.

CHAPTER XVIII.

FAITH AND FACT.

ON Monday evening, Mrs. John had Courtenay to dinner. The good fellow's constitution, strong from temperate living and abundant exercise, appeared to have entirely recovered from its fearful shock, and to have, if anything, taken on a little extra vigor from the unusual rest of the past ten days.

All the Fleuvemont people were over, though Nina had conquered some reluctance before consenting to go. She knew that they would meet Courtenay, and the idea of encountering her "victim," as Muriel had dubbed him, abashed her. Yet she realized that, before long, they must meet somewhere, and she preferred to have it over with.

On the afternoon drive over to the dinner, when they passed the Granzines', they saw Mrs. Granzine and Minerva on the little piazza—the mother standing, and Minerva seated, with a mass of flowers in her lap. Calmire saluted them with his whip, and Muriel raised his hat. These proceedings led Nina to remark the pair, but even before she recognized them, she had that vague feeling of something wrong that she had felt when they drove over before. The passing glance at Mrs. Granzine gave her a sense of shrinking that she sometimes had experienced regarding people whom she had afterward found dangerous, and when she recognized Minerva, she felt a certain relief, albeit confusion, at remembering the remarks she had overheard when Muriel was exhibiting himself with his cornet. Half unconsciously, she exclaimed: "She is certainly very pretty!"

Did Muriel blush? And what made him so slow in saying: "You mean that girl that we just passed?"

"Whom else should I mean?" said Nina, with some odd feeling of opposition.

"Oh yes, she'll do very well. See that hawk and the two little birds over there! Upon my soul, I believe he's getting the worst of it!"

They watched the birds manœuvring against the blue background, and flying along in front of them. In a few minutes, the three were out of sight, after what seemed a drawn battle.

Muriel then turned toward Nina and said: "How do you reconcile the work that was attempted then, with the goodness and omnipotence of your God? Either the poor little bird had to be eaten, or the poor hawk had to go home without any supper."

"How do *you* reconcile it?" answered Nina.

"I don't pretend to," Muriel answered.

After they were all in the drawing-room, Mrs. John said to Mrs. Wahring and Nina: "I'm disappointed in one guest whom I wanted Nina to meet. I think you know her already, Hilda."

"Whom do you mean?"

"Mary. She had to go to New York on some hospital business this morning."

"Oh, I want to see her so much!" cried Nina. "I caught a glimpse of her when we first came here. She was so lovely! I'd intended to ask about her before. Who is she?"

"My dearest friend," said Mrs. John. "She is—"

"Mr. Courtenay!" cried the butler, and that gentleman advanced toward his hostess.

The name gave Nina a little start, and she involuntarily slipped behind her mother, which brought her near Muriel.

After Courtenay had been introduced to Mrs. Wahring and shaken hands with the older men who came up, Mrs. John led him up to Nina. Before Mrs. John spoke, Muriel said: "I think you two have met before."

Nina promptly held out her hand, saying: "And oh! Mr. Courtenay, can you ever forgive the manner of our meeting?"

"Don't think of it in that way, Miss Wahring."

Men have their own ways of being "ready." The great generals, ready beyond other men, have not, as a rule, been very ready in mere speech; and men who have been very ready in speech are not, as a rule, very ready in real feeling. Courtenay was prompt in feeling, so prompt that the very directness of his emotion shoved aside that indirect approach to things which contributes to wit. Like the rest of us, he sometimes after the event, thought of the better things he might have said; but not often, for he was not vain enough to. Regarding this occasion, however, he did afterwards think of various antithetical observations with which he could have opened his acquaintance with Miss Wahring. He wished that he had said in answer to her plea for forgiveness: "Forgive it? I shall always bless it!" That was what, in his "Faith," he felt; and something like that, was what he thought Muriel Calmire would have said under the circumstances. The good man did not realize that that was just the sort of thing which, in its slight exaggeration and (as he would have been in earnest) its unblushing pouring of emotion into the ears of third parties, Miss Wahring would not have liked half as well as she did like the bashful parson's straightforward words. They showed, too, that he did not think of himself, but only of her.

Her eyes thanked him, and her answer was: "You're very good. And you have been doubly good to get well so fast, instead of giving me more of your illness to regret."

Muriel had managed to muster up enough unselfishness to move away, and Mrs. John did not find her presence necessary. Mr. Courtenay asked Nina if she would be seated, and got her a chair, instead of ordering her to sit on one before asking if she wanted to, as Muriel would have done.

When he was seated opposite her, the ardently-awaited situation was there, but it seemed strange. This eminently well-turned-out young lady in a very pretty dinner-dress, seated conventionally in a quite correct drawing-room, was certainly a most graceful picture, but she was not exactly an altar-piece; yet that was just what Courtenay's devotional habit had made of that glimpse of her bright face against the radiant heavens; and he had been worshipping before it in a very devoted but yet very professional fashion. He still felt the devotion, and it even showed itself in his eyes, but he felt a little as if he had gone into church to open service, and found his prayer-books missing; and so it came about that his first remark was:

"It has been a very hot day!"

"Yes, at noon it was," said Nina. "But we found it not unpleasant in driving over. I sometimes feel that our city sea-breeze must reach even up to here."

How easy she was! How she had given the little commonplace subject a suggestive turn, and how pitifully commonplace he had been! Was this life of his a very full life after all? Although he sometimes did go into society, he was at the opposite extreme from the regular society parson, and did not often talk with any strange woman except the wife of some new laborer who needed bringing into the fold, or some less doctrinal aid. He never was stupid in talking with *them*. And before he settled down to his work, he had not been stupid in talking with other sorts of people. All this went through his mind in a flash, but not to the relief of his self-consciousness. He jumped to the opposite extreme.

"Yes, it's an ill wind that blows us no good from the city."

Nina's balance had become the least trifle disturbed through her quick sympathy with his little perturbation, and she said, laughing, but a trifle nervously:

"Like that wind that blew my boat down upon you!"

This braced him. He was on the water, nothing before his eyes but her face with its loosened hair and the blue sky behind it. He exclaimed:

"Ah, I shall ever bless that wind!"

His fervor startled her. She heard the rings of the portières behind them click together, and Mrs. John approached, saying: "Mr. Courtenay, will you take Miss Wahring in?"

But after they got in, Mrs. John placed "her boy" Muriel on Nina's other side, although she had got Sallie Stebbins up from the judge's to make the company even, and had Muriel take her in.

Calmire was on Sallie's other side, and she liked to talk to him; and Mrs. Wahring was on the clergyman's left, and she preferred to have him, rather than Muriel, talk to Nina, so she occupied herself mainly with John Calmire, who of course had taken her in. This arrangement made Nina much of the time an object of competition between Courtenay and Muriel. To Muriel's ponderous self-assertive nature, this would have been an annoyance if he had not been in high feather, and feeling rather a zest for the rivalry. Courtenay's placid and unselfish soul was not at first conscious of anything in this conjunction unfavorable to his eager hopes. The possibilities of boredom and the possibilities of delight inherent in different arrangements of the same people at table, had not been realized among his limited sorrows and limited joys.

They were hardly seated when Muriel began, in his amiable way, to put his big foot right into the midst of things.

"Miss Nina, you owe it to Mr. Courtenay to make this dinner compensate him for a good many that he's lost."

"Oh don't let's think of them," said Courtenay. "Fortunately lost dinners are not like some other lost opportunities. I have had an extra appetite for a few days, that I think has already made up for mine."

"Your amiability seems equal to anything," said Nina. She did not mean to intimate that Muriel had imposed upon Courtenay's amiability, yet Muriel felt a little as if she did. Between them both, he felt a sort of compunction, and so set to work like a dancing elephant to improve matters.

"Well! All's well that ends well. We've ended in a good dinner. And if your running a man down, Miss Nina, has anything to do with the introduction of this Sauterne to these clams, I wish you'd do it every day."

"And I would echo the wish if it were needed to enable me to discuss these good things in your company," said Courtenay, looking toward her.

"Ah, then you find my company peculiarly appropriate to Sauterne and clams," said Nina.

"To anything good," was the best that Courtenay was able to say.

"To all things fragrant and inspiring—like this," said Muriel, tasting his wine, "and to all things tender and sustaining—like this," he added, drinking a clam from its shell, regardless of his fork. Then he looked at her, laughing, and said to himself, half surprised, "Blest if it's all chaff! She's lovely!" He had already attacked his second glass of Sauterne, and the emulation with another young man, felt now for the first time in her presence, was upon him.

"Don't you think there are flowers enough about the table already, Mr. Muriel, without drawing on your rhetoric for more?" asked Nina.

He looked at her significantly a moment, and then said: "Yes; emphatically Yes! Any that I or mortal man can make, would be superfluous here."

It was half mischief and half earnest. He would have said the same sort of cheap stuff to any attractive woman under the circumstances, and had often talked it for the sake of hearing himself talk. Nina did not know whether to be merely amused, or whether, if she should be anything more, to be pleased or displeased. She had never seen him in this mood before. She had got some sense of the deep current under the ripples of his nature, and she did not know whether to regard these trifling flashes as coming from the surface of the stream itself, or as mere will-o'-the-wisps of temporary impulse. But in reality, seldom if ever had Muriel talked the same sort of nonsense with quite the same feeling.

Once while Muriel was getting poor Sallie Stebbins out of breath with some disquisition more profound than Calmire's kind taste would permit him to inflict on that lady, Nina said to Mr. Courtenay:

"Won't you tell me a little about this work of yours that I interrupted so rudely?"

"Dear Miss Wahring," he answered, "will you

not try to banish your regrets over that harmless accident? For the sake of helping you to, I'm almost tempted to ask you not to speak of it again."

Nina flushed a little at even this kind opposition; but instantly answered:

"I *will* try, Mr. Courtenay, not to annoy you with it. Now tell me about your work, please."

"Most of it is Mr. Calmire's work, not mine."

Calmire, who had a faculty for following the conversation around him without losing the thread of his own, said to Mrs. Wahring, "Excuse me a second," and turning, smiling, to Courtenay, said: "I beg your pardon, Mr. Courtenay, but I couldn't help overhearing you. It ought not to be necessary for me to take the liberty of saying to you that honesty is even a greater virtue than modesty. Miss Wahring is able to realize that."

Then he turned and resumed where he had left off with Mrs. Wahring.

Nina returned to her attack.

"Well, as you were about to say regarding Mr. Calmire's work, which he allows you the privilege of doing for him?"

"As to the work which both the Messrs. Calmire make it possible for me to do, it's a good deal in the nature of leading the horse to water. They provide the water."

"And you pump it," interrupted Calmire again.

"Well, who's the horse, and what's the water, and how do you pump it?" asked Nina.

"Perhaps it would be necessary for Mr. Calmire himself to explain his part of the metaphor. I'll gladly explain mine. I suppose the ordinary functions of a minister to a laboring population must include much more attention to mere physical needs than mine do. Fortunately there is very little pauperism here, and very litle sickness. There is in the very air, a cleanliness and a spirit of industry and self-respect, and the sanitary arrangements of the town are perfect. So really I'm able to work more exclusively for the spiritual welfare of the people. Now I realize that making them religious is greatly helped by making them intelligent."

Muriel shrugged his shoulders.

"Now these people," continued Courtenay, "come here desiring neither religion nor intelligence. Of course there are exceptions, but I'm speaking of the mass and, naturally, most of the new-comers. But one thing they all do desire, and that is amusement. Now our programme is simply to give them what they don't want, by giving them what they do—to amuse them in ways that develop their intelligence, and to proceed from that to their religion."

"'Speak for yourself John!'" quoted Calmire with a smile.

Courtenay blushed and said: "Perhaps I ought not to have said '*our* programme' in reference to the religion: for I must admit that regarding that, Mr. Calmire's position has been simply that of a neutral—a friendly one, though."

"Perhaps," said Calmire, "if you'll pardon my interrupting you again, you may find yourself able kindly to say to Miss Wahring that you have not found my brother and me exactly neutral regarding the *moral* condition of these people."

"I can say so, most sincerely. The influence of these gentlemen, I need not say their example—except in staying away from church," he interjected in a good-humored way—"has of course always been on the side of good morals. But, also of course, I'm bound to believe that their influence would be even better, if it went farther in the direction of religion."

"I can't see how anybody is *bound* to believe anything," again interrupted Muriel.

"Ah, I feared so," said Courtenay, amiably.

"I'm afraid you'd find it a little difficult to support the proposition you hint at, Muriel," said Mr. Calmire.

"Why?"

"Why, if we don't believe what we know to be true, all basis of action falls to pieces, and certainly we're bound to prevent that."

"Yes! 'What we *know* to be true.' But Lord! that's not what gentlemen of Mr. Courtenay's cloth mean when they say, 'bound to believe.'"

"His expression is not under discussion, but yours. You said you could not see how anybody is *bound* to believe *anything*. Now I think a man is morally bound to believe, for instance, that two and two make four."

"Yes," answered Muriel, "and that three times one are three?"

"Certainly."

"But," said Muriel, "Mr. Courtenay says there

are circumstances under which three times one are one."

The explosion of this careless bombshell was followed by silence. Courtenay was flushed, and all, even Muriel himself, were annoyed. After a moment, Nina's clear voice uttered :

"Mr. Courtenay, will you kindly tell me a little more of who is the horse, what is the water, and how you pump it?"

The table broke into a laugh, and good feeling was saved. Calmire looked at Muriel with a smile that bordered upon a frown, which Muriel answered by raising his eyebrows, while some heavy lines took shape about his mouth. Then Calmire at once began talking to Mrs. Wahring, throwing Miss Sallie upon Muriel's attention, and leaving Courtenay free to continue with Miss Wahring.

"With pleasure," Courtenay answered. "The horse is, of course, the people here; the water is the material provided in the library building, more especially in the lecture-room; and when Mr. Calmire is good enough to say I pump it, he refers to my attempts to provide lectures, concerts, and magic-lantern shows."

"Delightful! But do you mean me to understand that it's hard to lead your horse to such water?"

"It ought not to be, and has not always been. But just now I am encountering an unexpected difficulty."

"What's that?" asked Calmire, who this time was in a temporary pause of conversation.

"Ah, I haven't had an opportunity to tell you

before. I have felt it, but only learned what it is yesterday after church. I understand that the Catholic priests are getting jealous of our influence over their people, and are prohibiting their coming to our entertainments."

"Why, there's been no attempt at proselyting their people, has there?" asked Calmire in a sudden way that for years had been growing less frequent with him.

"Unfortunately I have been able to make very little," answered Courtenay.

Calmire's face grew cloudy, and he said: "I fear the attempt to make any, may have impeded our efforts to do these people good."

Courtenay answered: "I have not thought it right to neglect their highest good."

"Ah, my friend," said Calmire, "the only way to the highest good is through the attainable good, and the highest is very seldom immediately attainable."

"The Catholic Church does not hesitate to proselyte, and we must fight her with her own weapons," answered the clergyman.

"I'm not convinced that we must fight her at all, at least directly," said Calmire.

"And let her have her own way?" asked the clergyman.

"Sometimes that is the most dangerous thing people can have," answered Calmire.

"Well, what am I to do?" asked Courtenay. "Here are these people opposing our efforts for the good of the poor and ignorant in this town!"

"Make allies of them."

"Impossible!" answered Courtenay.

"Perhaps. Have you tried?"

"No."

"It may be worth trying."

Nina had become much interested, and was turning her bright face to one speaker and the other, awaiting their replies. Calmire, who was opposite, noticed it; so did Muriel, who was at the angle of the table. "Watch out, parson!" he said to himself.

"I had never thought of making allies of them," said Courtenay, aloud.

"Neither had I," said Calmire. "I'm not sure that they would co-operate if you were to try. But there can be no harm in trying."

"I'm not sure of that, I'm sorry to say."

"Why, the worst you could do would be to fail."

"No! It might be worse to succeed," said Courtenay. "I believe it would inevitably spoil the work for the Catholics to take part in it."

"It might limit its range," Calmire admitted. " But it begins to look now like a question of limiting its range, or limiting the number of people whom it is to reach. I think there would be range enough, though, in fields that the Catholics would not object to."

"You'd have to keep away from History," said Muriel.

"Not necessarily," said Calmire. "The history most necessary for these people to know, Catholics and Protestants are agreed about. They can vote on all questions likely to be before them, without knowing anything of Savonarola or Bloody Mary, or even of Christopher Columbus."

"Yes," said Courtenay; "but I should hate to have our work kept away from such history as bears upon religious points. I hope I don't want to be narrow in *any* direction."

Nina looked up at him with a smile which somehow he felt he only half deserved; and Calmire responded:

"So should I hate to have our work limited at all. But I have found few things that are not limited, in spite of all we can do; and we generally have but a choice, not exactly between two evils, but between two limited goods. The choice here seems to be between influencing only a few of these people, or being a little discriminating in selecting methods which may influence them all."

"You mean between letting some of them go, or working with the Catholics?"

"It looks as if it might come to that."

"Well, then, for my part, I'd let them go. I couldn't work with the Catholics."

"Well, I hate the Catholics pretty well," blurted in Muriel. "But I'll be hanged if I'd be above using them!"

"They might use you!" quietly observed his uncle.

"And then again they mightn't," said Muriel. "You're not afraid they'd use you, are you, Mr. Courtenay?"

"I had not thought of that," said Courtenay. "I simply could not work with them."

"Some of them are admirable people, as the

world goes," Calmire quietly rejoined. "Of course I don't mean that their views are congenial with my own; but," turning his eyes full on Courtenay, "congenial views throughout, are not necessary to enable one to honor a man and work with him."

"You don't insist upon people believing with you, Mr. Calmire. The Catholic priests do insist upon it."

"I thought," exclaimed Muriel, "that you'd been trying to make some of their people believe with *you.*"

Courtenay's face reddened. Nina Wahring's interested expression changed into a look of disapproval, of which, however, she gave Muriel a portion, and Calmire said, promptly:

"Well, fortunately, our course need not be determined to-day, and we can determine it when our discussion need not trouble anybody but ourselves."

Mrs. Calmire arose, and as the ladies followed her into the drawing-room, it was with a feeling of strangeness that Courtenay saw Nina disappear. Surely it was unnatural that they should have so long been side by side without the tie which God himself had placed between them being recognized and even mutually acknowledged. Yet there she was, wandering off from him as unresponsively as any other young woman whom he had ever taken in to dinner.

He knew, though. The hope and faith were in his soul, and in the good time of Him who placed them there, they should be vindicated.

CHAPTER XIX.

COURTENAY AND HIS SISTER.

Though the day had been hot, the evening was cool, so the men smoked in the dining-room instead of on the piazza, and Courtenay, though he did not smoke, stayed with the men. When they joined the ladies, it was only to say good-night, as the Fleuvemont party had their drive before them. Courtenay, however, lingered to see the last of Nina, and placed himself beside her to walk out to the carriage. This aroused a little resentful feeling in Muriel, though whether it arose solely from Courtenay's appropriating what for the nonce Muriel considered his property, he did not stop to consider. His feeling of even a proprietary interest, would have surprised him a little, if he had been in the habit of examining his feelings.

On the drive home, he sat behind with Nina, as before. His first remark naturally was:

"Well, how do you like the parson?"

"He has simply the most beautiful face I ever saw," she answered.

"Nice thing, that, for a man to have!" was his comment.

"I don't think it lacks firmness," she said.

"No," said Muriel, "I shouldn't be surprised if it

could even get as far as stubbornness. But how do you like the man himself?"

"He appears to me very noble!" she answered. "Perhaps he's not as catholic-minded as some people, but we can't expect everybody to be very much so."

Muriel came as near wincing as he was capable of, and changed the subject.

"Do you think he's as beautiful as his sister?"

"As his *sister?* Why, I never saw his sister."

"Why, didn't I tell you," ejaculated Muriel, "that Mary is his sister—that woman you admired so the first day you came here?"

"Impossible!" exclaimed Nina. "Why, they're no more alike than the two poles!"

"The two poles are very much alike, I suspect," answered Muriel, "at least in a certain family resemblance—probably a great deal more alike than Courtenay and Mary."

"Well, do tell me all about them," said Nina. "They're the most interesting people I ever saw."

"Thank you!" said Muriel.

"Oh you egoist!" exclaimed Nina. "You unparalleled egoist! Are you *always* thinking of yourself?"

"Well, I'll be blessed if I know. I know that lately I've sometimes wished I didn't. But I've generally been so awfully *by* myself, you see—friends enough, but not many to be with and think about all the time—like parents and brothers and sisters."

"You poor boy! And yet the first time we drove over here, you wouldn't let me pity you. Perhaps you don't like me to now."

"Yes, I do. Do it some more!"

"Stop your nonsense and tell me all about Miss Courtenay."

"I wish I could. There's history written all over her. But I can't get at it. There's religious trouble in it somewhere, I judge from several things. I suspect Uncle Grand knows all about it, and perhaps Aunt Amelia; but nobody ever pumped either of them in this world, or ever will in the world to come, if there's any such institution."

"What a horrid, horrid infidel you are! But anyhow, tell me what you know about her."

"Well! She lives all alone and keeps a little school for the better children. And she also runs a sort of hospital for all sorts of broken-down people, especially for city brats and their mothers in Summer."

"But where does she get the money to do that?"

"Oh, I suspect Aunt Amelia knows. But she never tells such things, neither does John nor Uncle Grand."

"But why does she live all alone?" asked Nina. "I should think she'd keep house for her brother."

"Well, that's one of the mysteries about her," Muriel answered.

"Don't she and her brother get along?" asked Nina.

"They seem to—perfectly. But she never goes to his church, though."

"How very strange! But I'm surprised that people trust their children to her, then."

"Oh, that's because it's the fashion, I suppose.

Aunt Amelia started with her brood, and all her friends followed suit. Besides, everybody loves Mary, though I understand that she has fits of the dumps, when she'll have nothing to do with anybody but the children and poor folks, for days at a time."

"Not even with Mrs. John?" asked Nina. "I should think it would relieve any burdened soul to be near her."

"No, not even Aunt Amelia. But I forgot that even at such times, Mary likes to see Uncle Grand."

"Won't she even see her brother?"

"I have an idea not. But this is all largely conjecture on my part—made from putting this and that together."

"Why, you seem interested in her," said Nina. "But I don't wonder. I never was so drawn to anybody by a mere glimpse."

"Yes," said Muriel, "if she weren't nearly old enough to be my mother, I think I'd be in love with her."

"Why, do you know her very well?"

"About as well as I know the Virgin Mary. She always seems to me just about that far off, but just about as benign and lovely."

"You don't mean that you never spoke to her?"

"No, but I do mean that she always seems above our world—at least above my world," the boy added, in a tone that was very new in him.

"Mr. Muriel Calmire," exclaimed Nina, "you're the strangest man I ever saw! Is this humility, that you're treating me to a glimpse of now?"

"I don't know. It's something or other inspired by a lovely woman. They always make me good.

I've suspected you of doing it once or twice. Why don't you keep it up?"

"Because I've been lovely only once or twice, I'm afraid," said Nina, simply.

"Is this a glimpse of humility you're treating *me* to?" said Muriel, with a little laugh.

"I don't know," she said, in the same quiet and utterly simple way.

"Well, it's something rather nice, whatever it is!" exclaimed the boy.

"Thank you!" she answered, and they both laughed a moment and were still. After a little she asked:

"Haven't you any guesses, even, regarding Miss Courtenay's history?"

"Oh! of course she lost a lover once! That goes without saying."

"But it's so queer," said Nina, "that she doesn't live with her brother."

"And doesn't go to church," added Muriel, "especially as she's a parson's daughter, as well as a parson's sister. A queerer thing is that she never goes to see her parents, and her father never comes here. Her mother has been here."

"Well," said Nina, "Mr. Calmire has got to tell me that story sometime—if it's right that I should know it."

"Perhaps Mary will tell you herself," said Muriel. "You seem on the way to be great friends with her."

"She *is* 'friends' with people, then?"

"Certainly," said Muriel; "everybody in trouble goes to her—especially lovers and sich, and she and

Aunt Amelia and Courtenay take care of every sick cat in town."

"A proceeding which you don't seem to approve very heartily," said Nina.

"Oh, I don't know! I don't bother my head much about it."

"And yet you do bother your head over some serious things," she persisted.

"Oh yes, the big things," he answered; "but I'm not much on sick cats and that sort of thing!"

"Have you ever been sick any yourself?" she asked.

"Do I look like it?"

"No, nor talk like it either."

"Yet," said Muriel, almost as if musing aloud, "the best fellow in our class didn't seem ever to be quite well."

"He wasn't the same sort of a good fellow that you are, was he?"

"Not by a long shot. Guess he's a better fellow than I am."

"And there you go again!" exclaimed Nina, approvingly. After a little while she asked: "How good a fellow is Mr. Courtenay?"

"Oh, he'll do, in his way. But he's rather hidebound."

This irritated Nina a little, and she answered:

"Are you sure that he's more 'hidebound,' as you call it, than some young men who differ with him?"

"Mean me?" asked Muriel.

"Does the cap fit?"

"Of course not! I've outgrown all that stuff, long ago."

"But haven't you grown into any other stuff?"

"Not the kind that makes a fellow hidebound."

"Well, I'm not so sure about that," she said.

"Why, what do you mean?" he asked.

"Simply that you sometimes appear as blind to the good on his side, as you would say he is to the truth—or what you call the truth—on yours."

"I don't know; I hope not," said Muriel in a quiet, candid way that surprised Nina. "I hadn't thought of that."

"'It's worth thinking of'!" She smiled as she reiterated the old formula for the dozenth time, and they both laughed.

CHAPTER XX.

THE ALL-INCLUDING.

AFTER some alternations of silence and indifferent chat, they got into the open country and under the dome of the stars. It was a thoughtful night—not one with moonlight's constant challenge to admire and enjoy, or with deep darkness's gloom and appeal to inherited fears; but a night when the stars have an individuality, not only of size, but of distance, so that one seems to realize them not merely as spots of light, but as tangible bodies near and far.

After the two young people had pondered quietly for a while, Nina said:

"Who made the star-dust?"

"The same man that made the stars, I suppose," Muriel answered.

"I thought you fought against the idea that anybody like a man made either!" remarked the lady rather impatiently.

"How exceedingly literal even the brightest women are!" ejaculated the youth, and after a little pause, continued: "It was out of deference to your opinions that I used the word man. Far be it from me to limit the cause of this universe to anything our intelligence can grasp. Spencer suggests, you know, that the universe may be due to something as far transcending intelligence as intelligence transcends mechanical action."

"I didn't know," said Nina, "though perhaps I ought to have known. The idea appears to me immense and vague."

Calmire turned from the front seat and said:

"Doesn't it look as if ideas must grow vague as they grow immense? I wonder if that's not one reason why the farther we get in comprehension of the Infinite, the farther we are from believing that we comprehend it. The wisest men that I have known, have been the most modest."

Muriel went on to Nina: "That particular idea about the Power behind the universe won't appear so vague after you get used to it, but if people are honest, they've got to be content with many vague ideas on subjects that are beyond their grasp. People who are not, manufacture the religions."

"Dogmas, you mean!" Calmire interjected again.

"Confound your omniscience, Uncle Grand!" exclaimed Muriel. "Can't you help hearing everything that everybody says? I can't talk for Miss Wahring and you too."

"Don't try," said Calmire, laughing. "Talk to her. Anything worth her hearing, is worth anybody's."

But during the rest of the talk, Muriel did have a little consciousness that his uncle would hear without listening; but, though that may have kept him a little more careful than he otherwise would have been, the sympathy between him and his uncle was too great, despite Muriel's boyish tangents, to permit any serious embarrassment.

"Well, Miss Nina," he resumed, "do you really want to know about the star-dust?"

"Certainly, unless it's one of the subjects which you alluded to a moment ago, that my mind can't grasp."

"Look here!" he exclaimed, "I didn't mean your mind any more than anybody's else. There are lots of things which we've all got to be content not to know."

"To be agnostic?" she queried.

"Yes, just exactly so. But there are things about which it's legitimate to guess, and others about which it's foolish to guess."

"Is it legitimate to guess about the star-dust?" she asked.

"Yes, because we see things actually going on that suggest what it is."

"What is it, then?"

"It's smithereens!"

"Now, Muriel Calmire! can't you ever be serious two minutes together? What in the world do you mean by that word, if you mean anything?" It was the first time she had addressed him without the "Mister."

"I'm perfectly serious," he replied. "Smithereens is the very entirest, most completest smash that anything can be knocked into. Didn't you ever hear of a gentleman proposing to knock another gentleman into smithereens? that's what star-dust is. It wasn't made by Jack Heenan, though, or even by any of the more pious people, such as Torquemada or the Duke of Alva, who liked to hash up their neighbors for conscience' sake."

Nina could not help laughing with him a little, and then said:

"Well now do be serious and tell me how it *was* made. Of course you know, as you know everything."

"Madam, I am an agnostic. The foundation of my creed is, that I don't know everything, and, what's more, that I can't. The foundation of my moral character is modesty. The trouble with you is, that you don't know when I *am* serious."

"Well, I confess that it takes more penetration than I'm mistress of," she admitted. "Now if that satisfies you, go on and tell me how the star-dust got knocked into smith—that ridiculous word."

"It wasn't the star-dust, but the stars," he said. A lot of them bumped into each other and had a general pulverization."

"Well, I'd like to know who was there to see it, or how he survived to tell the tale," laughed Nina.

"Of course we don't *know* it," said Muriel, "even as well as we know that the Sun flung off the planets, or the planets the moons."

"That depends upon what you mean by 'know,'" broke in Calmire. "Some wise men think we do."

"So we do!" exclaimed Muriel. "Thank you, Uncle Grand."

"But watch out now, Muriel," said Calmire; "you're getting on disputed ground."

"Well," continued Muriel, "what I was going to say looks mighty consistent anyhow, and the men with the biggest grip take it in, whatever the dry-asdusts do. It's denied only by a lot of duffers who haven't any imagination."

"Don't be too sure of that," Calmire cautioned him again. "If you began to realize what harm imagination has done, you wouldn't blame anybody for using it cautiously. You're now among a lot of hypotheses that few working astronomers are yet quite ready to call proven."

"Don't you believe it, Uncle Grand?"

"The rhythms of evolution and dissolution?" asked Calmire. "It looks very tempting—provided," he added with a laugh, "one's sympathies are not pained by the thought of so much dissolution. But that's a thought that we've got to harden ourselves against anyhow, for it seems plain, at best, that every orb in the universe is going to become cold and dead some day, like the moon."

"Well, the 'hypotheses' suit me," exclaimed Muriel after a moment's musing.

"So do my faiths suit me," said Nina, "and haven't I as much right to them as you to your guesses?"

"Heavens, no! Why, I've something to guess on, but you believe lots of things that are made out of the whole cloth."

Well," said Nina, partly as if resigning herself, "tell me your guesses."

"Lord, they're not mine!" ejaculated the boy.

"Modest again!" exclaimed Nina very pleasantly. "But go on with them, please."

"Well, you see," Muriel went on, "we've reason to believe from the laws of physics, though we haven't had time for actual measurement, that the moon is slowly approaching the earth; and the earth, the

Sun. So presumably all the other orbs in the system, and in all systems, are approaching each other. The little ones will inevitably fall into the big ones some day, and when they do, they'll become star-dust again. If the moon were to fall into the earth now, it would be dissipated into nebulous matter that would reach beyond its orbit."

"Gracious Heavens, Cousin Calmire!" exclaimed Mrs. Wahring, who had been listening since Calmire last spoke, "do drive under cover somewhere!"

"I don't think we need to hurry," said Calmire. "We've some millions of years yet. Besides, if the moon hits us, or if we tumble into the Sun, the attraction of the larger body will hold the substance of the smaller one in some form or other—perhaps atmospheric. To get a bump big enough for a fresh start all around, the two bodies would have to be of near the same size. So you see our individuality, at least as part of our system, is not in such immediate danger."

"Oh I'm so consoled!" said Mrs. Wahring.

"But I'm afraid you've got to come to it sooner or later," insisted Muriel. "It looks very much as if, after you're part of the Sun, you'll go bumping up against some other sun some day and then, I really am afraid, your physical identity, even as part of the Sun, will be disturbed beyond recovery."

"Well, I'm glad my poor husband isn't here to be harrowed by this tale," exclaimed the lady.

"I'm here, mamma," observed Nina, "but I'll stick by you—even then."

After their little laugh, when Calmire had resumed talking to Mrs. Wahring, Muriel went on :

"You see, after enough of these things fall together—"

"But why should they fall together?" Nina interrupted.

"Why, if they keep on attracting each other, they've got to, haven't they?"

"But they attract each other so little—'as you do me, for instance,' to quote your illustration of the other night." Her manner made the speech agreeable despite its touch of sarcasm, and it was a pity that he could not catch the expression of her face.

"Then they've got to be just so much longer about it," said Muriel, too intent on his topic to invent a prompt reply to her badinage. "But it's got to come all the same"—"Just as some other things have," he was surprised to find added in his mind. But his imagination was constantly rounding out things in that way, and young as he was, he had made some progress in suppressing its suggestions, though he got into a good many scrapes from not suppressing more. He put this one under, not very summarily however, and went on: "We're going for some sun in Hercules now, you know, just as Uncle Grand said. Probably we're too far off to have picked out the exact one, but when we get there, there'll be a dust raised, I can tell you!"

"Oh Muriel," exclaimed Calmire, "we don't know that. We haven't had time to see whether things are really working in that direction."

"Well, isn't it a healthy guess?"

"Herschel felt pretty sure of it," Calmire answered, "and some of the rest are nearly ready to accept it. Yet most hold out against it as 'not proven.'"

"There's a mighty sight more reason for you to believe it, Miss Nina," Muriel continued, "than to believe lots of other things that you do. Well, just as I explained to you the other night, the star-dust rushes into suns, planets, moons, and then again, in time, those moons, planets, suns, will rush together and make new nebulæ, and "—here Muriel's voice began to sound like his uncle's, and he spoke meditatively—"so have come, and so will come, evolution and dissolution—evolution, dissolution—through times and spaces before which our intellects are absolutely powerless— this ineffably beautiful infinity above us and including us, throbbing with rhythms beside which our lives are vastly less than the smallest star is beside that milky-way; and yet those vast rhythms are but the pulses of the Universe. I don't know which moves me the more—the immensity or the order of it all. I suppose that's about the vastest conception the human mind has yet attained."

"Yes, stupendous!" exclaimed Nina. But after a little awed silence, she added: "And yet, Mr. Muriel, it seems to me a hopeless sort of conception, tremendous as it is:—nothing fixed—nothing permanent—nothing really attained!"

"Well," answered Muriel, "we've attained the Iliad—and Miss Nina Wahring! And I won't admit them to be nothing."

"But the Iliad has got to go too!" Nina modestly objected.

"There's a great deal to be said on that question," interrupted Calmire, turning again. "But the fact that the conception Muriel has been recounting raises the question, interferes with its being really the vastest conception yet attained: There are conceptions just as wide, which are more certain and not so mechanical, and, perhaps you would say, not so hopeless."

"Oh give me one!" cried Nina. "This tremendous dream of constantly recurring death smothers me."

"There's not time to-night. Let Muriel give you something else to catch your breath with."

"Well, what shall I tell you about?" asked Muriel.

"Oh I don't know! *Anything*. Yes," she exclaimed after a moment, "there *is* one thing you told me the other night about the way the stars were made, which puzzles me a great deal. Why did the dust get hot when it rushed together? Why do my hands get hot when I rub them?"

"Don't you know anything about the law of the Persistence of Force?" he asked.

"Oh, in the way that, I'm beginning to find, girls always know things! At school I studied a little about what my book called the Conservation of Energy. The teacher asked us questions, and we told her what was in the book, all in half an hour, and that was the last I thought about it. I wonder if it's what you mean?"

"Probably," said Muriel, with an inflection of despairing pity. But an idea struck him: "Weren't you telling me the other day that you once went to see a place where they made electricity?"

"Yes."

"Well, where did your people get their electricity?"

"From the steam-engine," she answered.

"Well, that steam-engine gave out nothing but force, did it?"

"No, it supplied the force that whirled the things that made the electricity—something like dynamics, they call them."

"Dynamos, you mean," he said, laughing. "Now don't you see that (to put it roughly) the force was turned into electricity, just as, later, the electricity was turned into light? And if you turn the electricity into heat instead of light, and put the heat under the boiler, you'll get back again to mechanical force, and can start the engines over again."

"Why, how interesting!" she exclaimed. "It's 'swingin' round the circle.'"

"Yes," he answered. "Now you see how force and heat are but different forms of the same thing, and it's not so hard to understand how the force of the star-dust rushing together was turned into heat. But what I've given you, is not the most interesting circle that Force swings around."

"No? What is?"

"Before the engine developed the electricity, where did it get its own force?" he asked.

"From the steam."

"And that?"

"Well, it must have had something to do with the fire."

"And that?"

"From the coal."

"And that?"

"Now you're too hard for me."

"Well, you know that the coal is ancient vegetation. The matter composing it was brought together in plants by the heat of the sun. In separating, in the fire, it gives off that heat again. To put it a little more precisely, the union of the plant's elements was effected by the sun's heat turning into chemical energy. The separation of the same elements is effected by turning the chemical energy that holds them together, back into heat."

"Electric light is sunlight, then!" she exclaimed.

"Certainly, a form of it. So is all other light on earth."

At the time of the publication of this narrative, the learned do not interchange the terms "force" and "energy," as freely as was often done when Mr. Muriel attempted his demonstration; and the new views of electricity also tend to make that demonstration appear rather primitive. But those views, after all, only confirm and widen the general principle he expounded, which is the main point.

He went on with his topic. "But even making electricity is not the most interesting way that a plant has of disposing of the sun's energy. When the plant is eaten by an animal, its energy becomes part of that of the animal, and helps do his moving, seeing, hearing, tasting, feeling, and thinking."

"Why," said the girl, in wonder, "I knew that eating plants, or eating animals that have eaten them, made us grow and enabled us to take exercise; but I didn't know that our thinking and feeling had anything to do with our eating."

"Well, it has," said Muriel. "But Lord! how ignorant they let you girls grow up!"

"Did you know these things when you were my age?" she asked.

"Why no!" he exclaimed after a moment's reflection. "We didn't have them till Junior year."

"Well, this is my Freshman year," she said, laughing. "Now tell me some more about food and mind."

"Don't you know," he resumed, "that you can't think or feel without matter in your nervous system changing place, and that that change is made by the force you get through your food and air?"

"No, they didn't teach us that at school," she responded. "It's very wonderful."

"I suppose they didn't teach that, because it's what they call materialism," said Muriel. "It's true, though: thought's nothing but another mode of force."

"Check there, Muriel!" Calmire interrupted. Then he excused himself to Mrs. Wahring, and continued to Muriel and Nina, a piece of noiseless road making it easy for him to be heard:

"Thought is *not* a mere mode of force. Why, with sufficient instruments one could see all those changes in nerve, but one could not see thought. The thought accompanies the nerve-change, but it is about as reasonable to make them identical because they are simultaneous, as it would be to make thought identical with change in countenance or voice, because they also are simultaneous. The realm of force and matter is one thing,—visible, tangible, or at least measurable,—and nerve and nerve-changes belong in it. But the realm of thought is invisible, intangible, unmeasurable. We can keep track of the matter and force as they go into your brain and as they come out, and some day we'll really measure them and the changes which take place in them while one thinks and feels —in fact we can measure the pulse-beats stimulated by our feelings now: but we can't measure the feelings themselves, except by inference. You can't even think of feeling as measurable like nerve-function, and there's no bridge between the two. All assertions to the contrary are but forms of words, and the idea of applying an instrument to thoughts and feelings, or of treating them in any way as we treat the nerve-changes collateral with them, is simply inconceivable."

"Well!" exclaimed Muriel, "if thought is not a mode of force, what is it then?"

"That's exactly what we don't know," answered Calmire. "But we know very well what it is not, and it's not anything we know of, but itself. It is as nearly an ultimate fact as force or matter—more nearly: for it is behind all our notions of them. By the way, though, perhaps I ought to say that *consciousness*, rather than thought, is behind those notions, but for the purposes of our talk, it's hardly necessary to go into such distinctions."

"Guess I'll wait," said Muriel, "and not up set what you've had to say, *this* evening. Yet I know lots of fellows who think as I've been thinking."

"Oh well," said Calmire, "there's a stage at which fellows jump at anything new, if it's only startling and subversive enough. But it's odd that that stupid blunder should deceive anybody. Saving your presence, I don't know that it ever has deceived any really eminent person, though eminent blatherskites have done a deal of chattering over it."

"Farther instruction in materialism from me," said Muriel to Nina, "is indefinitely postponed, until I've had a little time to examine my opinions. But," he continued, "I suppose you'll admit, Uncle Grand, that we know nothing of thought except in connection with nerve-change?"

"Certainly," said Calmire. "And we know nothing of the sensation of light except in connection, direct or indirect, with incandescent matter, but that does not make the sensation of light the same thing with incandescent matter." Then he continued his chat with Mrs Wahring.

Muriel resumed to Nina: "Well, force is still a fact that accompanies everything, and in a sense at least, causes everything. Even if it is not thought, it starts up thought, through vibrations that strike our eyes and ears and other organs, and if one is going to think at all with reference to one's relations to the universe, the first fact to realize thoroughly, it seems to me, is that through all, without us and within us, everything—the motions of the stars and their heat and light; the processes of our earth, its clouds and storms, and the growth of the plants they feed; the growth of its living creatures and all they do; the life of man—his senses knowing the universe, his intellect understanding it, his feelings toward it and toward his fellows, his loves and hates and aspirations—all depend, so far as we know, on processes in various forms of the same boundless force. It pervades all, sustains all, inspires all."

"It, then, is God!" exclaimed Nina.

"Yes—God, Pan, Brahma, Ormuzd, Osiris: wherever men have vaguely guessed regarding it, they have given it a name. It has had thousands."

"But, Mr. Muriel, Brahma and Osiris are idols."

"Oh fudge!" he exclaimed. "You've been in Rome, I believe? Wish I had."

"Yes," answered Nina. "But you mustn't say 'Fudge' to my simple ideas. It's not polite—or kind."

"All right! I beg your pardon, and I'll try not to do it again. Well, did you see any images of 'God' in Rome?"

"Yes."

"Then where's the difference? Call them, and images of Brahma and Osiris, idols or not, all are efforts to express to sense, the all-pervading power."

"Perhaps so," Nina admitted, "but nobody in Rome worshipped the pictures and statues of God the Father."

"Did they worship images of any other divinities? Even of men?"

"Yes, they did," said Nina. "But somehow that didn't seem idolatry."

"But it was, all the same," Muriel asserted, and added: "And now, I tell you, Miss Wahring, any sort of anthropomorphism is idolatry."

"What does that awful long word mean?"

"Why, it's simply made up of two Greek words"

(which the young gentleman was pleased to show his scholarship by pronouncing and translating). "It means the effort to narrow down the illimitable power behind the universe, to the form of a man. To my mind that's a step toward idolatry, whether the idolatry turns up in Italy or India: at best it's only the result of early man's incapacity to imagine a force not proceeding from a man or an animal. The early man wasn't quite ready to understand gravitation changing into heat, or into the later forces —winds and lightning and tides and vegetable growth and the mind of man and the grace of woman: and so at first he referred each manifestation of the All-including Power to a separate god: and to get a better grip of his ideas, made images of them—gods of fire, of light, of lightning, of wind, of sound, even of strength and beauty and intellect. But as men's minds grew more capable of general conceptions, their gods became more general. The Greeks, who had more gods than pretty much anybody else, got, in Pan, a conception almost as general, though of course not as exalted as the Hebrew Jehovah, or the Indian Brahma, or the Egyptian Osiris that I was just speaking of."

"But," asked Nina, "wasn't Pan merely a god of inanimate nature? You spoke of the All-including Force as moving our minds and souls. Jehovah was much nearer that than Pan."

"The best of the Greeks too got higher than Pan," Calmire interrupted, "—as high as anybody in those days; and so did many of the Romans."

"Yes," said Muriel, "but I was speaking only of the general conception. And as to the power that moves the visible universe, moving also the soul of man, the East Indians, and the Egyptians too, had at least a very distinct notion of the man's soul being absorbed in the universal soul *after death*, but they didn't comprehend that the force that impels the soul in life, is the universal force. Yet there were frequent guesses in that direction, all around, as there have been toward most of the recent generalizations."

"Well, I find it terribly bewildering," said the girl, " but inexpressibly grand."

"Yes," said Muriel, " it *is* grand—perhaps *it* is what Uncle Grand would admit to be the grandest thought possible to us—to feel that the throbs of those farthest stars and the throbs of one's own heart are impulses from one all-including, ineffable Power!"

"That is grand, but not yet the grandest," said Calmire.

When the ladies said good-night, at home, Muriel grasped Nina's hand with something more than the feeling of gallantry which had moved him early in the evening.

More than once that night, she was conscious that this proud, strong Muriel Calmire was yielding something to her, but she felt nothing more responsive than a little feminine triumph. Of Courtenay, she hardly thought before she was quietly in bed. Then she felt a disappointment at not having heard more of the details of his work. Next she realized that her disappointment was due, in a large degree, to Muriel's interruptions, and she felt a little indignant at Muriel. Her indignation increased with some such reflection as: "What right has that great lazy creature who does nothing but blow his cornet and amuse himself, to interfere with this noble gentleman whose whole life is full of self-sacrifice and devotion to the highest things?" Then came a lazy consciousness that Muriel had talked with great interest of some things which seemed to her very high. Then came a realization that when Muriel had interfered with Courtenay, he had sometimes been almost brutal, and then a recognition that he had generally been correct, and that Courtenay's spirit had not been any too liberal. Then she grew sleepy, with a dreamy feeling of sympathy with Courtenay in the hands of Muriel, who was so big and unsparing, but who was withal so true. Her last consciousness before her sweet slumbers, was of these two preparing for some game of strength and skill, and behind them she saw Calmire, who, she was impressed, had more strength and skill than either, and who would be umpire and see the match rightly played. But just as her half-dream faded into complete repose, that figure itself stooped to take up some of the implements of the game.

CHAPTER XXI.

AT A TENNIS MATCH.

COURTENAY was not the only person who had been disappointed in the results of the meeting between him and Nina: Nina was disappointed too.

Of course but a small share of the talk she participated in or listened to, is reported here: the very atmosphere in which she lived was permeated with germs of thought new to her. Her mother, having the indifference of a woman of the world to all such subjects, hardly realized what was going on, and if she had, would probably have thought the considerations in favor of staying at Fleuvemont more important than the dangers to the orthodoxy of her daughter. The poor child had, however, begun on the task which drove Hugh Miller mad, and she was beginning to feel the strain.

Calmire had avoided protracted conversations on the subject, knowing that they would tend farther to "unsettle" her, and feeling, though somewhat vaguely, that it would be against the duties of hospitality to exercise such influences under his own roof.

For a variety of reasons, she did not for some time seek farther conferences with Muriel. She had a doubt whether he would be quite fair. This doubt, so far as she cared to analyze it, was not that, abstractly, he wanted to be fair, but she had a vague feeling that he was too enthusiastic, perhaps too prejudiced, to be able to be so. Under the doubt was, too, that sweet maidenly shrinking that she did not feel regarding the older man.

She had not yet formed any habit of serious reading, and of course still less had she any idea of how to "hunt up" things in books. Calmire had reintroduced her into the library a few days after her arrival, saying: "There's one little alcove, that I call mine, which contains more worth knowing than any one man is ever going to know. But if you merely want 'elegant letters,' you can play over half the place with them, and it's a very good sort of amusement, until you find you're in earnest about something."

Despite the somewhat Delphic and, possibly, somewhat narrow-minded character of these utterances, Nina had come to find herself "in earnest about something."

In the mornings, after Calmire had started on his gallop across country to the factories, she often fumbled about, principally in Calmire's alcove, but found little to suit *her* case: the scientific books confined themselves to their facts, often in language that she could not understand, and the non-scientific books were vague and frequently contradictory to a degree that but added to her perplexities Her mind was full of pretty distinct questions, but the direct answers she wanted, were seldom in books; and those that were, generally could be got at only by wading through much extraneous matter.

As she was unable, then, for various reasons, to quiet her mind through Calmire, Muriel, or books, it was natural that her thoughts should begin to turn toward Courtenay. He was the most accessible fountain of that wisdom which she had long thought inexhaustible, and so it was a pleasant surprise to find him, a couple of days later, at one of the neighbors', where the local tennis club happened to be meeting.

When the Fleuvemont party entered the grounds after a word with the hostess in the house, a goodly company was already in position on rows of camp-stools on both sides of the courts.

"Why, there's Julia Winterton," said Mrs. Wahring, indicating a tall, striking-looking woman who was the centre of quite a group. "You know her daughter is just engaged to the Earl of Bournemouth. We must go and congratulate her,"—and in two minutes, it was:

"Oh Julia, I was so glad to hear it! Blanche is just the girl for it, and it must be just what you want."

"Yes, Hilda, it makes me a very happy woman, and I think Blanche's happiness is certain."

"She's a sweet enough girl to deserve any amount of it," said Calmire. "Let me join my congratulations too. But it's time for these foreigners to stop robbing us of our prettiest girls. And you mustn't think me a bear when I say that I'm very sorry that now Blanche can't ever be the wife of a president of the United States."

"Unless," broke in Muriel, as his form of congratulation, "some one should be envious enough to kill off Bournemouth. No jury with eyes in their heads would convict for it."

"Thank you, Mr. Muriel. But, Mr. Calmire, isn't one earl in the hand worth two presidents in the bush?"

"Depends on the earl," said Calmire.

"Well, ours is a good one, and it's well to draw the two branches of the English race closer, you know; and it seems to me that for a man with a daughter married to a prince, your talk is very democratic this afternoon. I hope you don't regret the match?" It is barely possible that the lady was a little nettled at Calmire's qualified felicitations.

"Oh, Edelstein's a good fellow, and he loves Molly. I understand that your young man is a good fellow too, and if he is, he can't help loving Blanche. But perhaps I'm justified in saying in this connection that, fond as I am of Edelstein, the plain truth is that he's not half the man that either of my Yankee sons-in-law is."

"Well, for argument's sake, I'll admit," said Mrs. Winterton, "that he's not a fifth the man that either of your *sons* is. Where are they now?"

"In India the last I heard. That's nearly half around. But speaking of men, here comes one."

There was no doubt of that: for it was Courtenay who joined the group. Blanche, who was like a younger sister to him, had met him in another part of the grounds, and already told him of her engagement, and said that he was to perform the marriage-service.

"Well, Mrs. Winterton," he said. "I suppose it's

going to be too grand a ceremony for a poor little country parson like me!"

"Not if it were in Westminster Abbey, Mr. Courtenay. You would do it honor anywhere."

The good man blushed, and when he raised his eyes, they met Nina's smiling upon him. They braced him, as they always did. He answered promptly:

"Honor anything where Blanche is? 'Paint the lily, and gild refined gold'? Lord Bournemouth is said to be a man of sense. How proud he must be!"

The little ripples of laughter that had been running over the group were loudest at this, and Courtenay was glad to retire with the honors, beside Nina, who had already given place to others seeking to felicitate the "successful" matron.

Courtenay was not in knickerbockers (as the fashion then was), and Nina, having heard of his renown as a player, asked him why. He told her that Doctor Rossman had advised him to keep quiet for a week longer. In a few minutes, when play was about to begin, Nina said: "Of course you want to look on;" but after noticing that she was not dressed for playing, he said: "I think not. I have agreed to umpire the finals, and I think that will be enough. But don't you want to watch the play?"

"No," she answered, "I'll save my interest for the finals too. Those people seem to find it very pleasant on the settees by the edge of the grove. It's cool and shady there. Suppose we go too."

The seats were scattered at judicious intervals, at the shady edge of the wide sunlit lawn, and her opportunity for ghostly counsel was secured.

His first words after they were seated were:

"It seems very natural to be here with you!"

"So it does to me," she answered, too full of her own purposes to dwell on the significance of his remark: "for I've been wanting to see you."

He was ready to assume all the reasons for the fact that his fervid convictions furnished; but he was a gentleman as well as an enthusiast, so the exultant throb at his heart found no bolder expression than a grateful:

"That does me very high honor."

"I wanted to ask you," she resumed, "some questions. But I hardly know where to begin.'

"The beginning is usually a good place to begin at," he said, smiling, "though it's sometimes hard to find."

"Well, you've helped me to it," she said, "and I will begin just there. Do you believe the world was made in six days?"

The turn in the conversation was so ludicrously different from what his thoughts had dwelt upon, that he burst out laughing.

"Why, it isn't a laughing matter, is it, Mr. Courtenay?" she said, half hurt and half amused.

"Of course not," he answered. "I beg your pardon. But one so seldom expects such a question so suddenly. Now my answer will have to be that it depends upon what you mean by six days."

"Then," said she, "please let me ask you another

question. Do you believe in the divine authority of the Scriptures?"

"Why certainly. Why do you ask?"

"Because, as I've been thinking over these matters lately, it has seemed to me, that if God meant to say six days, he would have said six days, and if he had wanted to say six something else, he would have said six something else."

"Perhaps he wanted to leave us uncertain," Courtenay answered. "You know that the world and life are full of mysteries, yet they are God's work. Why shouldn't God's other work, the Bible, be also full of mysteries?"

"Yes, I've thought of that too," said the girl; "but as far as I can read Nature, she makes no distinct statements that are not distinctly true."

"Oh yes, she does," said the priest. "She says that the Sun rises and sets, while it only appears to, and it is the earth that moves."

The girl's face fell, and she looked puzzled. After a few moments, she said:

"No. Nature does not say that the Sun rises and sets: we say so."

"And isn't it we," he answered, "who say that the Bible says that the world was made in six days?"

"Do you mean," she asked, "that the Bible only appears to us to say so?"

"Why, what more can it do?" said he.

She was puzzled again, but after a little asked:

"Do you mean to say that we cannot be more certain what words are in the Bible, than what motions are made by the heavenly bodies? Why, any child can read the Bible, just the same as the wisest man reads it, but no child can read the motions of the heavenly bodies."

"But any child can see the Sun rise," he answered.

"Yes," she said, "but all wise people agree that the Bible reads as it appears to, and that the Sun does not rise as it appears to."

"Yes," said he, "I suppose there are differing degrees of certainty."

"You admit then that we have much more reason to believe that the words in Scripture are what they appear to be, than that the motions of the heavenly bodies are what they appear to be?"

"Yes."

"Then why didn't you say so at first?" she asked in a manner far less abrupt than the words.

"Because," he answered very promptly and quietly, "I suppose that in trying to defend the Scriptures, I took a mistaken argument. It was a bad effort in a good cause," he added with a smile.

"But it seems to me, Mr. Courtenay, that God would at least have been able to make his meaning so plain that one need not be in danger of making mistakes with reference to it."

"Well," he answered, "as I said, perhaps He didn't want to."

"Then why did He profess to?"

"I don't know that we're warranted in assuming that He professed to. Why might we not as justly say that He professes that the Sun rises and sets?"

She was puzzled again, but after a while said:

"But the Scriptures are everywhere accepted as

having been expressly sent for our guidance. It seems to me much more reasonable that they should be exactly what they appear to be, than that anything else we know of should."

"Yes, that may be, but we must not be too self-sufficient in judging them. It won't do, you know, to judge divine things by human methods. All Christianity is a miracle, and so we must expect to find in it things out of the reach of our reason."

"Then how can we judge that it's a miracle?" asked Nina.

"Oh that's very plain. Why, just consider that the whole civilized world had been prepared for it by the spread of the Roman empire: there was at last a universal language provided to convey it; then Rome's conquests had provided nations of oppressed and suffering people ready to welcome the new light. At the same time, the hold of the rich and powerful on their old faith had been weakened; they had begun to see the absurdity of the polytheism of Greece and Rome, and their minds were becoming clean pages ready to receive the new impressions. And then, when all these wonderful provisions had been made for His coming, appeared our Lord with his wonderful new teachings of the brotherhood of man, and of God as a single loving father over all; contrast his doctrine of the brotherhood of man with the prevailing notions of conquering captor and conquered slave; and his God with the selfish, cruel, and wicked gods of Greece and Rome. Have you never thought how miraculous all that was?"

"Only in disjointed ways; I never thought of

it all together before. It certainly is very wonderful. But, Mr. Courtenay, admitting the Bible to have been miraculously sent, if we can't depend on the impressions we get from it, what are they good for?"

"Ask the civilization of the last two thousand years."

"Are you sure we owe all that civilization to Christianity? I've heard a good deal of it attributed to steam and electricity and the compass and even gunpowder."

"But don't you see," he answered, "that all these blessings have come up under the Christian civilization, and certainly you would not deny the Christian civilization to the Christian religion? That would be a contradiction in terms. It is to just such confusions as that that one always comes in trying to question it. The only way is not to question it—to accept it as the great including fact of the world, and if the minor facts seem to our limited intelligence at variance with it, to assume that they only seem so, until farther knowledge reconciles them."

She did not reflect—perhaps did not know—that Christian Europe had had no monopoly in the discovery of some of the agents of civilization which she had named, and she did not realize that he had made his own "contradiction in terms" by applying his own terms: neither did he. Yet the reasoning seemed to her, somehow, hazy, though she seized on another point in his remarks:

"You believe, then, in sacrificing your intellect wherever it raises any questions in your religion?"

At a Tennis Match.

"I should not have put it quite in that way," he answered. "But since you do, what is my intellect that I should not sacrifice it for my faith—for my people? My Master sacrificed his life."

"But what are our intellects for, Mr. Courtenay, if not to seek the truth?"

"When we have found the highest truth," he answered, "the intellect has done its best. It can afford to resist all temptations to fly beyond. Such temptations must be delusion."

She saw no answer to this, and returned to another aspect of what he had been saying. Though she objected to his position, she felt the nobleness in his spirit, and yet she felt remonstrant.

"You spoke of readiness for sacrifice. May I ask—it is not going too far, I hope," she said, blushing—"if you have never really felt the abandonment of some of these questions to be a sacrifice?"

"Well, at times I have had to resist a spirit of inquiry, though I doubt if it is as strong in me as in some men, and I'm grateful that it is not. But I try to make my religion one of work. There's enough to do without inquiring, and the struggle against inquiry has always been easy when I have realized that I must keep my own faith clear and strong for my poor."

Probably the greatest reward he had ever received for his pure efforts, was the admiring smile with which she looked up at him. She said:

"You are very noble, Mr. Courtenay."

"Oh no!" he remonstrated, "there can be nothing noble in mistrusting the intellect in such matters. What has it ever done? Only built system after system to see them disappear. The intelligence of the world has followed and forsaken a dozen systems in the time that our Religion has steadily and majestically pursued its way."

They were interrupted here by friends coming up, and the conversation could not be resumed before Courtenay had to go and umpire the games. Then Nina, instead of going to look on, slipped off by herself into the grove, and thought it all over.

Her first strong feeling was: "Here is a noble, useful life—I never knew one more admirable—entirely free from the speculations which fill the brain of that useless Muriel Calmire....And, too, it is a peaceful life: for it is not troubled by the questions that have been disturbing this useless Nina Wahring....What is this presumptuous mind of mine that I should let its little curiosities disturb me? Why not quiet it as he does his, in the greater truth?....'If his Master sacrificed his life, why should not he sacrifice his intellect?' —True, generous soul!....I wonder if it ever occurred to that Muriel Calmire to sacrifice anything —for anything—for anybody!....Well, the wise course is open to me, and what a noble course it is! I will simply stop troubling myself any more about the whole thing....Why, there's the moon, and up beyond, a star visible in daylight. I never saw but one before. How it throbs!.... 'To feel that the throbs of that far-off star and the throbs of one's own heart come from the same ineffable Power.'" The words had often gone through her mind. Now she added with a feeling of impatient triumph: "And yes, Mr. Muriel Calmire, that power is God!" Then the triumph melted into sympathy as she mused: "'God, Brahma, Osiris'—what was it he said? Well, I won't bother over it any more. Even he admits that it is surely God." She felt contented and at rest, and turned back toward the tennis-courts.

As they drove home after dinner, she sat next Calmire. Both were in a mood for silence, and she soon lost herself in the beauty and mystery of the night. But the feeling of its beauty was habitual, and now there grew up for the first time, the deeper feeling of its order. With that, came a sense of reverence such as she had never before experienced. After some minutes of deep absorption, she realized that all her previous emotions toward Nature had had in them something akin to the enthusiasm we feel for human superiority. When they had been very intense, there was something in them not entirely unlike the passion of human love, as her pure nature had imagined it; with this, her mind came to the conception of the Creator—the gray-bearded man she had seen in pictures; and the contrast of this image with the immensity that had just filled her soul, gave her a start of something strangely like disgust.

This set her to thinking of her talk with Courtenay, and after a while she turned and said to Calmire:

"Mr. Calmire, Mr. Courtenay says that perhaps the Bible doesn't mean what it says, and yet that all Christian civilization is built upon it. Now I can't quite make that out, can you?"

"No. I suppose he would call it one of the mysteries of religion. I believe that's their name for all contradictions in what they say they believe."

"*Say* they believe!" exclaimed Nina; "why, don't you think Mr. Courtenay does believe what he says?"

"I've no doubt he thinks he does, but 'believing' means different things to him and to me."

"I don't understand," she said.

"Well," answered Calmire, "to him it means something superior to reason, to me it means something subordinate to reason."

"But, Mr. Calmire, where's the virtue in Faith if we're going to let it be upset all the time?"

"I don't know."

"You don't think it a virtue?" she asked.

"Not for all persons, in the sense you mean it."

"Not for me?"

Nina was not given to self-reference. Her falling into it now, showed that something very unusual was going on in her mind. Calmire answered:

"I don't know yet."

"Not for Mr. Courtenay?" she asked.

"Yes, I think it's good for him."

"Then what kind of people is it good for, and what kind of people is it not?"

"Ah, young lady," he answered with a little laugh, "I shall not tell you that unless I find out that it's not good for you. But if I ever find that out, you will know the answer for yourself, so I shall never need to tell you at all."

And thenceforward at odd moments for many days, the cup of her perplexity was full. Mr. Calmire, whom, in a timid half-unconscious way, she trusted profoundly, said that it was well for Courtenay to believe as he did, yet Calmire did not himself believe as Courtenay did, and doubted whether it was best for her that she should. She wished that she had asked him whether he thought it best for Muriel.

And as she thought more about it, she became perplexed as to how Courtenay did believe. Despite her admiration for the self-denial in his conclusions, she could not make his views consistent with each other, and she was astounded once to find herself saying to herself: "Is it right to be content with inconsistent views—is it honest?"

But some time later, she was brought to realize that, in some regions, the only way to avoid inconsistent views, is to have no views at all.

When they got home, after the ladies had retired, and the men had settled down for an extra cigar, Muriel said to Calmire:

"What were you and Miss Wahring talking about as we neared home?"

"About Dogma's last ditch."

"What do you mean by that?"

"About Dogma exalting credulity into a virtue. Science declares it a vice."

"What did Miss Wahring say to that?"

"What did she say to that? Do you suppose I told it to her? You young people never will realize that it's absurd to tell people things they can't understand."

CHAPTER XXII.

MURIEL TAKES A SHORT INNINGS.

NINA awoke late the next morning, but feeling very bright, partly because, despite her questions to Calmire, she had been set relatively at peace by Courtenay, through the regular professional demonstration of the miraculous foundation of Christianity. While taking a light breakfast in her room, she pondered this, and then ran downstairs and out on to the lawn, like a child with some new-found wonder in its apron, to show it to Muriel and convince him.

This tempestuous Muriel Calmire was a factor in Mrs. Wahring's Summer experiences that she had not counted on. But he caused her no anxiety regarding her great scheme: for she expected his loud irreverence to make him distasteful to Nina; and, so far, in some respects, she had no occasion to be disappointed. Yet Nina, while she had found his aggressive infidelity repulsive, had not found it altogether uninteresting, especially as she had realized that its aggressiveness was earnestness of conviction, and that its justification was not altogether denied by Calmire, who was himself so temperate and so patient. But unquestionably she would have been much more moved by Calmire's admissions, if the crassness of Muriel's assertions had not prejudiced her against his side. How much of a young man's enthusiasm against restraining doctrine, may be due to impatience of restraint, it had not occurred to her to inquire.

Muriel, of course, was a propagandist—when it was no trouble to be one. Such boys, no less than the best men in the church, always want people to think as they do. Probably Muriel would not have sought jungles, deserts, and lonely death for the sake of spreading his faith, or lack of it; but preaching to Nina Wahring at Fleuvemont was a different matter. So despite his uncle's cautions against disturbing Nina's faith, he was at least always ready to take up the cudgels at her invitation.

When she found him, she gave him briefly the points she had learned the day before, and ended triumphantly with:" So Christianity is miraculous after all!"

"Yes?" asked Muriel, with a provoking drawl, and then flashed out: "Confound their impudence! To make out Christianity the only religion, they're always making out Rome's the only civilization, when off there were India and China and Japan with art and culture that in many respects could knock Rome endways. But even that 'universal language' argument doesn't amount to anything. The gospels were not even written in it; and assume the empire of Rome to have been prepared miraculously, then I suppose the empires of Charles the Great and Napoleon were too?"

"I never heard anybody say so," answered Nina.

"Nor I either," said Muriel.

"Then what makes you talk that way?" she asked.

"Because the world was certainly in as favorable a state for each of those men, as for Christ. Don't you see that?"

"Oh, what does a girl have a chance to see?" Then she added in a contrasting tone that made Muriel think of the middle register of a clarinet: "Tell me what *you* see."

He briefly explained the situations, when she said:

"But God may have shaped the world for Christianity through natural causes, as he did for Charles and Napoleon; and then there were Christ's miraculous new and divine doctrines."

"'Natural causes' are not miracles: so over goes that claim. Now what doctrines do you call miraculous and new?"

"Why one God—a father, and all men brothers."

"Now just look at that!" cried the boy; "Will you just look at that? I declare it ought to be a criminal offence for a parson to get hold of an innocent girl and stuff her with that sort of humbug. Asia had those doctrines long before Christ was born; and even the claim that Christianity introduced them to the Western world, is all nonsense. Certainly the best of the Greeks and Romans had them before Christ, and about his time their old mythology was already played out, as Courtenay says: Cicero and Seneca, for instance, were as much infidels regarding it, as anybody now is regarding Christianity. But is there anything remarkable about that? Don't all religions play out?"

Disregarding his question, she persisted:

"But, Mr. Muriel, I always supposed that Christianity was the first religion to teach charity and the sacrifice of self to others."

Muriel gave something like a low whistle, then begged her pardon (a proceeding rather new in him), and said, "Come on to the piazza, please, and excuse me a minute." Then he went off into the library, came back with some books, and said:

"Now, listen to this," and he read, in tones that, despite the feeling of opposition that he had aroused, seemed to her like deep music:

"'Charity is found where man, seeking to diffuse happiness among all men—those he loves and those he loves not—digs canals and pools, makes roads, bridges and seats, and plants trees for shade. It is found where, from compassion for the miserable and poor, who have none to help them, a man erects resting-places for wanderers, and drinking-fountains, or provides food, raiment, medicine for the needy, not selecting one more than another. This is true charity, and bears much fruit.'

"That," said Muriel, "is from the Katha Chari, a Buddhist collection of the third century before Christ." He went on, selecting passages:

"I find here that Manu, about twelve centuries before Christ, among his ten duties named 'returning good for evil,' and said: 'Shun even lawful acts which may cause future pain or be offensive to mankind.' He also said: 'He who seeks the good of all sentient beings, enjoys bliss without end.'

"The Khuddaka Patha, of the third century before Christ, says:

"'Let the love that fills the mother's heart as she watches over an only child, even such love, animate all.

"'Let the good will that is boundless, immeasurable, impartial, unmixed with enmity, prevail throughout the world.'

"Confucius, in the sixth century before Christ, said:

"'The abject man sows that himself or his friends may reap: the love of the perfect man is universal.'

"I won't read," he continued, "a lot of things from the Hitopadesa, because this editor says that although most of its material is known to have existed in the third century before Christ, it was not put in shape until about the sixth century of our era, and therefore possibly may have felt the benefit of Christianity. I haven't any idea that it did, though. I also refrain from quoting the Talmud and the Old Testament, because they are claimed as part of the Christian system, though they contradict it in perhaps as many things as they anticipate it in. But I want to give you a little of what Greece and Rome have to say on the subject. It would have been a greater miracle than any yet recorded, if they had reached their civilizations without some of those ideas." He hunted in another book, and said:

"Take this from Isokrates, four or five centuries before Christ:

"'That which it angers you to suffer from others, that do not to others yourselves.'

"That's merely negative," Muriel continued; "but how about this? That same Isokrates, I find here, advised Nikokles, King of Crete, to behave to states weaker than his own, as he would have states stronger than his own, behave to his."

"Why, that's the golden rule!" exclaimed Nina.

"Seems so!" said Muriel, and went on:

"Seneca says the same thing:

"'So live with your inferior as you would have your superior live with you.'

"Elsewhere he said:

"'It is required of a man to be of benefit to men—to many if he can; failing that, to a few; failing that, to those nearest him; failing that, to himself.'

"It strikes me that that's even a little in advance of the golden rule; for it puts others *before* oneself. But here's some more from Seneca:

"'The brave and just man when he places before himself as the rewards of death, the liberty of his country, the safety of all, for which he sacrifices his life, is in the highest state of happiness.'

"And there," continued Muriel, "you get not only more steps beyond the golden rule, but you get patriotism too—something which Christianity doesn't go into."

"But it seems to me," Nina remonstrated, "that I've heard Seneca spoken of as a *Christian* moralist."

"Oh Lord, yes! The Christians tried to steal him, and even forged a lot of letters between him and Saint Paul, just as they later forged the dotation of Constantine. But that's all rot! His morals *were* Christian, or Christian morals were his. All Aryan and Jewish civilization had pretty much the same morals—improving of course as time went on: Christianity is but one name for the world's stock of morality, as Buddhism is another."

"But, Mr. Muriel! Mr. Muriel! How can you talk so! It wasn't Roman morality. Didn't Christianity have to come in to put an end to the Romans' cruel shows in the Arena?"

"So they say! But nevertheless, many 'pagan' moralists resisted them, some 'pagan' emperors prohibited them, *and* many Christians were very fond of them. Hold on! I'll hunt up the evidence here if you want it."

"No! If you've seen it, I'll take your word. What you have given me is enough," and she gave a little sigh that was half relief from her strained attention, and half regret at its results. "But," she added, "why, in the face of such things, have my teachers always told me that Christ was the first to bring the message of ' Peace on earth, good will toward men'?"

"Because they've been crazy with enthusiasm. They see nothing and seek nothing but what makes for their case. They won't tell you what makes against it. They justify the means by the end, too, whether they mean to or not. The Jesuits are not alone in that. Within a few weeks, a learned man told me that Christianity is the only religion which states the golden rule positively; that no other religion did more than Confucius in saying, 'Refrain from doing to others that which you would not that they should do to you.' I don't see, though, that the difference between a positive and a negative statement of it, even if that difference existed, would be of much consequence."

"Why," said Nina, "it seems to me that the golden rule is clear and positive in several of the passages you have read. But," she continued after a moment, "despite all you've said, there are the miracles that Christ himself performed."

"Great Scott! Why, I sometimes think that if there were no miracles in that religion, a fellow might believe in it."

"A great many fellows do manage to believe in it *with* its miracles," she rejoined. "Why do the miracles convince you against it, instead of for it?"

"Why, simply," he said, "because they reduce it to the grade of all other religions. Its morality, much as I had to say against it the other night, is ahead of the rest of them, unless perhaps Buddhism, but the religion has the same ear-marks that the others have. If it had only left the miracles out, I'd have thought it something distinct."

"But aren't its miracles different?" she asked.

"Why, bless you," said the boy, "pretty much all the religions have incarnations, miraculous births, and all that, not to speak of miraculous cures and feeds and all sorts of prestidigitation. And as to observances, lots of them use the sign of the cross and even most of the sacraments. Rome and the East had infant baptism, and at the Samothracian mysteries, a priest heard criminals confess and granted them absolution. And as to originality of dogma, Lactantius, a Christian, demonstrated immortality itself from Plato's arguments, without referring to Christ in his demonstration; and Arnobius, another Christian, speaks of it as a widespread belief, in the Church and out, which he himself opposed because it would logically make men reckless in this life."

"But," persisted Nina, "wasn't *practical* charity introduced by Christianity? I've been told over and over again that the ancient philosophers talked very prettily, but that they didn't lead anybody to *do* anything."

"Now just look at that again!" exclaimed Muriel. "It's flat lying."

"No," remonstrated Nina. "It certainly has been told me by people who don't lie."

"Yes, I suppose so," Muriel conceded. "They merely repeated the lies that dogmatic literature is full of. Why, the truth is that in the best days of Athens, nobody was permitted to want; and that in Rome, provisions, and even clothes, were distributed by the state, free schools founded for poor children, medical officers provided for the needy sick, and people giving feasts were required by law to do something for the poor. And not only that, but so far from its being true, as I long supposed, that gifts from outside to cities and countries in distress, were known only under our present Christianity, the fact is that classic civilization had many such instances. Hold on, my author says something about that business," and he hunted in his last book again and read:

"'There is indeed no fact more patent in history than that with the triumph of Christianity under Constantine, the older and finer spirit of charity died out of the world, and gave place to an intolerance and bigotry which were its extreme antithesis, and which still unhappily rule in its stead.'"

"But," said Nina, "'the finer spirit of charity' has certainly been revived. And there is the idea of one God: Greece and Rome didn't have that."

"Well, suppose they didn't. Nobody claims any more than that Christianity brought it from the East. But the fact is that the best minds of Greece and Rome did have it before. They regarded the various divinities, with their various names, as merely symbols for the various aspects of the one Power. Valeus Loranus, who flourished in the century before Christ, wrote of Jupiter, 'Deum Deus, *unus et omnes*'—God of gods, *one and all.*" And Muriel dived into his book again. " Here's Seneca says :

"'Call Him Nature, Fate, Chance—all are names for the same God in the various manifestations of his power.'

" All the early critics of Christianity, and many of the fathers themselves, claimed that there was nothing new in its distinctive doctrines."

"What made them spread so, then ?" objected Nina.

"The same influence, I suppose," answered Muriel, " which made the same doctrines spread over the civilized world before Christianity was thought of. Christ was a great man, though, and gave them a great impulse, but so did Buddha and Socrates and Cicero and Seneca and Marcus Aurelius, and hosts of others who were not Christians at all. The fact is that all over Mediterranean Europe and the Southwestern half of Asia (leaving out some of the vagaries of our friends the Mussulmans) there was a general consensus of moral doctrine among the wise and good, which India had as Brahminism and Buddhism, Persia as Zoroastrianism, Syria as Jehovahism, Egypt in its esoteric doctrines, and Greece and Rome in their philosophies; and this morality reaches us under the name of Christianity. It seems, too, as if modern Christian apologists had kept the share of other religions in that body of doctrine pretty well out of sight, though I see here that Clement, for instance, though he was a father of the Church, said that Greek philosophy was inspired of God, as truly as Christianity was; and Justin Martyr, another father, counted many of the philosophers as among the elect of God. That degree of tolerance hasn't been the fashion in Christianity, though. No! Christian writers have made too light of the religious thought of non-Christian civilizations. That's not a matter of opinion: for here are abundant citations which you can verify for yourself, to prove that the educated classes in Greece and Rome were monotheists; held essentially the same beliefs in Providence and design in Nature that Christians do; professed the same reliance in God's goodness, and resignation to His will; had the same hope of immortality, with the same inducements to well-doing for its sake (but without the same slavish fears of Hell); practiced the same charity and forgiveness, and vastly more toleration; and, with a few exceptions in the Bible itself, expressed their doctrines in a literature infinitely loftier than that of the fathers of the Church."

"Well, I didn't know all this," said Nina, with a second sigh, over both her old ignorance and her new knowledge. "Girls seem to be shown only one side. But after all, what you detract from the originality of Christianity, makes its great influence appear all the more wonderful. Surely there must have been something divine in Christ."

"There is in every great genius," said Muriel, with a reverent tone that sometimes came from that paradoxical youth. "Half the gods have been made of people's reverence for great men. Imagine the beautiful doctrines we've been talking about, brought to an oppressed people sorely needing charity and consolation, and especially to the lower classes, among whom such doctrines were comparatively strange; imagine them preached by a man of Christ's presence and genius and consciousness of power. Even if he were not, in any peculiar sense, the Son of God, would not the people, a few generations later, (especially the wonder-loving Greeks, in whose language the gospels were written, a good while after his death,) have been ready to make him a god, as they did their mythical heroes? Even if he had not claimed such divinity himself, as I'm not at all sure he did, would not his followers have claimed it for him, as I'm mighty sure *they* did, and have elaborated the claim by all sorts of 'supernatural' detail? Such claims were not received then as they would be to-day, despite the fact that people to-day admit the claims made then: but if the same tales were told as having happened a year ago, nobody would believe them. People have always swallowed things regarding the past, even a few generations past, that they would not admit regarding the present; and all that made it much easier for Christianity to spread."

"Yes, there's something in that," said Nina. "I've heard that almost every people looks *back* for its golden age."

"Certainly," assented Muriel, "when the fact is that in the assumed golden ages, our ancestors were brutes, and for the real golden age, we must look forward. But here's another reason why Christianity took hold so readily. You know that the religions which Christ found existing when he appeared—what was left of them, made few promises and very vague ones: but Christ, or his reporters at least, offered some sort of reward in nearly every sentence. They led every beggar to expect to be on horseback in a very short time. Every religion starts among the beggars, because they've everything to gain and nothing to lose: and yet you always hear the fact that Christianity did, harped upon as if it were something wonderful. Christ's parables generally made the good people poor, and the bad ones rich; the poor thought he was going to give them everything— that is, everything consistent with morality, and a good deal more laziness and irresponsibility than *are* consistent with it; the people took much of what he said about his 'Kingdom,' whether he meant it so or not, as offering them a new earthly dynasty, just as people offered a new religion generally do, and they were so full of it that they wanted the Roman empire destroyed to make way for it, and some think that the Roman Christians stimulated the barbarian Christians in that job. When it became plain that Christ's Kingdom was not to be looked for here, it was looked for hereafter, mainly at first, of course, by the people who had nothing to look for here anyhow. Partly to gain those things, and partly, no doubt, from better motives, the people practiced, more or less, the altruistic morality that Christ had impressed upon them, and that was good enough and, to the majority, new enough soon to commend the sect to the attention of the better classes. And so, you see, here you are a Christian, and nothing supernatural about it."

"Well!" exclaimed Nina, with a long breath. "It won't do to be sure of anything, will it?" Then she added, rebounding from the strain she had been under into a little playfulness: "You're very learned with your big books there, aren't you?"

"Yes, and you with the stuff Courtenay gave you. So we're quits. Quits! Quits!" he cried, laughing and jumping up and dancing around the piazza. Then, to make her come, he seized her hand, but got playfully slapped on his own.

"Let's take a ride!" he exclaimed.

"I don't know if mamma will let me. Can we have a groom?"

"Yes, but what's the use? Mrs. Grundy doesn't call for one here."

Soon, after a little demur from Mrs. Wahring, they were having some royal good gallops over bits of turf and soft road, or meditatively walking their horses through woods, or pausing on bare far-reaching heights; and they found too much in the sunlight and brisk air, and buoyancy of youth, to bother their heads any more about Napoleon or Charles, or the Man of Peace whose victories surpass theirs; or even about Nina's question: "It won't do to be sure of anything, will it?" They had not yet begun to hear the thunders which mutter under that thought.

CHAPTER XXIII.

AIDS TO MATRIMONY.

Mrs. WAHRING had not cared to startle her game, but she had now been at Fleuvemont long enough to sound Calmire's heart on her matrimonial projects. One evening as they were strolling in the grounds, she began speaking of the pleasant time the four were having together, "except, of course, the constant sparring of those young people, who were never made to agree," and then she said that her very enjoyment made her reflect that it could not last—that the time must come when she (somehow she omitted Nina) must leave Fleuvemont. "Of course, I have compensation in my own home and my husband's society," she said, "but you—" She paused, and then she plunged:

"Cousin Calmire, why don't you marry again?"

"Haven't had the chance."

"Ridiculous! Don't you want to?"

"Most assuredly."

"Then, why haven't you?"

"I've told you."

"Now, don't play with me. You know you could marry any woman you please."

"I haven't had the chance to please."

"You're too fastidious. You need to shape

some one to suit you. Take some one who is young enough, and you can make her anything you please."

"But what can I make of myself to suit her? I'm too old for a girl to marry. What right have I to tie a woman of forty to a man over seventy? That would be the case in twenty years if I were to marry a girl of twenty."

"You might not keep her tied so long, then," laughed Mrs. Wahring.

"Oh, my family lives to ninety. But," he mused aloud, "in that case, I should not."

"If you should not, then what wrong do you do?"

"The wrong of depriving a girl of the natural love of a person of near her own age."

"Is there any certainty of her getting it? And if she does, she gets the thoughtless impetuous treatment of a boy. In exchange, you give her your experienced and tempered care, and you keep her in contact with a mind to know which 'is a liberal education.'"

"Don't you be sarcastic! And above all things, don't you put too much confidence in any such nonsensical expression that may occur to you in regard to me. I'm reaching the age when men begin to ossify their opinions. A woman who wants an education had better take a younger man."

"But don't you see that it's your habit to let your opinions change with discoveries, and that it was not the habit of the men just before you, whose opinions you have watched ossify? You are not like us who have a Faith. Why, you experience a certain wild delight in finding yourself wrong."

"Hilda Wahring! Why don't you do your brains justice, oftener? Oh the world, the flesh, and the devil!"

"Thank you, especially regarding the last two. I'd rather be devoted to the first, though, with a little reservation for the next world, than to the wicked notions you're so stubborn in."

"Well, I'll apologize so far as concerns the flesh and the devil, except as they always follow the world, as sharks follow a ship. But as to my notions, I hope, to use your phraseology, that the Lord will give me strength to stand to some notions that you've attacked this evening. I've no business with a girl for a wife."

"Any girl whom you will make your wife, is to be congratulated."

And this sentence survived in his memory, while most of the arguments with which the lady had supported it, faded away. But, of course, Calmire was the first thoughtful and candid man who could be more affected by a generalization fastening itself upon his vanity, than by an argument attacking his reason!

Calmire was too old a fish not to recognize bait when he could see the angler extending it. Mrs. Wahring's conversation could not have been plainer to him if it had been condensed into the simple statement: "My dear old friend, I wish you would marry my daughter. I know you would make her happy, and I know no other fate for her that **I** so much desire."

And here Mrs. Wahring, though ordinarily a good tactician, made a bad move. There were two excuses for her: Calmire was an old friend with whom candor had been her rule, and with whom, in fact, candor was almost everybody's rule; then, moreover, she felt, and not wrongly, that her convictions about his marrying would have weight with him. Her mistake was in not confining herself to expressing them incidentally. He was enough interested in the subject to note them without requiring special emphasis. As it was, feeling his positions attacked, he aroused himself to their defence. He should have been tempted to abandon them by finding others more attractive. Moreover, aside from his convictions regarding women in general, he was put specially on his guard respecting Nina.

He knew that the girl found him interesting, and was glad that she did. But he determined that in one respect she should not find him too interesting. Therefore, not seldom when he caught her hanging on his words or found himself pursued by her intelligent curiosity, he abruptly drew the topic into some less fruitful field, or overturned it with a jest. This was because he had little sympathy, as he had intimated to Muriel, with the latter's attempt to set up a kindergarten in infidelity for Miss Wahring's instruction, and was certainly not prepared to teach in it while she and her mother were his guests.

This produced upon her interest in him, an effect like those of most artificial policies, as undesirable as the one it was intended to avoid. He became an object of tantalizing curiosity to the girl, and aroused in her a suspicion that he did not deem her worthy of his free confidence; and this, as she knew him to be devoid of conceit, made him appear to her all the more exalted.

The next day, Muriel being off on some devices of his own, Mrs. Wahring being disabled by a convenient headache, and there happening to be no other visitors in the house, Nina found herself starting out about five o'clock with Calmire alone in the dog-cart.

Of the dog-cart as an aid to matrimony, not all has been said that the subject deserves, though it is true that much is made of it in the novels of the fair Mrs. Higliff, *née* Deasent; and those who have had the opportunity for a season or two, frequently to see her in the park, exalted in the trap of her present happy lord, above the victoriaed and landaued herd, have fully recognized the potency of that method of locomotion in effecting the marriage which raised her from the circles of Presbyterian respectability to those of horse-racing aristocracy.

As promoter of the love which leads to marriage, the dog-cart cannot be too highly honored by all economists who oppose Malthus and race-suicide. But as a sustainer of love after marriage, its frequent inefficacy might delight the soul of Malthus himself. To the philosophic observer, there is something in the relation of the dog-cart to this whole subject, which may be interesting enough to justify farther elucidation.

It will be realized that the inexperienced driver of the *new* dog-cart is generally in mourning—of course, for the worthy relative whose money paid for the trap. When the novice first appears, it is apt to be about eleven o'clock in the morning, after most of the early equestrians are out of the park, and hours before the more experienced artists on the vehicle come out. The groom, or whatever functionary may wear the livery (also deep mourning, even crape around the boot-tops, in some instances), is perched by the master's side, instead of sitting backward on the back seat—a position known to be impracticable for some new grooms on account of its tendency to create sea-sickness. Especially is the groom apt to be by the master's side if a tandem be under treatment, it being then doubly important that experience should be at hand. A few days later, the trap is observable, at the same hour, with the groom in the position, not (as we were going to say) for which nature intended him, but to which fashion has dedicated him. A few days later still, the trap with the same arrangements, appears in all its glory at the time the world drives—as early as three if the owner be a systematic and fussy man, or as late as six if he be accustomed to let things take care of themselves. Whatever a man's characteristics—prompt or dilatory, they will be exaggerated when he first faces the world in a new dog-cart.

Within a fortnight, the matrimonial functions of the engine are first indicated. A young woman appears, generally in a bright costume finely set off by the sombreness previously monopolizing the vehicle: for she is not usually a friend with whom the young fellow is familiar in sorrow and in joy, but some one whom he met in society (and consequently not in mourning), shortly before the melancholy event which led to his own sables and dog-cart. The next day, a second young woman appears, the next day a third, and so on, until all the intimate friends have had a drive in the new trap. Then the first young woman appears again, then for a week some of the others, and so on, the first appearing with decreasing intervals, until she is there every pleasant day. At about this stage, a bunch of light purple flowers, indicative of either ebbing woe or rising joy, is sometimes seen in the horse's headstall, and even in the button-hole of the groom. After a short season of this sort of locomotion, a mighty change is noticed—the groom has disappeared! He has long been felt a burden to the confidences suppressed on the front seat, but Mrs. Grundy has kept him in his place. Now, Mrs. Grundy releases all three from their irksome situation: for the young people are engaged. It came near being all four in the case of young ——, for he, not having been reared in the midst of good precedents, began his matrimonial pursuit with two tigers, but was most ingeniously corrected by Miss ——, to whom, however, he did not feel sufficiently grateful to make her his ultimate every-day driving companion. Or perhaps she declined to be.

If smiles were water, and could be scattered from the rear of the vehicle as bounteously as from the front, the dog-cart with an engaged couple meeting friends, would render the present style of road-sprinkler superfluous.

The smiles are scattered till late Spring or late Fall, as the case may be, when the vehicle is laid up during the wedding-journey. After the return, it appears again for a few months, when it is again laid up, and after a brief period it is, for some recondite reason, replaced by a low victoria. A little later, the couple is lost to sight for a month or two, and when they reappear, the dog-cart alternates with the victoria, the husband's place in the latter generally being occupied by a woman in a French cap with a bundle in her arms. Soon, on the days when the victoria appears, the husband is apt to be seen alone in a road-wagon with a trotter, and the general tendency is for the old place of the dog-cart to be entirely usurped by the road-wagon and the victoria, or the landau for which, before many years, increasing family makes occasion.

The mission of the vehicle which founded the family, is generally here ended. In some rare cases, however, (with occasional intervals when so high a vehicle is not practicable,) the dog-cart holds its own through the lives of the couples whom it first brought together. In those traps, if in anything that conveys humanity, look for happiness!

Some day, however, all other vehicles give way to the hearse, and the impatient new generation begins the pretty experience over again, in sables and a new dog-cart of its own.

Whether Mr. Legrand Calmire was beginning the standard dog-cart experience on the day when, on the strength of his patriarchal years, he dispensed with the groom, and drove tandem alone with

Miss Nina Wahring, was a question which could not escape his calm but speculative mind. Earlier in life, among his sources of amusement had frequently been his own superstitions—inherited tendencies to draw auguries and to believe things that his more modern individual judgment pronounced absurd. The habit of rigidly following his reason, regardless of the diversions of impulse, had now so long been his, however, that he dismissed these inherited tendencies almost unconsciously; but sometimes, even yet, one would produce a distinct impression upon him. Such an one came just before he started on this drive. The afternoon was cool for the season, and he told Pierre to bring him a top-coat. Thereupon flashed through his mind a vague notion that if Pierre should bring a light-colored coat, the outcome of his chat with Nina would be favorable to the notions Mrs. Wahring had been putting in his head; but that if the coat were dark, it would be unfavorable. Pierre brought a mackintosh that was neither light nor dark, and Calmire had a quiet laugh at his own expense. The question faintly before him was a little complicated by a thought that had once or twice passed through his mind. That there was any question at all, annoyed him; and partly for the sake of getting rid of it, he attacked it, in the course of the ride, at the point where his own complication lay:

"What do you and Muriel quarrel most about? Going home the other night, I didn't hear half your talk, though Muriel seemed to think I did."

"We quarreled over everything, I suppose. We generally do."

"I congratulate you! I hardly expected so much scope in people so young."

"I wish I didn't give you the chance to laugh at me so often. I meant everything that we talked about."

"Ah! that's not quite so startling. What did you talk about?"

"Well, the most interesting thing was himself."

"To him undoubtedly; but to you?"

"Yes, to me: though he didn't think I thought so."

"What do you find so interesting about him?"

"His deformities."

"Ah! you hit me hard there, my child. I might have prevented the growth of many of them. Yet," he mused aloud, "I was not his parents, much less all his ancestors. It is unquestionably true that 'the sins of the fathers' *are* 'visited upon the children.' So probably," he said, laughing, "Muriel's ancestors are responsible for anything you don't like in him; while I'm responsible only for anything you do like."

"What a horrid set of infidels his ancestors must have been, then! Pity that half of them were your own!"

"Oh, that was the good half!" laughed Calmire. "Only it wasn't—perhaps not as good as the other half. On both sides there were some who would have been called infidels."

"Well," said Nina, "as to the present infidel—"

"Do you mean me?" asked Calmire; "because if you do, I think I'll have to trouble you to define the term."

"No, I mean Mr. Muriel. Now if all that he says about Christianity is true—all that you don't contradict, I mean,—one might even doubt its divine origin. But if it's not divine, how did it ever do so much?"

"For my part," he answered, "I can't doubt the divine origin of anything: though it's not often that two people mean quite the same thing by the word 'divine.'"

"What do you mean by it, Mr. Calmire?"

"I believe," he answered, "that Christianity was sent by the same Power that sends everything—the Power you call divine."

"Then, Mr. Calmire, you must be a Christian."

"So I am, on the same ground that all men are who accept as divine all that seems to them reasonable in the faith, and attribute all else to metaphor and accident. Christians vary, you know, especially as time goes on. Don't you remember your saying once that you would not accept the Christianity of five hundred years ago?"

"Yes. But, it seems to me that on your ground, pretty much everybody is a Christian."

"I don't know anybody who is on any other ground," said Calmire, "if he uses his reason at all."

"And that's just what Mr. Courtenay doesn't do!" exclaimed Nina. "He professes to give up even his reason for his faith."

"Well!" commented Calmire. "As good a man as Mr. Courtenay can afford to, perhaps. But those of us who haven't his goodness, have to find our way by such lights as we have. But we're wandering very far from our starting-point. All this talk has grown out of what you are pleased to term Muriel's deformities. I don't know how far they are to be divided up between his ancestors and his circumstances. Do you find his deformities very monstrous?"

"Oh no! They would not be worth noticing in an ordinary young man."

"What? You think him extraordinary?"

"I certainly do."

"So does he," said his uncle.

"I know that," she responded.

"There's one point at least," said Calmire, "on which you agree."

"Hardly," said Nina; "his opinion of himself is very different from mine."

"Well, what's your opinion of him?"

"That he's a very brilliant and profound young man, who turns out of his way very little for anybody or anything but himself."

His uncle's opinion of his brilliancy and profundity might not have been as favorable as Nina's. Calmire did not discuss that, though, but said:

"You do him injustice. He's the most affectionate fellow in the world."

"Perhaps," answered Nina, "—when it doesn't interfere with his convenience."

"There you're correct, and there's where I blame myself. I have not made the effort I ought, to keep him where he would grow up consulting the convenience of those he loved. You think he's honest?"

"Yes."

"He intends to be," said Calmire, "but it takes a strong man to be honest always."

"He's strong!" said Nina.

"He's young," answered Calmire "Well," he resumed, "you think him brilliant, honest, and strong. That's a good deal. Can't you humor a doting old man with a little more?"

"He's handsome as—as—well, as himself: none of the pictures or statues are like him, though they're no finer."

"And yet you find the most interesting thing about him, his deformities!"

They both laughed.

"Well," protested Nina, "he's conceited, selfish, lazy, and I suspect not very thorough."

"You seem to have studied him pretty well on so short an acquaintance," said Calmire.

"Oh, I see through people pretty well."

So far, Calmire had not got much light on his little complication. He attacked it directly:

"Do you like him?"

"I don't know."

"Do you admire him?"

"Of course, in some things."

"Would you trust him?"

"In everything where he could be deliberate."

Calmire turned square around and looked at her.

"What business has a girl like you making such a piece of character-analysis as that?"

"A girl like me," she said, turning toward him, and looking directly in his eyes, "does not always judge character well, though. I want you now to forgive me for mistrusting yours because I've mistrusted your opinions."

He returned her gaze smiling, and taking the reins in his right hand, put his left on hers, saying:

"Well! 'a girl like you' is a queer thing!"

She looked up, blushing and smiling, and the tandem trotted homeward bearing two friends for life.

The outcome of the talk had been as neutral as the color of Calmire's coat. He had been mainly occupied in teaching the girl a few of the simple things she wanted to know, and, so far as he thought about it, he thought that the function most appropriate for him. And yet—?

The quiet troop of long shadows had left the hillsides and followed the music of the birds westward with the Sun. Soon tree-toads and other plain-colored folk on the dark sides of the trees, began to tell that the nights were growing longer. Down in the pond, a big frog, thinking of his Winter-sleep, growled out: "Don't care. Let it come! Let it come!" He startled the other singers so that they all stopped, and it was so quiet that two or three little stars peeped out. Over where it was too bright for others to come, the sky was yellow, and under it the hills were deep, deep blue. The air began to be cool, and Calmire reached back for more wraps, and they both thought pleasantly of the deep dining-room hearth: not eagerly, though, for no feeling of haste could disturb that peace. All feeling was toward rest: to the children who loved her, the great Mother was opening her arms.

CHAPTER XXIV.

GENTLE MAGIC AND HARD PHILOSOPHY.

A WEEK or two later, the two Calmire households and Courtenay, with a different young lady in the place of Sallie Stebbins, dined again at John's. After dinner Muriel went to the ladies on the piazza, and, without any polite subterfuge, proclaimed to two of them that he liked their company less than that of the third, by asking Miss Wahring to take a little stroll.

Mrs. Wahring protested that it was late, et cetera, et cetera, but Muriel's heavy will crashed through all her little diplomacies, and he and Nina started off.

"Where are you going?" asked Nina.

" I don't care," Muriel answered, but did not take the pains to learn if she did.

"I've never seen the poor parts of the town," she said. "Are they dangerous at night?"

"Oh no! There's no very poor part here, but we can walk through such as there are, even before it gets very dark."

"Then let's go slumming."

Ten minutes later, as they were passing a row of very small cottages, they encountered a woman standing by a gate half open outwards, looking anxiously up the street. As they stepped aside, she said:

"Good-evening, Mr. Muriel. Have you seen anything of Dr. Rossman or Mr. Courtenay?"

"Oh! it's you, is it, Mrs. Walters? I didn't know you lived here, and it was a little dark to recognize you. I've just left Mr. Courtenay at Mr. John's."

"To-night my William was taken awful bad," said the woman, "and I sent off for one of them. I've been looking into the face of everybody that passed: that's why I knew you."

"What's the matter?" briskly inquired Nina.

"It's my poor boy, Miss; he got hurted in the mills near a year ago, and he gets light in his head and frightened like, and nobody can't keep him quiet but the doctor and Mr. Courtenay. There he is, takin' on now."

They recognized sounds of moaning and deprecation from the house, which had not struck their attention before.

"Let me go to him," said Nina, and, in her enthusiastic way, went right past the woman without waiting for the amenities.

The woman caught hold of her and said: "Mebbe he's not fit for you to see, Miss. Wait a bit till I go in." And she went into the house, leaving Muriel at the gate, and Nina a pace or two inside of it.

This was not what Mr. Muriel had bargained for. He had come out to enjoy himself walking alone with Miss Wahring, not to be troubled over an idiotic pauper, or to wait alone while she was. He said:

"Oh, come along! You can't do anything for the boy: so what's the use of bothering? The doctor or Courtenay will be along soon. The messenger must have found one of them by this time."

Nina looked hard at him with a shade of disappointment. After a moment, she said: "I don't know whether I can do anything for him—probably I can't; but it may be something to his poor mother to have somebody with her till the others come. I'm going to try, anyhow. I've done some queer things in the way of quieting pain."

"It's not so much pain with this chap," said Muriel, "but he has fits of horrors, as I understand it —something like jim-jams."

"What are jim-jams?"

"Why, don't you know? From drinking hard."

"Oh! Does he take too much?"

"Oh no! Nothing of that kind. It's from a blow he got on the head."

"Does he get no better?"

"I don't know; I don't know much about it, anyway."

"And don't care?" said Nina, impatiently.

"Not very much, I guess:—no affair of mine. If Nature will do such things, I suppose she's got to have her own way."

"Then I don't see what we've got hearts for."

"Oh, there are nuisances enough for them, without any such nuisances as this."

"It's not nice in you to look at it in that way," she remonstrated.

"It's not nice in Nature. Don't blame me."

Here the woman came half-timidly back, and Nina followed her in, while Muriel remained by the gate. While the mother had been in the house, the moaning had been more interrupted and had changed to occasional protestation. When Nina appeared in the door, it stopped.

Muriel shifted his position, and through the open window could see the boy—a fellow of some sixteen years, who would have looked very commonplace but for the paleness and emaciation of his face, emphasized by a great shock of sandy hair. He was gazing at Nina with pleased surprise. Muriel stepped near enough to hear him say, after a moment:

"Why, you'm not a bit like the others!"

"I'm glad I'm not, if the others frightened you," said Nina.

"Oh, but they did! They's awful! Where be they gone to?"

"I've tried to send them away," Nina answered, "and I don't think they'll come back."

"Oh, you know 'em, then," half wailed the boy. "Mother swears she don't."

"I saw some of them once," responded Nina.

"What in the devil's name does the woman mean?" muttered Muriel, half aloud.

"You did!" exclaimed the lad. "Did the big red one hit you on the head too?"

"No," said Nina, who by this time had gone up and shaken hands with the boy, and seated herself beside him. "It wasn't that way. I had a book full of green and red and yellow pictures, and when I looked at it till my eyes got tired, and then looked up, I saw the queer things dancing all over the wall and the ceiling."

"That wasn't like mine," said the boy.

"Not exactly," Nina assented; "but I think

they're a good deal alike. Mine came because I hurt my nerves a little, and yours came because you hurt your nerves a great deal."

"What's nerves? Is it only people whose nerves get hurted what can see 'em? Mother can't see 'em. Could she see 'em if her nerves was to be hurted? You know lots more than she does or doctor. Oh, here they be again!" half cried the boy, cowering back with an expression that was terrible to see.

"They sha'n't get to you," said Nina, taking his hand. "I'll get in front of you." And she moved her chair from beside the boy directly in front of him. This brought her back toward Muriel, and he got disgusted again.

The light from the mantel now shone through the increasing darkness full on her face, which was directly opposite the poor boy. This diverted his disordered imaginings again, as her entrance had done. She still held his hand and talked with him soothingly for several minutes. He gazed at her steadily, only uttering monosyllables, until at last he said:

"You'm not like anybody ever I seen, and yet you'm not like them neither. What be you anyhow?"

"Only a young woman who is very sorry you have so much trouble."

"No, you'm more than that. I guess likely you'm an angel."

Muriel said to himself, "Well, if here isn't another at it!"

Nina laughed low and musically, not with her

Gentle Magic and Hard Philosophy. 249

usual hearty peals that would have jarred the boy's distressed nerves.

"Oh, but it's pretty to see you laugh!" he exclaimed, with something more like vivacity than anything, except the fear of a moment before, that his tired face had shown. This started Nina's laughter afresh. A little after she subsided, the boy said to her cheerfully but beseechingly:

"Laugh again!"

This time there was a little intention mingled with the laugh, and he said:

"It was prettier before. I'm getting sleepy."

Nina said: "It's very easy for you to find things pretty. Do you like flowers?"

"No, I don't care much for 'em."

"What do you like?"

"Oh, I like girls, and angels, and dogs, and such things."

This started Nina's laugh again.

"That's it! That's it!" cried the boy.

"Don't you like some other things?" said Nina.

"Oh yes; before I got sick," he said wearily, "I had a jew's-harp."

"What tunes could you play?"

"Oh, I can't think now. I'm tired, and I can go to sleep. I'll tell you all about it, though, if you'll come again," he said, stretching himself and gaped, "if you'll come and laugh. Will you?"

"Indeed I will," said Nina.

Then the mother approached and said, "Oh, Miss, you make him feel so good!"

Nina exchanged a few words with her, and then said to her son: "When I come again, what shall I bring you? Have you still the jew's-harp? I might bring——" She had been moving to go, but her eyes now fell again on the boy. He was asleep.

"God bless you, Miss!" said the woman, following her to the door. "Nobody never quieted him like this."

"Why, it seems easy enough," said Nina, "if you'll only let him have his own way, and lead him gently to think of other things."

"Yes, but that's not so easy. You was something for him to think of, yourself, you see. I try that way, but he's used to me and all I can do. The doctor and Mr Courtenay tries it, but they're nothing but men."

"Well, I'll come some more until he gets used to me—and tired of me," said Nina, and shook hands and passed out.

Muriel, who was standing beside the door, stepped on to the sill, held out his hand to the woman, and said, "Good-night, Mrs. Walters." Then Nina heard a few words of a rather protracted discussion, Muriel insisting and the woman objecting, and finally yielding, after which Muriel, with two or three long strides, half jumps, placed himself by the gate after Nina had opened it for herself.

They went along in silence for a minute or two until they were met by a man walking almost at a run. They could see it was Courtenay.

"Come back!" said Muriel, seizing his arm as he was rushing past without recognizing them, "your work is done."

"He isn't dead?" exclaimed Courtenay, half realizing his misunderstanding before it was all expressed.

"Oh no! Miss Wahring has charmed him to sleep."

"Sweet wonder-worker!" said Courtenay, with a reverence that excluded all suggestion of presumption. Yet the expression nettled Muriel a little. For once, however, he kept still.

"Come back with us," said Nina, to break a silence that she was very quick to feel embarrassing.

"Thank you, I will, so far as my corner;" and the three walked on side by side.

Courtenay said in a few moments: "That's a strange dispensation down there."

"I can't see anything strange about it," snapped Muriel. "The fellow's head got hit, and it's addled. Nothing queer about that!"

"No. But that the only son of a widow should be selected!"

"You must keep pretty intelligent blocks of wood in this town," said Muriel, "if they select what heads they're going to hit."

"And certainly a very cruel one in this case," quickly added Nina, for the sake of diverting the conversation. She was conscious only of the sympathy she was expressing, and her tact was too immature to prevent her for the moment from unconsciously "taking sides."

"There's a Power behind the blocks of wood," said Courtenay.

"Must be a mighty stupid one!" commented Muriel, half *sotto voce.*

"It's not for us to judge it, Mr. Calmire."

"All right; I won't if you won't."

Victory, even when a little brutal, inspires a conciliatory disposition: so a few moments later, Muriel resumed:

"That poor chap seems to yield to your good handling, Mr. Courtenay. Isn't he going to get well?"

"His sufferings can be palliated, but the doctor says he can never get well."

"Then the sooner it's over, the better."

"His mother wouldn't think so," said Nina.

"And I'm not sure that I should," added Courtenay.

"You've a tender heart, Mr. Courtenay."

"And your tough opinions have not yet convinced me that you have not, Mr. Calmire."

"Well, that's very kind in you, but I think it's a man's business to govern his heart by his opinions, and not his opinions by his heart. Now if it's the height of wisdom to follow Nature, and she permits only the fittest to survive, why should anybody want an incapable like that to survive? I hate sick people anyhow."

"That doctrine of the survival of the fittest," answered Courtenay calmly, "I've often thought, tends to make people cruel, and raises a good many hard questions. But it's a very easy doctrine for a man of your proportions to get enthusiastic over."

"By that same token, sir, it ought not to be an unwelcome doctrine to a man of yours. But where is the answer?"

"I think there are a good many. But here's my corner, and if I walk on to preach to you to-night, my people will be in danger of short-commons Sunday. I'd like to talk it over with you some time, though. Good-night. Good-night, Miss Wahring. Perhaps you can set him straight. Women see these things better than men do sometimes."

As Courtenay walked swiftly away, Muriel said to Nina: "I sometimes suspect there's a good deal of man in that fellow, despite his cloth."

"Why, we really *are* getting catholic-minded," she answered.

"Thank you! By the way, if he'd stayed with that sick fellow, he'd have had to take as much time away from his sermon as to talk with me."

"Perhaps he considered the sick fellow a worthier subject than he did you—or, perhaps, a more needy one. Forgive me; I didn't mean to be pert."

"Sure?"

"Well, perhaps I did; but I was sorry for it afterwards."

"All right."

After they had walked a little farther she said: "I'm beginning to understand you a little. I find you're a hypocrite."

"Why, what, in the name of all that's preposterous, do you mean? If I don't profess anything, how can any of my professions be hypocritical?"

"Oh, you profess a great deal."

"For instance?"

"Well, you profess to be very savage."

"Well, ain't I?"

"What do you mean by coming out here, and talking big and black and fierce about wanting that poor boy to die, five minutes after you've been giving his mother money to keep him alive?"

"What makes you think I gave her money?"

"I heard you force it on her. You're always forcing something on somebody—money, or an opinion, or—or something."

"Hm!" was all Muriel had to say.

"Well," she resumed after a moment, "haven't you anything to say for your conduct?"

"I don't see why the beggar shouldn't die. I don't see why the doctor shouldn't put him out of his misery."

"Then what did you give his mother the money for?"

"Well, you wouldn't like them to starve, would you?"

"No; but you're trying to make out that you would."

"Oh no. I'm not as bad as that."

"Just how bad are you, then?"

"Well, I think Nature had better finish him up her own way, since she's begun, and be quick about it. She's pretty sure to make a botch anyhow; but I'm not going to stand by and let her make as disgusting a botch as starvation would be. I can stop that. I can't stop his jim-jams, though, or I'd tackle them too."

"Hm!" it was Nina's turn to say now.

She broke the silence later, as if in the midst of a train of thought, with:

"And yet you *are* merciless!"

"So is Nature, if you look at it in that way. She's always killing off the weak, and she does it painfully and cruelly. I'm a mighty sight more merciful than she is. I'd chloroform the beggar decently and in order, if I had my way."

"And yet his mother, who loves him more than you do, would not let you."

"That's because she's a fool—all women are, over things they love."

"Perhaps that's not a misfortune for the things," she commented.

"It is in this case. It would be better for the boy, and better for his mother, if it were all over with. She can't do all the work she might, because she has to stay home with him. She gets only half her share out of life, and he gets nothing, and a good deal less."

"But she has him, and caring for him is a happiness to her."

"Well, I beg leave to doubt that. It's not natural that it should be."

"Yes, it is—to a mother."

"Well, a mother is a queer institution. If I'd had one, I suppose she'd have spoiled me too, taking care of me."

"I suppose nobody was ever known to be spoiled for the lack of a mother?" It was a pity that the darkness hid the expression of her face.

"Do you think I'm spoiled?"

"Awfully near it."

"Would you mind telling me how?" These falls, from her, did not daze or irritate him any more.

"Well, one thing, in your having so little sympathy with feelings not your own—in feeling so few things."

"Hm! I don't care to feel things that will knock my judgment endways."

"But I suppose that when you form a judgment, you want it to cover everything in the case?"

"Hulloa! That sounds like Uncle Grand."

"Well, *don't* you?"

"I suppose I ought to."

"Surely so consistent and catholic-minded a person *must*."

"Don't be rough on a fellow! Do you know you kind of make me see that perhaps in this thing I didn't give weight enough to the mother business?"

"Now that's being very good," she said in a way that was like a caress. "Now be good some more, and see if there are not some other kinds of 'business' that you're not apt to give enough weight to."

"All sorts of feelings and sich, I suppose you mean?"

"Yes, other people's."

"I dunno." He had unconsciously tried to cover a retreat with a little buffoonery of expression.

"Well," ejaculated Nina, amiably, "it's some improvement to say that you don't know."

"Thank you. I'm glad your ferocity is going."

"Oh, it wouldn't do you any harm," she said simply and seriously.

After a little silence she exclaimed:

"See here, I've got it!"

"What?"

"Mr. Courtenay's reason. My mind has been fumbling for it ever since I began to think about you."

"So you do sometimes think about me?"

"Yes; but don't feel flattered."

"Well, what have you got?"

"Why this: you say our hearts were made only for happy feelings. Now pity, sympathy, self-sacrifice are not happy feelings, but they are all great things. Where would they be if there were no misery in the world?"

"I've often heard Uncle Grand talk about that," Muriel interrupted.

"Oh dear!" she exclaimed, "I wouldn't have to find out near so many things for myself if I could always talk with him instead of wasting my time with you. But that woman's misery has done good even in your case, whether my troubles with you do or not. The best thing I ever saw you do, was to give her the money to-night. And it's worth all the more," she said in the softest tones he ever heard, as she lightly touched his arm and turned a glowing face to him in the lamplight, "for all the big black talk you uttered after it. Now, how could you have done it, in face of your horrid opinions too, if it hadn't been for the misery there?"

"I don't see that there was anything in it to make a fuss about," he said.

He never had been quite so pleased in his life, but he showed his vanity by not answering her question, even though he nervously deprecated her compliment.

"Well, why don't you answer my question?" she persisted.

"I give it up," he said—about the first time he had ever been wise enough to "give up" anything.

CHAPTER XXV.

A BIT OF KNIGHT-ERRANTRY.

Woman's dependence on man's strength has been hereditary through too many rude generations, to be absent from any of the present "daughters of Eve." Some women love men learned, many love them wise, most love them good, but all love them strong. Yet there are already evolved many modes of strength besides the one that all appreciate.

Nina was now thrown frequently with three men each of whom she found more interesting in his own peculiar way than she had ever found any man outside of the three. On their parts: Courtenay felt that he loved her; Calmire, though he had lived beyond the stage of love's happy illusions, felt himself, regarding her, capable of all love's realities; and as to Muriel, more than once it had crossed his mind that here was the first young woman he had met who, if she were not "hide-bound" and stubborn, might be capable of rising to a comprehension of the deep speculations and lofty aspirations of even his mighty soul. But then his wife was to combine the grandeur of Juno with the ethereality of Psyche, the passion of Venus with the purity of

Diana, the simplicity of Cordelia with the worldly tact of Beatrice; she was to be learned beyond all the philosophies, and yet was to learn everything from him; her mere glance was to compel his allegiance, and yet her chief delight was to be in submitting to his supernal self: in short, she was to be everything and its opposite at once. Such a creature, and such an one only, could be worthy the fealty of Muriel Calmire—as he conceived Muriel Calmire. But lately, when he had dreamed of loving some grand creature like Semiramis, he had regretted that Miss Wahring was but five feet four; when he had dreamed that his love would be a little appealing Psyche-like darling that he could carry around as he would any other toy, he had been sorry that *this* woman consisted of a hundred and forty very pretty pounds; when his reveries ran on dark-eyed Eastern houris, he had begun to wish that his new friend's eyes were dark; and when, through some book, he had felt an echo of the passion that sacrificed so many men to Mary of Scotland, he had said to himself: "Oh, if Nina's eyes, too, were but gray!" Perhaps he was not in love with her. But it is a portentous circumstance for one of the few youths of his make, to draw so many and so serious comparisons between a special woman and his all-embracing desires.

Nina, for her part, though not the sort of a girl who is always speculating on the feeling toward herself of each man she meets, was woman enough to have in her sub-consciousness a set of feelings which, so far as they went, told her a little of the attitudes of the three men. But her intense maidenhood prevented her examining those feelings very closely. They told her enough, however, to give her a faint vague perplexity regarding Muriel, which corresponded with his own self-contradictory condition. Toward Calmire, her feeling was even more complex. All women are match-makers, and she had heard from her acquaintances many a speculation, often humorous, as to who would be the next Mrs. Calmire. She had heard his name coupled with those of girls as young as herself, and once had even been jestingly advised to "set her cap" for him. This was very repugnant to her. Though she had plenty of common-sense, she was not without imagination, and she was young. Love between one man and one woman, she had rightly placed as the best of human experiences; and if anything human was, in her eyes, worthy of immortality, of course that love was. It had not yet dawned upon her that even her ideas of immortality were, on the whole, incompatible with the conditions of *human* love. She had heard the facile disposition of the case: "There is no marrying or giving in marriage there;" but she had not coupled with it any real conception of a love released from all human limitations and glorying in all conscious being. Of course, then, like all young women who dream the dreams she dreamed, and are strangers to the thoughts she was stranger to, she found the idea of anybody making a second marriage, repugnant. A part of this repugnance inevitably drifted in between her and Calmire. She had never respected or admired a man so much, and the more she thus regarded him,—the more she felt the charm of his gentleness and strength and wisdom, the more there grew in her a feeling, of which she was but half conscious however, that all her high ideals of love demanded that her interest in him should not increase. The attraction and repulsion grew together.

But toward Courtenay, her feeling was the most complex of all. His pathetic beauty as he lay, cruelly marred and dead perhaps, by her hand, had made her pity for him an actual passion, much of which was self-reproach and sense of reparation due. So far as it included a certain responsibility to him, it was the germ, but only the germ, of a feeling responsive to his own wild inspiration. As yet, he had said no direct word to her, but she felt that he loved her. This gave her a perplexing disquietude. She had almost a notion that she ought to love him, and she did not. She realized the nobleness of his life and aims, she felt the loveliness of his character. Sometimes she contrasted his self-denying careful gentle life, with Muriel's self-indulgence, carelessness, and brusqueness; but she could not love Courtenay—at least yet; and she could not hate Muriel—yet at least. What was stranger still, she never felt toward Courtenay that emotion that women so love—as if she could lean upon him. When she thought of Muriel, that feeling was sometimes there. But when she thought of Calmire, the feeling was always there—as much a matter of course as the solid earth beneath her feet.

This is not saying that she realized all this herself

or gave it nearly as much thought as is needed to convey it. In complex cases, when action is demanded, how many of the dormant feelings that spring up and impel us, have we ever clearly comprehended before? How much better our friends often know their existence in us than we do ourselves!

It was some time before the sharp summons of circumstances brought Nina's real feelings to her knowledge, but of course events kept adding definiteness in one way or another. One such event came a few days after the visit to the sick boy, as she and Muriel were walking, at sunset, some distance from the house at Fleuvemont. They were talking about Courtenay's work and Muriel's—well, his not-work.

"You've pitched into me for laziness before," said he. "Now as I said then, I don't believe I'm altogether lazy. I work like the Prince of Darkness (since you won't let me name my old friend the Devil), at anything I care for."

"Then you don't care for other people, I suspect," said Nina.

"No, not for many of them. And now that I come to think of it, it seems to me that the fellows I've known who've gone in for charity and all that, have most of them been rather slow."

"Haven't driven four-in-hand, you mean."

"No, not altogether that, but haven't gone in for the things a fellow ought to go in for."

"Such as?"

"Well, say boating and tennis and riding, and music and society if you will."

"Unluckily for me," said Nina, "Mr. Courtenay goes in for boating; and he certainly goes in for charities. And I think I've heard that he's a good tennis-player. Isn't he a musician too?"

"Yes, something of one."

"Why don't you like him?" she asked quickly.

"I do like him, or at least I try to."

"Why do you have to try?"

"Because I don't trust him," said Muriel, and Nina had a queer feeling as of recognition. Yet she exclaimed:

"Don't trust him? Why, what can you mean?"

"I mean that I don't trust him to look at things squarely. I mean that I feel, when I'm talking with him, that he'll not take a fact for what it's worth compared with other facts, but that he's always weighing it in the medium of his dogmas instead of in the true air."

"Yes, but some things will float on water that won't float on air. His dogmas sustain a good deal that would fall to the ground without them."

"I doubt that. The real work is done by something older and broader than his dogmas—something that they're simply tacked on to."

"Well! It's all awfully puzzling to me!" exclaimed the girl. "Sometimes I think reason is on your side, and then when I look at your life and his, it seems to me, you must excuse my saying, that facts are on his side."

"You mean his doing so much good, and my doing so little!"

"Yes, if it must be put in that way."

"Well, I guess he'd do good anyhow, no matter

what he believed; and very likely I wouldn't, no matter what I believed. But a good many fellows who believe as I do, do lots of good; and a good many fellows who believe as he does, don't. If you'll just look—"

He was interrupted by a woman's scream from beyond a clump of bushes near by. He rushed through them. There he saw one of the maids from the house, holding on with one arm to a sapling, and shrinking from a man who stood before her with his arms folded. He was not a specially brutal-looking fellow, but had a mean, cruel face.

"What's this about?" said Muriel.

"It's my husband, sir," said the woman.

"Oh yes, you're Annie. I've heard about it."

"Yes, sir. He's trying to make me go back with him, sir."

"What made you scream?"

The woman did not answer.

Nina, who had followed through the bushes, saw a slight shiver go through Muriel, and his hands contract like claws, as he jerked his head toward the man.

"Did you strike her?"

"None of your business."

"Yes, it is my business. She's a woman, and I heard her scream."

As Nina watched Muriel, he seemed fairly to expand before her eyes, into something portentous and baleful.

The man answered: "She's my wife, and I'll do what I please with her," and he reached out his hand and took a step toward her. She gave a little cry and started back.

A Bit of Knight-errantry.

"Stop!" roared Muriel. There is no other word to describe it. But his aspect was more terrifying than his voice: that, indeed, at once fell to its ordinary volume. "Now listen to me," he said in tones that seemed made of steel, and he seemed made of steel himself as he stood rigid and immense. Nothing stirred about him but his deep chest, and his tense fingers strained apart and grasping slowly and separately to and fro. His face was pale with a tinge of livid green, his deep eyes took that horrible merciless look of a creature watching its prey, only that their beauty and intelligence made them just that much more fearful.

At Muriel's order, the man had dropped his hands like a soldier at the word of command, and stood facing him. He spoke again in tones whose deliberate calm was grim beside the awful aspect of his rage:

"Now listen to me. Whatever your rights over that woman may be, you have no right to abuse her. If you touch her, I'll kill you. I mean exactly what I say."

He had no weapon, but as Nina saw and heard him, she no more doubted that he would kill the man, than she doubted his presence before her. She felt herself strained up with part of his strength. Even her sex's fear was banished from her. She simply waited to see what was to be the next irresistible movement of this awful power.

A man may be coward enough to frighten a woman, and yet have a half-stupid stubbornness that keeps him up until the actual contact with danger. Such a man faced Muriel. He even had some blundering notion that his rights were being invaded. There was no more thought of fight in him than if he had stood before a tornado, and yet he put on a cheap bold front, and repeated after a few moments' pause: "She's my wife, and I'll do what I please with her. Who are you?"

"It's no matter who I am. Touch her, and I'll kill you."

The man knew that he would, and turned away.

"Go to the house, Annie," said Muriel, "and I will follow you."

Then he turned to Nina, but could not smile: his rage so possessed him through and through. He said:

"Let us go back."

He was breathing deeply and rapidly, almost with great sighs. This too he could not control, or did not seem to care to try.

Before they had gone many steps, he stumbled: the strain had used up his strength. Then he was able to laugh, and he said to Nina:

"It's too bad to have to put you through such a scene."

"You're something terrible," said the girl.

And so one step more had been made toward definiteness in her relations with the three men. She was afraid of Muriel Calmire, and he was the first thing that she ever had been afraid of. But she feared him as one fears Nature's forces: under such fear, is reliance absolute.

CHAPTER XXVI.

IN THE SAME BOAT.

LIFE at Fleuvemont continued during September in about the simple courses already indicated.

The ladies ran off for two little visits, once to a certain nook in the Adirondacks, and once to Lenox. The first time, Muriel was so lonely and ill-natured that Calmire, following an instinct of earlier years, went off to Saratoga for a couple of days, and took Muriel with him. The next time the ladies went off, Muriel, forewarned, made arrangements to travel on some devices of his own, and after he got started, felt almost as much at a loss without his Fleuvemont life, as he had felt with it when the ladies were away before.

Moreover during September, as some people were driven toward town from their more remote summer fastnesses, a few visitors had been drawn to Fleuvemont for a day or two at a time. They were principally lone men whom Calmire compassionated for a Sunday; and more than one of them, as well as some others at neighborhood gatherings, aroused in Muriel, as Courtenay had, regarding Nina, that congenital jealousy universal in strong young males, or possibly some jealousy a little more special.

October had come, and one warm night, as the

four at Fleuvemont were seated on the piazza silently watching the twilight and the clear moon, Muriel suddenly exclaimed:

"What a night for October! Come, Miss Nina, let's go on the river."

"Delightful!" exclaimed Nina, rising.

"I think best not," said Mrs. Wahring.

"It's perfectly safe in a rowboat," said Calmire, rising too.

"I—I'm afraid of the night air for Nina," rejoined the lady.

"Well," said Calmire, "let's at least walk around the piazza, and see if the sky is not as beautiful on the other side," and he offered her his arm.

The young people did not follow. As soon as they were left out of earshot, Calmire said:

"Why don't you let her go?"

"What! alone with that young pirate?"

"Certainly. Under any ordinary circumstances, I'd trust any really good girl with him, as I'd trust her with her mother. Let them go. We were young once!"

"Yes, that's just the trouble."

"That we were?"

"That they are."

'It's no question of convention here," he remonstrated. "Why, they're almost cousins, as we were when we went rowing, let me see, twenty-eight years ago this month. It didn't hurt either of us much."

"Didn't it?" said she, affecting a sigh and placing one hand over the left side of her matronly bosom.

"You Sapphira! you were engaged to Wahring at the time!"

"But you didn't know it!"

"*Didn't* I? But didn't you enjoy yourself, even if Wahring *was* in China?"

"Well, to be candid, perhaps I did."

"'To be candid, *perhaps*'! So did I. Well, give your daughter a good time too."

"Ah, but your nephew is not you."

"No, he's certainly better fitted to give the girl a pleasant hour to remember than I am now."

"Your modesty, like other diseases coming late in life, is positively incurable. I know she enjoys your society more than his."

"So did you Wahring's more than mine. Yet you had a good time."

He did not know whether he had deliberated the shot or not, but he felt that in comparing his own relation with the girl, to Wahring's with his *fiancée*, the shot was a good one. It told, and as they neared the young people, Mrs. Wahring said so they could hear:

"Certainly there are few nights like this."

"Too few to miss," responded Muriel. "Miss Nina's not afraid to go if you'll consent. I'll take good care of her."

"The night is milder than I thought. She may go."

The two were soon in the boat. After the usual chat on surrounding objects and the incidents attending their start, they settled into a not uncongenial silence, both gradually yielding to the meditative influences of the scene. At last Nina broke it by humming a little song to the rhythm of his oars, he improvising a florid and sometimes burlesque accompaniment. At last he got so boisterous with harmonious growls and explosions that they both stopped for laughing, and soon grew silent and meditative again. After a while, she said:

"The night is no longer restful to me. You have been too busy all Summer filling it with questions."

"And you're disposed to feel unkindly toward me for it?" he asked.

"Perhaps I ought not to. I've heard you and your uncle say a thousand times that one should trust truth, no matter where it leads. But what you've given me, so far, seems to lead nowhere," and her tone was sad.

"Oh!" he exclaimed. "Now you're talking in the commercial way. One should not weigh consequences. Truth for its own sake is the thing, I suppose: only that's a sort of truism. What it really means must be that we can trust truth to lead rightly whether we see the way or not."

"I don't know about that!" she responded, again sadly. "I don't find the leadings very pleasant."

"But, Miss Nina, you don't mean—"

"Yes, I do," she interrupted, and went on passionately: "I mean that all this Summer, the whole world I used to stand on has been crumbling under my feet; I mean that the beliefs, hopes, fears, if you will, that shaped my former life, are nearly all gone, and those of them that I still hold, I find I used to hold for wrong reasons. I find that most of what has been taught me, was taught by ignorance and often by virtual dishonesty. Those who taught me, thought it better to give a wrong argument for a right opinion, than to give none at all. You can't tell what realizing all this means to me, because to you it came more gradually, and half of it came without trampling to death anything you held dear before. But my old beliefs were old friends, almost old parents; I had taken them so much as a matter of course, that I did not know what they had been to me, until they began to disappear; and here I see them destroyed, and so little left me in their place! I feel deserted, unsupported, alone! I'm very wretched, Mr. Calmire, if you can understand that, when every doubt of your own seems only a pillar for your pride. *My* pillars are all fallen, and I sometimes feel as if the life were being crushed out of me."

Had a meteor fallen into the boat, the boy could not have been more astonished.

"Why, you astound me, Miss Nina! I knew that you were getting more patient with us, but I did not know that you were becoming one of us."

"I'm not one of you! You're contented and even conceited, if you'll pardon my saying so, in your position, and I'm simply wretched and very humble —how humble, my talking to you in this way, ought to help you imagine."

Now, among the virtues which Mr. Muriel Calmire intended to practice some day—when he should become old and superior to temptation, that is to say when he should have had all the pleasure that the exercise of such virtues might interfere with, he had lately begun to include humility and candor in acknowledging defeat. There were very few pretty things that appealed to his æsthetic sense in vain, and these pretty virtues, with several others entirely too beautiful for daily use, had already several times (especially in novels) been honored by his passing admiration. But they had never appealed to him with anything like the same vigor that they did when manifested in the proud and, as it happened, beautiful creature now before him—a person whose whole association with him seemed to be a constant demand for just such concessions from him as she was now astounding him by making herself. The boy's first emotion was triumph, and it had almost taken possession of his tongue, when there came rushing over him a flood of sympathy and contrition such as he had never known. The conflict of feelings started him into a hysterical laugh, through which he jerked out the consolatory observation: "Why, Miss Nina, I—I didn't suppose it could make such a difference."

But the girl understood his feeling, and was better satisfied to go on:

"I've thought and thought and thought, and for my soul's sake, I can't escape seeing that if half you and Mr. Calmire say, is true; and if one depends on reason alone without Faith, Christ's divinity, a personal God, and immortality itself are all dogma. There's no good proof for any of them. The moral law is, I suppose, after all the main thing: but with Christ and God and Immortality gone, I don't see why people believe in that. Do you?"

"Why, of course I do. But before I tell you, I want to stick a pin or two. I don't see that Christ's 'gone,' as you call it. I suspect he's a historic fact that you can't get around; and as to God: there's certainly something running the machine and keeping it in some sort of order; and as to immortality: well, we don't know so much about that. But this is pretty considerable of a universe, and we have a pretty significant share in it, whether we're immortal or not; and either way, we ought to behave ourselves just as we should if we were, I suppose: only it's such a bore to do so. But upon my soul, as you sit there, you look as if you ought to be immortal, whether you are or not."

"Thanks, very much!" answered the lady. "But suppose you take the trouble to keep serious a little longer. There's something better than compliments to be had out of you—occasionally. Now, about behaving ourselves, I no longer know if right is right, or wrong is wrong, or if each is not the other. I sometimes feel as if I could be wicked. But I won't."

"Well, why won't you?"

"Oh, I don't know. Why won't Mr. Calmire? He believes none of the things I used to. Why won't you, if you can help it? For I wouldn't be talking to you as I'm talking now, if I had not seen that in your way you do sometimes try to do what is right."

"I do try, Miss Nina, in some things. But I like to have a good time too."

"Yes, I know all that, but at bottom you're true. What makes you so? You're not so from love of God, or from love of anything else I can see, but your precious self, except, of course, your uncle."

"*Do* you think I'm true, Miss Nina?"

"Haven't I said it? Would I have said any of these things to you if I didn't believe that?"

"Well then, why have you always been so down on me?"

"Because you're so seldom just to yourself. You have a great, deep soul, and yet you lead a shallow, empty life. You are really that earnest, thoughtful man you appeared to be the first moment I saw you; and yet you have no aims, and you never work at anything: all the deep things you've told me, you either studied because you had to, or 'picked up,' as you say,—largely because you happen to have an uncle who drops them; but your life, as you've candidly described it to me, has been mainly one of idleness and dissipation."

"But I never expected to keep up those things: a fellow must sow his wild oats, but sometimes I do 'keep up a devil of a thinking.'"

"Mr.—" she began remonstrantly.

"Quotation-marks! quotation-marks!" he cried, dropping his oars and holding up both hands.

"Oh, well, I can't understand you men," she exclaimed. "You're weak creatures at best."

"Is my Uncle Legrand a weak creature?"

"He's had much practice in being strong," she answered; yet she pondered a little over some things she had seen in him. After a pause, she continued:

"But I never can keep you to anything. I want

you to talk to me. I want you to tell me how, without any God, you and Mr. Calmire have any notion of right and wrong."

"Mr. Calmire won't admit that he has no God," said Muriel, "and I don't know that I will, but I haven't much of an opinion of mine."

"I did Mr. Calmire injustice," she said. "But I can hardly think of any God unlike my own. But go on and tell me how it is that you have a right and wrong."

He had resumed rowing, but he stopped again, as he did afterwards whenever he got specially interested.

"Well," he answered, "we have all the experience of mankind at our backs, pronouncing certain things right, and certain others wrong. The religions don't really do anything more than pick up this experience and enforce it. Of course you're not so blind as to attribute all morality to Christianity. Men can't work together, at least in fine work, without being able to rely on each other. Slavery alone could build the pyramids, perhaps, but it couldn't build the Parthenon and the Taj. There were morals behind those two, and behind the pyramids also, I've no doubt: certainly there were religions. Now religions all agree pretty well on fundamentals, allowing for different degrees of civilization of course."

"But you don't admit any religion to be supernatural, and what you say only proves all that splendid morality to be human; and, after all, the heart cries out for something more than the narrow facts of our little lives."

"Unquestionably. And it's a very good heart for doing so. Else we should not have any 'splendid morality,' but should be still among the 'narrow facts' in the 'little lives' of anthropoid apes. All progress lies in that cry. The morality is here though, and we're not leading the lives of the anthropoid apes."

"But the enforcing of the morals?" she exclaimed, "the making men live up to them?"

"Well, I haven't seen that religion has much to do with that," he replied. "I'd trust the agnostics of my acquaintance to observe them just as far as I would trust the Christians, and so would you."

"Yes, perhaps I would," she admitted. "But why does *anybody* live up to them? Why, I've heard one of the best women I know, say that if she didn't believe in a hereafter, she wouldn't hesitate at any crime. She even said that—that she might run away from her husband."

Muriel laughed and said: "I heard Uncle Grand talking about something like that the other day. He said that he'd often heard such remarks from such people, and that they simply hadn't thought about what they were saying. Either your friend was mistaken in her own view of how she would act, or you are mistaken in calling her a good woman. Do you believe she really would do anything disgraceful?"

Now it was Nina's turn to laugh, and she said: "No! She couldn't if she tried, and wild horses couldn't drag her away from her husband."

"Probably she spoke of that, just because it was the most extreme idea that could enter her head," said Muriel.

"But," insisted Nina, "*why* does any person keep good without a religious faith—if any person does?"

"Without a dogmatic faith, you mean! Mainly from force of habit—a habit of sympathy with mankind and enthusiasm for justice, that has been accumulating through all the generations. Anybody inherits his share of it, and the whole gathered drift of it surrounds him and bears him on with it."

"But what started it?" she asked.

"First love, then family affection, then friendship, then the realization, more or less distinct, that the greatest good of each man is in the greatest good of the greatest number of men. This has been lived up to with more or less directness, but always with increasing directness, until now it is distinctly realized as a rule of conduct. What did I read to you long ago on the piazza?"

"But what *is* good?" she demanded. "There comes in just my trouble."

"Ah, yes," he said, "the dogmatic meanings are confused with the practical ones. You've been told that only that is 'good' which is pleasing in the sight of God, and even that if you act from any less motive than 'love of God,' you are not 'good,' though the same teachers tell you that you are good if you act from love of your neighbor, and the best-known teacher of them all makes the test of love for your neighbor, that you shall love him as yourself—he seems even to have tacitly admitted that there can be 'good' in loving one's self, up at least to the degree where one can love one's neighbor too."

"A Christian policy which most of us are entitled to the credit of following!" she quietly observed.

"Yes," he agreed, "because it's common sense, not because it's Christianity. But don't go to ironing me now. You interrupt the lecture. Where was I?"

"You're very good and amiable to-night," she said.

"You've made me so," he replied, "and yet I'm not 'good' for love of God or even love of myself. Yet, you call me 'good' all the same. Now, don't you see distinctly that you applied that word to my actions because you are amiable enough to derive satisfaction from my humble exposition—in other words, you call me 'good' because I'm giving you pleasure?"

"Yes, that's true. I say you're good because you act in a way agreeable to me."

"Well, now, Miss Nina, here is the centre of the whole subject, and you must ponder it carefully, because it won't be clear to you at once, or before you've gone over it many times. I defy you to find a definition of 'good' implied in any religion or system of morals, that doesn't depend upon the idea of increasing happiness for *somebody*. No man ever had any idea of good, but happiness. 'Good for goodness' sake,' like 'truth for truth's sake,' 'beauty for beauty's sake,' and all that run of cheap phrases really means nothing—the repetition of a word is no explanation of it. Actually, the most abstract motive to good conduct ever urged, is to please God—to add to his happiness—a motive in the right direction by the way, because it is away

from selfishness. The same is true, in being good
to your neighbor. But even the ascetic, whether
St. Simeon on his pillar, or the Hindoo under the
car of Juggernaut, is simply being good to himself
—increasing the sum total of his own happiness,
(at least he supposes so,) by throwing away a lot of
happiness here to get a great deal more hereafter."

"Why, this's all very strange to me, Mr. Muriel. I always supposed that the grand thing was
to despise happiness."

"That's all cant. Take till we next meet,"
(What did he know of when they would next meet?)
"to see if you can think up a good act that doesn't
tend to increase the amount of happiness in the
universe—somewhere, some time; or a bad act that
doesn't tend to diminish it. And conversely, try to
think of any act that would add to the happiness
in the universe (including that of God and angels
if you want to bring them in), and see if it's not a
good act; and think of any act that would tend to
diminish the aggregate happiness, and see if it's
not a bad act."

"There does seem a great deal in what you say,"
Nina admitted. "But why, then, should not a man
devote himself entirely to his own happiness?"

"Because," answered Muriel, with the superiority of philosophy to practice, so frequent in
youth—and after, "for one reason, the veriest ignoramus knows that that's not the way to get
it. Happiness is a faint star that one sees quicker
by glancing at the brighter one of duty which
lies near it. Guess somebody must have said that
before!"

"Why, Mr. Muriel, is this you? A month ago you would have quietly appropriated it to yourself!"

"Perhaps! I don't know. I like to be strictly true with you. Well, here's another new development. Somehow it no longer seems to me a mere abstraction of the text-books that selfishness does not bring happiness, even to the selfish individual. Yes! I *have* been changing! I think I see for myself now *why* working for the greatest good of the greatest number is, in the long-run, the surest means of each individual securing his own good. Such is the law under which we live, and all moralists have caught glimpses of it, more or less distinct."

"Yes, perhaps," she meditated. "But how are we to judge when duties are in conflict?"

"Just as we judge which oar to use in pulling the boat around—by experience, which of course includes teaching from previous experience."

"But it's so much harder in moral questions," she objected.

"I can't help that," he said. "The difficulty of navigation is no argument against the use of such methods as we have. You don't pretend that religion is an infallible help? Look at the Inquisition, witch-burning, and stewed Quaker. In fact, I'm inclined to think that religion is a fearful misleader."

"But in pulling the boat around," objected Nina, "there's no selfish element to fight against. There is in moral questions."

"There's a selfish element in most questions," answered Muriel, "even in pulling the boat around. You see that splendid constellation right by those clouds over the western hills? Now, I can pull this boat around so as to bring you face to face with it, or so as to bring myself face to face with it. I'm going to resist the bias of self, and bring you face to face with it: for I'm going to turn now. I haven't rowed very far while this trivial conversation has been going on: for a fellow can't talk fit for anything with all his blood in his muscles. But it's time to go back, nevertheless. I'll farther unfold the mysteries of our moral nature, on the way home."

"First let me tell you," said Nina, as he proceeded to back water with his port oar and to put a little extra strength into his starboard, "that I do think there seems some ground to stand on in what you've been telling me. I feel better for it. But I don't half like your speaking in a sportive way of such things, as you just did."

"Well, my dear young lady," he proceeded, as he settled down to his measured stroke, and she shifted herself into an easier and more recumbent position, and stuck her little right thumb over the side into the water, where the hand and wrist seemed to Muriel more dazzling than the moonlit swirl that the thumb threw up—" Well, my dear young lady, there are two reasons for that—two at least, as there are for most things. One is that I'm rather a sportive sort of chap, as you have frequently been complimentary enough to observe (in your own language, however); and the other is" (and here he stopped rowing and lifted upon her that ponderous look which somehow she had grown to enjoy bracing herself to receive), "that when I'm talking over these subjects, their depth presents such a contrast to the shallowness of the best opinions I or any man can form upon them, that it stirs my sense of humor. But, *don't* think again, when I speak lightly in such connections, that I'm feeling lightly. I'm only indulging in a little unwonted modesty regarding my own opinions."

"You caught that from your uncle, too!" she said.

"Thank you, I didn't know it merited such praise."

"I've heard you, too," she continued, "indulge your sense of humor pretty freely regarding other people's opinions on similar subjects."

"Then do vouchsafe me a little grace for treating my own in the same way."

"Yes, yes; you're not as bad as you were two months ago. Then you had unbounded respect for your own opinions. But your uncle has given you a good deal of judicious snubbing in that time, I fancy. Hasn't he?"

"So has somebody else, Miss. But my uncle always does it kindly, and somebody else has not always been as gentle as she is to-night. Perhaps she has learned something, too!"

"Merciful heavens! Haven't I told you that I have? But do go on. You've been wandering in your mind ever since you turned the boat around."

"That is," he answered, "ever since the moonlight has been shining on your face."

"Evidently," she retorted, "it has been shining on your brain."

If Nina's face could be taken as a test, the moonlight was rosy for a moment. Muriel went on:

"No, with my back to the moon, my brain is better protected than before."

"Well, then," she said, "perhaps you can go on rationally. You were admitting what I said—that there is a selfish element to fight in making nearly all moral decisions."

"So there is. But it doesn't follow from that, that we have any other weapons to fight it with than just those we have; and they have come through experience—always, of course, including that of our ancestors."

"But," she retorted, "you talk as if there were no such thing as conscience."

"Certainly there is such a thing," he replied. "But we got our moral sense from the experience of our ancestors, developed by our own, just as we got our color sense or any other sense. The sense of moral beauty was developed in just the same way as the sense of physical beauty, by sympathy with fit objects, and antipathy from repulsive ones. Evil is a repulsive object. I don't deny that religious enthusiasm has often been a good defence against it. I do assert, though, that it's often been a bad one. I assert, too, that most of the best men I know are getting along without it."

"Without enthusiasm?"

"I said *religious* enthusiasm. I meant the kind that hinges on a professed knowledge of the supernatural. I don't mean that they get along without moral enthusiasm: that's a natural thing, for morals are a set of natural facts right before our comprehension. There's nothing supernatural about *them*, though folks used to think so. Still less do I mean that we are without enthusiasm for our common humanity. Both these enthusiasms are possible without the slightest tinge of supernatural sanction."

Evidently Mr. Muriel's association with his uncle for the past two months had been expanding his information on the subjects he was discoursing upon so glibly, and possibly his association with Miss Wahring had been quickening his interest in them.

"But why," asked Nina after a moment, "do you object so to supernatural sanction? Surely, it would be a good thing if we could have it."

"Assuming that it would, which is clear assumption, we haven't got it, and as soon as men claim to have it, they prove they have not got it by showing that the samples of what all claim to be the same thing, are not at all like each other. One man's religion contradicts another's. Then they begin to quarrel. The worst bloodsheds in history have come from those quarrels. Dynastic and territorial wars and persecutions have been nothing to religious ones. So, too, the worst domestic and social quarrels are the religious ones."

"Well, perhaps it all may be as you say, but I never thought over it much."

"Girls don't. We're made to help 'em."

"Perhaps some of these days you'll see some things that girls were made to help men in, too."

"What things? I don't know anything but looking pretty that men can't beat women at. What else is there?"

"Sympathizing."

"Oh, I always thought any fool could do that."

"That depends on what you mean by a fool. You're not able to do much of it, I'm afraid. But now I'll give you a touch of your uncle," she added, resuming an upright position and wiping the water from her hand. "What's knowledge good for?"

"To increase happiness."

"Good! What are the arts good for?"

"To increase happiness."

"Good again! You see what a convert you've been making. Now, on your own reasoning, sympathy is the highest of the arts. It does more for happiness than any other art."

"I never thought of that."

"Because you never felt the need of it. Because you never suffered, even as I have been suffering for the past few weeks."

"Haven't I? Now, if you're such a believer in sympathy, why don't you exercise more of it on a poor devil like me?"

"'Poor devil' is good. You're the last man to admit yourself an object of compassion. Why, I began our acquaintance by pitying you, and much thanks I got!"

"But then I do have my tastes and feelings, and even aspirations; and some of them are not unworthy of even your interest; and yet you don't seem to have cared much for them—at least not until to-night, and then it seems to have been principally because you wanted to pump me."

"Oh, you stupid boy! don't you see that I wouldn't have 'pumped' you, as you call it, if I hadn't grown interested in what you have in you to pump? Haven't I told you so before to-night? But my not having made it apparent to you before, supports what I've begun to suspect—that I'm not blessed with a first-class genius for sympathy myself, and that such as I have, is not very well developed."

"Practise it on me, won't you?"

"I'm not sure you deserve it."

"I don't mind trying to deserve it. But you have seemed so awfully far off."

"And yet, Mr. Muriel," and her beautiful candid eyes looked straight into his, in the bright moonlight, while she said, "our opinions don't seem so far apart as they used to. Except that I believe more fully than you do that God is behind it all, most of the differences left between us, seem to me mere words."

"Upon my soul, I hope so. Do you?"

"Yes!"

CHAPTER XXVII

DEPENDENCE.

From the cleft in the hills away under the majestic clouds that Muriel had pointed out, came a puff of wind. The sky had been growing darker, not with that pervading mist which hides all the stars, but with more clouds and heavier, which made the stars between their rifts seem all the brighter. Over in the West, throbbed, almost gently, a glow that was the last of many reflections of far-off lightnings. The next time, the wind came, not with a puff, but with a burst, and the gentle glows in the western sky became swift-climbing flames that set the edges of the clouds on fire; and there was thunder, but muttered so low that they would not have heard if they had not been intent.

"It's coming!" said Muriel.

"Oh, how glorious!" cried the girl, and then again the western sky burned for an instant as if the sun had just set.

Then: "I come," boomed the thunder.

"It's glorious, glorious, glorious!" echoed Muriel. "But I'll be getting you wet."

"I'd like to know how you'll be responsible for it," said the girl.

"I always feel responsible for any woman I

have with me," answered the boy, as he bent hard to his oars. "And for you I feel *very* responsible."

She smiled at him, and hummed some contented little tune.

"How you do make the boat go!" she said. "I actually see foam come back from the bows." And then she said to herself: "How strong he is! And he's pulling so because he wants to save *me* from the storm." Muriel exerting himself, was a new Muriel, and exerting himself for somebody else, almost a strange one; but she liked the novelties, and felt as woman always feels when the man before her shows himself strong.

The storm came fast, and the black waves were high. The lightning was soon no play of reflections, but split great jagged rifts through the sky over the heights, and the flashes showed boats already cowering under reefed sails. The peaks flung the thunder to each other, and it rolled down the precipices.

"When the thunder rolls down, it will fall into the river, and can't catch us," laughed Nina.

"Almost anything can catch us at the rate we're making," said Muriel. "Why don't you get scared?"

"*Scared?*" with a long dwell on the *a*.

"Why, yes. Other women would."

"You don't know me," she answered very quietly from the darkness. For now they could not even see each other except as the lightning flashed.

"By Jove, I didn't!"

"But Jove himself has shown you to me," he added a second later, when the next flash came and showed her—not leaning back languidly, but erect against the glory, in her close white gown, her proud bosom swelling forward as her arms strained on the tiller-ropes, her beautiful lips set firm, her nostrils dilated, her calm eyes peering far to catch her bearings, and her hair made, by the lightning, a halo around her pure face.

Did you ever pull a boat *hard?* If you did, against wind or tide, or other men, you can understand how Muriel, seeing this image, recognized it but did not feel it, until quiet moments later. But in such moments, how often it came, and how vividly!

A big drop splashed on his left hand.

"Here it is," said he. "You must put on my coat."

"Oh no!"

"What?" said he, like the crack of a whip. "This is no time for nonsense. You'll be wet to the skin."

"So will you."

"It makes no difference if I am. Besides, the exercise will keep me warm. You can do nothing but sit there till your teeth chatter. Here!"

He took his Norfolk jacket from under his thwart, and crawled toward her. The boat was pitching about so that if he had stood up, he would have toppled over.

"Put this on."

And for the first time in her life, she yielded to compulsion, and she liked it.

"I don't want any cigars," she uttered between two little laughs. She had put her hand in a pocket while fumbling for a sleeve.

"Oh, there's a watch and a lot of things there," he said. "Let me have it a moment."

As he groped for it in the dark, he touched her hand, and felt an impulse to kiss it; but the boat was rolling in the trough, a little flurry of rain came, and his impulse hardly had a chance to become distinct enough for him to know whether he wanted to kiss the hand because it was hers, or simply because it was a woman's. He knew later, though; especially when he reflected that he had never in his life before wanted to kiss a woman on the hand.

"Now," said he, "I have the coat by the collar, and am holding the inside toward you. Feel until you know your right arm is in the right arm-hole, then I'll release it to you."

In a second he almost felt her in his arms; and afterwards he had occasion to realize how absolutely he respected her.

"Now you've made a man of me," she said, laughing, as she settled into the coat and into her seat.

"You didn't need it!" he answered, and turned to crawl back to his thwart.

He felt for his oars—and they were gone. In his impetuosity, he had neglected to stow them, and they had no stops. He was entitled, however, to the excuse, such as it was, that he was used to stops.

"Why don't you row?" Nina called.

"The oars— Wait a moment."

He wanted to spare her, somehow. A flash of lightning came and showed the situation. She said nothing.

"There's really no occasion to be alarmed," said he. "Nothing serious can happen to us. We'll be blown ashore somewhere pretty soon, at this rate, and even if I had the oars, I'm not sure it wouldn't be the wisest thing to get ashore at the very nearest point we can, instead of rowing down the river in the rain at a snail's pace, as I was doing before."

"Why didn't you tell me at first that they were gone?" said she.

"I didn't want to frighten you, and wanted to think."

"It wouldn't have done any good to get frightened," she said very simply.

"Well, you're just a trump!" he exclaimed, "and the queen at that."

"Not good for many tricks just now, I'm afraid," she responded with a little laugh.

"That depends on the hands!" he answered. "There's not very much at risk, I think, if you don't catch cold. Let me see!—I have it! I'm going to paddle with the bottom-board from the bow. You can steer against me. If that jacket gets soaked through, I'll give you another bottom-board to paddle with, and keep yourself warm."

"Aren't you going to look for the oars?"

"We can poke along to shore sooner than we could find them. The wind's with us."

He groped around and got the bottom-board out.

"This is a poor paddle," he said, "so you'll have to steer hard against me to keep her even. I'll change sides occasionally, to relieve your arms. Why didn't I know before what a regular-built, spang-up— Here goes!" and he set to work.

Another flash came with a deafening crash of thunder close at hand.

"Pray excuse my back. I forgot my manners in the dark," he called over his shoulder. He had turned on his thwart to use his paddle.

"Since we're transformed into a canoe," she responded, "I ought to be doing the paddling here, in the stern, and you, there, facing me at ease."

"Even at Mount Desert, they don't let the women do the work that way," he answered, "and women have their rights there, if anywhere. But the right to do the work, is one they've never clamored for, I believe."

The rain came down in sheets. It seemed as if the blackness itself were wet and falling on them. They went along, occasionally exchanging a few cheerful words, until he said:

"Of course you're soaked. Let me get you another bottom-board, to keep yourself warm with."

"No! We're almost inshore. But may I wriggle the rudder from side to side? That will exercise me."

"It would hold us back a little," he objected. "Why not pull both tiller-ropes at once and swing yourself to and fro, as on the vertical parallels in the gymnasium? You don't really need to pull alternately."

"You're a man of resources!" she exclaimed.

In a few minutes, a flash of lightning just prevented their being bumped into a wharf, and they ran past it on to a sloping shore, where, in the darkness, they did graze a boat hauled up on their right.

"Sit still," said Muriel. And he took the painter, jumped out through the little breakers that somehow managed to show white, hauled up the boat, straddled the bow to steady her, and said:

"Now creep to me, and be careful not to hurt yourself against the thwarts."

"Shall I unship the rudder?"

"It would be as well. Lay it under the seat, please."

She did as she was bid, and groped her way to him.

"Let me carry you through this mud," said he.

"No, I can't be more bedraggled, and it will be all mud going home, anyway."

"Take my hand then, and jump toward me!"

"Wait for another flash. I can't see where I'll land."

The flash came. She reached out her hand to Muriel and jumped. He held the hand and put it over his arm, she not resisting, and they walked up the bank toward the lights. One was from a waterside tavern. With their eyes opened to the absolute blackness before, they could now see quite plainly.

"Come under this shed," said Muriel, "and I'll go in and get you a hot whiskey that will expand your views of the universe."

"Must I take it?"

"You unquestionably must."

She waited, and Muriel went in. Behind the bar was a jolly old river-dog, who said:

"Don't take it hot if you've got to go out again. You're too wet. No use in opening up your pores. Hadn't you better put on some of my togs, though?"

Muriel pondered a moment about "togs" for his companion, and then said:

"No. It's only a little way home. The walk will keep me warm enough. I've a friend out here to whom I'll take this, and swallow mine when I come back."

"Why in blazes don't he come in?"

But Muriel had taken some whiskey and cold water and was gone.

"Now," he said, "if a man's coat has made a man of you, take this like a man." "Miss Nina," somehow, had dropped out of its dominance in his phraseology.

"I can't promise to enjoy it like a man. But 'Here goes,'—that's what you say, I believe."

"Yes, you're the queen of—trumps isn't good enough for you."

Flying about like the recent lightning, he ran back, gulped his own drink, flung down half a dollar, and was out of the door, having paid no attention to the old fellow's yell of "Here's your change!" or his after-reflection, "Blowed if that isn't the maddest cove around these parts! I've seed him afore somewhere!"

Then Muriel strode off with Nina's hand again on his arm, and said to her:

"You can dress like a man and drink like a man, now walk like a man."

"You'll forget that I'm a woman if I don't do something inconvenient."

"No, by Heavens, I'll never forget that! But weren't you afraid at all in the boat?"

"You would have saved me!" It had slipped out, but she did not even reflect that it had.

"I'm not a very good swimmer."

"You would have been."

"Miss Nina, I don't deserve this!" and he felt, for almost the first time in his life, sincerely modest.

Now it seems pretty plain that out there in the dark, with her depending upon him, that man was in love with that woman. Why then didn't he tell her so? Simply because he didn't know it himself.

He felt the emotion, but he doubted whether this—simply this, could be the occasion for which he had waited through all his thinking years. From boyhood, he had cultivated a beatific dream of loving some woman superior to any whom he had ever met or ever could meet—a creature full of all possible charms, half of which, of course, could not exist in conjunction with the other half. Nina Wahring, equally of course, was not such a creature: so how was he to learn all at once that he was in love with Nina Wahring? His Love, forsooth, was to be hail-fellow-well-met with him—more of a boon companion than any of his college mates, yet he was always to treat her with the deference of a subject to a queen: here he had been calling Nina a trump, and had made her put on his coat—simply *made* her. Of course *she* was not his pedestaled ideal!

Worse for him, while in the deepest sanctuary of his soul, that changing ideal had stood sacred behind its altars; in the outer courts of the temple, the priest had chucked the dancing maidens under the chin. He was not the first whose service within the hallowed walls had been passionately true, while his life outside had been, just as passionately, something else. In short, many of the sweet impulses that had drawn him, as man, toward Nina as woman, had become, for him, familiarized to baser uses. They were no proof to him that here was his Love. He had permitted them to lead him often where he had no thought of love. They had not been reserved for their true function—to guide him, unthinking, to that pure goal.

Not only, too, were his imagination and his passions all out of gear, but that deliberative, skeptical intellect of his—in great matters cautious, despite his impetuosity in little ones—must make its leisurely survey of the situation. More than once before, he had unthinkingly striven toward some big temptation, and when he had got squarely within reach of it, so that he could realize what a large part of his life it must absorb, he had quietly turned his back, and afterward called himself a weakling and a fool for not grasping what he had sought, and disregarding consequences. The pale cast of thought was inevitably so much a habit of his constitution, that it not seldom sicklied o'er the native hue of resolution, especially where resolution was portentous with possibilities. He was as incapable of being entirely carried away by floods of pure emotion, as he was of constantly dwelling on the safe heights of philosophic calm.

He was too young to realize that great junctures do not necessarily require great preparations, and that many of the culminating determinations of life have to be made at unanticipated moments. Vastly less was he able to realize that most tremendous fact in practical morals, that the only safety at such sudden moments, is in a character so drilled, in every-day life, to do the brave thing and the right thing, that, when there is no time to think, it does them automatically. But this is beside the immediate issue, which is simply that it was so much the habit of Muriel's mind to imagine what great circumstances must be, that he had virtually put them outside the possibilities of actual life, and might be in the thick of the greatest things that life can bring, without realizing how great they really were. Well! for all these reasons, and probably a great many more, (For what search will discover all the springs of motive, or what patience describe or even comprehend them all ?) Muriel did not yet know that he loved Nina. But as he strode along with her, following the storm which had passed them as contemptuously as it had caught and tossed them, he did get so far as to have one or two distinct questions whether in that majestic future where his imagination projected all great things,—and almost all great conduct,—he might not love her.

The sky was clear behind them, and even the moon threw in front their shadows arm-in-arm in most friendly fashion. Nina was a little worried over the anxiety she knew her mother must be feeling on her account, but that could not long repress the gale of high spirits into which such an experience always throws the young and healthy and brave. But Muriel, while alive to the fun of it, had two or three periods of deep meditation. He was also getting more and more under the undefinable power of Nina's presence—a power that, as he had begun faintly to realize, always brought out the best of any man that was with her. As they chatted, somehow he talked less slang, and his voice grew deeper, and he let up on their tearing pace—for they were in a glow—and the influences of the calm deep night began to fill his soul.

"Oh the ineffable order and majesty of it all!" he exclaimed. "How can people worship a God of freaks?"

"How could they make him other than a God of freaks," said Nina, "with such an experience thrust in upon the order, as we had half an hour ago?"

"Yes, very likely he killed somebody then, and out of pure wantonness. I don't wonder the savages sometimes beat their idols. What can we make out of it all?"

"Well," said Nina, "I've been told not to probe the mysteries; but I don't find that very satisfying. I found your talk in the boat much more so."

"See here!" broke in Muriel, "I've got a queer idea. Suppose these mysteries are simply of our own making! Nature is plain enough, or at least our ignorance of her is not superstitious and torturing:

we can study her. Now suppose nobody had invented any God to put behind Nature, then there are none of his mysterious ways to account for."

"Then I'd be lost!" exclaimed Nina. "Take God away, and there's nothing left."

The remarks were inconsistent enough with some things she had been saying, but such inconsistency was natural enough in her chaotic state of mind.

Muriel's comment was: "Nothing left? I've rather a better opinion of the majesty of those hills, that river, these deep, deep heavens and—and," he added, turning towards her, "of your fair though somewhat bedraggled self, gentle lady."

"Yes, Nature inspires one!" said Nina, after she had got through laughing at his complex compliment, "but I meant that without God, there would be nothing to depend upon."

"I don't know about that either. Don't you put any faith in 'the indomitable soul of Armand de Richelieu'? You're certainly no stranger to it in your own person; and as to Nature: there's unvarying Law behind it all. You can depend upon gravitation at least?"

"Yes," she said, "and I can meditate upon the procession of the equinoxes, I believe I heard somebody call it, though I haven't the slightest idea what it means: but I've no doubt they're something very responsive for a burdened soul to cast itself upon."

"Well, now there's Uncle Grand. He doesn't seem to have any other sort of thing to cast *his* soul upon. But perhaps yours needs something like the human, only more than the human, as all women's seem to—because they haven't the binomial theorem and the Pons Asinorum as we men have, I suppose. But nonsense aside, there's Uncle Grand, who I don't believe has said his prayers for twenty years, and yet he is good and calm and noble. Now why can't other people get along on what he gets along on?"

"Other people are not he," Nina answered. "Do you know that for a long time I wouldn't believe in him? And I couldn't make out how my mother did. I can't make it out yet, for that matter, as long as she professes to believe in some other things."

"Such professions of belief, in people of her age, are matters of habit," said Muriel. "People don't really think about them."

"Well, how about professions of disbelief?" asked Nina.

"If a person doesn't believe what's generally taught, it proves that he has thought for himself," Muriel answered. "People are not generally taught what you call the disbelief, as everybody is taught the belief. But what, after all, have we got to depend upon save what we *know?* We do know that this is a Universe governed by Law—not only this immensity of ponderable facts shining above us, but the intellectual and moral immensity within; and *that* Law—that no subterfuge can avoid and no prayer can change, is what we've got to rely upon."

"Oh, Mr. Muriel," exclaimed Nina, "no prayer can change? Hard—inexorable? No! don't let us say we know that! Most of what we say we know, we have taken on faith from other people. We can take the truths of Christianity in that way too, if we take other truths so."

"We don't take other statements so, when they contradict common-sense," said Muriel. "But I don't object to taking the truths of Christianity; I object to taking its untruths. You know perfectly well, as Uncle Grand said the first time we dined over at John Calmire's, that what were assumed to be the truths of Christianity eighteen hundred years ago, were not the same as fifteen hundred years ago, or the same then as at any later time. And a greater change in what are called the truths of Christianity, has taken place in the last thirty years than during all their previous history."

"Then how are we going to know what is the truth?" asked Nina.

"Oh," he answered, "I guess we'll manage to get along: we generally have."

"Perhaps! We'll hope so!" she said with a despondent sort of cheerfulness, "but," and she unconsciously increased her slight pressure on his arm, "my heart shrinks from all these uncertainties."

"Poor little heart! We've been burdening it pretty sorely." He spoke tenderly to her for the first time.

"It is getting stronger, and finding good help," she said, looking up at him with a smile.

They were at the steps, and after hurried explanations and reassurances to Mrs. Wahring and Calmire, they went in their wet clothes to their rooms.

CHAPTER XXVIII.

ABSENCE OMITS TO CONQUER.

NINA awoke late the next morning, feeling perfectly bright and fresh. When she got downstairs, she learned that Muriel had already gone to Calmire to attend to some sudden exigencies for his uncle, and that those matters would involve his taking the boat that night at its landing where the tributary joined the great river. There was no landing nearer Fleuvemont. She missed him, and felt keenly disappointed on learning that this sudden excursion would probably connect itself with a visit on Long Island promised for a few days later, and that he would not be back for ten days or a fortnight. "And he went without even a word for me," she was thinking, when Pierre laid a note beside her plate, saying:

"M'sieu Muriel has commanded me to give zees to Mademoiselle."

It ran simply:

"What a lot of time we've been wasting while we might have known each other better! I hate to waste more by going away. I hope you're quite well after last night. Mighty few girls would have behaved as you did. *Auf wiedersehen!* M. C."

Her first feeling on opening the note, was dissatisfaction at his omitting all form of address. This was not lessened by his including her with himself as having lost time. Then it *was* lessened by his saying that he hated to lose more. Then the fact that His Superbness really had thought about her health or anybody's, almost amused her. Then his just and straightforward compliment pleased her, and then his invocation for a reunion surprised a feeling that made her blush. Then she turned back to the beginning and, after reading the first sentence, said to herself: "Well! It may be conceited and it may be impudent, but it's true!"

Her mother noticed her blush and said:

"Is that boy up to more of his impudence?"

"A little," said Nina, laughing half nervously.

All that day, the spots she had previously frequented, somehow began to be individualized by "Here he said" or "Here he did" or "Here he looked" so and so. And the scraps of music that floated through her mind were more and more in the timbre of Muriel's cornet; and the songs that came through her lips were more and more those that she had caught from Muriel. She was not as conscious of all this as a more sophisticated girl would have been, but so far as she did realize it, it gave her a timid pleasure.

On the next Sunday, she and her mother drove over to hear Courtenay preach. Her mind was not very much on the sermon until this passage attracted her:

"And, my friends, this curse does not come to

the learned alone. Knowledge, it is true, has been a stumbling-block to the faith of many; but there is a form of ignorance aping knowledge, that has been a stumbling-block to many more. To such, to doubt seems worthier than to believe, and many an ignorant disbeliever looks down upon the wisest believers."

Here Nina commented to herself: "But not half as much as ignorant believers look down on learned disbelievers."

He went on: "Christianity need not be afraid of Science; but oh, my friends, do not cultivate the disbelieving habit of mind. Shut your minds to doubts as you would shut your ears to the songs of the fabled sirens who used to lure the mariners to destruction. When you read, why read books that encourage that habit of mind? The English literature that has stood the test of time, is a Christian literature: why read the infidel books that bloom to-day to die to-morrow?"

"Poor George Eliot!" said Nina to herself. "Is your place so insecure?"

"Do not seek doubt," continued the preacher. "Avoid it. Fear it."

"Muriel Calmire is too brave to talk like that," said Nina to herself.

CHAPTER XXIX.

IN ANOTHER BOAT.

THE night after he left, Muriel took the boat about ten o'clock. After he had got his stateroom-key and disposed of his traps, he walked aft to indulge in a luxury in which he specially delighted—a cigar by the stern-rail of a vessel leaving a wake of starlit water. Cigarettes, Muriel despised, except with the sorbet at a stag dinner and, it cannot be denied, at some dinners which were not stag.

Soon after the cigar was in successful operation, there came up in his mind, associated with the sky and river, the sky and river of the night before. Nina's pure strong face was opposite him in the little boat, and her expression of perplexity was melting into one of confidence, with occasional flashes of interest and sympathy.

These sweet visions were interrupted by a touch on his shoulder, and the question in a sweet contralto voice:

"I believe I have the honor of addressing Mr. Muriel Calmire?"

He turned and faced Minerva Granzine. The velvet-brown eyes were laughing, so were the soft pink cheeks with their dimples, and the red lips, which were parted; and the perfect teeth were brighter, perhaps, for the night, though the light from the cabin striking on one side of her face gave it almost its daylight radiance.

Poor Muriel, although he deemed himself very deep in the sex, had been "kicking around" too much, ever to have had the long and constant association with a noble woman which makes the presence of an ignoble one, even if she is pretty, disagreeable. Besides, Minerva was by no means altogether ignoble. She had made her little sacrifices in her time, was capable of her enthusiasms, and unquestionably had her charms. Few women, perhaps no young and good women, could realize the fascination she had for men. And probably few men could themselves quite explain it. Their general reason was: "She's so awfully pretty." But that was the smallest part of it. She was so awfully feminine—not in the miniature negative way—not in merely lacking things that men have, but in possessing so much that men have not. She was round and soft and tender and gentle and affectionate and, under it all, glowing with passion. Her smile was a banter, her glance an appeal, her touch a thrill. She was educated, after a fashion; and the democratic conditions of her village had thrown her with several men of pursuits superior to her father's—some of them men not without reading and aspirations—a young schoolmaster or two, and occasional students and professors off for vacation. She had been engaged to two or three of these, as well as to one or two of the best young men in the village, and all her suitors thought her, for a time at least, the very pearl of womanhood. But as she could very dearly love a good many people at once, and was too kind not to accept every offer made her by men whom she really liked, and as many offers were made, there had not yet been time for any engagement to result in marriage. But a very strange thing about her was, that not one of the men who had been engaged to her, seemed to bear her any ill will. She always got ·amicably off with the old love before getting professedly on with the new. She was too amiable to jilt anybody. Probably she let it be plain to each one, in some way, before she installed his successor, that, however fascinating she might be as a woman, she was not very desirable as a wife. Perhaps this was the easier to do because, generally, she had installed men of high requirements—men who would not marry where they did not entirely respect. Yet although she was, to put it mildly, so "inconsequent," she was so amiable withal, so charming, so kind and gentle, that on ceasing to respect her, and being unable to love without respect, one could not help still feeling friendly toward her. It was a very remarkable fact that, so far, all the men who had been very intimate with her, were among the best of those within reach. She could feel the heroic merits of Clint Russell, despite his profanity and his superiority to grammar, and had stirred his big heart; and before, even Courtenay had felt her charm, and for a while was devoted to her. Even since, he had seemed to take a pitying interest in her.

Among the men whom she had attracted, had been, a few months before, Muriel. She had found him a very odd fish among the others: he had not resisted her—no man of flesh and blood, with a free heart, could; he had become extremely intimate with her, but he had never professed to love her. With all his strong passions and all his ideals, he was very little of a sentimentalist. He took pleasure wherever he found it, and this soft round bright unthinking creature that threw herself in his way, was pleasure; but the oft-imagined lady who was to redeem and inspire his life, was quite another thing, though as yet a very varying and indefinite one. He never mixed the two for an instant, though, and he was too straightforward to give Minerva any notion that he did. But she loved him in her way, for the time being, perhaps more than she had loved anybody else: for, not to speak of advantages of person and position, he was so immensely above her—above any young man she had known, for that matter—in rude strength of character and intellect. He was mysterious to her and, despite his playfulness, at times almost awful. And probably she thought that *this* was the *real* love, as she had thought many times before. How long she would continue to love him, or anybody else, when she had begun, was more apt to be determined by the man than by her: she was always ready to go on loving. But what the "love" of such a creature is, is hard to make out. For *anything* that appeals to the affections, she was full of her soft warm passions. A year before, they had taken the direction of religion and she had joined the church, and for a week or two after it, was as *dévote* as anybody; and here again on the boat, they were making her radiant before the eyes of Muriel Calmire. Although of late she had met him occasionally, for a good while she had not seen him alone, and she had begun to realize the fact and ponder over it and worry just a little. It may be remembered that on meeting him a couple of months before, when he had taken lunch with them, she had found something to blush about. But among her rather unusual characteristics, was a capacity to deliberately say or do a thing, and then to blush over it, and then to say or do it again, and then to blush over it again, and so on interminably. In fact, she generally did blush—she was blushing now, as she looked up at Muriel with her bantering smile.

Promptly it drove away the pure vision which had been softening and inspiring him. Away deep ponderings and self-questionings and self-reproaches! Up surges youth's hot blood! Socrates could make Alcibiades thoughtful, but he could not prevent his being young.

Muriel rose and answered Minerva's mock-ceremonious question in the same vein:

"You have a slave of that name. What under heaven brought you here? I didn't notice you coming aboard, or on the train."

"I've been near the landing all day with Susie Janney, and I'm going down to New York with them."

"Where are they?"

"Susie and her mother went to their stateroom as soon as they came on board. The purser gave me one all to myself (He's a friend of mine), and it has a parlor, too! Won't you come and call on me? I've nothing to do but sit up and talk with you."

"'Wot larks!'" he ejaculated. But somehow, instead of attending to her bantering invitation, he continued: "Won't you sit down?"

She took a chair a step off, in shadow, and Muriel placed his beside her. No one was near them. She laid her hand on his, and said:

"Why haven't you been to see me?"

Muriel answered truthfully: "I don't know."

"You didn't want to come."

"That's not so."

He was perfectly sincere again. He had wanted to go several times, but, somehow, his desire had not been strong enough or steady enough to send him. The obstacles had perhaps been greater than usual, or even than he quite appreciated.

"Then why didn't you come?"

"Well, we've had company at our house, and Uncle Grand has had lots of things for me to do. He's been away a good while, you know. And I've been away some myself, too."

"Yes?"

One of Minerva's charms was, that she never made herself disagreeable. When other women would get jealous, she only got sad and went on loving—somebody else. But she was not yet even at the point where other women get jealous. The excuses were good enough—good enough, at all events, for an indolent and forgiving nature to accept in preference to disagreeable conclusions.

Nobody was near them. The side toward Muriel was in shadow. She laid her arm on his knee. The night was warm for October, and the sleeve was loose. What a wondrous great white arm it was! The wrist was a little large, but the hand was small, and the taper up from the round wrist was perfect. Why did not Muriel seize it?

"Oh, I do so love starlight nights," said the girl. "The moon is such a tell-tale."

"Yes, she's an old maid, you know," said Muriel.

"That's what I'm going to be."

"What?"

"At least—you know," and her ready blushes came again. "I'm never going to marry anybody."

"Bet you ten to one!" said Muriel.

"Well, it won't be you."

"I never said it would."

Then, seized perhaps by a bit of compunction for his bluntness, he did lay his hand kindly on the lovely arm. How cool it was! If the night had been cold, the arm would have been warm: such perfect balance had Nature given the rare creature.

"What makes you bother your head about such things, anyhow, Minerva? You'd never be happy married. Your heart's too big." Then he felt a little more compunction, and did not help matters much by adding: "You know you'd soon tire of any man."

"Not of *any* man."

"How many have you tired of already?"

"Never of the right one."

If she had ever tired of any man, and probably she had, the man had never been sure of it.

"Yes! Your tiring of any one proves that he is not the right one. But the right one doesn't exist; you don't want to tie yourself up. What's the use of bothering about it?"

"None, perhaps. At least I'm not sure there is. You're none of you worth it." And she laughed, but in a way that he thought of afterwards. She had put him a little on his mettle, though.

"No, we're a poor lot. What should we do without the women to keep us straight?"

"Yes, if you'd only condescend to deserve all we do for you. We don't spare ourselves."

"Or us either, when you're inclined to tease us a little, do you?" and he gave the arm a little pinch.

"Don't. You hurt. You make it all red."

And she raised it opposite his face, while the sleeve fell back to the dimpled elbow. White things showed distinct enough in the mixed lights of the boat and the stars.

"Pretty thing!" said Muriel. "Don't tire it."

And he took it by the wrist. A month before, he would have kissed it. Now he gently bent it down again on to his own knee, where, after a second, he relinquished it, saying:

"Wouldn't you like to walk the upper deck a little and see the stars overhead?"

"Yes, that would be splendid! Let's go this way."

And she sprang up the ladder before him, putting her little boots almost into his face.

"Hm!" said he to himself as he rushed up after her.

Then she took his arm. What a difference there is in the way women do it! One makes herself an inconvenience, another an inspiration, most produce no effect at all. Minerva's hand never rested on a man's arm without his realizing that she was a woman, and his realizing only the charming features of the fact.

But she put more than her hand on Muriel's arm, and her electric form brushed against him at every step. More than once he felt a glowing consciousness of it, but some half-realized reminiscence that was not of the spirit of this night, came and calmed him. Despite his slowness in great issues, or rather issues that he realized as great, under most circumstances he was careless of consequences, and eager to seize the joy of the moment. He had no clear realization of the counter-influences working within him now, and he felt half disgusted with the quiescence produced in him by the play of opposing forces.

The main thing which distracted him from the glowing ecstasy beside him, was a want that had never obtruded itself before: he had always taken her for what she was, been glad enough to find her, and thought in a healthy, though perhaps a dangerous, way, only of what the moment offered. But lately a new habit—a new requirement, had grown up within him—faint, little more than rudimentary, but distinct and delicious beyond anything he had known before. Sometimes when his soul was filled with the awful beauty of the night, and when he had marveled and triumphed in the sense that this speck upon a speck—this brain of man upon the earth, had learned a word or two of the infinite histories of the stars,—sometimes when he had caught an occasional glimpse of the philosophy to which those stupendous facts are the first stepping-stones, and all that was highest in his being had been filled with a sense of the Infinite Energy and the Infinite Law, he had lately learned the joy of supporting a woman's tender steps to those heights where most souls must stand alone, and he had had some foretaste of the sympathy which, at a word, brings the companion-soul into the communion of that lofty worship.

And now! Here he was under the holy night with this marvel of exquisite flesh!

He had much reason to feel a certain chivalrous responsibility for her entertainment, and, however much, at any time, he might be embarrassed and perplexed, it was never difficult for him to talk, provided the embarrassment and perplexity were not thrust upon him suddenly. Now he made it pleasant for Minerva and even for himself, in the face of distractions new to his experience. When, at moments, he forgot both attractions and distractions, his mind might glow up into some comment, perhaps on the infinity around them, that brought him a sense of chilling emptiness in her; but that for her, opened up vistas of thought by which she was puzzled and awed — awed, that is, as far as she was capable of awe, which was farther than are some women who have studied enough to dry up such rich juices as ran in her. She was capable of enough of it often to find herself lifted, when with Muriel, to planes that she was not conscious of with anybody else, and to have her passion burn all the stronger in their purer air.

For an hour he walked glowing and languishing amid her intoxications. Then she stopped, saying: "I'm tired. Take me to my stateroom."

At the ladder, she pushed him playfully and said: "Go first and catch me."

He obeyed mechanically. Before she touched the deserted lower deck, she threw herself backward into his arms. As they closed around her, his soul was full of hot battle. But in a moment, there came into his quick imagination a beautiful and noble face, whose eyes looked trustingly into his, as they had looked the night before.

His arms fell, he bade Minerva an abrupt goodnight, and to the bow of the boat stalked the puritan Nina had seen on the great staircase at Fleuvemont.

There he stood silent while the air, resisting the boat's swift motion, fanned his hot face. His pulses, quelled for a moment, were beating with redoubled fury. But soon the cool air and a revery into which he gradually subsided, calmed them.

The moon was just rising. A broad light trembled over the ripples before him. The hills were transfigured into mountains, towering, immutable, calm ; some late cottager's light on the bank made human the stupendous scene. It interfused itself with his own being. Though he stood long, he never afterward could recall anything that passed in his soul except a consciousness of the omnipotent loveliness, a strange feeling that it and he and Nina all were one, and his saying to himself, as he turned to seek his rest:

"I love her! Thank God! I love her! I love her!"

CHAPTER XXX.

GOING WOOING.

OF course a readiness, despite his unorthodoxy, to say "Thank God," or to use that venerable name in less reverent ways, was not the only inconsistency in Mr. Muriel Calmire. Consistency was apt to interfere with his ease, and, it may be suspected, he dearly loved his ease. Not only did he love it for his big and handsome earthly tabernacle, but also for the copious and not altogether ungraceful imagination therein enshrined. Although on calm nights he could discourse to Miss Nina Wahring on the infinite Law that no subterfuge can escape, and although he did not number Ser Tito Melema or Mr. Fred Vincy among his progenitors, if his blood had come through them, his imagination could not have been more incapable than it was of picturing the same evils resulting from his own acts that he knew often resulted from the same acts performed by other people. Calmire had more than once been anxious over this, and remonstrated with him in some such phrase as:

"You believe in the unerringness of natural law, I suppose?"

"Certainly I do," Muriel would very properly reply.

And then Calmire would utter, with a sadness which the boy thought a good deal of a bore, some such phrases as:

"Yes, evidently, in all lives but your own. It's sad that there, you can't learn it from books. It's a big truth, but there's no royal road to it. When there's temptation before him, every young fellow believes in at least one miracle—that the laws of Nature are going to be suspended in his case."

It was now all that Muriel could do to keep himself away from Fleuvemont. A month earlier, with the same eagerness in his heart, he would have rushed back as a matter of course, postponing his business and, if need be, cutting his social engagements; but now, somehow, there was a new conscience in him. By a display of energy which, if it was not unnatural in him, was certainly unusual, he finished his business in half the time he expected. He also found that his visit could as well be made earlier and shorter than at first intended, and within a week he was on his way back to Fleuvemont on the same train that had taken Nina there nearly three months before. A block on the road detained it several hours. Muriel had not expected to leave New York so soon, and he was so preoccupied with what the night on the boat going down had revealed to him, that he forgot to telegraph for a trap to meet him at the station. No public conveyance was there, but he hardly noticed the fact. He gave his hand-bag to the station-keeper, told him that he would send for it and his trunk in the morning, and started off up the hill through the moonlight with the gait of a young panther.

His heart was full of singing birds, as some good old poet hath it, although the voice which gave the songs utterance, as he swung himself along could have issued only from the throat of a strong and happy man.

At the house, he saw lights in the ladies' windows, and in the library, which was habitually reserved to the master's use. A servant was closing the front door.

"Has Miss Wahring gone to her room?" was Muriel's first greeting.

"She went an hour ago, sir."

"My uncle is up, I suppose?"

"Yes, sir; I just left him in the library, writing."

Muriel started for the library, whence Calmire, having heard his voice, was coming out to meet him.

"Oh, Muriel," he said; "I didn't expect you so soon. I was just trying to write to you."

"'*Trying* to write,' and *to me*. That's good! Why, what's the matter?"

"Come in and sit down."

Calmire waited to say to the servant: "Tell Pierre not to go to bed until I tell him to. Leave word at the stables that I shall want to catch the down train at 2.17." Then he followed Muriel into the library, closed the door, took a seat opposite the young man on the other side of the smouldering fire, and began:

"Well, Mr. Stubbs, we're in a scrape."

Because Muriel never was a little fat fellow, but a lank and rather puny child, Calmire long ago, on the principle of *lucus a non*, had nicknamed him Mr. Stubbs. The name had gradually fallen into disuse, but on occasions of hilarity or distress—of any considerable feeling, in fact, it was apt to come to the surface.

"What is it, Uncle Grand?"

"Do you want to marry Minerva Granzine?"

Muriel shivered, and then his blood was like flame. At the same moment he felt that sinking weakness that sometimes comes before battle. He would have given his right hand to be away, but would have given his head rather than go. He did have cause for fear: for although he had controlled himself a week earlier, there had been times, before he knew Nina Wahring, when he had not. He managed to say:

"Certainly not. Why do you ask?"

"Because her mother came here to-day to tell me that it is time—high time, that she were married to somebody, and that you are the man."

A cold perspiration burst out over the youth, and he remembered the prophecy regarding the wretch who should pray that the mountains might fall on him and hide him. Then between his ancestors began the conflict in his soul that Calmire had once warned him of. Should he ignore these responsibilities, or should he meet them? But though he did often shrink before possible consequences, it was not his habit to deliberate over moral questions, except in the abstract, and it was his habit to trust his uncle. He had hardly grasped the situation before he exclaimed:

"Great God, Uncle Grand! What can I do?"

"If you want me to answer that," said Calmire,

"of course I must know your side of the story too. I've only heard Mrs. Granzine's."

Muriel sat silent, leaning forward, his head down, his forearms on his knees, his hands clasped in hopeless perplexity and dread. Shame was covered out of sight by the heavier emotions, but through his brain rushed a dozen mean schemes of escape, which he had not strength enough left either to harbor or to scorn.

"Do you want my hand in this business?" continued Calmire.

"Do I what? Why, Uncle Grand, I—" and he could go no farther.

"Because," calmly resumed Calmire, "while the interests of the family are, to some extent, my interests, and while your interests are certainly mine as far as you are willing they should be, I should be very sorry to seem intrusive."

"Oh! stow all that! You know perfectly well that if I'd known the trouble first, I'd have come to you with it."

Calmire's face beamed. He drew up his chair, and put his hand on Muriel's knee, saying:

"I hoped so, my son, I hoped so. I'm very glad. I've known more than one young fellow come to grief by taking a different course."

"That's because most old fellows are such fools," was Muriel's reply.

"Yes," assented Calmire, "the old fools beget the young ones, and then have no mercy for their folly. Now tell me who's to blame for this, if that question is not too much for human nature?"

Muriel had recovered himself a little under Calmire's handling. He was almost nonplussed by it, however, and let two or three thoughts shape and oppose themselves in his bewildered brain, before he burst out :

"Why don't you blame *me*, and raise an infernal row ?"

"There seems to be row enough already. Nature attends to that side of the case without our help. I prefer to take care of the other side if I can, and keep the misery down. There's sure to be enough without any from me. Now, if you want me to do anything, you've got to confide in me. Do you care to ?"

"You're good, as always. But this is not a matter of my confidence alone."

"I trust I can appreciate the reticence of a gentleman," said Calmire. "But I don't see that it's called for here. Of course you'll acquit me of any idle curiosity: but I've heard Mrs. Granzine's statement of the case, and if I'm to have any such opinions as the subject demands, I must hear yours."

"But, Uncle Grand, I've been told, by yourself for aught I know, that it's a man's duty to lie, even, rather than betray the confidence of a woman."

"I'm not sure that I ever took it upon myself to pronounce on that question. But don't you see that it doesn't apply to this case ? The revelation, if it be one, has already been made by the other side."

"By her consent, do you mean ?"

"Her distinct assertion."

Muriel paused. Without the little stimulus of

discussion, he could not fix his thoughts. At the first mention of Minerva's name, Nina's image had seemed to come up in his mind even before Minerva's; and now it kept thrusting itself into all the things he tried to shape, and confused them. He realized with perfect distinctness, or thought he did, that all the possible joy of life had been snatched from his grasp, and his future loomed up black and terrible. Yet he was hardly conscious of any pain. He tried to grapple the facts and group them into intelligible shape. But he was unequal to it. He got up, walked to and fro two or three times, stopped, and leaned on the mantel.

Calmire, to help him on, spoke again:

"To come to the point, do you care to tell me, without details, whether she led you on? It's a tough question, but you're honest."

Muriel hesitated, and at length said:

"I must say I think she did."

"Was the first thing that would not have taken place if a third person had been present, her doing or yours?"

"Hers!"

"You've been to her house, of course? Was her mother surprised to see you?"

"She didn't seem to be."

"Always pleased to have you there?"

"Well, it did strike me that she was."

"And she left you alone?"

"Yes."

"And kept doing it?"

"Yes."

"I thought so," said Calmire, settling back in his chair in the comfortable way that naturally follows the demonstration of one's own prescience.

A pause. All sorts of reminiscences and speculations began running through Muriel's brain. Pictures, now loathsome, whatever they had been before, in which the pretty girl had borne a part, mingling themselves with others more loathsome still, of scenes yet to come in which she might bear a part too. Yet of all these, he seemed to be a mere unmoved spectator. Calmire called him back to himself.

"Now one or two other things. Did you ever profess to love her? Pardon me, I don't believe you ever did. Of course you praised her beauty, and fed her vanity. You never talked of marriage?"

"Of course I didn't," said Muriel, looking into Calmire's eyes almost indignantly, and then settling himself into another chair.

"Hm! It didn't seem possible that you had; but—" Calmire paused and pondered.

"Had you ever suspected her character before she led you on? What was your opinion of her when you began philandering about her?"

"That she was awfully pretty."

"Yes, that started you. But did you believe her an innocent girl?"

"Probably I'd have kept away from her if I'd felt sure she was."

"What? If she had seriously attracted you?"

"But she only attracted one side of me. There's not much of her but her beauty."

Another pause, in which Muriel realized that he was in pain—horrible pain. A woman of whom there was much besides her beauty, filled his soul; and she was lost to him! And then the phantasmagoria in his brain began again. But in another moment he felt the torture renewed, and then he burst out:

"Oh, my God! Haven't I fled temptation—fled this very woman's temptations, and all for this!"

"Muriel, Nature doesn't play laps and slams. Each game counts by itself." The statement was couched in terms singularly inconsistent with the serious tones in which it was uttered, but it fitted the occasion.

"Uncle Grand," cried the boy, "I love Nina!" and he went over and put his arm on Calmire's shoulder and leaned his head upon it.

Calmire gently passed his hand over Muriel's hair as if it had been that of a woman or a child. He said: "Yes, it is hard, very hard. But how you young people do jump to conclusions! This matter is just opened, and yet you regard it as finished. Of course I can't tell how it's going to turn out, but you assume at once that you can. We won't give up yet."

Muriel straightened himself, and went back to his chair, saying:

"What's my duty?"

"It's too soon to tell about that. One thing is plain: you've got to clear out."

"What? Run away?"

"Keep out of the way—out of *my* way, if you prefer."

"But here's a responsibility that may be mine. *My* child! And," he said in a lower tone that was inexpressibly sad and bitter, "I've longed for children as women do! Well," he added after a moment, "at least I don't propose to shirk."

"Poor fellow! Of course you don't. But the first thing, is to find out what's the best way to handle the situation. If you want me to do that, clear out and leave it to me for the present. I don't want you within the reach of these people. You're too complex: there's no knowing what you'll do. You may marry the woman or murder her. When I want you, I can send for you."

"I must go anyhow." His frightened conscience said: "I can't face Nina's awful eyes."

In a moment he went on: "But at least give me some idea of what you think best to do."

"I don't know myself. The case is so complicated, I want time to study it."

"Ought I to marry her?"

"Ought you to desert *it* ?"

"Oh, I don't know. Of course I could provide for it."

"Provide what? The care its father owes it?"

"Oh, what can I do? What *can* I do?" cried the boy in his agony.

"You can't do anything very satisfactory. But you must do the best you can. I'm not sure that marrying the mother or deserting the child are the only alternatives. And I'm not even sure which of the two is the worse, even for the child. It is better that a child should be at peace among strangers than in a discordant home. The plain truth is, Muriel, that you have taken the responsibility of the life of a human being for whom it is impossible for you to provide what every human being needs—and what your having been without, has had much to do with bringing you just where you are."

"Oh, Uncle Grand, I took no responsibility. I didn't think, I didn't realize, and here I'm hemmed in by hell-fire on every side!"

"There's no need of my preaching to you, my son; but I must tell you that you're learning what I knew you would have to learn sooner or later—that most of our great disasters come from crimes that the codes don't deal with."

"You think me a criminal, then?"

"Certainly not by the world's present standards. And after what you've told me, I'm not disposed to heap unmeasured blame upon you myself. I know what temptation is, and I know what youth is. But I think the world ought to judge more by consequences. Certainly by that standard, such an act, instead of being omitted from most codes, would be placed among the gravest crimes. But I don't want to add my preaching to the other bad results; I only want to help you deal with them."

"Well, anything but this vague misery. For pity's sake let me give it some shape. I feel as if I could fight definite prospects better. Tell me what you think *now* about my marrying her."

"If I were her father, I'm not sure that I should want you to."

"But *they* want me to. You can't put yourself in their place, and they surely have some rights in the matter."

"Why, Muriel, self-sacrifice is a new rôle for you!" exclaimed Calmire.

"If I'm to lose what I most care for, what does the rest matter?"

"You're a boy! otherwise you would never think that 'the rest' is of no importance."

After a little silence, Calmire said, half musingly, "No. If the girl were my daughter, I don't think I would let her marry you, at least now."

"What? I could be good to her."

"You could resolve to be. But you're the last man in the world to keep such a resolve, at least among the men who could make it."

"Why, Uncle Grand, I'm not such a bad fellow."

"No. You're rather a good fellow, or you would not entertain these ideas. But you're a candid fellow, and an irritable one. You'd sting her to death without intending it, provided her counter-stings did not kill you first. Your home would be Hell on earth. She'd probably leave it."

"Well, what difference would that make to me?"

"To you? Why, you're proud!"

"Perhaps I have been."

"There you go again! You're proud, I tell you. Do you suppose that *anything* that doesn't kill or maim, can change a man's character in an hour?"

Muriel was silent a moment, and then said:

"This thing makes me a maimed man. I shall never get over it."

"Yes, you will. I meant physical maiming: I've seldom known anybody not to get over any trouble unless he died of it." And there was a reminiscent sadness in his tone that went far to contradict his assertion. "I don't mean to say," he went on, "that people are always the same after great catastrophes as before them. Of course, they're changed, but not half as much as you suppose, and it takes time for even that. But festering wounds kill: if they don't, they stop festering. This one is not going to kill you: you don't come of stock that suffering kills." And there was again a touch of melancholy in the tone that uttered the boast.

"And there's Johnny!" said Muriel after a moment. "Do you suppose he'll want to fight? He's a gentleman, whatever his parents are, and I'll fight him if he wants to, and let him kill me. That would settle the whole miserable business."

"No it wouldn't," said Calmire, "not by a great deal. But Johnny's above all that. His early education was not in a fighting community, as yours was."

"No, and his character isn't what mine is either," ejaculated Muriel in a tone of regret. It was the first confession of inferiority that Calmire had ever heard the boy make.

"Now lie down on my lounge and go to sleep," he said. "You're gaping now. It's lucky that we Calmires can sleep when we need to. That's one reason we don't die before we're ready; sometimes even when we are ready. I'll tell you in an hour what you've got to do next."

He flung an afghan over the boy's feet, left the room, and afterward was surprised to find that he had locked the door behind him, as if he had had some sub-conscious idea of keeping the secret safe.

CHAPTER XXXI.

BANISHED.

CALMIRE went into the dining-room, rang for Pierre, and ordered him:

"Have a bottle of Burgundy, some cold meat, and something to make it taste good, here in an hour. Mr. Muriel is going back in the 2.17 train. By the way, roll up a couple of sandwiches for him, in case he should not care to eat before starting. And don't go into the library. He's asleep there."

"*Pardon, M'sieu!* Will not *M'sieu* take some supper? John said *M'sieu* would take the train."

"No, I shall not go. Mr. Muriel has come, and he will go. He is younger than you and I, Pierre."

And Calmire laughed, not entirely at the little pleasantry which he allowed himself with the old retainer, who had followed him from Switzerland nearly thirty years before; but partly from the cheerful consciousness that he had quite involuntarily started among the servants the impression that Muriel was hurrying away to attend to important business for his uncle.

While Pierre thought his master was laughing with him, the master was thinking to himself: "If the beggar would only get his impression to Nina's ears! I shall not hurry myself to breakfast in the morning for the sake of preventing him." Then he said aloud: "By the way, Pierre, as I'm to be up so very late, if I succeed in sleeping over in the morning, make my apologies to the ladies, and explain matters."

"*Parfaitement, M'sieu.*"

Months before, in a talk with Nina, Calmire had declared himself a superstitious man; and he often half-humorously admitted himself superstitious regarding the truth. Some people would think that that attitude was illustrated now, as he said to himself: "How am I going to explain Muriel's absence to Nina? She's such a penetrative minx! Yet suppose that I could lie to her, and she should believe it: how do I know that it would be for the best? In these complexities, how can I arrogate to myself power to see beyond the end of my nose? How can I tell whether a lie will do more good than harm?" and he went on musing: "How, for that matter, can anybody at any time? Truth is natural: a liar goes against Nature, and sets up for a prophet in the bargain; he needs not only a 'long memory,' but an infinite foresight. But how am I to stave her off?"

The good gentleman need not have troubled himself—even to lie. The question was settled without his help, and if he had lied, as some people thinking themselves wiser would have done, he would have been found out, and the existing chaos would have been worse confounded.

Calmire told Pierre to put another log on the dining-room fire, and then seated himself, musing, before it. In five minutes he, like Muriel, was asleep. In fifteen more he was awake. Among his first reflections was:

"If I were as terribly wise as some people, I suppose I should not have given that boy a word of sympathy. While pitying him as much as blaming him, I should have let him see only the blame, and while intending to do what I can for him, I should have professed to throw him upon his own weakness and inexperience. That was the 'good old-fashioned way,' I suppose. Ah, these are degenerate days!"

Then he fell into a long meditation, making a few notes on an envelope from his pocket.

At half-past one, Muriel had a dream. He and Nina were in the row-boat, down upon them came the yacht that Nina had steered that bright day somewhere away back in another life. Mrs. Granzine was at the helm. Nina had just said, "Most of the differences between us seem to me mere words." She had smiled, and was looking into his eyes with that glance of recognition and trust. *Crash* went the yacht into their little boat, just where Nina sat. He saw her face marked like Courtenay's, and she sank. He tried to pull the boat around with his port oar, to where she was sinking, but some nightmare force held his arm and interrupted him. Nina was there drowning. He tried madly again and again to pull to her, and could not. In horrible agony he awoke. Calmire had been gently moving his arm to arouse him.

"Oh!" he cried; "is it *all* a dream?"

"What have you been dreaming?"

"Nina!" he exclaimed. "Yes, I remember now. Never mind. I'm ready. What am I to do?"

"Come and have some supper."

"I can't eat."

"Go out into the lavatory and dash some cold water over your face. Then come into the dining-room."

In a few minutes they were opposite each other at the table. Muriel was ready for a glass of wine, but he poured out half a goblet of the carefully tempered Burgundy, filled it up with ice-water, and swallowed it at a gulp. Then he filled his wine-glass. Pierre had withdrawn at a sign from his master.

"If you don't eat something with that," said Calmire, "your head will be reeling."

"All right," said the boy, and helped himself to some cold chicken and bread, and before he knew it, was relishing them.

"Now," said Calmire, "have you plenty of money?"

"Did I ever have?" asked Muriel.

"Never long. What have you about you?"

"Twenty or thirty dollars."

"That will start you," said Calmire. "Go to some place within six or eight hours of here, where you are not known, and which is not small enough to make you an object of remark. But you can't cash checks at such places, so take this." He tossed across the table a wad of bills that he had taken from his fob. "In three days write me where you are. For three days to come, I don't want to know. Then I'll tell you what to do next."

"All right," said Muriel, and after a moment added:

"Oh! I hate to leave you with this uncertainty hanging upon me. For that matter, I hate to leave at all. It seems cowardly."

"It is best."

"You promise me on your honor that you will do nothing to prevent my ultimately facing this thing like a man?"

"Need I?"

"Forgive me, Uncle Grand, my brain whirls."

"Now, Muriel, one thing you are to understand. There's no room for heroics in my philosophy. Self-sacrifice is a great thing—in its place. But I don't believe that a man who has spoken slander, can remedy it by wearing a hair shirt, or that a man who has robbed, can better things by shaving his head or going on a crusade. The world has so long been educated in such notions, however, that when a high-spirited youngster repents a wrong, his first impulse is to do himself some harm. If there's a chance to do it under the guise of doing somebody else some good, or what appears to be some good, so much stronger the impulse. Most of the time, there is, at bottom, some notion that in that way scores can be cleared off and matters made as they were before, at least from the side of justice."

"But, Uncle—"

"Don't interrupt me, please. I don't say that this is deliberately your individual way. I simply say that, in the present stage of evolution, it's largely human nature. Now all that way is mainly humbug. Harm done, is harm done. There's no undoing or offsetting it. The only reasonable thing is to attend to the consequences, and try to shape them to the least pain for all, and to confine that pain as nearly as possible where the blame lies. This trouble is too complicated to judge hastily. I can't tell you yet what to strive for. Perhaps I said too much in the library. **Leave it to me, and I'll try literally to *judge* it.** When I ought to send for you, I will send."

After a few moments of meditation, Calmire asked abruptly: "Whom did you supplant?"

Reflecting a little, Muriel answered: "I can't be very sure, but as probably Clint Russell as anybody."

After another brief silence, Calmire asked: "Have you a diary?"

"Only a very fitful one."

"Take it with you to consult if I want to ask you any more questions."

"It's in my trunk at the station now."

"Well, it's time for you to go there too. Telegraph me in three days. Now, Muriel, remember this. It won't mean much now, but it will later. Make the most of this time of misery. It is in such times that character grows. Good-bye."

"Good-bye."

Calmire walked with him silently to the steps, and pressed his hand. At the turn of the road, Muriel looked back to Nina's dark windows, then buried his face in his hands, and down the hill which, a few hours before, he had scaled in triumphant hope, he was driven beneath the waning October moon, inert and despairing, burdened for the first time with the ennobling curse of care.

CHAPTER XXXII.

"DU SOLLST ENTBEHREN."

AFTER Muriel left, Calmire went in and sat before the fire. His thoughts ran somewhat: "I suppose some wise men would have sent that poor boy off without a single gleam of hope. Ah, me. Perhaps a youth without follies is apt to mean a manhood without inspirations."

Then instead of continuing to ponder, as weaker men would have done, he said to himself, as his habit was: "While I sleep, it will shape itself," and went off to bed.

He awoke late next morning, but with a pretty clear idea of what point in the situation he would touch next, and while dressing with the happy impulse of physical vigor that, whatever his state of mind may be, a strong man often feels in the morning, especially in early Autumn, he told Pierre that he should need his saddle-horse at ten.

As he went to the front door, he found it open, and saw Nina sitting on a bench in the sunlit lawn. She was braiding some bright Fall leaves around her hat. In pulling it off, she had loosened her hair, and the red-gold stream rippled down over a deep green dress of some soft substance that fitted close to her graceful curves. On a tree near her, waited a few birds who had postponed going South to look at her, and they were chippering sweet praises of her to each other. Her profile was toward Calmire, and its firm delicacy stood out against some dark evergreens. Her face was absorbed in her work, but was relieved by an expression of deep content, and she was humming to herself a little song which he could not clearly catch.

While life and temptation last, who shall say with final assurance: "I have conquered"? Calmire had renounced the sweet dream that had been floating across his mind for many weeks, and had determined that though the rest of his days might abound in sympathy and peace, he should know the fires of joy, only as reflected heat. In his life, passion, possession, exultation, all had blazed glorious and triumphant. He had felt all that man may feel and keep strong, and he had said contentedly: "I have had my share: let me make way for others now." But he was a man still: he stood regarding her as men who are both strong and good are apt to regard women—with some such expression of mingled discrimination and reverence as a sincere Egyptian priest, if there was one, would have regarded a creature which to him was both flesh and God. At first the trained habit of Calmire's soul to lose itself in any object of beauty, made him unconscious of all but the æsthetic side of the picture before him: but as he watched Nina's unconscious loveliness, there grew in him the man's yearning to possess and cherish. Back in his consciousness, but undefined, rumbled that deep note which underlies every human symphony, and which means incompleteness and abnegation; but so far as he was conscious of it, it only aroused that savage impulse to crush all opposition, right or wrong, which seems to have come down with all great strength, from barbaric fathers. In Calmire, as in all other men of steady power, the barbaric tenseness was under perfect and involuntary control. It never attained even the definiteness of motive, but it often filled his soul with a grasping eagerness.

While he stood thus with all his nature unconsciously reaching for her, she overcame some little difficulty with her wreath, and held it up on a level with her eyes, humming her little tune with a certain triumphant energy. Some maidenly instinct kept her from uttering the words, but Calmire remembered them.

"Er kommt! Er kommt! Mein Lieber kommt.
Mein Lieber kommt zurück!"

Was this a flash of triumph that passed through Calmire, as he said half aloud: "No, he won't"? Whatever it was, the next instant the honorable gentleman bent his head, and his cheeks were red with shame.

Then he turned and went into his library and closed the door, and walked up and down heavily a few times, and then seated himself in anxious thought by the window which commanded the barren hills with their stones and mullens. And circle as his thoughts would, they always came back to the point: "It may be too late now to be generous for him, and her need of me may be final. There's no one for her but him or me. And now he, poor boy!—"

Soon Nina came running in to learn if he was up, and found him at breakfast. Her large instincts told her that there was something wrong, though Calmire's attempts to conceal that fact were among the great efforts of his life.

Mrs. Wahring came in too, and said: "Why not only are *you* late, but Mr. Muriel is losing some of his new punctuality. I suppose he returned last night?"

Evidently Pierre had not been subjected to any inquisitions.

"Yes," said Calmire, who had learned that the best way to conceal essentials, is to leave as little room as possible for inconsistency between non-essentials. "He came, but new matters had arisen which forced me to send him right back."

"Oh!" exclaimed Nina, and Calmire thought how comfortable it would be to be dead.

But just at present, he had no time for comfort in that way or any other. He had got to go to Calmire and survey the situation. He told the ladies that he was going to ride over. One reason why he had ordered his horse saddled, was that he did not wish any company.

"Let me ride with you," said Nina; "I must go to-day."

"Unfortunately I'm in great haste, and must go across country," answered Calmire. "Won't you take the victoria?"

"Oh, I can go across country."

"There are high fences," said Calmire, almost impatiently.

"You mustn't take them, my darling," expostulated Mrs. Wahring. " It's bad enough for Cousin Calmire to risk his own neck. You're not fit for a long ride, anyhow: you've been a little sleepless of late."

" But I'm very fit now!" urged Nina.

Calmire was half tempted to make some compromise with her, but restrained himself by reflecting: "I've got to gag that she-devil of a Granzine, and that's a job that'll give me enough to think out, without having to parry this child all the way."

Mrs. Wahring had a headache, and so it came about that Nina drove over and back alone. She had a good time with her own thoughts—so good that she drove over alone more than once later, and thus the little circumstance of her going alone this day, had some results; or perhaps it would be better to say that the place of this little circumstance in the infinite web of causes and results, eventually became more noticeable than at the time would have appeared probable.

As Calmire started to ride across country, the old-time suggestion of augury came up in his mind, and as he dismissed it, his smile was very sad. He thought of a similar suggestion that had come when he started to drive tandem with Nina far back on the other side of this great gulf of trouble. It is strange, before one stops to reason over it, how remote even yesterday appears, when there is a great event between it and to-day. Calmire's augury to-day was : "If I jump an even number of ditches, this affair will come out right; if odd—!" But he forgot to count the ditches, and that was the last of his habit of augury.

CHAPTER XXXIII.

A LITTLE DIPLOMACY.

THE first thing Calmire did on reaching the office, was to send for Clint Russell, the gentleman whose difficulties with the bass tuba, and interest in African colonization, were alluded to very early in this narrative, and who was one of the most important foremen in the mills.

This Clint Russell was a character. When a great lank boy of twenty, he had come to Calmire from the army. Muriel's grandfather asked what he could do. He answered: "Anything that don't need book-larnin'," and Mr. Calmire found out that he had substantially told the truth, as he always did. But he had since shown his ability to do some things that did require more or less "book-larnin'," and had provided himself with not a little of that enervating commodity. Yet, as is not seldom the case with such men, his speech, especially at exciting moments, retained much of the twang and many of the solecisms of his youth, as well as a very undue proportion of the oaths he had, boy-like, cultivated in the army. But at bottom he was a gentle and reverent soul, rugged, but strong and reliable as his native New England hills.

When he came in, Calmire, with a diplomacy foreign to his character, but, like many other arduous things, within his powers under great necessity, got Clint into a communicative mood, then led gradually from a business talk, through some inquiry about Granzine's functions at the mills, to comments on the family, and at last managed to bring in, in the most natural manner in the world:

"I had a notion once that you wanted to marry Minerva, old man."

He had affectionately called Clint "old man," when none of the other men were by, for many years.

"And have that damned woman for a mother-in-law? Not if I know myself, sir!" was Clint's prompt reply.

In the rest of the conversation, he had abundant occasion for his pet adjective, and its various forms as verb and substantive, but the reader need not be bothered with them.

Calmire laughed in spite of his heavy heart.

"Why, Clint, what difference does the mother-in-law make, if a man wants a girl?"

"Not so much with your sort o' folks; but it's different with us. We mostly have to live together, and crowd close. Old Granzine's peterin' out, and never amounted to narthin' in his own house nohow; Johnny's gone to college, and won't be doin' much for quite a spell. I'd soon have the old woman on my shoulders, and I hate her."

"Why, Clint, you didn't always feel this way. But pardon my meddlesomeness."

"Oh, as for me ever hav'n' anything to pardon in you, it's too ridiculous. Yes, I did kind o' shine up to Minervy once, and that woman she kind o' led me on until, I may as well out with it, when Mr. Muriel come home one holiday, and the woman got her blasted neck twisted over him."

"Which woman?"

"The old 'un. The young 'un might ha' kep' along straight enough if the old one had had sense enough to let her alone. But she ain't much of a critter to go alone nohow. It might ha' been right enough though, if the old woman hadn't interfered. But mebbe it's all for the best."

"Whether it's better or not, Clint," said Calmire, "I'm sorry you think Muriel was the cause of any trouble. But I've never known of his being with her a great deal. He certainly has not been since I've been home."

"Guess that's so," said Clint. "Well, if it hadn't been him, it might ha' been somebody else, and that too, perhaps, when my job got far enough to make it hurt."

"Then you've no grudge against Muriel?"

"I ain't had no call ter! He hadn't been here: so he didn't know what I was arter, and he didn't do narthin' I wouldn't ha' done."

"Well, if you wanted to marry her, you're pretty liberal to him. But that's just like you."

"Oh, we wasn't reg'lerly keepin' company. I was only sort o' shinin' up to her."

"Well, it's strange you hate the mother so much, if you didn't love the daughter just as much."

"It's God a'mighty's own work to hate that woman anyhow. None of us people ain't good enough for her; yet at bottom she's not as good as the worst of us. She's always makin' trouble. She nearly bust up the library while you was away.

Oh, I know her! But I didn't think so awful much about it till she tried her stuck-up airs on me."

"You didn't think much about what, if I may ask?"

"Sorry I can't tell you, sir." But he told enough for Calmire before the interview was over.

Calmire could not have talked with any other subordinate in the works as he talked with Clint. But the characters of both men made such intimacy possible without any intrenchment on their respective positions, and Calmire not only liked, perhaps it would not be too much to say loved, the man, but found him an unfailing source of sympathetic amusement, and often indulged in chats with him. Calmire found it very congenial with his feeling toward his trusted henchman to learn that, after all, Minerva Granzine did not appear to have more deeply stirred the giant's great and simple heart.

But Calmire was no sentimentalist, and perhaps he did not allow quite enough for Clint's involuntary New England reticence. He knew, though, that there are too many close intimacies where hearts are not involved, and he had more to search for, with hope and fear for Muriel's sake. His cautious inquiries, however, elicited nothing to relieve his perplexities. Yet there was much more of the conversation, some of which eventually served him.

He led the talk over a wide range of topics concerning the work-people, and the various organizations for their benefit, bringing in a variety of personal gossip, and getting side lights on his main points as best he could without arousing suspicion. To close the interview, he looked at his watch and said:

"Well, we've used up a lot of time, but I've been so busy since I got home, over back work and with guests in my house, that I haven't really had a good gossip about our people before. You've given me some points about the way things have been running, especially at the library building, that I think may be of some use. And," he added laughing, "if your friend Mrs. Granzine wants to stir up any more seditions there, or make any trouble of any kind, am I to understand that I'm at liberty to refer her to you?"

"Yes, *sir!*" said Clint. "Just you do anything you please. We all know you don't take no wrong twists on nobody. Good-morn'n'."

As soon as Clint had gone out, Calmire wrote to Mrs. Granzine, asking for an appointment a week later, and expressing regret that many engagements prevented his giving the subject the consideration it deserved, in less time.

CHAPTER XXXIV.

THE ENCOUNTER.

ON Friday, the twenty-first, promptly at seven, Mr. Calmire presented himself by appointment at Mrs. Granzine's. That lady opened the door herself, and asked him to walk into the "drawing-room."

When they were seated, he began:

"I hope I needn't tell you again, Mrs. Granzine, how much I deplore this affair, and how ready I am to do anything and advise anything that will make the burden lightest for all concerned."

"There need not be any burden about it, sir. All that is necessary, is for Mr. Muriel to marry Minerva. All will be happy. Providence orders everything for the best, sir."

"So you attribute this state of affairs to the designs of Providence, do you?" Calmire could not help saying in a tone of sarcasm that Mrs. Granzine was too intent on her own ideas to notice.

"How can we doubt it, sir?" she answered. "Does not God do everything?"

"I don't know: we seem to do some things ourselves. But I believe the people who claim to know, find it convenient to have a devil to do a part."

"The devil has no chance where we do our duty, sir. Everybody's duty is plain here, and through this mysterious dispensation, good will come."

"Well, I regret to say that I don't see anything at all mysterious in the 'dispensation,' and I do find a great deal that's mysterious in the question of what we ought to do about it."

"You do not mean to say, sir, that you have any doubt as to Mr. Muriel's duty to marry Minerva! There can be only one end to such doubts, sir, and I do not see how you can doubt at all."

"Simply by trying to consider your side of the case as fairly as my own."

This nonplussed her. She had never known anybody to be troubled in that way before. After a moment, she said:

"It is perfectly plain to me, sir. May I inquire into the considerations which prevent its being equally plain to you?"

"Well, to begin with the point you are most likely to be interested in: I doubt if it would be the happiest thing for Minerva."

She was dumbfounded, and her eyes took an ugly look.

"Did you come here to play with me, sir?"

"Not at all. Shall I give you my reasons?"

"Yes."

"Then you must pardon plain speaking. It is but natural for you to suppose that what money and surroundings Muriel could give a woman, ought to make her happy."

"And why not?"

"Any newspaper will prove to you that money cannot secure happy marriages—that wretched ones are as frequent, proportionally, among the rich as among the poor. Marriage must depend on the persons themselves, and in unhappy marriages, the woman inevitably suffers more than the man. Now what sort of a preparation for a happy marriage is the present state of affairs?"

"If a man has the least spark of decency about him," she exclaimed rather irrelevantly, "he would do his duty by a woman under such circumstances!"

"Softly, madam. We are simply inquiring what his duty is."

"I say it's to marry her and be good to her."

"'Be good to her' is an easy thing to say, and perhaps an easy thing for an inexperienced man to think he can do. There might be some confident eagerness to begin it, in some generous young men. But when the humdrum of life begins, and new experiences come to the front, the first chivalric feeling is driven into the background, and soon the question becomes the same as it is in all other marriages: Are the two people fitted for each other?"

"But—" she interrupted.

"Bear with me a few moments more, please. Now here, that question has some powerful considerations against it. First and plainest, the different experiences of the young people. These are of vast importance, not only as regards their relations to each other, but their relations to the world: and the two relations affect each other. But it's not an agreeable point to enlarge upon now. Next, and stronger, comes the different cast of their minds. Muriel's is very peculiar. I never saw half a dozen women who could live with him happily. Then comes the all-important fact which we cannot afford to blink, that to make a woman happy as the head of his house, a man *must* look upon her with eyes which it is impossible for the man to have for the woman in this case."

"What way do you mean, sir?"

"I mean that the present state of affairs would have to be forgotten, and some men could never forget, and Muriel happens to be such a man."

Mrs. Granzine drew a long breath, and got up and walked the floor. At last she burst out:

"Yes, you ruin us, and then despise us!" Then she threw herself upon the sofa and burst into a flood of angry tears.

Calmire felt as much sympathy as men usually do before women's tears, but he always felt his convictions more persistently than most men can. His lips twitched a moment, and then he unconsciously uttered a little nervous laugh. He rose and approached the sofa where the woman's face was buried in her arms, resisted an impulse to lay his hand on her head, did lay it on the arm of the sofa beside her, and said, very quietly:

"Compose yourself, Mrs. Granzine. We must consider this matter with calmness, or we can do nothing."

She sat up, clinched her knees with her hands, and glared at him through her tangled hair.

"Consider it calmly! Do nothing with it! Your nephew and adopted son comes here and ruins my daughter! You refuse justice, and ask me to consider it calmly, and you speak of doing nothing with it! What do you call yourself?"

At first the question concluding her tirade did

not move Calmire to any response, but during the silence that ensued, it somehow found lodgment in his mind, and in a few moments he answered her in a sad slow voice:

"An imperfect man who hopes he loves justice and wishes to do it. But," he added with a sudden quick firmness, "no amount of excitement on your part is going to help me one hair's breadth."

She had but one idea, and had had but one for six months—to marry her daughter to Muriel Calmire. That idea seldom slept, unless she slept; it had been first in her dreams, and had greeted her first of all things when she awoke. Monomania was a mild name for it. That she had not forced it into every sentence of the interview, was an illustration of the strength of her nature. Now the floodgates were down. She rose to her feet and half screamed at him:

"Will you make your nephew marry my daughter?"

"Probably not."

Mrs. Granzine flew to the first alternative:

"Then I will."

"You'll have to find him first. It may not be easy, even then."

"Oh! He's run away, has he? The coward! Then I'll disgrace the name of Calmire from one end of the land to the other."

"At the cost of the name of Granzine?"

"Oh, what's the name of Granzine?"

"You seemed to consider it a good deal just now, when you spoke of the danger threatening it."

"Well, the name's going to the dogs anyhow!"

"Not if I can help it!"

She dropped into a chair and looked up at him.

"Not if *you* can help it? What can you do?"

"Send you and your daughter away from here in comfort until the future is past question. Meantime determine what is best to do then."

This was not what she had been burning for, for six months. She felt, though, that force would not give her that, and Calmire's "Not if I can help it," had surprised one of the little loop-holes of even her dark soul. She sat a few moments perplexed and, for her, softened. Then she began: "Where's the justice? Where's the justice for the woman, anyhow? The two commit the same wrong. The man goes free, the world pardons and receives him. The woman bears her burden and her disgrace, and the world turns her off. Oh, it's unjust!"

"It's no such thing!" exclaimed Calmire. His mind had lately been full of the subject and it overflowed. "I've heard that sort of rant on the stage and off, until I'm sick of it. It will pass among old maids, but you're too experienced for it. You know what a man is, and what a woman is. You know that a young man's passions are to a young woman's, as lightning to moonshine, unless the woman is perverted: and you know that if she is, she can heat and mould the man like wax. You know that no man has the same control over any woman that almost any woman has over almost any man. You know that it's as natural for a young woman to fly, as it is for a young man to pursue, that the only defence for either of them, is in her reserve, and that if she does not use that defence, the fault is hers. You know that it's her business to protect them both, and that a good woman always does. You know, and I'm going to indulge myself in saying that I don't believe anybody knows better, that most of these miserable scrapes are made by women perverted from their nature, and men who only follow *their* nature. Don't talk to me about the man being as much to blame as the woman! There may be one case in ten where he is. But that's not this case, and you know it."

"I don't know it, and he's got to marry my daughter," persisted the woman. Long nursing of the idea seemed to have rendered her incapable of relinquishing it, yet it was far enough displaced to make room for the idea of revenge. "If he doesn't," she added, "I'll disgrace you all."

It was a little strange, but not unnatural, that her resentment had not directed itself more specifically against Muriel; but she had a sub-consciousness regarding his share of the responsibility: and of the obstacles to her ambitions, the principal one seemed to be Mr. Calmire.

He reflected: "Confound the woman! In her madness she's just as apt as not to do something which will publish the whole affair. I must stop her mouth." Then he said:

"Mrs. Granzine, suppose we suspend our argument long enough for me to tell you a little circumstance that may influence your views. A friend of mine, who was a sergeant in the First Maine Cavalry some twenty years ago, told me that the surgeon of his regiment got hit once while attending to the wounded under fire. The surgeon was a brave man, though not exactly what my friend calls a 'straight' one. Well, my friend carried him to the rear and set him down against a tree, and the surgeon said: 'It's a pretty bad case, and if I don't get over it, I want you to take these things'—and some of them were pretty valuable things—' to a patient of mine up in Sandsville.'"

Mrs. Granzine's muscles grew a little more tense.

"My friend said that he took the things, was himself left on the field for dead that night, found himself robbed when he recovered consciousness, and never saw the surgeon again—"

"Well, Mr. Calmire, what in the world has this to do with what we're talking of?"

"Never saw the surgeon again," resumed Calmire, "until the surgeon came to this town last week. Now, Mrs. Granzine, you needn't care to know the rest of the story, and it will never be told unless I should be forced to illustrate the laws of heredity a little by citing their application to the case of Minerva Granzine."

The woman leaned back in her chair, with a face so pale that only her hair and her great gray eyes seemed to stand out from the white "tidy." In a few seconds she bent quickly forward with her hands clinching her knees, looked piercingly at Calmire, and ground out between her teeth:

"I'll kill that Clint Russell! How did he learn it was I, and what made him tell you?"

"He learned it naturally enough, and I learned it naturally enough, without his intending that I should. But if you had acted more wisely toward him, I never should have happened on it. But if you really mean to continue your unwise course so far as to kill him, you've made a mistake in making me a witness to your intention. Such testimony hangs: so to be safe, you'd have to kill me too. I've no particular objection to your doing that, but I don't believe it would be good policy."

Then he arose and continued: "Mrs. Granzine, you're a sorely-tried woman, and I'm sorry for you from the bottom of my heart. Of course you will believe that, or not, as you please. But permit me to advise you to believe it, and to let me know that you do, and then to command me in anything that I can approve which will lessen your troubles. Good-night."

His tones were kind and earnest. If there had been any sarcasm or hardness in them, she would not have felt so sure that her game was up.

Calmire had not got half way to John's before he met Clint Russell. He stopped for a word, and at parting said: "Clint, perhaps I ought to tell you that your having put me on the track of more of Doctor Leitoff's history than you intended, need give your sense of honor no further misgivings. It has done good service."

"Then," broke out Clint, with a very just feeling, but, as has been the case with more than one other good man, with a very mistaken idea of what he was talking about, "Hurrah for our side, and Mrs. Granzine may go to the devil!"

CHAPTER XXXV.

ANOTHER ENCOUNTER.

THE next morning, Mrs. Granzine, in a neat gray morning-gown, was by her window trying to compose her distracted mind by reading one of Ouida's novels, when the noise of a carriage caused her to look up, and she saw Miss Wahring pass toward the green. Her face assumed an expression of hate as tragic as anything in the intense volume before her.

"You took him away! I know you did! I know you did!" she exclaimed, so loudly that Minerva called from the next room:

"What is it, mother?"

"Never mind, my child."

Mrs. Granzine let her book lie, her finger between the leaves, and fell into a brown study. Suddenly she said: "I'll do it," rose, put on her bonnet and shawl, which were noticeably tasteful though inexpensive, and started down the street. Arrived at the green, she saw that Calmire's victoria was not before his brother's house. She walked past the house, around the green, and past the house again. Then she walked about for half an hour, frequently going where she could see John Calmire's house, and peering into all the shops as she went by them. At last, she entered a drug-store where one of her few special friends was clerk, and said to him:

"William, I desire to write a letter. May I have the privilege of doing so here?"

"Certainly," he said. "Mr. Einstein will not be in for an hour. Come right back to his desk."

She went and spent three quarters of an hour in producing, after various abortive attempts, a document covering but two sides of a sheet of notepaper. She addressed it, and started to go out, when she saw Nina Wahring talking with the drug clerk, whose sentence she caught up at: ".. perfume it very mildly: I should say about ten minutes. Will you wait?"

Nina said yes, and seated herself. The clerk went back to the prescription counter. Mrs. Granzine said: "Thank you, William. Good-bye," and passed outward into the store. The room was long, and before she reached the front, she began to shorten her steps and to peer at various objects in the showcases. Opposite where Nina was sitting, she seemed to find something of deep and peculiar interest. After appearing to contemplate it for perhaps five minutes, her hand all the time in her pocket fumbling with the note, her features set, she crushed the paper, turned, and abruptly walked over to Nina, and said in a low tone:

"Excuse me, Miss. I have observed you frequently interested in conversation with a gentleman who has no right to have any young lady but one interested in him, and I feel under a moral responsibility to make you acquainted with the fact."

"I don't know that I've any need of any such facts," said Nina, very calmly.

She did not like the woman. Before Mrs. Granzine spoke, there was something chilling about her neat cold cut; and her grandiloquent language and especially the expression of countenance which accompanied it, were repulsive. Nina's antipathy was a pretty good substitute for apathy, but probably if Muriel's name had been mentioned at the outset, the substitute would not have been as efficacious.

"The person is not a proper person," reiterated Mrs. Granzine.

"Oh!" said Nina, but very imperturbably.

"I mean Mr. Muriel Calmire," said the woman, impatiently.

"Yes?" said Nina, with rising inflection, but the same exasperating calm.

"He has ruined my daughter," ran on the woman, stung beyond any power of restraint.

"Yes?" said Nina, half mechanically repeating the expression with the exasperating rising inflection which had already served her so well, but she had a faint grateful sense of the support of the counter.

"And he has run away; but he shall be forced to come back and marry her and support her child," almost screamed the woman.

"Yes?" again said Nina.

This was more than Mrs. Granzine had bargained for. She had expected to overwhelm the girl—not only to destroy all fear of her being in the way of Muriel's marriage to Minerva, but to make her suffer for the innocent part she had presumably taken in warping Muriel's inclinations away from the unhappy girl. Here, for her life, she could not make out whether Nina was agitated by such communications, whether the revelations appeared to her of consequence enough to affect her relations with Muriel in any way, or whether (worst thought of all) Muriel had not, with that almost shameless candor of which he was spasmodically capable, already confessed and been absolved. With her communications received as of no consequence, and herself treated contemptuously as a meddler and, she felt, an inferior, Mrs. Granzine had gratuitously poured the family scandal into another pair of ears. Somehow she had, from the outset, no fear that it would go farther; but nevertheless, she felt the deepest humiliation that she had endured in connection with the whole humiliating affair. The instinct of self-preservation asserted itself, and she said:

"I trust you believe, Miss, that nothing but a conviction of moral responsibility would have induced me to make this disclosure."

" Yes ?" again.

Mrs. Granzine disappeared. Nina took her purchase, paid for it without counting her change—a very unusual thing with her—and left the store.

Then what had been said to her began to take on more detailed meaning. While listening, she had felt and known little but that she must hold herself in hand. Now she began to realize what it was that she had been bracing herself against. In horrified amazement, she recoiled from it with a start that shook her whole soul and changed the relations of all things in it. To her eyes, were opened vistas that had been shaping themselves deep down under her consciousness, and now fell into coherent aspects under the new law which had assumed control of her being. She voiced it all in a questioning cry that welled up from depths of her nature far below will or purpose, and that, in the frequented street as she was, almost escaped her lips:

"Muriel? Muriel? *My* Muriel?"

She would not believe it. What she would not believe, she hardly knew. She only knew that far out in some inconceivable region, beyond even the bounds of modesty, there was some vague form of evil which cursed the human race, and especially her half of it, more heavily than any other blight. She knew, too, that associated with this evil were often, on the man's part, deceit and cruelty. But deceit and cruelty were not Muriel, so how could *he* have done the wrong? The problem was too much for her. She puzzled and puzzled, until at last one fact, or set of facts, began to assume horrible distinctness. Another woman had a claim on him. Then she clearly felt what, before, she had half unconsciously uttered to herself, that *she* had a claim—the claim that a strong and lonely soul has on a kindred soul when, by rare chance, it meets one on its pilgrimage—a claim intensified a thousandfold when the ardor of youth and the infinite sweet allurements of sex enforce it. Muriel was *hers*, and she was his. Now she knew it. And here was her one immeasurable, ineffable possession, claimed, and claimed with some dread vague right whose mystery made it doubly terrible, by a person who could no more appreciate the thing she claimed than the gorilla could appreciate the human captive it was alleged to make. The comparison came from a picture in a book which she had glanced into that very morning. It took possession of her overwrought brain, and started a horrible and bizarre sequence of fantasies. Muriel was in hiding to escape the gorilla, and yet (and Nina almost fainted as the thought came to her) perhaps he was under an obligation that he could not disregard and still be Muriel, to come back and yield himself up. Then the picture changed. Muriel could not be the captive. He was too strong. He would subdue the horrid thing, and for the rest of his life would be its keeper. And outside the cage where they would dwell, would pass thought and art and high ambitions and sweet love—Nina herself was its image, though pale, white-robed, with flowing hair and wan eyes—and as they should pass, Muriel would see them all and yearn for them, but yearn less and less every day, perhaps, until he should cease to care for them, or even to know them; or perhaps he would yearn more and more, until he would try to break his chain of duty, and Nina could not let him break it, and then they would both go mad. And she wondered if she were not mad already to have such strange phantasmagoria running through her brain.

Dragging along, sometimes under such nightmares, sometimes with a seeming absence of feeling or interest in the matter, she reached John Calmire's.

At lunch, she was gayer than usual, but little Mrs. John saw or felt something in the gayety that made her uneasy.

CHAPTER XXXVI.

A SOULLESS UNIVERSE.

THE next morning, Nina awoke too early after a restless night. But she saw definitely before her many distinct facts which she had hardly recognized in the confusion of the evening before.

The strangest one was that she still loved a man who had been guilty of the one, to her, unnamable crime.

Next in strangeness, was that while, at the first knowledge of the crime, she had instinctively dissociated from him all thought of deceit and cruelty, she had never in her life before thought of the crime as other than absolutely and unqualifiedly black. With this, she remembered some men's talk to which she had at the time paid very little attention, about "degrees" of burglary and murder.

Perhaps, then, there were degrees of this unnamable crime! And now her simple easy world of applied dogma—of snap judgment from a ready-made supply kept in stock, was gone, and gone forever.

Nina had no special intellectual genius—she was a woman at best: but that best is the very best, though it may not do the things—often relatively cheap things—that are heard of. Yet she could do much that the commonplace would call impossible. One such deed, was forming her present feeling regarding Muriel—considering, on the *ex parte* case before her, and in face of the vague and bitter sentiments of a young girl regarding the aberrations of which he had been guilty, whether his wrong, great as she felt it must be, had necessarily involved any violation of his honor; and judicially deciding that that could not be. That she was helped to this feat by love, does not detract from its greatness.

On one point, her judicial conclusion (it would be better to say her judicial inspiration: for there was not very much reasoning about it) nearly broke down. At first her mind had been filled solely with thoughts of Muriel's separation from herself: when the idea came that he had been unfaithful to her, it was a sudden revelation, and for a moment was accepted with the faith usually inspired by such. Soon, however, her characteristic justice asserted itself, and she said aloud: "What claim have I on him?" Then she added to herself: "He never gave me a word or sign or look of love." This led her to ponder over the details of the evening before he went away. "He praised me," she said to herself; "he showed deep sympathy with me; he regretted that we had not known each other better earlier. But *I* did not exist, to be known, much earlier! I am not the same woman that came here. That night in the storm, I think— Well, whatever he felt toward me, he carried away with him: he saw no other woman before he went."

In a moment more, she sprang from her chair, clasped her hands, and said with a radiant face: "He left me that letter! He left me that letter!" Then she flung herself on her bed in a flood of tears.

But what was this other cloud of whose presence she had been but very dimly conscious, but that now, as the day came on, rolled up until it shut out whatever gleams were in her uncertain sky, and left even her present universe of strained ideals, dark and hopeless? Muriel, her teacher in morality, had been immoral. Slowly it became perceptible, and grew plainer and plainer with horrible and overwhelming distinctness, that the new basis of conduct and life and faith which he had lifted her to after her old one had disappeared, had, in its turn, broken down, and broken down under Muriel himself! Nothing was left, then—no purity or goodness on earth, no God in Heaven. There was nothing for her to rest upon: the universe was but an infinite shifting sea, no land under foot, no star overhead; and here in her first great misery, when she most needed all the dear consolations that she had had in her girlish sorrows, the consolations were gone, and she was alone—alone—no God—no Muriel.

She flung herself on her knees and strained her eyes out to the steel-blue Autumn sky, and as she peered into its vacant depths, moaned in her agony: "Empty! empty! empty! Some miles of air; then black cold space; then off, off, off, another world perhaps, with more air; then more space; and so on, and on, and on, till my brain whirls— here and there more worlds—more suns—all growing cold and dark—but no Heaven and no God! Only cold, cold, cold and dark, dark, dark!"

Shuddering, she repeated the words over and over again in a half-dazed fashion, braiding her hands in her long hair and straining against it as if it might be some such spiritual support as she had been yearning for, and rocking herself to and fro, until one knee which rested on the hard floor beyond the rug, began to pain so as to recall her to herself. Then she exclaimed:

"What? I?"

Putting one hand on the dressing-table, she raised herself, and said:

"I can at least dress myself, instead of maundering here like a lunatic."

But the torturing thoughts would crowd. She felt a cold little gleam of comfort when her girlish timidity was invaded by a nebulous impression that some preachers of the old faith had sinned too. But all grew doubly black with the thought: "That simply proves their faith baseless. And the new faith is baseless, and there is nothing, nothing, nothing! Why, I wonder that even the floor supports me."

When she looked into her mirror, she exclaimed in a hoarse whisper: "God! What a face!" But she went on with her toilet, without ringing for her maid, and the rush of her thoughts kept on too.

Suddenly she flung her brush on the table with a start. She had thought:

"Muriel will be coming back soon. I must go away. I must escape! Where shall I go? What shall I do?"

She began rocking herself to and fro again on the stiff chair where she sat, and repeating the words until, after a while, the sentences began to lose their meaning, and grow into a faster and rhythmic sing-song of "Where shall I go? What shall I do? Where shall I go? What shall I do?"

When the feeling had spent itself, and she began to reason again, there came the question of how to induce her mother to go, and how to explain their hurried departure to Mr. Calmire. It had been understood, with Nina's glad concurrence, that they were to remain at Fleuvemont until her father should return in November. Now the question of how to get away, was a torture; she had become so nervous that everything was a torture. But this question made her think of explanations to Calmire, and the thought of him was always restful to her. She grew calmer with a vague realization that he too must know all the terrible facts of this godless universe which completed her despair, and that he was cheerful in spite of them. Perhaps he could help her! So she decided to ignore the question of departure, at least for a few hours until she could tell him that she had no more faiths for his talk to disturb, and so lead him to cast any light he could on that blank darkness in her soul where her old faiths had been.

CHAPTER XXXVII.

MURIEL CALMIRE TO LEGRAND CALMIRE.

WHILE Nina was suffering alone, Calmire was reading and answering the following letter:

"Oct. 13th, 18—.

"Is there no way of easing up this torture, Uncle Grand? *Was* my crime as great as my punishment? *Are* men's punishments in any way proportioned to the evil they intend? It's not remorse I'm suffering most from, at least as I've always imagined remorse, nor even realization of the consequences of my crime—or fault or misfortune: for I'm not always quite ready to admit it a crime. Yet sometimes, when I judge it from its consequences, it seems as if it must be the blackest crime that man ever committed.

"But over and above all—remorse and dread and personal misery—I'm simply in Hell because I realize at last what a mass of lies and snares this universe is. Beauty and pleasure lied to me—everything lies. The blue water out there on the lake, with its white-topped waves dancing in the sun, is only a treacherous lie: beneath it are the bones of men it has drowned. It woos me to come to it: and it would drown me too, if I did not fight it with my superior human skill and will.

God knows I'd like it to, often enough! It's a lie! All things are lies! The glib philosophies that used to make things seem good and beautiful are as much lies as the religions. This misery has made me realize that much wisdom at least.

"Look at the hills. What are they but piles of dirt? To the unthinking man, they may seem grand or fair. But to us who know, and have sense enough to keep our knowledge before us (And it's only fools who ignore such knowledge, and that's why only fools are happy)—to us who know, and who are manly enough to face facts, these hills are but relics of horrible convulsions, when earth seethed and shook and burst and yawned, and heaved up horrid ridges where even yet men lose their lives. Why, in Switzerland the other day, a whole village of simple folk, who had done no wrong and meditated none, while they were in the very act of saying their prayers to the merciless being who launched all these terrors, were crushed, smothered, mangled, by an avalanche of these same mountains that I have been fool enough to find joy in. Some few escaped maimed, and a babe unhurt—its mother dead, and no living breast left from which to draw its food. Probably the poor little thing sickened and died too. And this is what is done by the hills, to which that simple old fool Solomon looked up saying that from them came his strength!

"Oh, my God, (His name is now Satan, Ahriman, Siva—anything that is *honestly* bad, which Jehovah and his troop were not,) how I do hate cant! How I do hate that milk-and-water spirit that prates of good—good—good, in a world whose very lying crust of sham beauty rests over lava-fires!

"And if this murderous Nature tires of her big brutal weapons, what mean and disgusting poisons she plays with! And whom does she kill with them? Not those who have had their full share of the deceitful farce called life, but the children, and the weak and wretched—those whose innocence or whose misery would evoke some pity from the meanest soul of even mean humanity. But Nature? Pity from her?

"And beyond this seething ball whose cheating crust swarms with Nature's victims, what have you? More lies! Those clouds and sunset glories—what are they but painted lies? Get into one of them, and where are you? In a fog—chilled to the bone, damp, seeing nothing, sure of death if the thing be long continued. And yet, there off on the horizon lies one (*lies* one, I say) that some damned fool of a priest would call the gate of Heaven; or some damned fool of a poet would yearn for as a bridal couch for him and the mass of flesh and bones and blood that he calls his Love. Why, take a very woman—the form of all these lies that has cheated me most, and what is she but a mass of the things I've named, hidden and gotten up to lure men to their doom, by a pretty skin which you can't go into even as far as you can into a man's, without drawing out the disgusting blood it hides, and making the infernal mechanism squeal? What is that pearly rosy coloring, but the same sort of a lie as the painting on a cloud, or as this ocean-covered, hill-ribbed earth over the hell seething underneath? Take the lovely-seeming skin itself—what is it? Old Swift knew. There was an honest man! You remember how the princess (Glumdalclitch, wasn't it?) of the big people, to Gulliver's finer sense was covered with pits and offended his nostrils. Our women are beautiful and sweet to us, simply because we're fools—weaklings; our perceptions are not fine enough to see what they are. Yes, and I suppose I could be just idiot enough again to kiss one of them—*one* of them! As if I dared kiss her footprint!

"And yet sometimes I don't care, now, for even her. My very love was but one more lie!

"And of all the hideous cruelties of this reeking earth, I'm among the worst, I'm not merely recreant to love, but I meditate murder every hour, and it is only because I couldn't hide it—and forget it—that I don't commit it.

"Oh, God! Uncle Grand, I shall go mad!

"Oct. 14th.

"I couldn't go on yesterday. I was tired. I never knew what it was to be tired in my mind until of late. Besides, the feeling had written itself out. I had a momentary notion that I was wrong somewhere: one is not always strong enough to be loyal to painful convictions. But I've read the whole through calmly to-day, and I see that it's *true*—deeply, damnably, hopelessly *true*.

"But as I read, I couldn't help thinking: But what does the whole cursed farce amount to anyhow? In a little while it's all over; and that fact would take all the meaning out of it, even if it were good for anything while it lasts.

"Uncle Grand, I did think you were an honest man, and a brave one. How then, have you let me grow up in such a veil of lies? What if the veil did shut out Hell? If we're in the midst of Hell, isn't it best to know it? I'm not afraid of Hell, even; no, nor of the fiend who made it, whether you worship him as God, or, like the more honest Persians, as devil. They're not honest either: for a man who knows enough to worship a devil, as they do, must know too much to worship a god too, and they do worship one: in case of mistake, I suppose.

"Oh, how it sickens me when I think of our lying, canting professors there at college, trying to cover the whole thing over, as the skin covers over the fat and blood and skeleton of the woman! It's so queer that they should think it their duty to lie so! Some of the old fools do seem to be kind and even honest in their way. They 'think it's all for the best,' I suppose, as their predecessors thought the inquisitions and excommunications. The honest old church-people would burn and torture for their faith. The church-people of to-day are too weak: they merely lie.

"Oh, for the robust old times when a man could kill if he wanted to! There must be a delight in it! And perhaps somebody would kill me!

"Write to me, Uncle Grand. Probably you will have something to tell that will come as near killing me as anything can. But nothing can! There's not mercy enough in the universe for even that.

"M."

PART II
KOSMOS

CHAPTER XXXVIII.

LEGRAND CALMIRE TO MURIEL CALMIRE.

"Oct. 16th, 18—.

"I know all about it, my poor boy. I told you it would come. But I still say that you'll get over it. You're simply enduring one of the curses of—I won't say genius, but of the type of mind which, with certain exceptional accompaniments, is genius. A man who takes little from tradition, but investigates the universe for himself, seldom settles into the mature convictions he lives by, without going through just such a crisis as you're in now. Weaklings, it kills, sometimes driving them to kill themselves. Strong men live through it; and only after living through it, do they enter upon their full strength, and therefore upon their full capacity for happiness.

"I have known, and now you know, what it is to envy those whose necessities are simple enough to be met by the simple creeds. But this envy did not last in me, nor will it in you. You will again rejoice in dwelling on your lonely heights, even amid the storms that sometimes enclose them. I know as well as you do, how lonely you feel there now—how there is no light in the sky, how the sun, if it appear at all, shows itself only as a smouldering horror; how the far-off homes and peaceful ways of men, not lit up by the natural glow, seem distorted and contemptible. I know it all, my boy. The loneliness is one of the most terrible things about it. But realize that others have been there, and have come to regard this racking time as but an episode, from which they have come back to life as joyful as before, and strengthened against a return of the same despair.

"If you can get hold of a copy of Sartor Resartus, read the chapters 'The Everlasting No,' 'The Centre of Indifference,' and 'The Everlasting Yea.' The 'No' but seemed everlasting. So far as human needs go, the 'Yea,' when reached, *is* everlasting. Possibly you have read the chapters before, but probably they produced little effect upon you. To get anything from the profoundest experiences of others, one must bring profound experiences of one's own.

"To Carlyle, all seemed seething flux—no point in the universe whereon to stand. The first fixed thing that came to him, was a realization that he could fight. Whatever the forces controlling things might be, he knew that they were simply torturing him, and he felt that he could at least return torture with struggle. There was work, at least, and work with a big inspiration—the right to fight one's way, the right to one's self. For ordinary work he was too ill—one always is in such crises. I dare say that, with the titanic nerves of our family, you have never before felt that anything attacking them could break your health. But I shall be surprised if I do not soon receive word that you're ailing all over. Carlyle came out of his crisis with a dyspepsia that lasted him for life. I don't think you will: for you are not Carlyle. Neither was I, but most of the few ills that my flesh is heir to, I trace back to those evil days. Perhaps if I'd had the soul to suffer as he did, my body would have been as badly racked as his. Well, as I was saying, he found *something to do*, though it was only gnawing his file, and probably then began the realization which he expressed in that wonderful sentence: 'In idleness alone, is there perpetual despair.'

"Of course your turning-point probably will not be his. It may be nearer mine, which I will tell you. With much the feelings you have described, I was on a hill-top, looking over the face of Nature, no longer fair to me, but just as you described it—the hills, dirt-heaps; the waters, chilling and deceitful death; the clouds, fog-banks; the sun itself, a mere hell, hotter than the science of my boyhood enabled its theology to express. 'God' was the cheat who had made all these lies. Suddenly there came into my mind the thought: 'God or Devil, whatever made this universe, made out of those fog-banks, clouds of glorious beauty; made those dirt-heaps, the mountains which were once among my noblest joys, and have been the inspirations of poets from Solomon down; made that water not only beautiful, but a means of the greatest recreation and strength; and made that sun, hell it may be, a hell that I, at least, can't fall into, and has tempered it so that, at this very moment, it is life and, in spite of myself, vigor to me and to all the happy throngs around.' 'Why, they *are* happy!' I remember saying to myself with surprise, 'and I am probably the only wretched one of the many in sight.'

"From that moment, Muriel, this has been a different world to me. My crisis was not all over: no moment (the novelists to the contrary, notwithstanding) changes all one's habits of thought and feeling. Before I could again count myself a happy man, I had to go through many a period of darkness, when the facts I had acknowledged to myself on the hill-top, were as juiceless as the binomial theorem. But I have never been any more able to doubt their truth, than to doubt the truth of the binomial theorem. Since that crisis, I have endured anxieties and miseries greater than those which plunged me into it—as great as can be thrown upon man, and he be left alive and sane —my eyes have been blind to sweet sights and my ears deaf to sweet sounds, most of my reason has been paralyzed, (In our race it never all goes); in short, there has been little, for the time, but a realization of that fact which is as indestructible as any fact in human consciousness can be, that out of the materials called base, Nature is constantly producing beauty. But with that in mind, a man can't find things wholly bad.

"And along with that fact, comes a troop of other facts equally indestructible and equally sustaining. For one: Nature makes haste to hide her ugly work: wander for hours, and the chances are that your senses will not be offended by what she has killed. For one bird slain, you see and hear a myriad beautiful and happy. Their lives are hours, weeks, months, years of joy; their deaths, but moments of pain. So through all animate nature, even to man with his Atlas-burden of thought. You know that at a given hour, most men are happy. This I have had to acknowledge to myself at moments when my soul was full with all the misery it could hold. I have doubted, as every reasoning man undergoing the ordinary fate of mortals must sometimes doubt, whether life holds joys enough to compensate its inevitable woes; but these doubts, candid men, with very few exceptions, will tell you are the experiences of but moments in days, or but days in years, or perhaps of years in lifetimes.

"But Nature who has made the beauty you *can't* escape, has made the organism which feels it, and has made that organism so that under the vast majority of conditions, if in health, it will feel the beauty. You who have hitherto been well and happy, have never before had occasion to realize the importance of that provision. But the truth is that the machine that takes in the beauty or enjoys the sensation of whatever kind, can only do it when in order: and nothing throws it out of order more effectually than sorrow and anxiety. What you call your disloyalty in love, is simply shock and fatigue of your nervous system; and because it is sometimes incapable of feeling even the emotion of love, you are morbidly suspicious of your loyalty. The fact is: that even the healthiest man, is not keen for anything at all times. If his attention is absorbed in one thing, he cannot often instantly turn all the enthusiam of his being to another.

"In this connection, take that part of your

letter whose perverse ingenuity hardly justifies its unsavoriness, though it makes me feel the agony which caused it, and pity you with my whole soul. To the Brobdingnagians, Glumdalclitch was beautiful. You admit that, to your tastes, though trouble has disordered them for a time, at least one woman is sometimes beautiful still. Now what you were finding out-of-joint, was simply a disturbance in nervous relations. All happiness, whether derived from woman's beauty or any other source, is simply a question of the relation between the recipient and the external cause, and when the nerves are in order, they keep those relations correct. The swine's correct relations make them glory in what disgusts you: give them your senses, and what disgusts you would disgust them too. There are other creatures who glory in what the swine discard: give them the senses of the swine, and the things would disgust them too. Glumdalclitch pleased the Brobdingnagians: she disgusted Gulliver.

"But be very careful not to let what I have just said, blind you to the all-important fact that there *are* a positive and a negative. The man is superior to the swine; the swine, to the creatures who live on what swine refuse.

"Yet while we know a positive and a negative. we are not made to know an absolute. All we can attain, is relative: for us, at least, there is no ultimate. The astronomer talks of enormous distances, but so does the microscopist. What makes either distance great, is simply its relation to a less one. Now as we cannot really conceive an absolutely great or small, so we cannot conceive absolutely agreeable or disagreeable. Happiness depends almost as much upon capacity to ignore some things, as upon the capacity to enjoy others; and every normal person under normal circumstances, possesses that capacity to ignore: its absence is one of the first marks of an abnormal condition—the droning bee of the Summer noon, which helps the loiterer's revery, grates on the ear of the man whose nerves are all on edge. That ill health and sorrow so upset our nerves, is one of the worst of the maladjustments that we have to face. Sometimes the very things which we most need to resist, are the ones most fatal to our powers of resistance. But so it is, and we have to make the best we can of it.

"You see I don't attempt to blink facts. Find all the fault you please with your theological friends for doing it. To the healthy man, under average circumstances, there is no need to blink anything: with keen senses and clean conscience, he finds enough to occupy him in real things, and does not bother himself much with the questions that tempt to blinking. Most of them are insoluble, and the wise man acknowledges the fact. When he is ordinarily well and happy, he can be consistent enough to leave those questions alone. When he is too young or too blind to realize their insolubility, of course he fools with them, and when he is ill or wretched, it takes more than the strongest man's strength or the wisest man's experience, to keep his hands entirely off them. The churches knew that the speculations on sin and death must come from the ascetic's sick body.

"You've even got the theological prejudice against the law of the survival of the fittest—or the destruction of the least fit. The law was not known in my early time of trouble: if it had been, probably I should have misread it as you do. But surely, as death is here, it is most merciful that it comes quickest to those who have no dread of it, and to those who have least to lose by it. Muriel miserable invokes it: Muriel happy shunned it.

"As to your bloodstained conscience, don't let that bother you any more. A repenting man is always morbidly conscientious. It is inevitable to a man of your imagination that nearly all the possible ways out of a complication should present themselves, but it does not follow that he is any more willing to adopt the bad ones, than if he were too stupid to imagine them. You couldn't kill anybody, unless it were deserved.

"What a long letter I've written! I've been interrupted since the last paragraph, and will leave some more of your points calling for notice, until my next.

"Affairs here are *in statu quo*. On one thing I am clear, however—clearer, if possible, every day. You are under no obligation to pretend to right your wrong by sacrifices which, even to the people you are bound to stand by, would result in more misery than happiness. The best that can be done, when we determine what it is, will be bad enough; but your making a mutually destructive marriage is not yet demonstrated the best.

"Our friends are with me still; and it will do you as much good as harm, to tell you that the younger is sad. I know that you would not have her lied to, and that that very fact is at the root of at least half your hopelessness. Could she once get hold of that fact—of what I know to be true of you, my boy,—that, whether you are God or Devil, you would not be, to a woman you love, other than yourself, there is no knowing what her great nature is capable of.

"You'd better leave that place where you are, and 'take to the woods.' I don't want anybody to know your whereabouts just now, and in a big town somebody may happen along and recognize you. Keep in the open air all you can. But when you are housed, take up something that will divert your mind. Your tendency will be to read your one subject into everything. Try not to. I wish you had a taste for mathematics. Couldn't you work at logic? You need actual *work*, if you can grasp hold of it now, which I'm not sure you can.

"Oh! You'd better write so that your letters would convey to a third person nothing that you would not wish them to. There's no knowing where a scrap of paper may go.

"You know I love you."

This letter had no signature or form of address, but only a date; the place of writing, even, was not named.

CHAPTER XXXIX.

REVELATION.

Nina's restlessness had brought her downstairs before her mother or Calmire, who was busy with the foregoing letters; and a little walk in the sun amid the bright leaves and the few lingering flowers, made her vigorous youth assert itself, and sent her to the breakfast-room in better case than half an hour before would have seemed possible.

She saw now what a woman of but ordinary womanliness might not have seen, and she realized that it had been true for a week—that Calmire was in trouble; and he saw, as he had suspected the night before, that she was; and each saw what the other saw. Calmire felt his large gentleness and pity stirred, even before he asked himself whether his own trials, of which he supposed her ignorant, might not also be trials in store for her. She felt a shrinking from talking with him as she had determined, but with her tendency, when anything was to be done, to do it, she brushed the reluctance aside in her large way, and having sent her mother off on some pretext, while Calmire was on the piazza with his cigar, she came up pale and languid, in terrible contrast to her usual sprightly way, seated herself squarely in front of him, and said:

"You must talk to me!"

His pulse stopped. He was so full of one subject that, before he reflected, he thought she must be alluding to it. But he fixed his eyes on his cigar, knocked the ash from it, realized that he had no grounds for his suppositions, and in a second turned to her, smiling, and said:

"Commands from such a superior should be cheerfully obeyed. What am I to talk about?"

"About everything, it seems to me."

"Where am I to begin?"

"Mr. Calmire, I want you to tell me what keeps you calm and good when you don't believe anything. There's nothing to keep me so. I don't believe anything any more. You needn't any longer be afraid of disturbing me. Talk to me now."

"Well," said Calmire to himself. "So Muriel's kindergarten has turned out a graduate! Ah me! I've got to take hold at last!" He little realized for how much more than mere intellectual disturbance, Muriel was responsible. He had, however, a quick return of the suspicion he had intimated to Muriel—that Nina's trouble was deeper than creeds go, and he was anxious as to the cause; but without wasting time in conjectures, he determined that it was best to follow her lead right on. So he answered:

"Though you say I don't believe anything, I probably believe many times as much as you ever did—as you have yet had time to. Nevertheless you know most of the truths that help anybody to be 'good and calm,' as well as anybody knows them. But you don't appreciate that *they* are the truths which really do the work, and you are letting yourself be disturbed over some other notions which people have associated with those essential truths. Possibly those notions are of some value to some people, but not to the woman you are growing to be."

"But who's to decide what's really true?" she asked. "People differ so."

"That's a big question—the test of truth," he said. "In the first place, we have to determine what we mean by truth."

"Are you going to be very tiresome, Mr. Calmire?"

Her bantering way of saying it was so charming that Timon himself could not have been offended. Calmire laughed heartily and said:

"I hope not, dear, but I'm afraid I may, and I see plainly that you're not feeling well. Hadn't we better put it off?"

Eager as she had been for something to tie her poor little boat to, she was not eager, with her aching head, to have it dragged after a long-drawn analysis. She had the yearning natural to one who has been depending on alleged short-cuts to truth, for some new short-cut across the waste of her perplexities. She wanted a "saving word." She did not realize that no brief word can contain what she needed; and the slow, laborious construction of a system, however impregnable, was scarcely in her mind, and not to her taste at all. Yet, so far, the talk had diverted her a little from the tortures she had been enduring, and the prospect of relinquishing it, even to escape some tedious logic, brought her face to face with the tortures again. She eagerly begged Calmire to go on.

"Well, dear," he said, "some people say there are two kinds of truth, human and divine. That seems to me plainly impossible. I can conceive of only one kind of truth, and the portion of it which we have, we have had to learn from experience. It is, of course, largely incorporated in the religions. But it is contradicted right and left by some statements in the religions, and so their followers try to make them out to be a superior kind of truth."

"But, Mr. Calmire, mere human truth is so limited. One can see so little for oneself."

"The trouble about your beliefs, is that you have supposed it necessary to believe a great many things that you *can't* 'see for yourself.' What you can see for yourself, is limited, I admit; but human experience is the only source cf truth we've got, and when we imagine that we have any more, we get into trouble. All the substantial operations of our lives are conducted on experience; and all our blunders come because we have not enough of it. We've enough for practical purposes, however, or at least enough to secure all the happiness at present within our reach: for experience, and experience alone, does just that."

"What? The faiths don't help?" she asked.

"Only," he answered, "that portion of the faiths which are pointed to by experience: though it is claimed, with doubtful justice, that some people couldn't get that portion without the fanciful portion. For instance, experience really says that, within reasonable limits, 'it is more blessed to give than to receive:' but religion says it too, and as it's not a very obvious truth, a great many people believe it (or think they do), not as matter of experience, but as matter of religion. Now that's all very well, so long as they don't profess to believe *against* experience: for then harm comes —the wastes of asceticisms, religious wars and persecutions, human hearts torn out on the altars of imaginary gods, both physically and emotionally —like poor—" He hesitated, but some impulse prompted him to add, " poor Mary Courtenay's."

" Mary's! Oh, I've so wanted to know her life. Can't you tell me of it?"

" Perhaps, some time. Let me go on now with what I was trying to make clear to you. Do you suppose the so-called mysteries of religion—its preposterous assertions and self-contradictions, made the saints and martyrs, and make so many good men in the church to-day? Do you suppose it was that part of religion that men have died for, or, even if a few have, that it was that part which sustained them in dying?"

" Well, in pity's name, what was it then? For it seems to me that I am dying too—for want of it."

" It was not often dogma, if ever, but what lay under the dogma—the morality that men have been learning through all their experience, and the simple faith in the Infinite Power and Infinite Law, which, in the religions and out, under the name of every beneficent God ever worshipped, has inspired the best men through all history."

" Yes, Mr. Calmire, and it is just that faith which I have lost. In some respects my mind since I have been here has been widened. I have grown to a cold intellectual recognition that love for mankind is the noblest basis of right-doing, if any basis is good for anything; and that there are no freaks in the merciless Power that governs us. But I have not the kind of faith in any of it that can sustain and comfort anybody. I've gained Altruism, and I've gained Law, and they're two very big-sounding words for a girl to be able to use, but—I have lost God."

"That 'cold intellectual recognition,'" he answered, "will grow into something warmer, and those 'big-sounding words' will come to mean more to you, perhaps, than any other words have yet meant. And as to losing God: you mean, that you have lost a lot of primitive and gratuitous notions regarding God."

"I have lost all I had, and where God was, there is now nothing but unfeeling machinery. My deepest soul finds nothing to respond to."

Calmire pondered a moment and then said:

"I suspect that it has pretty much all to respond to that it ever had, but that communication has been interrupted. We must see if we can't open up some new lines: but that's not the work of a day. Suppose, though, I give you something to think about. In many days, it may come to have a meaning to you."

"Give me anything—a straw: for I am drowning."

Calmire pondered again, and then turned toward her with a curiously complex smile, and said:

"Shut your eyes and stop your ears."

"What? Oh don't play with me now."

"My poor child," he said, taking and caressing her hand, "I never was more serious in my life.

Besides," he added, looking up and smiling again, "I'm only asking you to do what the orthodox teachers ask: they want you to give up the use of your senses. Now try to do the same for me a little while. I really do want you to shut out all sight and sound, and to remain in that condition as long as you can. Can you imagine yourself deaf and blind?"

"Imagine it? I've known it."

"Why, what in the world do you mean?"

"Once in the Pozzi at Venice, I wanted to see how it must have felt to be imprisoned there, and I lingered behind my friends, and put out my taper."

"There's not another girl in creation who'd have done that! Weren't you frightened?"

"No, I didn't think of that: I knew my friends would come back for me."

"Well, how *did* you feel?"

"There was no world left, and it seemed as if I had extinguished my soul."

"So your soul seems to be largely a matter of sight and sound, doesn't it? But in those dungeons, you couldn't experience exactly what I have in mind. I want you to try it again here—to get your mind and senses as nearly vacant as possible —to obliterate yourself as far as you can, and when thought and memory insist on reasserting themselves, yield and open your eyes. It's too light out here, come into the hall."

They went in out of the glare. Calmire gave her a seat, and she closed her eyes, and put her little hands over her little ears. She succeeded so well in losing herself in the silent darkness, that in about four minutes, which she supposed fifteen, she had almost lost consciousness; but then she found herself thinking, with a sort of horror, how black and empty such life would be, and opened her eyes.

Before her, under the arch of the doorway, was the infinitely deep blue sky; far off, near the horizon, it grew softer and touched the hills mellowed by the Autumn haze. They were still green, with faint patches of brown and yellow and dark forests of pine, and here and there the subdued flame of an Autumn maple or the gold of an elm. Under the hills, the river was a little misty too, but nearer, it reflected the blue of the upper sky, save for one dot of white sail; and in the foreground was the soft curve of the hill of green lawn, with bold masses of nearer flame and gold and red-bronzed oak and dark green pines. On the outer edge of the hill, over the rich brown line of the road, came patiently two great shining white and yellow oxen with their cart. Contrasted with the darkness and vacancy Nina had just emerged from, Nature's beauty appealed to her as it had never appealed before. After some moments of rapt silence, she said quietly:

"How inexpressibly lovely! It is a revelation!"

"Precisely!" answered Calmire. "And it was because I wanted you to realize it as a revelation, that I got you to shut yourself out from it. It even surprised you, though you were familiar with it. Now try to realize (as you could not have done ten minutes ago, though you have thought of it often) what a revelation sight must bring when an oculist gives it to a blind person. Just think it over a minute. I have a purpose in all this," he added with a smile.

After a little time she said: "Well, I think I have some such realization as you wished me to get. It must surpass anything anybody ever dreamed. It must be so with hearing too, and to some extent with the other senses. But why have you made me do all this?"

"Partly (but not mainly) to try to get you to recognize that the revelations we get from Nature, direct through our own senses, are not so much to be despised after all. You said a few minutes ago, that without certain dogmas of your old religion, there was nothing left. Yet you also said that shutting out light and sound extinguished your soul: so, after all, your soul seems to get a large part of its significance from light and sound, as well as from your old dogmas. Now the fact is that even when the dogmas are gone, everything *real* is left. Think it over a moment, and then I'll try to give you some farther points more significant still."

After a little meditation Nina said: "Yes, I have been wrong—stupidly, foolishly wrong, in underestimating what we have outside of the religions. I had been taught to believe that without Christianity the world must mean nothing."

"That Egypt and Greece and Rome and India, and China and Japan meant nothing!" exclaimed Calmire.

"Yes!" said Nina, "and now what *can* you tell me more significant than showing me my foolish blunder?"

"Well!" responded Calmire. "We have used the word 'revelation' several times, in connection with your appreciation of what Nature shows us of itself. Now I want to help you realize that the word was no metaphor, but that all we know is actually a revelation from an infinite Something under what we see and hear and feel, and pervading it all—a revelation that it has taken millions of years to bring to what it is, that is still increasing, and that we can increase for ourselves."

"Why," exclaimed the girl, "that's all very grand, but very bewildering: and yet somehow it doesn't seem altogether unthinkable."

"Of course it's not," Calmire answered; "people have had glimpses of it as long as they have guessed, but we've got much new light on it of late years, and if you ever get a clear realization of it, you won't talk as you were just talking—about having lost God, and having nothing left: you'll find new reasons to believe that you can't lose God, and that everything means God. Now, to begin with, do you believe in evolution?"

"I don't like to think that we're descended from monkeys."

"Now do try to get rid of that cheap prejudice! I'm afraid that some of the ancestors we're forced to acknowledge, were worse in *some* respects than even the monkeys: I never heard of an assembly of monkeys enjoying seeing a lot of their own kind killed by stronger beasts; or worse still, enjoying seeing a lot of their own kind kill each other. But so long as we are what we are, what difference does it make what our ancestors were? I did not ask you, however, whether you like the doctrine of evolution. I asked whether you believe it."

"I suppose I've got to."

"Well then, don't make faces over it as if you were biting a lemon, but glory in the progress your family has made. Somehow women don't seem to welcome truth—to believe that it *must* be better than any mistaken conviction, no matter how deeply cherished."

"Do all *men ?*" asked Nina.

"Oh certainly, certainly !" said Calmire, laughing. "But let's assume that you believe in evolution, as, of course, all *men* do. Now try to follow me closely, please. Millions of years ago, your ancestors, you know, were far humbler than the monkeys —bits of protoplasm or floating jelly, with virtually no senses, no thoughts, no feelings. Try and imagine what the universe must have been to them— blank darkness and silence, somewhat as you felt it in Venice, and tried to feel it, or rather to be insensible to it, a few minutes ago—virtually no universe at all—nothing revealed, no 'revelations.'"

"Yes," she responded, "I experienced a little of what they must have found it."

"No," said Calmire, "I doubt if we can begin to realize the vacancy they lived in: we cannot get rid of our memories of sights and sounds, and our highly evolved sense of touch. But a creature who never had any senses, could not have even memories. To the first creature that had a sense, though,—say only the faintest sense of touch, the universe had some little meaning—a little something of it was 'revealed.' To the one who first felt a difference between heat and cold, more was revealed; more still in the difference between sound and silence; still more when one could feel a difference between light and darkness; and then, by slow additions, were revealed the differences in sound and color. So by insensible degrees, from generation to generation, new revelations have been added, with new capacities for receiving them, until at last you've reached your share, and to you are revealed such things as this beautiful scene before us, and all I tried to get you to realize a few minutes ago."

"But what does all that prove?" Nina interrupted.

"Simply that, as every experience is a revelation from the source of experiences, where there are revelations, there is a something to be revealed. All we know, is a mere film over Something beneath, which we cannot measure—something to which we can assign no bounds—an Infinite; and through our senses, It has been to some degree revealed to us, and revealed naturally and truthfully."

"But that's all merely material," objected Nina. "What has it to do with making people good?"

"After a while, you won't so despise the 'merely material,' and it happens to be by comparing the 'merely material' truths revealed by the senses, that we have learned the higher body of truths which 'make people good': moral truths are primarily revelations from the same Infinite Source with the material ones. *All* truth grew up by the slow degrees I have indicated. *All* truth is revelation. Your immediate trouble is that men have asserted so many imaginary and unnatural revelations, that when the fancied revelations are proved mistaken, one is driven, as you have been, to overlook the true ones. But the true ones are there, they are the only body of truths on which all men, so far as they know them, agree: and the source of those truths does exist, and is the only actual reality corresponding with what you have been in the habit of calling 'God.' There have been a myriad conceptions regarding it: for all sorts of divinities and anthropomorphic fancies have been put behind the actual revelations of Nature; and now, simply because much that was mistaken in your conceptions, has disappeared, you feel that the fundamental Verity behind the conceptions has disappeared too. But it is there all the same, and much clearer to us than it was to Moses or Buddha or Paul. But you have got to learn to recognize it with *our* eyes, and not with theirs. Now I am forced to leave you, and I have but barely opened the subject, but we will talk this over some more this evening."

She gave a start, and put her hand on her heart.

"What's the matter?" asked Calmire.

"Oh, nothing! Some little stitch in my side." But she kept him until she learned (quite diplomatically, she flattered herself) that Muriel would not be back that evening.

CHAPTER XL.

THE NATURAL AND THE SUPERNATURAL.

AFTER dinner, Nina furnished her mother some pretext for going away, and that lady was of course always ready to leave the girl with Calmire. When they were alone before the logs in the drawing-room, she began by saying:

"I don't know that I said 'revelations' this morning, with any real feeling that they were revelations. It was simply a fashion of speaking. I see what I see, and hear what I hear, but, despite your reasoning, the idea that there is anything more than I hear or see, does not yet really take possession of me."

"Of course not," answered Calmire. "It's too new. It needs looking at often, and from many sides. Now, if it won't bore you, let's begin again with our 'protoplasmic ancestor.'"

"Charmed to renew his acquaintance," said Nina.

"Well," continued Calmire, "I have the honor to introduce to you, not one, but those, generally, who first had any consciousness of differences in things outside of themselves. Let's go into their experiences a little more in detail than we did this morning. Of course I won't attempt to give the exact chronological order, especially as no one knows it, but will merely try to give the subject in a general way. They must have found some things pleasanter than others—soft contacts pleasanter than harsh ones, even surfaces than cutting ones, light than darkness, and warmth than cold. Those, for instance, who had a distinct sense of temperature, must have found it preferable to float in the warmer places. Well, when their descendants came to have added, say, a sense of taste, they could have a good time, lying where the sun falls on the water, and feeling the motion of the waves, and enjoying their food—the universe was revealed to them to a degree of considerable significance. But how infinitely fuller became the life of the creature who had added the sense of sight! Think of his greater happiness, even before any enjoyment of beauty came, in avoiding danger and finding food. Of course at the beginning it wasn't sight as we know it, but mere recognition of light. Then it probably took thousands of generations to develop any notion of color, and thousands more to develop discrimination of many colors."

"But," she interrupted, "how do you know all these things about the creatures that came before man?"

"Why, we not only find fossil remains in successive layers of the earth, that indicate the progress; but we see much of it going on now. We still have almost all grades of animals with us. And just as the astronomer calculates from the eclipses we know, that certain reported ancient obscurations of the sun and moon were also eclipses, so the biologists know early processes through contemporary ones. This is a very different thing, mind you, from accepting gratuitous statements—like those credited to Moses, for instance—which contradict known facts."

"Yes, I can see that," she said, "and now let's go back to Grandpa."

"So you acknowledge your poor relations to-day, do you? Well, after some of your very-very-great-grandpas had got pretty susceptible to light, some of your grandpas not quite so great, must have got susceptible to, say, the difference between red light and white light, and to the difference between red light and blue light, and gradually to other differences of color. Else, where did *you* get your capacity to recognize such differences? These susceptibilities must have been developed pretty late, because we find many human beings, and intelligent ones too, in whom they are not developed yet: you know some color-blind people. Now to some rays, we are all color-blind! for the prism gives us some that nobody's eyes are yet far enough evolved to be susceptible to; we know them only because they have certain chemical powers, some of them of use in photography, I believe. So, many rays that we see, could not have been seen by our humble ancestors; and therefore (Here comes the great point) it is fair to presume that the rays not seen by us, must be visible to our posterity. Now think what the grand sights open to them will be! Only we can't think much more definitely about those sights, than we can about the rest of the Infinity yet unrevealed. As with sights, so with tones. Our ancestors who first heard noises, of course developed, generation after generation, a capacity to recognize differences between noises as well as sights. One of the proofs that this capacity has been so evolved, is that we find it now, like susceptibility to shades of light, in very various degrees of development. There are plenty of people who hear well, and yet cannot distinguish between two tones differing by fifty vibrations a second; while on the other hand, there are some musicians who will recognize a difference of half a dozen vibrations, and I think less. Moreover, just as the color-scale contains shades beyond any existing eyes, so the sound-scale contains tones beyond any existing ears. Average people recognize notes four or five octaves above the treble clef; musicians recognize them an octave or so higher still; but soon there comes a point where vibrations are too rapid for any human ear yet evolved to hear. Some naturalists have suspected that some insects communicate by notes too high for the human ear, and whales by notes too low. I suspect that's all rather mythical, though, especially the whales: for when vibrations get too slow to be recognized as tones, they are perfectly audible as separate beats. But aside from single tones, take the 'overtones,' whose abundance in some instruments makes those instruments so much more beautiful than others: some people are conscious of many more than other people are—actually hear things in the present music, that other people can't. How will it be then with the real 'music of the future'? Try again now from this point of view, what you tried from another this morning—to imagine the possible revelations of sound."

"Oh, it's too much—it's too much!" exclaimed Nina. "Inexpressibly grand, but inexpressibly bewildering. It makes my head whirl."

Had Mr. Calmire attempted his argument a dozen years later, he could have given it new depth and beauty from the discoveries that the waves of which we recognize a few as light, really include not only those of the spectrum Calmire knew, but are already shown to extend into a spectrum ascertainable only by other means than direct sight, and infinitely larger than he had any idea of—some of its waves presumably long enough to reach beyond our universe and all our conceptions, while others are so minute as to be equally beyond our faculties. And it is but a little fragment of this graduated infinity, that our senses can grasp, as light. The capacities of our early predecessors could respond only to fragments vastly less, and we can assign no limits to what may be appreciated by our successors. It is suspected that light and heat are other waves in the same boundless series, and also that what is now found regarding that series of waves, seems true of another series, among which we apprehend a few as sound.

But Calmire, not anticipating these discoveries, and so making Nina's head whirl more, answered her:

"Let's stop: if you're tired, you can't take in more."

"Yes, I can. And besides, you've given your poor creatures about all the usual senses already."

"And your word 'usual' anticipates one of my objects in doing it. Why shouldn't there be more than the 'usual' senses?"

"Why, I never heard of any."

"Neither did the creature with but one. Yet even now," Calmire said with a smile, "the societies for Psychical Research may be on the track of one new to us."

"Are you joking?"

"Not altogether. Some people really seem to get knowledge from other people's minds, in ways different from those already well known—by a sense of intellectual touch, as it were, just as the first creatures with a sense of physical touch, got knowledge in ways not known to their predecessors. But our own contemporaries who are advanced in this respect, hardly seem to get any *new* knowledge, however,—any that they do not appear to read from the mind of somebody else. Yet that much would show a new sense."

"Tell me more about it!" exclaimed Nina.

"Well, there isn't very much to tell yet. You know how a suggestion will make a sleeper dream?"

"Yes, I've heard how the clash of shovel and tongs makes one dream great battles; and turning on the gas, makes dreams of great conflagrations."

"Well," continued Calmire, "there's an artificial sleep, or rather state of waking dreaminess, called hypnotism, into which some people can readily be thrown, and in which they will dream and feel and do anything suggested by the person who puts them into that state."

"Why, isn't that something like mesmerism?" asked Nina.

"Certainly. It's the modern name for, apparently, the same thing. Well, the influence of the hypnotizer—or the mesmerizer if you will, appears to be communicated sometimes by mere will, without words, and even at a distance. People vary very much in their susceptibility to such hypnotic communications: some seem so sensitive that they apparently get impressions from other minds without any conscious effort on either side. I've had persons get from my mind, very strange things that they could not have known in any other way that I can think of, and they have been able to get still farther impressions by both sides concentrating attention on the subject."

"Such as what?" interrupted Nina.

"Oh, impressions of facts in my history, names of those dear to me, and many things that I may tell you sometime. But now you see that *if* this susceptibility to such impressions is normal, it is going to become more general and more intense, as delicacy of physical touch has, and develop into a distinct new sense. And," he continued, laughing, "as aptitudes tend to concentrate themselves in the nerves best adapted for them—to locate some of the senses in special organs, we may yet have an organ to read each other's minds with, as we now have organs to read each other's faces and voices."

"But how ugly we'd be with a new organ!" exclaimed Nina.

"You're expressing the jelly-fish's opinion of a creature with eyes, aren't you?" said Calmire.

"Great Heavens!" Nina ejaculated. "How narrow all our every-day notions are! But if we can read each other's minds, we can't keep our secrets," she exclaimed, after a moment, becoming again conscious of one that was burdening her very sorely.

"I don't know about that," Calmire answered. "It looks as if nothing can be read against its thinker's will. But it's all very uncertain yet."

"Well, it's wonderful anyhow, even as far as it's got!" exclaimed Nina.

"I don't know," said Calmire, "that it's half as wonderful as any one of the senses that we already have, would appear to a man lacking it, if he were suddenly put in possession of it. Try and think a moment of such 'revelations' as you had this morning, coming to a person to whom they would be new."

"That's true, all true!" exclaimed Nina. "It brings up again the stories of people blind from birth being suddenly cured."

"Now go back," said Calmire, "and tell me if you, with your five or seven senses (for you realize that some of our senses are still in such a vague state of development that people don't even agree how many we have), wouldn't be almost as foolish to deny the possibility of more, as would the creature with only one?"

"Why, yes! I never thought of that before!"

"Really?" said Calmire, with a quizzical laugh, and then continued: "Now here, my child, to sum it all up, is what I want you to think about some more and often:—the first beings were absolutely vacant of knowledge. To them and to their descendants, the Infinite has been revealing itself little by little, through countless generations, until it has made possible such revelations as human beings have. The sum of these revelations, is what we call the natural world—this vast assemblage of woods and hills and seas and stars and deep vault of heaven, and the busy, thinking and enjoying creatures, and, through all, despite some drawbacks, Order and beneficent Law. All this has slowly been revealed through the senses we have. *But*, and here is the point of it all, the evolution we know, gives us abundant reason to believe that the Infinite which we touch on all our sides with our imperfect senses, could go on revealing, to finer senses, unlimited new truth, beauty, orderliness, happiness. What we know, must be as nothing to the great beyond that we do not know. We are getting hints of it all the while which we cannot clearly comprehend. To one it suggests itself in a strain of music; to another, in some dear face—to one, in the majesty of mountains; to another, in the mystery of wooded vales—the hunter feels it beyond the misty morning; the poet, beyond the sunset—in some way, at some time, most highly organized beings have felt that ineffable thrill."

"Yes," cried Nina, "I have felt it! I know it! I know it!"

"Now," said Calmire, "that Infinite Beyond—surrounding on every side the Nature that we know, is the real *Super*-natural. But it is unknown, and, except as we gain little by little from it through experience and study, it must, so far as we can judge, remain unknown. Myriads of men have professed to tell of it, but everybody believes that all but his own chosen few, drew wholly on fancy. This of course goes to indicate that all drew on fancy. But though we know nothing of that all-pervading supernatural, faith in it is one of the fundamental conditions of right thinking. All this may mean but little to you now. But it will come to mean more."

"It seems to mean already, Mr. Calmire, that you have proved to me what I have before supposed we had to take wholly on faith—the existence of the spiritual world."

"Of course! Oh, it's a delight to teach you!" exclaimed Calmire. "Yes, some anthropomorphic 'spirit' has always been supposed to be behind every new manifestation of that unknown Infinity. You know that even now, the hypnotism I was telling you about a minute ago, is called 'spiritualism,' and the spiritualists call their hypnotic visions 'revelations.' And quite lately, electricity was attributed to spirits, just as savages have always attributed wind and rain to them. But as soon as such specimens of 'spiritualism' get sifted from the false notions they necessarily start with, and from the humbug that the designing always promote with them, all notion of 'spirits' in connection with them is abandoned, and what is left takes its natural place in the body of knowledge. Yet such knowledge has always come to us from that mysterious Infinity on whose surface we live, and which has had almost universal recognition in some such phrase as 'the spirit-world.' Now don't think of this any more before you go to sleep, but think it over hard when you wake. Good-night," and he kissed her forehead.

CHAPTER XLI.

AN OUTSIDE ARGUMENT.

THE efficacy of teaching often depends as much upon personal relations as upon doctrine; and at this stage of Calmire's expositions, a circumstance occurred that greatly increased Nina's susceptibility to his influence.

The next afternoon, he proposed to take her riding, but she was languid because of the heavy feelings and unaccustomed thoughts of the preceding few days, and so a compromise was effected. Calmire put the ladies in a victoria, and started out beside them on Malzour.

I don't know much about a horse, but that one was like some other rare beings—no education was required to appreciate him.

His sire was an Arab who had been given to Calmire by some oriental diplomatic friend, and the name had been "kept in the family." His dam was a great three-quarter-bred Kentucky mare. He was big and black, and seemed to have a sunshine of his own. He was as proud and fiery and gentle and reliable as his master. He liked to have children pat him: yet he was as ambitious as Bucephalus, or as Alexander's self; but while he was always ready to do all a horse can, he was always content to do only what his master wanted. The front of his head was straight and generally upright; his nostrils were open and red; his little ears most always pointed forward; his long neck, though generally arched, was *not* like a swan's, for a swan's is sometimes ugly; his breast was so broad, his chest so deep, his forearm and quarter so powerful, and his back so straight and short and firm that it would have seemed a waste for him to bear a weight less kingly than Calmire's; where the bones were indicated through his shining skin, his legs seemed slight, but that was only in contrast with the great muscles above; his pasterns were rather long, that is why he and Calmire seemed to move on as if the horse were a thing of springs or waves, rather than one of unyielding bones with joints; his feet were round and firm, and pointed straight forward, but they were not small; his tail, on top, was a continuation of the nearly straight line of his back, until it gradually drooped into the rich flowing curves of the hair, and when he was going fast, it was almost the only horse-tail I ever saw that it did not disgust me to have compared to the train of a meteor.

Among the various high questions which, at quiet hours, had claimed the discourse of Calmire and Muriel, the cutting of that horse's tail had held a prominent place. Muriel had seen so few revolutions of fashion, and had got such a one-sided grip of the truth that, to us, the beautiful is largely the conventional, that he urged the conforming of Malzour's tail to the prevailing mode. But Calmire had got hold of the truth that as we leave the artificially-enfolded human figure, and go through the brutes out toward inanimate nature, our respect for convention decreases. This he

illustrated with such facts as that only in the most
degraded times, such as those of the *Ancien Régime*,
have many trees been trimmed into noticeably artificial shape, and that it took as colossal a fool as
Xerxes to think of carving a mountain into a form not
its own. Calmire's principle being established by
this induction, he proceeded to apply it by saying
that, much as he enjoyed contributing to the content
of so artificial a creature as Mr. Muriel Calmire, most
of whose person must necessarily be covered by
art,—willing as he was, therefore, to enjoy that gentleman's countenance despoiled, as it was, by the
razor, he would not inflict on Malzour, whose privilege it was to go as Nature made him, the artificial
incongruity of banging his tail.

Well, the grand horse certainly justified his master's principles, as he was led up in front of Mrs.
Wahring and Nina. And as Calmire mounted him
as lightly as Muriel would have done, and rode off
with them, Nina exclaimed to her mother, much
to the latter lady's delight:

"There go two noble creatures!"

Malzour knew that Calmire would not let him
out for the first half mile, and danced along contentedly enough until, when they got upon the
main road at the bottom of the hill, by sundry uneasinesses he called to himself the attention of
his master.

Calmire said to the ladies: "Excuse my running
away a few minutes to calm Malzour down," and
then said to the horse:

"All right, old boy," and with an unconscious
pressure of the leg, he brought the horse's croup

toward the middle of the road and let him go over to the turf by the side. There he pressed him with the other leg; for if he had not, the horse would probably have gone to the fence and over it, supposing that was what Calmire wanted. He always did, as nearly as he understood it, what Calmire wanted; but he also occasionally had a desire of his own, as he had respectfully intimated before Calmire took him off the road. When he felt the second pressure, he brought himself around again parallel with the road, and Calmire pressed him with both legs and lightly touched the curb, when the graceful mass started off in a canter lighter than Vergil's verses.

It soon got to be a tearing pace, and after they had had a mile or two of it, including two or three very pretty jumps over ditches beside the culverts and an occasional détour where the roadside was impracticable, Calmire said : "We're not in a hurry this afternoon," and gently drew him in, and sauntered back to meet the ladies.

After walking quarter of a mile or so (for Malzour was one of those rare horses who, though they pick up their feet with the spring of a good pianist's wrists, nevertheless will walk), Calmire saw the victoria with the two ladies approaching, and set forward at a slow trot to meet it.

He turned, and was at Mrs. Wahring's side of the carriage, and, by a touch of the curb, moderated Malzour's desire to trot with the other horses, into a gentle canter which grouped the most beautiful of all Malzour's beautiful possibilities, and would have made the veriest tyro in the saddle look a thing of grace. What Calmire looked, Nina never forgot. Yet strange to say, always in recalling horse and man and that afternoon, she was more apt to imagine Muriel in the saddle than Calmire.

Suddenly the off horse in the victoria, on Calmire's side, made a plunge.

"What is it?" said Calmire to the driver.

"The young horse is a little fresh, Mr. Calmire, sir. If you'd just please go on the other side!"

In a minute, one rein (which, it was discovered later, the coachman's monkey of a boy had been stropping his father's razor on) snapped, and the bits of both horses were held on but one side. The colt, who would have been safe enough if the harness was, proceeded to do what he could towards running away, and there were not fit means to prevent his steadier companion from going with him.

"Don't be uneasy!" said Calmire to the ladies, "I'll take care of it."

But Mrs. Wahring, though she could endure anything for which she was prepared, was not a woman for quiet counsels in emergencies. She began to scream and to show decided symptoms of intending to jump out of the carriage. Her screams frightened the horses more.

"Sit still, I tell you!" thundered Calmire, with a voice and look that Nina thought were the finest things she had seen in him that day.

The poor lady, astonished and cowed, shrunk back to her seat, and quietly awaited death. Nina felt rigid, but her anticipations stopped in dependence on the big black horse and his rider.

In two seconds Calmire was around the carriage again, with his left hand on the wild young creature's rein at the bit, and his right restraining Malzour, so that at times the faithful fellow's hoofs were plowing ridges in the road, as the two carriage-horses, for both were now running away, fairly dragged him with them. Malzour was literally being dragged by Calmire's arm. No human frame could stand it long. The speed was checked a little, but Calmire felt that a few more seconds would finish him. They were at the foot of a gentle hill, and Calmire saw with joy that near the summit the road had been cut into the side of the hill, leaving a bank on the left. But the left rein was broken. It could not turn them in. He pondered a second, then his face suddenly fell into hard lines and turned deadly pale. He called to the man:

"Drop the rein, leave it to me."

Then a glow that seemed almost to contain a smile, spread over his face, as he released the frightened horse's bit, put spurs to Malzour, and went up the hill at a speed compared with which the runaways were slow. At the summit, he stopped a little toward the right side of the road, and turned Malzour square across, facing the bank. The horse arched his graceful neck. Calmire, with such a face as great inspirations bring, leaned over, patting him, and said: "Steady, old fellow, and goodbye, if we must." And then he waited. His most definite thought was: "I hope it won't be maiming! Death has got to come sometime, and I suspect it's pretty much of a humbug anyhow."

It was not long as his watch would have counted

it, but long enough as his crowding memories did, while the mad destruction rushed towards him. When it was within a few paces, he waved his hat. The horses veered to the left. He plunged right against them. In three bounds, all three horses were down against the bank.

"Jump, and take their heads," called Calmire to the coachman, and by the time the man had the near horse by the bit, Malzour, from whom Calmire had sprung as they touched the bank, was standing safe by the roadside, and his master was at the head of the off horse.

Calmire's leg was a little bruised by the tug-irons, where he had struck the horse when he rushed against them. No other living thing was scratched.

He had probably saved the ladies' lives, and at the imminent peril of his own, and Mrs. Wahring's quick mind did not, on the whole, regret the risk.

CHAPTER XLII.

THE ESSENTIAL RELIGION.

NATURALLY the ladies went to bed early that evening, but the next morning after breakfast, Nina came to Calmire on the piazza with a weary smile, and said :

"Night before last, and even yesterday, it seemed to me that I really felt toward that Infinity which you have shown me to be behind all things, something that might take the place of my old feeling toward God ; but when I awoke this morning, I had no more feeling regarding it than if I were dead. It's a very ungrateful recognition," she added with a charming mixture of banter and earnestness, "for your risks in preventing my being really dead, as well as for your trouble in teaching me."

Calmire gave a cheerful little laugh, and said :

"Of course you don't find your feelings on philosophical truths very brisk this morning. Such a little shake-up as we had yesterday afternoon is apt to divert currents of emotion, and your current of that class of emotions hadn't been running long enough to wear a very deep channel. But even in the old times, if you had questioned your 'love of God,' or your love of your mother, or of any one else, you would have found many a morning when you did not absolutely thrill with it, especially if you had been very tired the night before. Don't let such a perfectly natural circumstance disturb your new faith, and don't keep pulling the faith up by the roots to see if it's well started."

"Well," said Nina, "certainly a new horizon has opened to me, but faint and vague. My view is full of uncertainties and perplexities."

"That's entirely natural," Calmire responded. "To have its full effect, the subject must color every fibre of your intellectual being; but it has hardly had time yet to get below the surface, and it is too tremendous to be assimilated all at once, anyhow. The significance of these commonplaces of modern philosophy that I'm trying to teach you —the bearing of the scientific facts on the moral principles, never is found as obvious at first as later; and perhaps the added light will not come as often when you seek it from deliberate thought, as in odd moments, by side-flashes from every-day experience. It's going to take a good while, too, for you to truly *realize* one point which is easy enough to understand without realizing—that one's religion is simply what one thinks and feels regarding the Power behind the universe our senses know; yet one *must* realize that fact before getting the relation to the Infinite which transcends all relation to an unseen personality."

"It has seemed to me very strange," she said, "that the facts relating to the very beginnings of life, which you have been telling me, should have a bearing upon our relations to that Infinity. But I see that they do, even from what you have already told me."

"Unquestionably they do," he said; "and the fact seems to have been realized almost universally. Every religious system but some very primitive ones, deals with 'the very beginnings of life,' in some cosmogony, more or less absurd. A religion is but a theory of life, and the questions of life are but questions of our relation to the universe (including man, of course), and the forces behind it."

"But, Mr. Calmire, all that you have told me about, was, after all, mere sensations, not the high thoughts and feelings where religion dwells. I've always been taught that God sent us those directly, or that the devil did," she added with an expression which proved that the devil did not send them to her often. Then she continued: "You did hint something yesterday about intellectual and moral truths coming from physical ones, but of course you didn't expect me to understand that."

"Why, that isn't hard to understand. Most truths which you call intellectual and moral, are merely statements about physical matters, and perhaps, in the last analysis, all are. Take a few at random—for instance, the first of our great 'glittering generalities'—'all men are born free and equal.' It simply means that no physical force should be used to seize another man's material goods, confine or injure his material body, or hinder his freedom of speech—which is simply to hinder his using material type, or vibrations of material air, to affect another man's material eyes or ears so as to influence certain material motions in the nerve-matter of that other man, with which (and here we blend into the immaterial again) his opinions are associated. 'Do as you would be done by,' has a similar set of implications. There's no hard and fast line between the intellectual and the moral and the physical, Nina, any more than there is anywhere else in Nature. Why, even what you call 'matter' is simply a name for a lot of mental impressions of size, color—possible odor and taste, and of that resistance to pressure, which you call solidity. But an electric shock or a hypnotic command would oppose about the same resistance to muscular pressure, and yet there's nothing which you call 'matter' there."

"But then a thing's a thing, Mr. Calmire. When I see a thing, it's because there's something there."

"Yes," Calmire answered, "there *is* 'something there'—something everywhere, Something Infinite and Inexpressible, causing all our sensations; and when you express a certain set of them, you call that set, matter. You call another set, lightning; but the lightning is not what you mean by 'matter,' and yet it is as much a manifestation of that same Something, as resistance to muscular pressure is."

"Well, there seems reason in what you say, and yet it's so queer. I can't get hold of it."

"It takes time and frequent turning over," Calmire responded. "But it will make the task easier, perhaps, if I try to give you a notion of how thoughts and feelings arose. Or are you getting bored?"

"Not a bit, not a bit! Do go on, please."

"Well, I can only do it very roughly. Our knowledge of the subject is yet very new, and we've only had time to make ourselves a mighty poor stock of words to talk about it with, and I don't want to bother you with the big ones. And at best it's very hard to put the case with absolute consistency: for when we talk of thought and feeling, we have to talk in words that all come more or less directly from sensation, because thought and feeling themselves came from sensation. The words themselves prove it—our very difficulties prove our case—the very word 'feeling' even yet remains connected with the sensation of touch; and we say that a man hasn't any 'sense,' when we mean that he hasn't any mind. Moreover the truth that thought and feeling arose in sensation, differs so from our ordinary impressions, that it takes many illustrations and much pondering to make it clear. But, though all thoughts and feelings start from sensations, we regard thought and feeling as advanced, in proportion as they have advanced away from sensations."

"Well, I can't half understand it," persisted Nina. "Do you mean that our loftiest emotions—love, for instance—are built up from mere sense?"

Calmire burst out laughing. "Why, my dear child, that is the very feeling of all the great ones, whose connection with sense is easiest to trace. In the vast majority of mankind, it has hardly got beyond sense yet—and a single sense at that: with most people it's mainly an affair of the eye. With a few rare souls, it is a sympathy in great thoughts and great feelings; but all the same, those thoughts and feelings had their seeds, ages ago generally, in sensations. Take something vastly more abstract than love:—reverence. What started it but the sense of grand *things* (and grand processes)—suns and skies and mountains and oceans and storms and the strength and beauty of living things?"

"Well," said Nina, with a little sigh, "it does seem as if it might be so, after all."

"Then let me try to show you a little of *how* it's so. Let us go to our humble ancestors again—to the first of them who ever felt sensation, and look for a notion of how thought starts. His consciousness of his thoughts and feelings, we can't account for: it's beyond us—with God, if you want to put it so. But we're up to some of the relations of his thoughts and feelings with the outside world and with each other. Now until that first fellow felt the first sensation, there was, so far as we are concerned, absolutely no thought, no knowledge. The first sensation, whatever it was, was knowledge—was a revelation from the source of all our knowledge—reaction between something in us and the Universe outside. It may have been simply knowledge that the creature's progress in a certain direction was obstructed, or that one current of water was warmer than another, or that one place was darker than another."

"You speak of a creature floating in water. Were all the earliest creatures marine?"

"Probably. Most of the primitive forms we now have, are. That's the reason the biologists like to study by the sea. Now suppose one of those creatures barely capable of feeling heat, when he floats into the sunlight. He has then mere sensation—no *thought* about it. But if he recognizes that sensation as the same he felt yesterday, that putting of the two together, is more than a sensation:

it's a thought. There's some reason, though by no means conclusive, to believe that our word 'thought' started from a root that meant to put things together; and we have a way now of saying of a man who thinks well: 'He can put this and that together.'"

"Taking one consideration with another," sang Nina lightly from "The Pirates of Penzance," and then flushed at having been so unconscious of the sombre undercurrent of her thoughts.

"That's it exactly!" said Calmire. "Now suppose our very-great-grandfather going a step farther on. Suppose his food most abounds, as it generally does, in light places. After getting accustomed to find it in such places, the creature has fitted together frequent sensations into a general thought of light. (Of course the beast can't think the man's thoughts, but he must have some processes like those of a man's mind when it is hazy and nearly asleep: I suppose you won't object to its being a thought of light, because he doesn't give that word to it?) But to continue: Now he has fitted together certain other sensations into a general thought of food. Then he gradually gets a farther step and fits the thought of light to the thought of food, and so gets a thought higher than either of the first ones. Suppose one of his descendants far enough evolved to be capable of *seeking* his food, instead of merely absorbing it as it comes. He must get into the way of going about after it in bright spots. But fallen leaves and branches float about in the water, and so, a few generations later, do other creatures which prey on our friend, or even creatures of his own kind in his own generation may do it: so he or his descendants must in time get to distinguish between these small moving shadows, and the great fixed ones of banks and rocks and trees."

"But why must he get to make these distinctions?" asked Nina.

"Simply because he'll get eaten up if he doesn't."

"But," objected Nina, "the one whose senses are evolved first, must be smart enough to eat up the others."

"It's not generally the smartest that eats, but the biggest; and the little fellow develops smartness in getting away from him. Man is not descended from the biggest creatures. My child, do you know that there you have touched the fundamental mystery of our moral evolution? Even way back there and way down there, prevails the rule that danger and suffering and cruel necessity develop soul."

Nina's face became a beautiful study.

"Now," continued Calmire, "let's run over it again. Frequent experiences give a thought of light, frequent experiences give a thought of food, later experiences give the thoughts that where light is, food is, where moving shadow is, danger is: light is salutary, darkness is to be dreaded. A jelly-fish reaches that generalization after thousands of centuries of inherited habit, and children display that identical generalization early, which means that the generalization was evolved in our early ancestry. Expand that generalization a little farther, with experiences a little higher, and you get the early man's notion of a good god of light and an evil god of darkness—all built up by obvious sequences from the most primitive sensations.

Now perhaps you see that the probabilities are tremendous that all our thoughts and feelings were built up from sensation in similar ways—that no man ever knew anything that he or his ancestors had not built up in that slow fashion."

"But oh, Mr. Calmire!" exclaimed Nina, "this is bringing religion itself down to mere sense!"

"Bringing it down, my dear child? If I tell you that a flower grows from earth, and is limited by the kind of earth it grows from, do I bring the flower down to earth?"

"No, I suppose not, after all. Go on, please."

"I don't want to go on until I get you to realize a little better, how your sympathy with what I am trying to explain, is obstructed by prejudices and cant phrases of prejudice, which the world has evolved with the old order of beliefs. You objected lately to the law of evolution, on grounds of family pride; and now you don't want matters of religion made matters of sense; and so on. But your objections are all beside the issue. It ought not to be a question of what a doctrine interferes with, but simply a question: 'Is it true?' If it is, we can rest satisfied in it: for unwelcome truth always turns out a blessing in disguise. But you have had too few opportunities to realize that. When you have realized it oftener, you will not have any preferences whatever as to what dress truth comes in, but simply an eagerness for truth in any dress—just as selfish an eagerness as for any other thing that will add to your happiness."

"I do hope so, but it seems very strange. I feel very weak and desolate, and what you have been saying to me still seems a kind of narrowing down even of the little standing ground that was left me. I've been brought up to despise the things of sense, and here you want to convince me that my whole mind and soul are made up of them."

He reached over and gently stroked her hand as he went on:

"Not a bit of it! They're made up of things of consciousness, which originally were awakened by things of sense. As we've said more than once before: thought—emotion, are the highest things we know—at the summit of our evolution. Here they are: what matters it how they got here? Patience! Patience! and all will become clearer. I've been 'narrowing down' a good many of your old conceptions, it's true. That was sure to be done by somebody—by yourself if by nobody else. But I hope I've given you some better ones in the place of them. I want to get you out of that sadly mistaken way of despising *anything* in Nature. Exalting thought at the expense of sense, is all a mistake, and is primarily responsible for the horrors of asceticism. It was the sort of fool who does that, that Luther sang of in 'Wein, Weib, und Gesang.' How splendidly the knowledge of to-day confirms his inspirations! Is not sense the medium whereby the external Infinity communicates with the internal one, or as you would put it, whereby God informs Soul? Is not sense, then, just as near to God, at one end, as it is to you at the other? Is it not simply our senses, that have led us on a little way into that mass of order and beauty to which we cannot assign any limits?"

"And yet," said Nina after a little reflection

"every-day religion, which satisfies most people's needs, is not made up from study of Nature, but from the inspirations and meditations of holy men."

"So it is, my child. But their 'inspirations and meditations,' so far as good for anything, result from experience of Nature (which of course includes human life) by themselves and their ancestors. True, they tell us other things, but of doubtful value. You know that even the church itself has had to decide what to accept and what to reject."

"Well, what is the right test?" asked Nina.

"Simply the correspondence of what men say with what Nature says. Nature is the only source of truth: of course I mean Nature in the large sense—including human nature."

"Yes, that's just it, Mr. Calmire. Aren't the minds of holy men original sources of truth?"

"Certainly; but just as all 'sources' (you know the word originally meant springs) furnish water which has fallen from elsewhere. Nature pours truth upon us in our daily experiences—in woods and under skies, in laboratories and observatories, before organs and orchestras, in minds and hearts and in social organizations. But the monk in his cell, the hermit in the desert, the old-fashioned German dreamer in his closet, have not been content with what Nature pours upon us, but have generally imagined absurdities and chimeras; and their vagaries, fastened on to more or less of the truth, have done much to shape the religions.

"We should never forget," he continued, "that the

mind of man is irregular and fallible, while Nature is unvarying and reliable—that though she initiates and sustains man's soul-force, she still leaves him enough independence to run counter to her own laws—of both the external world and of mind. Thus he makes his own opinions proportionally unsafe. As soon as men get to fancying beyond Nature's plain revelations, there are all degrees in which they speak truly and falsely, and all ways in which even the best men contradict each other. Socrates believed that the immortality of the soul will be the solution of all human ills: Buddha believed the same of its virtual annihilation. The fact is that neither of them either knew or could know anything about it, Nature being absolutely silent on the point. Now in the hosts of such cases, as there was no possible way of proving either side right or wrong, the original method of avoiding tedious discussion was for one disputant to roast the other. That way being out of fashion now, however, they get together and have a little amusement that they call a 'heresy trial,' where both sides assert a lot of things that neither can prove, and then the majority decides that one is right, or sometimes that both are: for the world is growing so amiable, that the latter way is becoming quite frequent."

"But, Mr. Calmire, you don't mean that all 'the work, the beauty, the poetry, the exaltation' of the church has been the fruit of error?"

"By no means! At bottom they have rested on Nature's own truths; but I'm afraid a good deal of error has been the fruit of the poetry and exaltation. Like all great forces, they're dangerous things:

they often substitute false emotion for true; they often draw their nourishment from men's fancies rather than from Nature and active life. All healthy mental stimulus, not only as it comes to us, but as it came to the first creature that reacted with the outside Universe, originally proceeds from without—from Nature, as I just said (or God if you prefer to put it in that way), or from other human beings. But it won't do to mistake the reactions of one's own mind for the utterances of God. The mind's stimulation of itself is as dangerous as the body's."

"But all the body's stimulants come from outside," Nina objected.

"Not all," he answered; "But that subject is not pleasant, we can't go into it, and you couldn't understand it if we did. Just bear this in mind, though: there are but two sources of truth open to us—the outside Universe, and minds evolved by healthy reaction with it: not minds 'inspired' by their own fancies."

"But," said Nina, "somehow this doesn't seem to come from above—it all seems so awfully mechanical and unspiritual."

"That depends upon what you mean by spiritual. It comes, as everything does, from the Mystery under all our knowledge, which the other day you called the 'spiritual world.' And in that sense, it must be absolutely spiritual; but if you mean that it does not profess to understand anything more of that awful Mystery than the little revealed to our senses, it is *un*spiritual. If, though, you mean by spirituality, the really highest range of thought and feeling which that mystery has yet yielded from itself, if you mean the great emotions which the contemplation of mystery generates, if you mean the 'sacred thirst' for more of such experiences, you will find in what I have been indicating, room for all that—though it will involve some change in your tastes. But, either way, you still have everything man ever really knew, and every reasonable longing he ever felt—from that coming sunset, back through all the beautiful truths painted or carved or in any other way recorded."

"But," she insisted, "there are truths that we can't paint or record."

"Yes, dear, an infinity of them! But until we can paint or record them, it won't do to claim that we have them. If those we haven't got, are what you mean by spiritual truths, why, so far as our minds are concerned, there are none. Yet don't let us for a moment forget that in another sense *all* truth is spiritual: in a unified Universe, truth is necessarily one—the revealed as much as the unrevealed."

"But what does it all mean when we speak about so many of the best men having devoted themselves to finding and teaching spiritual truth? I don't mean men engaged with bugs and stones and such things that we talked about once," and she suddenly turned pale, "but the men we speak of as 'spiritually-minded.' What does that mean?"

"It means a great many things—everything between the wonderful moral insight of Christ, and the arrant nonsense talked in Alexandria in Hypatia's time."

"But there you go again, Mr. Calmire: 'insight,' into what?"

"Into this marvelous mass of experiences and reactions between them, which we call the human soul."

"Well, isn't soul, spirit? Isn't that spiritual?"

"Not in the sense I think you're struggling over now: you want something beyond the human 'spirit'—something of those outside spirits that the savages think of. We can only know the human spirit, and it may be made a very ennobling study. But even with that study, as with a good many other pursuits, the dangers have been proportionate to the advantages."

She uttered a wondering "How?"

"Because it has been the direct road to most of the idiocies. As long as people are studying visible, audible, and tangible things, they are using their longest-evolved and therefore most practiced and reliable senses, and so are least apt to wander into error. The thing is 'right before them,' as we say, and keeps their minds pinned down to it. But when we come to examine our thoughts and feelings, not only are the faculties we use comparatively new and unexercised and weak, but the objects of our study are as elusive as our powers are feeble. So the results are largely vagaries and confusions, and although people have been writing about them ever since they began writing of anything, it is only very lately that we've begun to get them into any sort of shape. At last, though, we've fastened them on to nerve-function, where we could bring our reliable old senses up to help us, and now we're getting ahead."

"Are you coming to my question pretty soon,

Mr. Calmire?" she asked with a fascinating little *moue*.

"You mustn't ask such deep ones, if you want me to get to the bottom of them quickly. I'm nearly as far as I can go, though. I've been telling you all this to show you how our knowledge of our own little 'spirits' is necessarily so vague. Our own spirits are invisible and intangible, and men have gratuitously and irreverently assumed so much resemblance between them and the Invisible and Intangible Infinity behind phenomena, that they have professed to be able through them to study It. So they have got mind and morals hopelessly jumbled up with speculations on the Unknown behind all we know, and have got in the way of calling the whole chaotic mass 'spiritual truth.' Why, when I was a boy, the border between what our minds can do and what they can't, was so ill-defined, that we were actually told that there was such a thing as a *science* of ontology, or pure being, as distinct from the manifestations of it, which are all that finite creatures know: and yet their very term 'science' meant something *known*. I believe they're actually talking such nonsense in some schools to-day."

After a little pondering, Nina asked, "Nevertheless, isn't the 'spirit' of God made manifest through His works *and* through our own souls?"

"Undoubtedly," assented Calmire, "only there's no more made manifest than *is* made manifest; and all that is made manifest, is just our good old reliable experience, which we've had to gain as much in the sweat of our brows, as we've had to gain our bread. But there's a type of mind that always acts as if it could get ahead of the primeval curse: it despises the slow ways of investigation and discovery, and claims some sort of insight into something that no two of its votaries agree upon, except in calling it 'spiritual truth.' And it is just this ' truth ' that makes up the vast mass of human error, of wasted power, of fruitless contention, of wars and inquisitions in earlier ages, and of grown men spending their time on ' heresy trials' in ours."

"I begin to understand now," said Nina, after a moment, " something you said yesterday morning about the woman I am growing to be, and also something else you said once when we were driving home from a tennis-match—it seems as if it must have been many years ago, before I was born. You said you didn't know whether Faith, according to my old ideas of it, was good for me, and that it *was* good for Mr. Courtenay. Of course I always knew why it was necessary for many people. I may not be very bright, but I know that most people could not understand what you and Mu—what I have learned here," she substituted, changing color again. Then she continued: " But it seems a pity that people should be hugging false ideals, and worshipping idols and pictures and Bambinos."

"Well," Calmire answered, "rag babies have often soothed bereaved and demented mothers. The point for you to realize, though, is that just as fast as humanity was able, it has got rid of anthropomorphic conceptions of the Infinite. The Greeks, you know, did not merely have an anthropomorphic god as the source of the Infinite Power, but had a special anthropomorphic divinity to account for each revelation of Nature—a universe full of gods fighting, loving, lying, and stealing, just as the Greeks did themselves. The Hebrews, while they professed to have but one Supreme being, had, like the Greeks, no end of supernatural ones—angels and devils and translated prophets. Then the early Christians added the Virgin and the saints, with altars and churches built to a great variety of them: Rome is certainly among the idolatrous cities of the world."

"But now, Mr. Calmire," she said, " you're talking of the Romish Church."

"Oh! The later churches," he answered, " much to their credit, have been practically reducing the number of those anthropomorphic conceptions and idolatries—those images—material and ideal; and that simply goes to prove what I said—that as fast as humanity can get some conception that the Power behind our lives is absolutely ineffable, it diminishes its attempts to express it."

"Haven't I seen somewhere," asked Nina, " the word Unknowable, with a big U?"

"Yes," said Calmire. "And in one sense, I think it a very unfortunate word. Of course only what is revealed to us, is knowable by us; and so the Revealing Power, except so far as revealed, is correctly called Unknowable. But as we know more every day, the Power is, in that sense, eminently knowable, and so far as the other word implies that it is not, the word is incorrect."

"How splendid—inspiring," cried Nina, " to realize that It *is* knowable, and that each little step in knowledge is a step in knowledge of the Infinite, of God."

"Yes," said Calmire. "I don't wonder at the enthusiasm of the great investigators, when it has such inspirations behind it. That enthusiasm was never as great as in our day, as the inspiration has never been so clear. I think you have now some idea of the 'Religion of Science.' It's so much decried, because it's so little understood."

"But," Nina expostulated, "I don't yet see how it can make people good. You said that you would come to that."

"So I will. But we haven't time now. You were getting toward it yourself a little faster than you suspected, when you exclaimed a moment ago that it was 'inspiring.' If you've recovered God and the spiritual world, suppose you try to take the rest for granted for the present."

"Yes, I've recovered something, or at least I have something new. But something is gone, something is gone!"

"Yes, my child, something that you supposed was there, but was not. As we grow older, something seems to go every day. But if we keep our souls open, something greater comes: we are on the surface of an Infinity, from which each step of evolution or discovery, brings a new revelation. Call it God or Nature or what you will—no sane man can escape the might and order and beauty of that Infinity, no skepticism can. It is here to-day, as it was before you felt uncertain about it. Doubts and disappointments and the contradictions of mistaken creeds, but affect the power to realize it: it endures despite them all. All our knowledge, all our inspirations, all our joys come from It; the laws under which we receive them are absolutely unvarying, absolutely consistent, and we can study them and benefit by them. Though we cannot yet know All, and cannot even conceive knowing *All*, we can have *faith* in the Infinite Power, Order, and Beauty from which our souls emanate, and of which, in limited measure, they partake; and so we can have faith that to use our little fragments of will in accordance with Its laws, is growth and happiness, and that opposition to them is destruction. That faith is founded on the evidence of our senses; it is unavoidable, and it is the foundation of all right reason and of all true religion."

Both sat silent some moments, when he said musingly: "Perhaps such broad outlooks make life more impersonal, but they make it more calm —but," he added in a moment, "the young do not care for calm: they want joy."

"I have done with joy," she said. "I came to you to ask the secret of your calm."

Calmire smiled with a skeptical feeling regarding her ignorant young despair, but thought best not to contradict her, and merely said:

"Well, really, dear, I believe the great secret of calm is the realization of the pettiness of all that can disturb our lives, in contrast with the immensity that includes them."

"Is that another name for Faith in God?" she asked.

"Faith in God is one of the names for it."

CHAPTER XLIII.

MARY'S STORY.

As Calmire mused over his talk with Nina, there kept coming up in his mind one sentence of hers: "I have done with joy."

"This is no mere religious upset," he had already said to himself more than once. "She never was *dévote*—she never was so attached to her old conceptions that the mere breakdown of them has afflicted her so. There's other trouble somewhere." Then he thought of his own great trouble over Muriel, and suddenly reflected that Nina had started to pronounce Muriel's name, changed color, and altered her phrase. "It must be there!—For some reason, it must be there!" he said half aloud. But he could not imagine any way to account for her knowing of Muriel's difficulty, and so dismissed the subject. But of course it would keep coming up.

One afternoon, they were out with the tandem again, and passed Courtenay driving in a low phaeton with his sister. As salutations were exchanged, the two women, though their goings and comings had happened to prevent their meeting yet, looked directly into each other's eyes with sympathetic recognition, and really bowed to each other, rather than to their actual acquaintances in the respective vehicles. After they had passed,

Nina said to Calmire: "She's so lovely! Why don't you tell me her story?"

He had already deliberated whether he should tell it to Nina, and, of course, he realized that it is always a relief to sorrow, to sympathize with the sorrows of others. He now felt, too, that Nina had reached the point intellectually where his objections to telling the story would not apply. He turned toward her and asked: "Do you want the gist of it, or the details?"

"All that you'll tell me."

"In that case," said he, "let's wait till we're quietly at home where there won't be so much to distract us. I don't want to have my mind too much off my leader this afternoon anyhow, for he's new to the position; or too much off my story either, for that matter, when I tell it."

They had started right after lunch in the brisk October afternoon, and got home long before sunset. It was warm enough to sit in the sunshine on the piazza in their wraps, and he began the story there.

"Well! When Mary was about eighteen, she fell in love with Arthur Woodleigh—a bosom-friend of mine, and the finest man I ever knew. They worshipped each other, and you know enough about Mary to realize that it was for good reason; if he was her equal, and he was.

"On leaving college, Arthur expected to preach, though he was like anything but the typical divinity student of that time. He was as splendid physically as Courtenay is now; but, unlike our St. John, he had had a pretty good crop of wild oats to sow, and had sowed them with a generous hand, as he did everything. He was full of love for all things that live, so when he outgrew his nonsense, the first serious question he put to himself was: how he could be of most use. Strange as it may appear to you, politics was seldom thought of then as a career of beneficence. There was not as much taught in the colleges about American history and politics, as about those of Greece and Rome: virtually all the colleges had been founded to make clergymen, and the ministry was the one career generally turned to by those whose first wish was to serve their fellow-men. So Arthur thought of preaching, and this, you can realize, made his suit for Mary particularly congenial to old Mr. and Mrs. Courtenay."

"Was the father a preacher too?" asked Nina.

"Yes, and the grandfather and the great-grandfather, and, for all I know, so on back through a line of savage medicine-men. But Mary's not that way, though. She takes after her mother, who was descended from the grandfather of Thomas Jefferson. But we're getting away from the story again. The old people favored the match, as I said. The facts that Arthur was rich and well-born, were not considered obstacles, though I believe the old gentleman did think his clothes fitted rather too well and were of rather too worldly a cut. Well, when Arthur got out of college (They were engaged during his Senior year) he began to study theology."

"Why didn't they marry?" asked Nina. "You say he was rich."

"Her parents persuaded them to wait until he

should be at least on the road toward his profession. But the road toward it proved the road away from it. Quantities of things that he had taken for granted until he stopped to think about them, he found he couldn't take at all."

" Such as ?" asked Nina.

" Well, he's told me that the very first thing that aroused his skepticism, was the attempt of the catechism to make him responsible to keep a promise which had been made for him by somebody else without his knowledge or consent—I mean the promises of his sponsors in baptism. Then, I remember, he and I had our doubts about eternal punishment, even at that time."

" Even at that time! Why, it was not so very long ago."

" About four hundred years, I think," said Calmire; " that is to say: that counted by revolutions in thought, it is about as long since the time when people began really to get hold of the idea of the Conservation of Force, and when Darwin's Origin of Species and Spencer's First Principles appeared, as it was before that time to the days of Luther."

" Well!" said Nina, with a long breath. " Perhaps I've begun to understand a little of that since I've been here."

" You see," said Calmire, " that the books which everybody reads now, or rather the echoes of which everybody reads, were then read only by very few. I had read them before Arthur had. He was a youngster in college when I was a man of thirty. He got to his skeptical attitude from the inconsistencies of what he was studying, and almost independently of modern science. Geology and Astronomy were in those days 'explained' away with more or less success. It was not really until Darwin began to take hold, that the new revolution began. But aren't you tired of having me talk all around Robin Hood's barn, when you simply want me to tell you about Mary and Arthur?"

"Oh no! We'll get to it in time, and I'm interested in all you're saying. Why, most of your outside talk has been simply in answer to my interruptions."

"We won't get through the tale to-day," said Calmire, "if I try to give you a detailed history of Arthur's mental development. To make a long story short, he soon came to look upon Christianity simply as upon other religions, admitting it to be the best, of course. But in those days, it hardly entered Arthur's head, or anybody's else, that there could be Religion pure and simple, as distinguished from the Christian religion or the Buddhist religion or the Mahometan religion."

"But," asked Nina, "by 'Religion pure and simple,' don't you mean the religion you have been showing me in Nature, and isn't that what I have often seen alluded to with respect by orthodox writers as 'natural religion'?"

"How our flowers do grow!" exclaimed Calmire, smiling. "No, the two things look a good deal alike, but they have important points of difference. Orthodox Christians have respected only so much of natural religion as supported their dogmas, and the discovery of the law of Evolution has so expanded natural religion as to make it virtually a new thing that destroys many of the dogmas. Very few orthodox writers have yet really tried to use it, though most of them have heartily abused it. Well," he continued, "of course Arthur's views of religion did not suit old Mr. Courtenay, and he regarded Arthur as on the way to eternal perdition."

"And that's Mary's story!" exclaimed Nina.

"Oh no: that's only the beginning of it! Of course the match was broken off, not by any means as a matter of conviction by Mary, but as what she considered a matter of duty. The worst of it was, that the more she tried to reason with her father, the more she convinced him that Arthur's notions were leading her to perdition as well as Arthur."

"What did Arthur do? Why didn't he take her?"

"Largely because she wouldn't go. She would make no promises to either side. At times, she would hope that her father would look on it differently, and she would cheer Arthur by counseling patience. At other times, she would simply preach submission, and poor Arthur's soul was being worn out of him by alternately climbing the heights of hope and being dashed into the depths of despair."

"But she must have suffered more still," said Nina.

"I'm not so sure of that," Calmire responded. "Men and women in love are spurred by widely different necessities—far more so than you can realize. To some men—probably to the manliest men, such a state of affairs is worse than it can be to women of corresponding womanliness. After two or three years of it, Arthur went off to the war. He had always felt it something of a duty to go, but he did not want to go away from his terrible problem."

"How did she feel about his going?" asked Nina.

"Oh, of course she thought him rather too fine for 'food for powder,' though she always said: 'If it comes to the point where such men are needed, I must submit.'"

"Why," said Nina, "weren't the best men needed? I thought brains had something to do with making wars short and merciful."

"And in so thinking," said Calmire, "you show yourself possessed of more of that article than most of your sex—more, probably, than poor Mary had at that time, though your heart is not juggling with your brains, as hers did. Her father was a parson, too; yours was a soldier in his day, and so was your great-grandfather, who was my great-grandfather too."

"Didn't you go to the war too, Mr. Calmire?"

"No."

"Why?"

"One reason was having so many relatives and associations on both sides, and having also a weak habit of looking on both sides of any question:—and there were other reasons. But if one could see the merits of a matter from in front as well as from behind, I think I should have gone in spite of all the reasons. Arthur went, however."

"Yes, from despair," said Nina. "How many went from pure patriotism?"

"That," said Calmire, "is not for a man who stayed at home, to judge. But you don't quite do Arthur justice. Despair certainly was in his heart, but there were other things too. And, in a short time, they included a bullet-hole."

"Of course!" said Nina, grasping the arms of her chair.

"But not one of the 'of course' kind," said Calmire, "or perhaps I would not have spoken of it quite in that way. The hole was not all the way through, but a graze on one side. It was an almost miraculous sort of wound, for a trifling difference in position, even if it had not perforated the organ, would have made the heart-beats so painful as to soon wear a man out. But this was a wound for a man with any decent show, to get well of."

"Oh he *must* have got well!" exclaimed Nina, leaning forward with a glowing face, her hands still grasping both arms of her chair.

"Ah, my child! my child!" exclaimed Calmire, "Nature doesn't work on your basis. The doctors said he would get well, and soon began to wonder why he didn't, and after some days, one of them told me (for I went down to Arthur) that they were satisfied something was preying on his spirits, and that he never could get well as long as it did. I wrote to old Courtenay. His answer was, substantially, that he was as sorry as I was (and I believe he was sincere), but that he could not see the gain in sacrificing Mary's eternal life for a few years of Arthur's earthly one.—That finished what little orthodoxy there was left in me!" said Calmire, "though I've recovered some of it since. But I was simply in a blind rage. I went to Arthur, and told him I was going after Mary, and that he must hold on till I should get back."

"Where were you?" asked Nina.

"Down in Virginia at a little farm-house near Spottsylvania. Arthur asked me if the old man had given in, and I told him, saving your presence, that the old man might go to the devil, that I was going to bring Mary. I can see his pale face now, as he smiled to thank me, but there was no hope in his smile.

"Well," continued Calmire after a little pause, during which Nina did put out her hand and take hold of his, "it was not a very quick journey—all sorts of obstacles in war-time, you know. But after three days, I was up at Mary's home. I had telegraphed her that Arthur would die if she did not go to him, and that I would be after her on Thursday morning—I think it was. The old man met me at the door, and she stood behind him with her bonnet on. I pitied the poor fellow almost as much as I did her. He was a saintly man, but a narrow one. He shook hands and said nothing until I was in the house. Then he said: 'Mr. Calmire, this is terrible!' 'Yes, I rather think it is!' said I. 'What are you going to do about it?' Perhaps I would not express myself in quite the same way now. I think I must remember every word of that interview. He answered: 'It seems to me the greater sin to let my daughter go.' 'What are *you* going to do, Mary?' I asked her. 'I'm going!' said she. 'My daughter! O my daughter!' cried poor old Courtenay, the tears streaming down his face, and I heard Mrs. Courtenay sobbing in the parlor. The old man turned and put his back against the door, and stood there crying, but as firm as a rock. I call him old man from the habit of that time, though he was really not over forty-five. I thought of our ages very distinctly, because I had to say to him: 'Well, Mr. Courtenay, we've barely time to catch the down train. Are you going to let us out?' 'I must not! Oh, I must not!' he cried. I shall never forget the feeling that came over me then: I was in a hurry, and I was not born a patient man, so I said to him (I wish now I'd put it milder): 'Mr. Courtenay, the rights of conscience and the rights of parental control can be carried to extremes. The line has got to be drawn somewhere, and I draw it at murder. You must let us go!' 'No, I must not! I must not!' he said, but stopped crying and began to look ugly. I was fool enough in those days to let another man's ugliness make me ugly too, so I said: 'Stand aside,' and went towards him. He said: 'If you take her, it must be by force, and force against the minister of God defending His law.' 'There's no time for cant,' said I (I'm sorry I did), and I put my hand on him. Mary grasped my arm. I told her that I shouldn't hurt him, but that he must let us go. Something in her eyes quieted me, and I said to him: 'Mr. Courtenay, I do respect your earnestness of conviction, and hate to have to oppose it, but I'm going to take Mary through that door; and unless you doubt it, to try to prevent me is simply cruelty to all concerned.' His eyes looked like blue steel, for perhaps ten seconds. Then he said: 'I cannot doubt it, and I may as well yield now as later; but all the same, I yield to force,' and he stepped aside. Mary kissed her mother, who now stood in the parlor door, and turned to her father, who seemed prepared to kiss her. She stood still, however, and said: 'Father, what can I say to Arthur?' He answered: 'My child, if my poor life could settle this question— could save his—I would give it, over and over again, but I cannot tell you anything else to say to him.' She said: 'Good-bye, Father,' and went out of the door without touching him. She has never seen him since."

"Can *she* be so unforgiving?" exclaimed Nina.

"It's not that," Calmire answered. "Or at least it's not entirely that. He has not since taken squarely any attitude that entitles him to forgiveness. Mary is no sentimentalist. The usual 'kiss and make up,' unless there's more behind it than there can be here, is the way of children. It's doubtful whether her seeing him would justify the pain it would bring upon her. Well!" Calmire continued after a moment, "he came to me with the strangest face I ever saw, and held out his hand. I had to take it: I don't remember that I ever rejected a proffered hand. He came to the door and said to us, so that Mary, who was already down the steps, could hear: 'May God bless you both and—and—' I think he said 'spare him,' but his voice sank and I'm uncertain. When I got Mary into the carriage, I noticed that a terrible change had come over her face. It was set and cold. She said, after I got in, 'Thank you, Legrand!' and grasped my hand so that it pained me, and held it until we had driven seven miles to the station, only answering me in monosyllables, until I saw that it was better not to talk to her.

"Well, we got down into Virginia. When we were within a few miles of the house where Arthur was lying (we were riding in an ambulance, and that, by the way, was the first time I saw Clint Russell: he was driving it) Mary pointed to a man in an army hat but a black coat, and asked if he was a chaplain. I told her I supposed so. Then she asked if there was one near Arthur, and when I said it was doubtful, she told me to ask if this one would go with us."

"She wasn't pestered about his soul?" exclaimed Nina. "Oh! she meant to marry him!"

"Yes. When we got to Arthur, the doctor told me he was just alive. I went into his room. He did not give any sign of recognition. I sent Mary in alone. She told me some time afterwards that his hand had closed on hers—that was all."

After a minute or two, Nina wiped her eyes and said:

"It sounds like two hundred years ago. Fortunately such things have grown rarer."

"Yes," said Calmire, "as dogma has lost its hold. It was not religion that made this trouble, but dogma—going outside of all real questions of moral life into a lot of factitious ones, and assuming as facts a lot of statements and theories on subjects that we know nothing about."

"But, Mr. Calmire, where does dogma begin and religion end?"

"Just where common sense and experience end. There's enough in the Bible that conforms to both, and it's easy enough to see how the rest got there."

CHAPTER XLIV.

COURTENAY'S FAITH.

But why had Courtenay been standing all this time with his feet pointing toward Nina and the grass growing under them? By September, he always needed a vacation, and always deserved it. This time, the nervous shock of his accident made him doubly need it. After he met Nina at the tennis-match early in that month, he met her but two or three times more, and where private chat was impossible; and then he was off, by previous arrangement, to spend some time with his parents. He had intended to get a chance to see Nina before going, by running over to say good-bye to Mr. Calmire. But an hour before he expected to start, he met that gentleman on the street, and in response to his interested inquiries, had to tell him of his intended vacation, and to receive his good-bye on the spot. This made him think of postponing his departure, but his faithfulness to appointments where others were concerned, made it natural for him to go, even had not his love for his parents made it unnatural to disappoint them. And toward them, he felt something more than ordinary love and duty. His father's relation to Mary inspired the son with an almost yearning pity. Years before, Mary had said to him: "Father probably admits no question of forgiveness; but tell him that I think I have conquered all bitter feeling, and that I will see him when I feel able to." But she had not felt physically able to, and Courtenay knew enough of the condition of her nervous system, to realize whenever she said this, that it was true. The father's condition, though he would not admit it to himself, was one of remorse. If he had been able to admit it and seek forgiveness, the occasion for Courtenay's pity for him would have passed.

As Courtenay thought of leaving the neighborhood of Nina, he said to himself: "The Lord will bless my following my duty," and he unconsciously made the fact that he had had this opportunity to follow duty in the face of his desire to see her, a half-realized argument that he and she were destined for each other.

Courtenay had but just returned from his vacation two days before Nina saw him driving with his sister, and it was not unnatural that two days later still, he should appear at Fleuvemont to "report himself" to his patron, though neither of them would have used that word.

This time, Fortune favored him. Calmire was away, and Nina was on the piazza in the warm October sun, when Courtenay approached the house. He had gone over by rail and walked up from the station.

When Nina recognized him, she felt a little shrinking; but it was too late to run away without hurting his feelings, and she did not wish to do that, nor is it certain that, all in all, she really wished to run away. She even had felt a desire to talk over some of her skeptical troubles with him. So she was perfectly truthful when, advancing to the top of the steps and holding out her hand, she said:

"I'm glad to see you, Mr. Courtenay, and especially to see you walking with such a vigorous step. Of course you're quite well?"

Perhaps her speech was a little more elaborate than it would have been if her self-consciousness had arisen only from the recollection of her "attempt to murder him," as Muriel had come to call it. But the sight of him had at once brought up not only what she felt of his sentiments toward her, but the thought of Muriel—or rather that thought intensified: the thought itself, with all its terrible complications, had seldom left her during many days. It made her life a double one.

"Oh yes, I'm perfectly well, thanks," Courtenay answered simply.

"Your vacation has done you good! Then you have enjoyed it."

"Yes, in a way I did. But I was impatient to get back."

"Why? Was not your work going on right?"

"Oh, it was not that." He had reached the Rubicon, but his plunge was an awkward though an honest one. "I wanted to get back to you."

"I should think you had had more reason to want to avoid me," she laughed, half nervously.

"No, no! God himself sent us to each other!"

From where he had seated himself, against the post at the edge of the piazza, his face was turned up to her with the fervor of conviction and adoration. It was very beautiful, but it struck her with misgiving. Expressions of adoration, she had known before: but the confidence in this man's face and speech was strange and startling. She had long felt that Courtenay loved her: but, young as she was, she was not a stranger to feelings of that kind. She was a stranger, though, to such confidence in an admirer: she had met him oftener than has been detailed here, but not often enough to account for this. Her blush was as much that of confusion as of modesty, when she answered, half at random:

"I don't understand you."

"You have been made the instrument of death and life to me. I was away from earth. When I came back, I came to you. When I stayed, I stayed for you. That I love you, is but the half. I live in you. You are my condition of being."

"Why, Mr. Courtenay, you hardly know me!"

"What is knowledge?" he asked, and, too absorbed to notice her startled shrinking, went on: "The pride of it is leading the world to destruction! One does not need any such mole's-wisdom to comprehend you. You do not need to be known: you are like the angels, for faith—and worship!"

No woman was ever indifferent to such address, and no devoted face ever glowed from canvas with more loveliness than was in Courtenay's as it yearned up toward her. For an instant, she was lost in his fervor and his beauty. Then there seemed to come to her a voice, calm and quiet, and with some reminiscent associations of the Infinite Order. It simply said:

"*Is this thing true?*"

And the answer she made was:

"*I*, a thing to be worshipped, when worship means what it does to him!"

All this went through her mind so fast that Courtenay hardly noticed her pause before, flushing, she said:

"Mr. Courtenay, you have done me the greatest honor that—"

"No; it's not that," he said, interrupting her, "it's not in that way—I don't do it: God appointed it. I don't deserve it, perhaps of myself I would not feel worthy to ask for it. But as God has sent us to each other, I humbly, but oh so gratefully, turn toward you."

Perhaps, as a woman, she would have been better pleased had the man thought more of his own feeling, and less of God's will; and certainly, as the woman she had recently become, she would have been better pleased had he had less confidence in his own ability to interpret the Infinite, less readiness to attribute to it any swerving aside to any special man from the courses laid out for all men; and less readiness to assume that if it were so to swerve, it would specially devise such kind and dignified means of introducing a country parson to a city belle, as having her run him down in a boat. But though she might have been better pleased, she was not quite displeased. She had too much healthy vanity to suppose his devotion quite limited to religious enthusiasm, and she could not be insensible to his merits or his charm.

Her natural candor, or unconscious tact, brought a diversion by letting him see this.

"Yet I respect you enough, Mr. Courtenay, to feel that the interpretation you have given to God's will, does me honor, even if I—if—if it's not on a strictly professional subject."

"Oh, my profession covers everything, or ought to. I'm a weak and fallible man, but surely if my office is to be useful in anything, it should be most useful in what most concerns the deepest feelings. But you know that I'm not speaking to you as a priest, but as a man, and as one who loves you.'

"But when I said that in doing so, you honored me, you disclaimed doing so."

"Yes, there is more than that."

"Now, Mr. Courtenay, listen to me." She did not at first speak with the tenderness that such women are apt to use when they have similar things to say. There was a certain assurance in his manner which seemed superior to the need for tenderness. But with her next sentence, her natural self had occasion to come forward. "I know what pain is, well enough to make being the cause of it hurt me. But I know we are apt to make it greater by trying to shut our eyes to painful things. I know you love the truth, or at least you love a great many things because you hold them to be the truth: but I believe that the way to truth is not by believing things because we find them pleasant, and still less by giving the beliefs we make for ourselves, a superhuman authority. For my part, much as I honor you, I'm not ready to flatter myself that Nature, or God if you prefer, has adapted us for each other at all. Probably to adapt us to each other," she added, smiling, "Nature would have to make me a much better woman."

"I know that you are as good as it is given to humanity to be," he protested. "And I know that Heaven sent you to me. Why, everything has been different to me since my eyes opened upon your face—my work, my faith have all been inspired by the very thought of you!"

She reflected what this meant in a life like his, and she contrasted with it, protestations which, young as she was, she had heard more than once, that her companionship *would* inspire lives that she knew had been empty, and were made to remain so. Here, without her even willing it, she actually *had* been made by this good man a helper in his beneficent work! What had her influence done for that other man who had broken her own life? In her girlish ignorance, she had not realized that Muriel's fault could have been committed before her influence touched him. Her life *was* broken, and yet here she was of use in Courtenay's. There still lingered in her, enough of her old enthusiasm for his faiths, to glow up under sympathetic stimulus. Those faiths were at the basis of his noble life, and she —actually she—had been a helper in that! She had not willed it. She had not deserved it. Her voice faltered as she said:

"Mr. Courtenay, I am unworthy of this. Even your goodness has not made me worthy of it."

"As if anything I could do, could be worthy of

you!" he answered. "But perhaps you will make me able to deserve you!"

That tone of confidence again! It was not arrogant. It certainly was not insincere. But *was it true?* She sat still for some time, pondering, leaning forward a little, her right hand turned upward lying in the palm of her left, her eyes steadily gazing over the river and the hills, as if the little hieroglyphs that the changing foliage was dotting over them, held hidden some answers to the riddles of her life. The past was pain and chaos, and seemed to have reached a definite and hopeless end. Here seemed offered her, order, usefulness, peace. The two visions opened before her, but only as two domains belonging to strangers—for contemplation: not, at the moment, with any sense of ownership actual or to come. But after she had regarded them a few seconds, abstractedly, almost listlessly, Courtenay being too gentle, and perhaps too confident, to interrupt her, she awoke, as it were, with a start, to the realization that the two realms were clamoring for a decision from *her*, and she deliberated a little more regarding them. To enter one, would be to condone a horrid wrong and to do a grievous injustice. That one was closed. But oh, how fair it seemed! How much of the pain there, was birth-throes of mind and character! All the heights were there, and over them, all the stars. The other was a flat noonday land, with farms and factories and schools and hospitals and work and stupid peace.

Then over it all, a quick cloud came and a thunderbolt fell: one was Muriel's land, and the other somebody's else! She did not care if it was God's; she would not enter it. She could not enter Muriel's, but she could remain a denizen of nowhere, if she must, and beat the universal air with tired wings all her days.

She turned to Courtenay. His face had become anxious now, pleading, and almost pathetic.

"No, my kind friend," she said, taking his hand "It is not always given to read God's will aright. Even were I to go into your life, I should spoil it."

"Why? How?" he exclaimed in astonishment.

"My friend, your thoughts are not my thoughts, and I fear that even your enthusiasms, noble as they are, are not my enthusiasms. I am interested in much that interests you, but I am more interested in things which do not interest you. Moreover, the things which interest you most, are not those which interest me too. To spend part of our lives together, but the best part of them separate, would be to wrong the best part of them."

"Why, I cannot even conceive what you mean," he answered.

"That but proves me right," she said with an almost regretful gentleness; "and to make you know what I mean, would bring no agreement, and might needlessly pain us both."

He was not very well-used to having people reticent with him, and he was somewhat used to overcoming what he called "difficulties" in the opinions of others. He was a little tempted to essay the same thing here.

"But, Miss Wahring," he said, "I am sure that if you will consider these difficulties with me, they will disappear. There can be but one truth, and surely if we seek it together we should find it."

"At the very outset, Mr. Courtenay, I do not believe that we could agree on the ways of seeking it."

This answer went a little deeper than he was used to, and he fell back on the remedy universal among doctors of the soul, as well as among doctors of the body, when the danger is not pressing—time:

"In time you will consent to discuss the subject. You live with people who, much as I honor some of them, are apt to confuse your leadings. Otherwise it would all be as plain to you as to me. I will say good-bye now, but I hope you will not find it disagreeable to see me in future."

"Not unless you make it so," she said with a faint smile, giving him her hand. "I am sorry to have had to—" she was going to say "pain you," but something in his confident air prevented, and she substituted "disagree with you."

"Oh, my faith is strong!"

He said it kindly and modestly, not aggressively.

And as he went, she pondered: "His *faith* is strong. Ah me, I fear I'm only a woman! How stupid men are! It would have made no difference though. He's so good and gentle! I hate to hurt him! But—but—but it ought to hurt him a little more!" And she laughed. Then she pondered and grew very serious, and said aloud: "I could not *depend* upon him."

A moment later, she asked herself, thinking of Muriel, "Could I—could one, depend upon *him?*"

CHAPTER XLV.

THE MORAL ORDER.

Mary Courtenay's story was followed before many days by Nina's meeting Mary herself. The two women became friends at once, all the more readily because Mary had been through much of the spiritual experience that Nina was now undergoing. But their sympathy in this regard was felt, rather than expressed, and when expressed was confined to incidental remark, because Nina feared to arouse painful reminiscences in Mary, and Mary no longer morbidly sought them.

Nina's mind was very full, however, of Mary's cruel history, and also reverted not seldom to the disappointment she had had to inflict on Mary's brother. These thoughts, added to those for which her own life was giving her abundant occasion, soon made her very conscious of a need not yet met in Calmire's efforts to prop up her faith.

One rainy evening Mrs. Wahring had left them alone by the library fire, when Nina broke a little congenial silence with:

"I've often thought lately about your quoting, once when we were all out in a shower, that the rain falls alike on the just and the unjust, and you added that lightning is no more apt to strike a bad man than a good one, and made fun about your being as safe as anybody. I know myself that wrong-doing often hurts the victim more than it hurts the wrong-doer, and often hurts the innocent outsider as much as it hurts the people directly concerned. Now in all this jumble, I can't yet keep up any steady faith in right and wrong and in a moral order, without a God to say what is right and wrong, and to punish wrong—if not here, hereafter."

Calmire answered: " There *is* a God, if you prefer that name, to 'say what is right and wrong,' and to reward right and punish wrong. But those things are not perfectly done, any more than anything else in this world is. Your trouble is an old, old fallacy. Lots of anthropomorphism is built on it. Because the natural course of things is not perfect as concerns morality, you're disposed to shut your eyes to the fact that it nevertheless does conserve morality, as far as morality is conserved at all. Of course the world is not evolved up to ideal morality, but it has got as far as passably good working-morality, and is constantly improving."

"But," Nina objected, "'the rain falls alike on the just and the unjust' still."

"Yes; but there are not so many unjust for it to fall upon."

"But Nature is blind—the power behind it is blind!" said Nina, mournfully.

"We're getting into terribly deep water," said Calmire, "but it won't do to forget two things—the first is, that rain and lightning don't include the whole question."

"Yes, I've thought about that," said Nina.

"After all that rain and lightning do, doesn't the moral man get along better than the immoral one?"

"Yes, take it all in all, though to the superficial glance, he doesn't always seem to. But it's really a truism to say that he does, because when you come to boil it down, morality is but a term for the conduct which experience has found, in the long-run, in closest conformity with Nature's laws, and therefore that which we get along best on. Those laws, imperfectly as they have yet got our planet evolved, generally catch the violator of them pretty promptly, whether observers realize that he is in their grip or not. I often think of what an eminent artist told me after painting the portrait of one of the richest men of our time, who had made his money dishonestly, but had all the externals of happiness. The artist said that in studying the man's face, he had found more misery in it than in any other that he ever saw."

"That's very interesting," said Nina. "I wonder if he finds as much happiness in the moral faces!"

"I don't remember certainly," said Calmire, "but I have an impression that he said he did; but such an impression would be very natural from the experience of all of us."

"Yes, that's true," Nina assented. "A man can't escape his sin, after all,—or his virtue."

"There you go again!" said Calmire, smiling. "You persist in asserting half the time, though you deny it the other half, that the adjustments are perfect. The fact is, that many a graceless dog and many a saint both escape their deserts."

"Yes, so they do!" she exclaimed. "But most people get them, after all. But what is the other point you want me to bear in mind?"

"That beyond the graceless dog and the saint, though including them—taking the Universe at large, morality can't be escaped, unless by accident. It is a fundamental condition of all things and of all law—as much as gravitation is."

"Why, that's awfully strange and interesting!" exclaimed Nina. "I supposed that morality only had to do with man, and pretty civilized man at that. Tell me more of it, please."

"Well," Calmire went on, "you're ready to say 'good man' and 'bad man,' aren't you?"

"Certainly! Why?"

"Never mind why, just yet. And you'll say 'good dog' and 'bad dog,' won't you?"

"Yes."

"And 'good fish' and 'bad fish'?"

"Well, I don't know about the goodness or badness of a fish. I can't conceive a fish having much moral character."

"The 'much'ness of it is not what I'm after," said Calmire. "Have you ever heard of a whale (though he isn't a fish, by the way, but he'll do)—of a whale in a rage—stubborn and unreasonable, when all that gentlemen required of him was to be killed in an amiable and accommodating spirit?"

"Yes," Nina admitted. "And I suppose the carp at Versailles who used to feed from the king's hand, had their willing days and their sulky days, and were called 'good' or 'bad.'"

"Unquestionably," assented Calmire. "And now don't be very critical just yet, but answer my questions simply. As to fish: you would say 'good hook' or 'bad hook,' wouldn't you?"

"Yes."

"And 'good steel' or 'bad steel'?"

"Certainly."

"And, as to the components of the steel, 'good iron' and 'bad iron' or 'good carbon' and 'bad carbon'?"

"Yes."

"And you could go on to say 'good' or 'bad' carbonic acid gas, or hydrogen or oxygen, or anything else?"

"Certainly, but—"

"Never mind the 'buts' just now, we'll take care of them later. Now I want you to see what quality all these things, from gases up to man, have in common, that makes you willing to apply the terms good and bad to them all."

"I shouldn't say 'from gases up,'" responded Nina, "but *from man down*. I suspect we apply the terms good and bad to the lower things only metaphorically, and that their true application is only to a moral being."

"Oh what a Nina you're getting to be!" exclaimed Calmire, approvingly. "But, my bright girl, you're wrong all the same, unless you're ready to contend that the first grunt of approval from which our word good is descended, was aroused by some companion of the creature who gave it, rather than by its food, or a soothing ray of sunshine, or some other contribution to its creature-comfort."

"Wait!" cried Nina. "That's too much all at once, make it easier, please."

"Well, that grunt meant 'good,' didn't it? Now do you suppose it was first applied to another animal, or to something to eat? If the latter, its later use toward man was metaphorical from its first use toward the food: and even if the former, its application to man grew upward from the beast."

"It wasn't a grunt at all," said Nina, "but a bird's song!"

"Ah, my sweet little poet, the facts are too plain! The bird was evolved long after that sound. True, we can hardly corral the very *first* grunt. There were probably a good many simultaneous ones for very different reasons and of very different kinds, some of them not audible to such ears as ours. But what did all those that meant approval have in common?"

"A feeling of satisfaction, I suppose you mean," Nina answered.

"And what did the objects which called them forth, have in common?" asked Calmire.

"Why, the capacity to arouse feelings of satisfaction, of course," responded Nina. "But you're not going to claim that that's a moral quality: why! the objects of men's vices—the very act of murder, have that."

"Good for you, my child!" exclaimed Calmire. "But don't go too fast: remember that a thing may be good or bad for a thousand reasons. Brutus thought Cæsar's murder good: Cæsar, so far as he had a chance, undoubtedly thought it bad. But take a simpler case: one glass of brandy is taken to produce inebriety, another is taken to save life; the toper says: 'The brandy is "good" to make me drunk,' and the invalid says: 'The brandy is "good" to make me well.' Now, as you said before, they are both 'good' to produce feelings of satisfaction, but what is the difference in the feelings of satisfaction here, that makes one immoral and the other moral?"

"Why, one's bad and the other's good!"

"But *why* is one bad and the other good?" Calmire asked.

"Why, in the long-run one does harm and the other does good," Nina answered.

"Don't use, in an explanation, the term that needs explaining. Think and try again."

"Oh, I'm too stupid!" exclaimed Nina. "Won't you help me out?"

"No, you're not stupid, but you poor girls don't get any training. Now is one bad because it tends in the long-run to lessen the man's happiness and that of others; and the other, good because it tends to increase the man's happiness and that of his friends?"

"Certainly."

"Well now is happiness—? But I won't ask hard questions any more just now. We've got back to the standard test of morality—effect upon the aggregate happiness. But weren't there good iron and good oxygen on the planet before there was any happiness to be affected by them?"

"Certainly."

"Why do we call them good? But I'm questioning you again."

"Never mind!" said Nina. "That's plain enough. It's because they had in them the possibility of contributing to happiness."

"Well now, hasn't everything?" asked Calmire.

"Why, where would evil come from, then?" asked Nina in return.

"Simply from misuse of the good things. Let's take a string of 'horrible examples'—suppose, for instance, that a rat eats a wounded humming-bird; a rattlesnake kills a man; a disappointed office-seeker shoots a patriot: don't you think of anything not unmitigatedly bad in those cases?"

"I see," Nina replied, "that although the humming-bird was a finer thing than the rat, the rat's appetite was a good thing for himself."

"And wouldn't it have been a good thing for everybody," asked Calmire, "if he had only eaten as he usually does, matter that might otherwise become offensive? So after all, wasn't his eating the humming-bird, merely a misuse of the good? Now how about the politician shooting the patriot?"

"I can't find any good at all there," Nina answered.

"It probably took some courage, and skill with his weapon, didn't it?" asked Calmire.

"Yes, but the motives directing them were wholly bad."

"I'm not so sure of that. I suspect that, at the bottom, they were motives of self-preservation—and a desire to support his family, and a rage at anybody trying to keep him out of a place, like that of a tigress at seeing her cubs' meat interfered with."

"It does look like it," said Nina. "What's the key?"

"Simply deficiency of other good motives to restrict the rat and the rattlesnake to victims inferior to themselves, and the politician to less objectionable methods; and, too, deficiency of ingenuity to devise such methods. It's our deficiencies that cause our evils—all the powers that we really have are intrinsically good, only we have not enough to keep action always in a good direction. Death itself is only a lack of powers: it is not a positive thing. Yet, the world over, they've regarded it as a positive thing, and got up angels or devils, to produce it, when, after all, it's only life that can be produced. Death is merely the absence of it."

"But evil is here all the same, Mr. Calmire, and inasmuch as it *is* here, what difference does it make how it got here—as you said about our worthy selves, some time ago, when you were talking of Darwinism?"

"All the difference in the world: because how it got here determines how it's going to get away from here. If evil is only a bad adjustment of good things—such as the bad adjustment of your good needle to your good fingers, when you prick them—we know how to improve our adjustments and decrease the evil. We don't attempt it any longer with incantations, relics, and holy water; nor do we need to pester ourselves over the old questions of how God can have all the power there is, and yet the devil have nearly as much, and why God doesn't kill the devil."

"But," expostulated Nina, after a moment, "however we try to decrease the evil, we can't restrict all animals to vegetable food. Some creatures have always got to be killed to feed others."

"Quite probably, until the others stop being fed—until, in short, dissolution is well under way: but that doesn't concern us very closely. I didn't say, however, that evil would ever disappear from the planet entirely—at least until good does: as long as there's anything going, I suppose it will sometimes get out of order: I only said that we can make evil constantly decrease: creatures that live by the destruction of others, are being hunted off the earth themselves."

"But," said Nina, "a partiality for game-pie is not yet set down among the capital offences."

"No, and I don't say that it's going to be. I do say, though, that your ancestors, before they became tillers of the soil, lived on other animals to a vastly greater extent than you do; and I do say that the modern states pay bounties for the destruction of dangerous creatures."

"Then," said Nina, "the evil days of the snakes and tigers have come."

"Yes," answered Calmire, "but they are more than proportionally better days for better creatures. Don't think, though, from anything I've said, that I set this up for a perfect world—now or prospectively. It's an imperfect world—a very imperfect one I suppose, though I don't know where anybody venturing on that statement, has found his standard of a better one: but imperfect as it is, it's not a positively evil world; but only negatively evil—good can be permanently advanced in it, and evil can't. Everything, properly used, can do more good than harm. In other words, the proper use of anything is moral: and here we are back to the subject we started with: for as every act uses something, so every act is moral or immoral."

"But Mr. Calmire!" objected Nina. "There are a great many acts that we never think of calling moral or immoral."

"Yes, my child. In most cases the moral quality is so nearly balanced or so slight that we don't notice it—sometimes we even mistake it, but it's there all the same, and we can't escape it. Every possible act of man or process of nature, is legitimately open to the question whether it tends in the long-run to increase or diminish the happiness in the Universe. On that fact, man's moral nature rests: his conduct inevitably must be shaped with reference to it, and always has been. So has the conduct of every other creature capable of conduct, of course at first very blindly and in very few particulars, but gradually increasing in complexity. Our old friend the jelly-fish was moral, as far as he went, in seeking the light places—and would have been immoral to stay in the dark ones where food was scarce, and where colds were to be caught, assuming him subject to that disorder. The beaver is moral in making his dam, and a beaver who won't work at it, is an immoral and reprehensible little beast. A squirrel who lays up a store of nuts for himself and his family, is as moral, in that particular, as a man who does a similar thing, and a squirrel who does not, deserves to go to the poor-house. Bees and ants are cited as moral examples by the greatest teachers. In short, the Universe, or our share of it, is so ordered that creatures *must* be moral to a certain extent or die.

"But the higher moralities flow just as inevitably from the operations of the Universal Law. Food, shelter, defence, are necessary. They can be had better by coöperation than by solitary effort or by mutual pillage. The law that makes it to the advantage of the beavers and ants and bees and even wolves and jackals and elephants to help each other, is the same law that, in a higher evolution, makes it to the advantage of men to help each other. Human society is but these lower societies evolved—patriotism, philanthropy, altruism are but the evolution of the social virtues that we see starting in the lower creatures. To make the higher society possible, children must be educated in the family, and the family, conjugal fidelity, the lofty ideals of love, all have their sources in the demands of the higher social evolution. Patriotism and the civic virtues follow in here, as a matter of course. In short, looking over the whole field of conduct, it grades insensibly from the lowest act of self-preservation up to the highest act for the amelioration of the race. You can't draw the line anywhere between the jelly-fish seeking the light places, and Washington devoting himself to liberty. Thus morality, in its various forms, has grown up inevitably in the universal system of things, as stars and planets, and all the forms of life, have grown."

"Then do you think," asked Nina, "that morality is on the other planets just as it is on ours?"

"Not *exactly* as it is on ours: that can't be; but morality must be, in some degree, everywhere. Let's look into it a moment: for your view can't be too broad. We know that the other bodies floating in space, are under the conditions of time, space, matter, and force, just as we are. We know that they contain many of the same chemical elements that our planet does. We know it absolutely, only of some of the suns: but the planets are pieces of the suns. We know, deductively, that all those spheres have been evolved from some comparatively homogeneous form of matter, as ours has—in short, we know that they are subject to the law of evolution. To assume that they all are not inhabited by sentient beings, is harder than to assume that some of them are; and, under the law of evolution and dissolution, those beings have got to die and others be produced to take their places. Now we are not apt to think of morality as coming in before the human family, but there are very decided and very beautiful moralities in the conjugal and parental relations of many of the lower creatures. There, you have the elements of moral evolution; and the evolution is recognizable as soon as there comes a subordination of the present to the future, a devotion of parents to children, and some sort of public opinion and regulation. These may not be higher than they are in a band of coyotes, but they are morality, all the same. And, you know that, going way below family relations, the lowest animals and even the vegetables must have some capacity of adaptation to their futures and to each other's existences. In fact, the laws which make a stone on the hillside roll when the stone propping it is removed, and continue to roll until other stones are interposed, and to stop when they are interposed, are not only mere physical laws, but are also laws adapting the stone to the other stones around it. But bless me!" he broke off, "this is getting awfully long-winded. But I'm coming out at something. Do you think you can live through it?"

"Try me," she answered.

"Well," he went on, "as there is that side to the laws which regulate the stone, I don't know that we can deny the germs of morality to the stone, although, of course, we do not ordinarily dissociate them from consciousness. Now to carry it even a step farther back, I don't see but what the germs of morality must be in the simple stardust that first begins to whirl into suns. Certainly, to deny to the star-dust the germs of morality, would be to deny the law of evolution—to say that, later, the germs of morality had been *created*, and that is something that, despite Genesis, we simply can't conceive. Morality must have been evolved, with everything else. The whole universe, then, must always have been moral, though in a rather small way here and there, especially between evolutions of systems. Of course, now, we don't call any of the functions of inanimate matter, morality, any more than we call a hundred and fifty pounds of inanimate matter, a man. But the man is evolved out of the inanimate matter all the same, and so must the morality be evolved from its corresponding primitive conditions. The conditions for both the man and the morality are in the inanimate matter and the primitive law. Well, then, it seems pretty plain that morality is, potentially at least, throughout the universe, just as matter is, and must appear in corresponding degree wherever evolution sets in. The claim, then, that any man or set of men have brought it on earth, or that it depends upon the system of any lawgiver, is absurdly belittling. Its sources are wide and remote in the very foundations of the universe. The claim that the fading away of any categorical system of it, is going to remove it from among men, is of course equally belittling. Hundreds of its codes have risen and fallen, but it has remained and increased; and for all I can see, despite the impression of many that our immediate traditional religion is losing its hold, morality was never as high among us as it is to-day. And moreover, I don't know any good reason for supposing that the morality of spheres whose evolution is older or faster than ours, may not be as far in advance of ours, as ours is of the coyote's."

"Do you know what you've been doing for me?" asked Nina,—"better even than saving my life?"

"I know what I've been trying to do. I've been trying again my old, old task, of showing you that anthropomorphism belittles the Source of all things —of morality with the rest; and that all the ideas we most value—now the idea of morality, as before, the idea of a God and of a spiritual world—rest on foundations broader and deeper than any that human attributes can express. Now you can judge for yourself whether you would rather have your morality on this basis—that all our talks have been leading up to, or on the command of an anthropomorphic God. You see that it does make a difference, even in every-day morality, whether one believes in a Universe of infinite Order under the control of Law—a Kosmos, or in a Chaos with order depending on the whims of some arbitrary, vacillating, even revengeful creature like a man."

"I see it now and feel it," said Nina, "just as you want me to, and just as I want to myself. But I know that my realization of it is going to grow weak again."

"Why bless me!" exclaimed Calmire. "Haven't all the saints in the calendar always prayed for the strengthening of their faith? And though they did not have a chance at modern views of things, some of them were tremendously strong men. Don't expect more from yourself than they were able to reach."

"Yes! But our faiths are on broader and surer foundations than theirs, and ought to be firm."

"But yours are assailed by foes that theirs were not," said Calmire. "Comparatively few of them had to make such a transition as you are making. But you'll be helped if you try always to realize this: Morality is not narrowed to any one doctrine or system. *All* law is moral: so much of it as we succeed in learning, it is moral to follow."

"And all this," said Nina to herself, "is not so different from what Muriel told me."

CHAPTER XLVI.

MISERY MAKES STRANGE BEDFELLOWS.

OF the various unhappy people with whom this narrative is concerned, certainly not the least unhappy at this stage of their experiences, was Minerva Granzine. The strain was beginning to tell upon even *her* health. Dark hollows were appearing around her gazelle-like eyes, and her springing step was becoming heavy. Strange as it may appear, part of that strain was an honest sense of shame. Such a sense is not inconsistent with many an impulse which leads to occasions for it: both can be fervid in a fervid temperament: the only question is: Which is the more fervid? Minerva's mother, while in some ways kind and forbearing, was possessed by a burning ambition, more destructive, if possible, to the peace of all the household, than any passive lugubriousness, or even any bursts of temper, could have been. The idea of marrying her daughter to Muriel Calmire had become a monomania that would have lasted even if the shame had been entirely out of the way. Despite her impotent threats to Calmire, she still hoped to cover the matter up, feeling that she had risked no farther exposure in forcing her secret on Nina Wahring. Such was her state of mind, however, that in any way to remind her of the subject, even by the mute appeals for sympathy so natural to her unhappy daughter, was to start her on a tirade of conjectures, fears, hopes, and abuse of Muriel and all his race, which even Minerva's rudimentary conscience was sometimes stirred into feeling excessive.

The state of affairs in the Granzine house was so far known only to the mother and daughter. The elder woman's strange strong character was superior, or perhaps inferior, to any irrepressible craving for sympathy or counsel, even from her husband. His relation to his wife and ostensible daughter, which Calmire and Clint Russell knew, illustrated the weakness of his fibre. The wife did not care even to lay her own burden upon it, much less to admit it to a share in the responsibility of supporting her ambitions against the house of Calmire. The time might come when she would have to; but should the secret once be opened to the public, there would then be, even to Granzine's timid nature, less temptation for retreat.

Minerva, then, was worse than alone in her misery. At least she would have been, but for one strange string of circumstances. Living in a little cottage behind a wood passed by a by-road, some four miles Northwest of the Granzines', was a girl named Huldah Cronin, who, a year and a half before, on taking her wages one Saturday evening at one of the mills, had said to the cashier: "I shall not be back Monday, Mr. Blakeman. You may as well take my name off the roll." On her way to her boarding-house, she had surprised a flashy friend of hers at Botts's livery-stable, by requesting him to send a carriage for her at nine o'clock. When the carriage came, she asked the driver to go to her room and take her trunk and bag, and while he was performing that operation, she called the landlady into the hall and said: "Mrs. Orange, I want to bid you good-bye. You're entitled to a week's notice before I leave my room; I prefer to pay you a week's rent instead. You have always been kind to me, and I thank you." Then she passed into Mrs. Orange's hand, bills which represented all of the wages she was known to have drawn, but two dollars, which she subsequently gave the hackman; and without waiting for a word from the astonished woman, she followed the hackman to his vehicle and was driven off to the cottage where she had lived since. From that time, she had never been in the town of Calmire by daylight, and had refused, through a middle-aged negress, to see two or three of her old cronies who had traced her to her retreat. In Minerva's country walks, in some of which she had not been alone, she had occasionally passed Huldah driving in a pony-carriage, but had not, apparently, been noticed by her.

One moonlit Saturday evening, soon after Muriel had gone away, Minerva was walking home from the early choir rehearsal alone and rapt in revery, when, not far from her own home, she was aroused by hearing her name spoken. Beside her at the curb, was standing Huldah's pony-carriage.

"Get in here," said its occupant.

Minerva, as was her custom when commanded, obeyed.

"It's a beautiful night," said Huldah; "we'll have a drive."

"But, Huldah, what makes you take me?"

"I'll take you home in ten minutes, if you want me to."

"But you're so queer!" exclaimed Minerva.

"You can't tell me anything about myself that I don't know," said Huldah, "and I sha'n't tell you anything that you don't know: so neither of us will make much out of that subject, and we'd better talk of some other one. I'm sorry for you, Minerva Granzine; and that's all I'm going to say on *that* subject: so we'll have to take up another one still. Have any new books come to the library this week? I sent for some Saturday, and they were behindhand."

"But," exclaimed Minerva, startled, and with her usual flush, "why do you say you're sorry for me?"

"Because I am."

"But what makes you so?"

"I've watched your face. That's all I know, and all I care to know. Can you tell me about the books?"

"I don't know. Yes—that is, I believe mother said this morning that a new bundle had come."

"Do you read much now?" asked Huldah.

"I never did very much, you know," answered Minerva. "I haven't much lately, either."

"Your mother does," said Huldah. "I should think she'd make you."

"Well, I don't know. She doesn't seem to care much to have us read her sort of books. Johnny hates 'em."

"Queer fellow, that Johnny!" Huldah exclaimed. **"There's more man in him than in any boy in Calmire."**

"Yes! He's like mother in some ways, but he's soft and gentle like father too. Johnny used to think a great deal of you."

"The first foolish thing I ever heard about him!" commented Huldah. "Do you sing as much as ever?"

And so the talk went on, gradually getting into a natural flow, and several times ten minutes had elapsed before Minerva's strange entertainer, who had made the poor girl nearer happy than she had been for many days, and who had kept out of town during most of the drive, drew up on a side street between the church and Minerva's home, while saying:

"Come to the powder-house field beyond Jim Miles's Tuesday, at two, and I'll give you another ride."

"Oh! I'll be so glad! You're very good to me."

Then said the other:

"Good-bye. I've let no woman kiss me for two years, but you may as well."

And Minerva did it, and, wondering, went home where her mother, used to her delays with her young companions, received her without remark.

On the Tuesday, which was a beautiful day, Minerva, not, strange to say, more than three minutes behind her appointment, met Huldah, had a delightful drive, in which the latter neither asked nor told anything personal, and was set down near four o'clock about a mile from home, at an intersection with the main road. This was repeated the next Tuesday, Huldah always fixing the same time. On that occasion Minerva, feeling

Misery Makes Strange Bedfellows.

helped by the drive and the sympathy, walked along homeward with steps more light and careless than she had taken for many a day, until, after about quarter of a mile, stepping on a displaced board over a culvert, her foot slipped, she felt a twinge of terrible pain, fell, and fainted.

When she came to, she felt dazed, but soon tried to rise, and was prevented by the pain in her ankle. Then she began to look around and wonder who might come to help her, when what should appear, coming from town, but two prancing horses in a victoria with two men on the box, whom she soon recognized as in the liveries of Calmire.

"Not that! not that!" she exclaimed aloud. "I *must* not be seen lying here by them!"

She made an effort to rise, that would have done even her mother credit, fell and fainted again.

Her eyes opened on the face of Nina Wahring, who was bathing Minerva's forehead with a handkerchief which had been moistened by the footman, in the rill under the culvert.

Minerva uttered a faint scream, and ejaculated:
"My God! *You?*"

Then she closed her eyes again, not altogether in weakness: for she tried to cover them with her hands.

Nina, infinitely distressed, was for a moment dumb. Then she said:

"You must be much hurt, poor child. I want to help you."

"Oh, no! No! No!" cried Minerva, with as much force as could well be left in a woman who had just fainted twice.

By this time, Nina was herself.

"Blossom," she said to the footman, in her calm sweet tones, "perhaps you and Williams had better go back to town for a doctor." But as soon as the man was at a safe distance on the box, she called out to him: "Stay where you are for the present. I may want you more than the doctor."

Then she bent over Minerva, and said, while she gently stroked her forehead: "You *must* compose yourself and tell me quietly what it is. Did you fall?"

"Yes."

The pain made the answer spontaneous, but she would have yielded, as usual, without it; and she was already soothed by the calm spirit beside her.

"Are you in great pain?" asked Nina.

"Oh, yes. It throbs fearfully."

"Where?"

"My limb." (Mrs. Granzine's elegances had not been entirely wasted on Minerva.)

"Your leg? Which one?"

"The left. Oh, it hurts so! down by the foot."

"Blossom, bring a cushion, and put it under her head," called Nina. "Do you feel too faint for it?" she asked, turning to Minerva.

"No, I think not. How good you are!"

The transfer was tenderly made. Nina got Minerva's handkerchief, told the footman to wet it and any he and the coachman might have, and proceeded to take a look at the injured member. The ankle had already begun to swell, and a touch to it was agony.

"I wish I knew whether to cut the boot!" mused Nina aloud.

"Oh yes, do open it!" said Minerva.

"I think we'd better not," concluded Nina. "I think we ought to bandage it tightly. The cold water will prevent its hurting you so much."

"Oh, it will hurt so to tie it!" cried Minerva.

"I hope not," said Nina. "I'll squeeze the water over it gently first, and make it numb."

"Oh! Oh! Oh!" cried the sufferer, a few moments later, as the first drops fell. But soon the cooling influence so gently administered began to tell, and in a little while the fair surgeon had the soothing bandages in place.

"Now do you feel stronger?" she asked.

"Oh, so much better!" said Minerva, looking, for the first time, into the face of her benefactor, and bursting into a fresh torrent of tears, with which physical pain had very little to do.

"We must let you rest a little, and then put you into the carriage and take you home," said Nina.

"Oh, no, no!" protested Minerva. "Not in the Calmire carriage! Let the men send somebody for me, *please* do!"

"No. It would take too long. Such things always take longer than one expects. You might catch cold lying out here, and I don't think that ankle is a good thing to catch cold with. It's getting late too, and it's no longer Summer."

"And you think of all this for me!" blubbered poor Minerva, again weeping copiously.

"You're not safe from cold there now," was Nina's answer. We must lay a cushion under you, but that will make your head lower still, and it's too low already: so we must have two, and I will sit on one, and hold your head in my lap."

"Oh, don't touch me! Don't touch me! I'm not fit!" moaned the girl.

"Blossom! Come and help me!" called Nina, who had managed to keep the man out of easy earshot when not needed.

"Oh, I'm so much better! I can help myself!" sobbed Minerva. But a little help was not superfluous in establishing her on Nina's lap, where she lay quietly weeping and wiping with some sort of a coquettish little apron, the few tears that did not eventually trickle over upon Nina's devoted costume. At times she moaned: "I don't deserve it!...I'd rather you'd killed me." And Nina simply soothed her with some such phrase, gently uttered, as "Hush, child!" (The 'child' was several years older than Nina.) "If you don't keep calm, you'll not be strong enough for us to get you into the carriage."

What Nina felt during the strange time while this was going on, she never clearly knew. She was inclined to think that she did not feel anything at all, except sympathy with a creature in pain, and the necessity of getting the girl home. Whatever she felt, she sat and stroked the girl's hair and cooed little soothing nothings to her, until after about ten minutes, Minerva looked calmly up at her and said:

"You dreadful angel! I think I'm strong enough to be moved now."

Then she reached up, seized Nina's hands, and covered them with kisses and a fresh burst of tears.

And Nina, for the first time, felt something too. It was as if a hand grasped her throat, and there was a drop on Minerva's forehead that did not come from her own eyes.

Soon she was lifted in Blossom's burly arms, and transferred to the carriage, Nina all the while holding the leg above the hurt ankle.

Then Nina, the labors and dangers over, felt the second emotion that she afterward could recall. It seemed impossible for her to get into the carriage. But without violating truth, she could say gently, as she stood beside Minerva:

"You seem very safe there, but your leg is bent. I think you will be easier if you sit more cornerwise, and we move your feet more to the left. I can walk beside you just as well as not."

Then occurred the strangest thing of the whole experience. Minerva leaned over, at the cost of some pain, and murmured so that the man holding the door open might not hear:

"It makes me miserable to have you touch me. And yet if you will sit beside me and hold my hand, I shall be stronger and better the rest of my life, and God will bless you!"

Nina got into the carriage, with a feeling as if she were entering a church.

Somehow, she never remembered quite how, she got Minerva home, and got back to Fleuvemont.

There she escaped all the household but Calmire, who felt that something had gone wrong with her. She took his hand with a smile that made his heart ache, then walked mechanically to her room, threw herself face downward across the bed, and moaned: "My God! My God!—My lost God!"

CHAPTER XLVII.

THE UNKNOWN GOD.

WHEN Nina went to her toilet-table to prepare for dinner, (she was not addicted to convenient headaches, or to yielding to inconvenient ones,) she started to see there a note directed in Muriel's hand. It ran simply:

"It may be some time before I see you, and I want you to know something *now*. You have done for me, from the first, much that I did not realize till very lately. You have made me a better man. Since I first saw you, I have been Galahad.
"M. C."

She had picked up the note, trembling and deadly pale. She read it once impatiently without taking in its significance; then she read it again more deliberately, and at the last word, the color rushed to her face. Her hands dropped, both holding the note. After a moment, she said aloud: "He can't have supposed that I knew", and in another moment, she said to herself: "Perhaps he thought I might come to know!" Then she read the note again, kissed it passionately and put it in her bosom.

That night, it may well be supposed, was a restless one for Nina. From Muriel's note, she had gained a strange sad exultation, and notwithstanding her outburst on reaching her room in the afternoon, she had found a certain peace in the recollection of her Samaritan-like ministrations to the girl who, responsibly or not, was the one baleful shadow on her life; she even got something like comfort from that poor creature's " God will bless you." But who was God—what was God—to bless? This diverted her thoughts to the aching questions she had taken to Calmire, and they alternated with questions of her future and Muriel's.

Should she answer his note? No, not now! It called for no answer, and there was nothing to say. He could not know, and she could not tell him, that it meant to her already what, he plainly feared, he might some day have occasion to wish it to mean. But was fear of future possibilities his only motive? Plainly not: he might, perhaps would, have written the same thing, had such possibilities not existed. He was grateful to her—and there was more than that. For her pure mind, his almost shameless candor held no repugnance, and despite her misery, she felt very proud—proud of what she had done for him—proud of him and almost grateful, in her turn, to him, and she felt the impulse to write and tell him so. But no, it was impracticable now. Oh, what was practicable —what could become practicable?

The idea that he had ever loved Minerva had not once entered Nina's mind, and with this letter proving his regeneration, she could "forgive" that mysterious crime of his, if it really was a crime calling for forgiveness: in fact, as she all at once recognized with triumphant joy, it had not been a crime against *her* at all. But there would be that other woman and her child! Could they be shut out of Muriel's home, and she feel a right to share it? Besides, he had not asked her to share his home. But she knew! Alas! She knew, too, where his duty was. *What* it was, was too vague for her to think out: but *where* it was, she had a woman's intense conviction. All she could do for him now, was to keep him there. She had done something for him, he had told her so; she might have done everything, but it was now too late! Too late! But she could hold him to his duty, and that she would.

And of course she would do it with a woman's passion for self-immolation.

Then, as she peered into the mysterious future, questions of Providence and God, came up again and filled her mind.

After she had lain many hours wearily pondering all these things, she yielded to the temptation that the gleams of dawn had been sending through the blinds, and arose and opened one.

She uttered an exclamation at the scene.

Just below Fleuvemont, the river widened and made a great backward curve by some obstructing hills, so that Nina's window in a South-East turret commanded a view of the heights where the sun was coming. It had just begun to color the long stretch of sky and stream: above the line of hills, the heavens were a dark dull scarlet, like faintly glowing iron, and they shaded up, growing less translucent, into the deep, deep blue of sapphires—almost as dark as night, where the light seems contained rather than given forth. The hills themselves were defined in the same deep blue, but thick, opaque, intense and unspeakably rich, and edged like metal against the dull red sky. Under them, was the wonder of it all—the water, intensely blue like the hills, though glassy against the deep texture of the land-color: but quarter of the way across the stream, some current cut the dark blue with a much lighter shade, nearly gray, like that of polished steel: then, after another line of the deep blue, was another grayish current, and so the whole surface was broken into irregular bands of contrasting shades, like some of the refined miracles of Japanese art. The effect was emphasized by great oaks in the foreground. There was not yet sunlight enough to show their bright Fall colors, and their rugged branches here and there thrust broad dark dashes into the transcendent picture. Between some of the dark branches, Nina saw, lying across two of the blue and gray streaks of the river, the graceful black mass of a great steam yacht, silent, her lights still burning, her spars black against the deep red sky; and far down the river, where sky and water met in a misty harmony of tints, was faintly defined against them both, the colossal shadowy mass of a coming steamer and its smoke.

All this wondrous picture met Nina's gaze when she first looked out, but after she was lost in it a few moments, she let her eyes range away from its intense colors, to her right, where, half around her horizon, all sky and river faded into faint translucent blue and pearl, clean cut below and ruggedly gashed above by the dark hills: and there, high above them, glowed and throbbed immense, the white purity of the morning star. But while she was contemplating it, she became conscious of a fainter brightness pervading the sky far, far up, and raising her eyes, she saw toward the zenith, clear, calm, cold, the waning moon. Near it was one little star.

But these gentle lights only emphasized the grandeur of the scenes below, and after Nina had wonderingly surveyed the whole, her gaze returned and rested there.

She wrapped herself up warmly and, opening the window, seated herself by it. As she raised her hand to support her cheek, the loose sleeve of the green plush robe fell back from her round arm. The robe went admirably with the red-gold hair that tumbled over it, and her strong sweet face added poetry to what, had the face been soulless, would still have been beautiful. It would have been hard to choose, even for lofty inspiration's sake, between the picture she made in the window and the picture she saw from it.

Nina soon ceased to note the details of the scene, and began to lose herself in the harmony of the whole, just as one feeling great chords of music has no thought of the separate tones: the harmony is something which they are not. So in the greatest aspects of Nature, is given something which material things are not—which an artist may paint each thing forever without expressing; which only the greatest artists express at all, and to express which, whatever else he may fail in, makes any artist great. People have tried to indicate it by the word "atmosphere," but atmosphere is only one of its mediums. Others call it light, but it does not appear often where there is much light, but oftenest when the Sun is gone, or before it comes. It is that which is more than light or air, more than skies or mountains or seas—which includes them all, and all that is upon them, in an integral whole. And it is from this vast unity that comes the vastest feeling known to man—a feeling which not only fills the soul, but includes it—makes it one with Nature, or, as has been said, one with God.

Nina's troubled thoughts had all passed away like vapors, and her whole being was interfused with the mighty beauty before her. When her power of feeling flagged enough for her to think, her first definite idea was: "How mysterious it all is!" Then, after another period of the ineffable feeling, she thought again: "But what *is* the mystery—what is behind it all? All this glory is only an aspect of something beyond, which I feel, as one feels a soul behind a face.—Yes! It is that Reality, for which Mr. Calmire said one name is God."

Then her thoughts became vague, and were soon absorbed again in the emotions through which Nature blended its soul with hers.

In the next recurrence of definite ideas, she said to herself: "I have received my message! I have received my message! No words of any creed could ever carry this!"

After another interval, she felt:

"It seems impossible to believe that there is not a conscious intelligence behind it all!—Yes, and a beneficent one! But never again will I try to narrow my feeling of that Intelligence into any other limits that human attributes can express!"

Nina did not go downstairs until she had had a long and refreshing sleep. When she left the breakfast-table, and her mother had gone to write some letters, she caught a glimpse of Calmire on the piazza and ran up to him with:

"Oh Mr. Calmire! If you had only seen the sunrise this morning!"

"Why, I did: they're so beautiful at this time of year that I manage to see them pretty often."

"I wonder if you felt it as I did?" she asked.

He looked at her with a grave kindness and replied:

"What did you feel?"

"That it was Holy, Holy, Holy!"

"Yes, dear, but wasn't there something besides that, and more definite—something that I think must be generations in advance of our language—something that a man can't express, unless he can write great music or paint a Sistine Madonna?"

"Why, Mr. Calmire, how strange! I did have just that feeling before the Madonna. And you did too?"

"Yes, one sometimes has it before the greatest art of any kind—where what they call 'the divine in man' expresses itself. Just as the Divine outside of him expresses itself through Nature."

He paused a moment, apparently reflecting, and then asked: "Did you hear any music?"

"A bird or two."

"Nothing more, though?"

"Why no! Did you?"

"Not this time."

"Why, what do you mean, Mr. Calmire?"

He hesitated a moment and then said:

"I don't often talk about it, but I thought you might know. There's more than we see—in two senses. But I think we see better than we hear: sight is probably the older and better-practiced sense. There's music there, though. I didn't hear it this time, but I've heard it before." He spoke very solemnly.

"Mr. Calmire! Really? What was it like?"

"More like the deep choruses of men's voices than anything else I can recall. Yet the bird-songs blended with it, but vastly better even than the violins do with the pilgrim motive in *Tannhäuser*." He paused again, but evidently overcame some reluctance, and went on: "You know I'm not what you call superstitious, Nina, but there were some strange things about this. I've heard it two or three times. It was when I awoke in the very early morning, and I think that each time there was death in my house, or impending over it."

Nina felt a sense of awe that kept her silent.

"That fact," Calmire continued after a little while, with a marked change of expression, "may have been mere coincidence. I was anxious, my nerves overstrained, and I awoke early. But, mere coincidence or not, the fact is as I have stated it."

"Did you never hear it at any other times?" asked Nina.

"Not that I can recall. I suspect, though, that the great musicians must hear it often, and that if my experience was not fortuitous, it was because the circumstances had developed in me some special nervous sensibility that the great musicians often experience. They do not make the music, but Nature sends it through them. It is always there in Nature, whether we hear it or not, just as the greatest pictures are, whether our eyes are open or not; and, for that matter (as I've tried to show you in all our talks), just as all great things are—great beyond our perceptions or our dreams."

"And God behind them all!" exclaimed Nina.

"Let us rather say, 'God *in* them all,'" responded Calmire. After a moment, he said: "No people who could feel what we felt this morning, could have more than one God. It may seem eccentric, but sometimes, especially after such an experience, the use of that word 'God' arouses in me feelings very like those which orthodox people have regarding its use profanely. The word has so long done duty for such limited and base conceptions of the Ineffable Power, that to me it often calls up repugnant associations."

"Well, what word shall I use?" asked Nina.

"Oh, any!—that one, if you please: no newer one comes natural so often."

After a little silence, she spoke up: "Mr. Calmire, why should not the Ineffable Power (that term comes more natural than the old one this time, thank you),—why shouldn't the Power which manifests itself in everything, manifest itself as a human being?"

"I don't know," he answered. "I'm credibly informed that it does, in some fifteen hundred million instances, to-day."

"Oh, is there *anything* that you won't tease about?" she exclaimed, smiling in spite of her impatience. "You know what I mean! Why, after all, shouldn't there be behind all we see, a Cause like a human being?"

"I can't imagine," answered Calmire, "anything like a human being pervading all Nature, or even the portion that we saw this morning, and I don't think you can. But assume that there is such a self-contradictory Being, why should he be more like an inhabitant of earth than like an inhabitant of Neptune or Mars or any other of the countless heavenly bodies? None of their inhabitants can be like human beings: their air is denser or thinner than ours, their days and years longer or shorter; their heat great enough to burn us, or their cold to freeze us; their light to blind us, or their darkness to incapacitate us; and their gravitation so great that our muscles could not move us against it, or so little that perhaps one of our jumps would carry us over their moons. So they can't be like us, and it's just as reasonable that God should be like any of them, as like us."

"But," she persisted, "you showed me the other day that there must be intelligence and morality everywhere."

"I don't see why not," he answered, "and there's certainly not the same absurdity in making a moral and intelligent God, if you're going to make one at all, that there is in making an entirely anthropomorphic one. The notion of a God narrowed to a specific form, which could be distinguished from other forms, and therefore must be less than the whole, seems to me belittling. But if you want to indulge your fancies wider, there's not much difficulty in forming an impression that, as man includes all inferior earthly types, from the cell of protoplasm up, so there may be some form of existence higher than any other, which includes all other forms, man's among them."

"I don't quite understand that," said Nina.

"Why, you know, (But of course you don't,) that in the egg, the higher animal develops, in a rough way, through the forms of those below him—the highest being, in the egg, at one time, we'll say, like a fish, later a reptile, then a bird, and then a quadrupedal mammal. And a man's thoughts and feelings also, include, to a considerable extent, those below him : there's not much that the lower creatures do and feel, that he doesn't. Now the universe (I don't mean merely the little universe revealed to us,) in fact does include *all* forms of being, in a wider way than the man includes the forms below him, and so the whole universe may be, in some sense too wide for us, a higher form than all the rest. So, I confess, I'm pantheist enough to have a frequent feeling in regard to the entire universe (so far as I can hold the conception) not entirely unlike the feelings of those who worship an anthropomorphic God."

"Yes, Mr. Calmire, though you do not revere a

'person,' you are an intensely reverent man. But I hardly know myself when I say it. And this morning I felt some of the reverence which I find you full of. But did you have the same kind when you were as young as I?"

"Perhaps. But it has grown as I have grown. I remember riding one Fall morning, when I was little more than a boy, with Nature spread out before me—there was a gray sky with a band of yellow light under it, far off; I saw it under some great trees that I was passing, and I was pondering on the contradictions and absurdities of the creeds, when a realization came over me that not in the written creeds, but right there before me, in the universe itself, was the place to seek God. From that place, all the faiths had been built: they were simply composed of the impressions, combined and recombined, that the universe had made on different men. Then I thought: 'My creed shall be the impressions the universe makes on me!' I often think of that ride as being to me what a certain ride of Saul of Tarsus was to him. So, pondering upon the immeasurable universe, of which only some little manifestations reach us through our senses, I have got into the way of feeling toward it, much of what you have felt toward 'God,' and, as I told you the other day, of feeling toward each advance in knowledge, as so much more knowledge of God. I don't believe that any person evolved to knowing the feeling we had this morning, really needs an anthropomorphic God."

"But, Mr. Calmire, that's all so abstract and unhuman. I want sympathy."

"Did you experience anything like sympathy this morning?"

Nina meditated and answered: "Yes, I did."

"Don't you suppose that if you were more highly evolved, you would have experienced more? Reflect that some thousands of generations back, your ancestors didn't experience any."

"It does seem as if one might."

"And wasn't there a sense of something that includes the human, as well as transcends it?"

"Yes."

"And yet you want to bring it down to the human! That may do for those who never felt the soul behind Nature."

"Ah well," sighed the girl, "this is all so new and strange! I've been so used to hearing of the absurdity of 'Nature-worship.' And in those days I didn't feel what is behind, any more than the scoffers did. I supposed that what we see, was *all* of Nature; and that God was a man sitting off somewhere away. I waver a great deal yet, but I've really grown beyond that."

"*So* big!" said Calmire, holding apart his hands in the way that always accompanies that expression with children, and smiling sympathetically. "But you mustn't think of God only as behind *external* nature. What power made our ancestral speck of floating jelly contract when it touched something? What made that responsive tendency pass down from generation to generation, and increase until it reacted to heat and light and color and sound and music and words and every influence we know—until the descendant became man himself? And even then, what power sustains man? He is not self-existent or self-dependent: his every pulse beats without his will; his very brain, wherein resides his most essential self, works by forces which he cannot half control. What are those forces? You saw God behind the Sistine Madonna—an image of the human: have you never had the same feeling in relation to the human itself?"

Nina pondered, and there came up before her Calmire's face as he sat on his horse before the runaways; and then, with a contrast that almost terrified her, though it did not displease her, came Muriel's, in his just but awful wrath when he defended the woman in the shrubbery. The images passed, and she looked up with a complex expression that puzzled Calmire, and said: "Yes."

"The truth is," he went on after a moment, "that there ought never to be a question of God behind Man or Nature, but only of what sort of a God; and if the anthropomorphists would but stop manufacturing one that Man and Nature both contradict, and be humble and patient enough to learn of the real one from the manifestations through all real things, (among which, of course, I include all mind consistent with external Nature, and not warped by this mysterious free-will of ours,) there wouldn't be any more quarreling—the 'reconciliation of Science and Religion' would come. But even so far, despite all the quarrels regarding details, few people really doubt that under all things, is the Unknown God—that same Unknown God to whom Paul found an altar inscribed in Athens."

"But," queried Nina, "wasn't that altar supposed to be raised by polytheists who feared they would leave some god out?"

"Yes, it was so supposed; but it seems to me more likely to have marked one of those splendid Greek, or Egyptian, guesses, which modern knowledge is all the time confirming and developing. So man has made his guesses and built his altars all over the world; but after all, it is largely in his laboratories that God has become less 'unknown.' Many of Paul's lofty inspirations are splendidly confirmed, though, by our knowledge. He preached, apropos of that same altar, a great deal that applies perfectly to our conceptions of the Ineffable Power—that God is not like images of metal or stone, and 'dwelleth not in temples made with hands'; that he is 'not far from every one of us'; that 'neither is he worshipped with hands, as though he needed anything'; that 'he giveth life and breath to all things'; and that 'in him we live and move and have our being.' I recall a mediæval Latin hymn which expresses the same feeling. The old monk called his God

> "'Super cuncta, subter cuncta,
> Extra cuncta, intra cuncta.'

"Do you remember Latin enough to get the points?"

"Not to be sure of them. You'd better give them to me."

"Well, it means simply 'over all things, under all things, beyond all things, within all things,' and yet I haven't the slightest doubt that the man who wrote it, had, running parallel with it, an entirely anthropomorphic notion of God—that he fully believed the statement that Moses had seen 'God's back.' I haven't any doubt that he 'believed' (in his way) two utterly contradictory propositions—that his God was a man whom he could see and shake hands with, and that he was at the same time '*extra cuncta, intra cuncta*,' and the rest of it: the mediæval mind was doing such things all the while. There are plenty of such minds cotemporary with us, just as there are still savages in the stone age. Even Paul was so: he began that splendid discourse on the Unknown God, by calling the worshippers of the Unknown God, idolaters, while they are really the only people who are not—who make no idol, in imagination or in matter. But despite his hard words, Paul loved to feel the Universal Presence as we did this morning, in the 'temples not made with hands.'"

CHAPTER XLVIII.

GOD AND MAN.

AFTER a little pause, Nina said: "All that you have been telling me is very interesting, and seems very true. Perhaps I shall grow up to it sometime. But yet I yearn like a child for God as a loving father, and feel lonely in a world that seems to have no one to take care of it, and no one to take care of me—where there seems so little to keep men good, and very much to tempt them to be bad."

Under his deep brows, Calmire shot a look at her which seemed to come from Muriel's eyes. "What does she mean by that? Can she possibly know?" he said to himself. Then he reflected: "Even if she should, there's nothing I can do now, but go on and build up her supports, and divert her as best I can." But then, despite poor banished Muriel, there raised itself, like a beautiful serpent's head, the idea that, lovely as she was, it would be a joy to instruct and uphold her always. He put his heel on the thought, and went on with his earlier themes.

"You say the world is not taken care of. Assume that it takes care of itself, and not very good care at that: all the same, there has been enough care of some kind to make it grow from a planet inhabited only by 'the fearful dragons of the prime,' into one graced by a few such creatures as yourself. I don't think that you're ever going to get back the idea that there's anything outside of human relations, corresponding to the care of a parent for a young child; and you've got to face the facts and get along without it. Nature does provide us with parents during our childhood, but when we are old enough, she leaves us to ourselves. It's the only way we can conceive of, to ensure our intellectual and moral development, and such freedom of the will as is possible under our circumstances. For that last, we have to pay the standard price of freedom, in vigilance, self-denial, and effort. It's the true wisdom to say: 'Here are Nature's laws. They are all I have, and, except as I learn more, all I can have. I know I can depend upon them absolutely. Here am I, with a given power to know them and use them. It is power enough, rightly used, to make life on the whole worthwhile, and to enable me, perhaps, to make it worthwhile for some to whom it would not otherwise be so. Let me take my life, then, happily if I can, but bravely, whether happily or not.'"

"Ah!" said Nina, "but so few of us are that strong—especially so few women. We need the good God over all."

"Some women are that strong, and you are going to be. I've not said that there's no 'good God over all.' I simply say that if there is one, he gives us his care in a certain way, so much of it, and no more. For my part, I can't enter into the mind of any well-informed person who thinks of

God as interfering and tinkering with the universe at all. Why, even a great human administrator proves his ability by organizing a set of agents and principles to do something, and then leaving them, with occasional oversight, to do it."

"You allow room for occasional oversight, then?"

"Not on the part of an organizer great enough to do without it."

"I prefer," said Nina, "to think of God as constantly watching over me, as a father would who could always be with his child."

"Yes, dear. But what we 'prefer' is one thing, and what we have, may be another. The only thing that it's reasonable and honest to 'prefer to think', is whatever happens to be the true thing. Now thinking of God as constantly watching over us as a father watches over his children, is against the evidence: for the axes have fallen, and the faggots have burned, in spite of all the martyrs' trust; and men have been lost, and children have died, in spite of all the women's faith. It all may be essential to the development of the race; it may all fit in with some scheme wider and grander than any human father could conceive; but look at it squarely, and there's little in it like the human father. Whatever the All-father may be, he has put us off to boarding-school, possibly for our own good, and never comes to see us. He may sometimes hint his existence, though, as perhaps we may assume he did this morning, and send us great inspirations with the hint."

Nina pondered a few moments, and then said:

"But can't the administrator be great enough to make the law go down to the minutest particulars of our lives?"

"What a girl you are! Do you know that you have asked the question that puzzles me more than all others? Certain illegitimate ones might puzzle me more, if I would dwell on them, but that seems a legitimate one. Surely every one who has suffered much has found, if he has tried to do his best, that the suffering—the loss, the apparent neglect and cruelty of God, if you want to put it in that way, has had *some* beneficial effect on his character, and he even may have sometimes found a more or less compensating side in the circumstances themselves: so probably he has at least believed that it's an ill wind that blows no good, and been tempted by the doctrine that 'all's for the best!' There's no sort of doubt that what appear to be the blind general forces of the universe, do go much deeper into the details of our individual lives—both outer and inner, than thoughtless people realize."

He paused, meditating a moment, and Nina, with a little sense of possible victory, said:

"Well, Mr. Calmire?"

"I've watched it as closely as I could, my child, in my own life and others, and I've thought upon it as deeply as I can. My conclusion is, that, whatever evolution may be tending toward, so far, the universal forces are not enough specialized to go much deeper than the *general* features of our lives. All evolution is specialization, you know, and there's no knowing how far, even down into the special needs of character, the external influences may yet go. But for the present, I have to content myself with the boarding-school view. It may be the very best thing for us. If there's a Father who sends us off here, he may be a better Father than if he coddled us more. The school has its merits: there are no freaks in the management, and no excuses are received. My only objection is, that there's no way of learning all the rules, and we're constantly getting into trouble for violating rules that we have had no chance to learn. That, if you are going to hold a 'person' responsible for it, is not fair play. At this stage of evolution, though, perhaps we get into more trouble for violating rules which we do know than for violating those we don't."

"Yes, I've often heard Earth called a school for Heaven," Nina interrupted.

"It may be, for all we know," Calmire assented. "But intellectual health requires us to realize that while we are off at this school, no Father who sent us here has anything more to do with us *directly* than if he didn't exist; and therefore, if I were to reason anthropomorphically, I should assume it to be His wish that we are not to spend our time and strength over questions regarding Him, but to busy ourselves in doing what He has given us to do, and enjoying what He has given us to enjoy. We have more than enough to occupy us, and I've seen enough of the results of illegitimate speculation. Whatever may be the nature of the Cause, the only revelations of it that we have are through Nature and human nature; and they come best incidentally to our work there. And it seems to me that the greatest teachers taught just that. Christ himself was full of the duties of human life: I can't imagine anything more alien to his own example than the protracted seclusion and exaggerated self-communion and asceticism of so many of his professed followers. The world owes a great deal to its saints, but I suspect it owes more to its investigators. The church admits something in that direction," he added, with a laugh, "when it proposes to make a saint of Christopher Columbus, and something of the same kind when it made one of Charles the Great.

"Now," he continued, "to sum it all up, what *have* we to go on? We know that there is a Power which we cannot conceive as limited. We know that it works in accordance with laws that we have never known to vary (of course I leave miracles out of the question, as absurdities common to all the religions); we know that we can study those laws, gaining by the study; and—most important and very strange!—we know that as fast as we learn its laws, we can ourselves use that awful Power—that it then submits itself to our commands—that, so far from being, as it appears to the savage, a remote God to be assailed by prayer, it is as it appears to the scientist, a familiar friend, and even servant, of unswerving faithfulness, to be controlled by knowledge."

"What?" cried Nina. "God our servant!"

"The idea only illustrates the absurdities of the anthropomorphic conception," Calmire answered. "or perhaps the absurdities of our contemptuous notions of service: though we do look down upon it, once a year certain sovereigns wash the beggars' feet. However, I did not say anything about God, except to state the savage's idea. I only spoke of the motive Power of the universe as we know it. Nearly all savages place a God behind it. An increasing number of civilized men refuse to try to go behind it at all: the strongest intellects of the time declare themselves too weak to. But, to go back: I didn't mean by the Universal Power, mere brute force: for certainly in the operations of the Power, we must include all the normal functions of man himself—thought, emotion, conscience, aspiration, Nature is the source of all those things, even if she has added a certain paradoxical freedom of will to use them, or even if she has been educating us from the very beginning to control herself. You don't find any human parents as generous as that! All the same, however, that pretty fancy, like every other one regarding that infinite subject, raised by our finite capacities, is nonsense: for there is no generosity in giving when infinity is left; and that very sentence, too, you see, is nonsense: for how can infinity be left, when it is less than infinity by so much as has been taken from it? So let us mark again the constant lesson that it is foolish for us to speculate on the nature of an unlimited Power: our limited faculties are only for its limited manifestations. No matter in what direction we attempt to get beyond them, we always find ourselves swamped in paradox. If you try to get out of the scrape by putting an out-and-out human God behind it all, you have the father educating his children to unite with him in the control of things, and giving them control as fast as they learn how to use it. But then you see you must limit his power or his kindness: for if a human parent could effectually educate us without pain, he would: so we're in paradox again.

"The only reasonable course is to find content in knowing that the manifestations of the Power work for the constantly increasing wisdom, goodness, and happiness of the human race; that while around us misery and ugliness are frequent, they do not prevail, but that happiness and beauty are, on the whole, characteristic of our world; and that, in all conceivable probability, behind all the happiness and beauty of which we are conscious, is infinitely more—infinite material for higher thought and loftier emotion, some of which, our descendants, with finer capacities than ours, will enter into. Moreover, while, without, there is the Divinity we see and feel; within, there is the same Divinity which, without seeing, we feel more really still—that Divinity including us, but distinct from us, and we distinct from It—even controlling, in our little measure, the very forces which are the manifestations of it. True, that little measure so shades into the including Immensity, that we cannot tell where It resigns control, and we become free agents: it's the old, old mystery of fate and free-will. But despite the mystery, we have the certainty that, in some undefined degree, we are free moral agents—each with his own share of the Universal Power. Now are we to be glad of what we have, and do our best to increase it: or are we to count it as nothing, because we have not more?"

CHAPTER XLIX.

MORE CORRESPONDENCE.

Muriel Calmire to Legrand Calmire.

"Oct. 18th, 18—.

"THE misery has begun again. I started to address you as usual, but I remembered your injunction to write nothing that an outsider could identify. I suppose, though, that I may as well be honest in such a lying world, and tell you that I did not think of your caution until I hesitated over writing the word 'Dear', because it seemed as if even you had joined the conspiracy of the Universe against me. The first time I read your letter, I got a lot of comfort from it. But as I think it over, how do I know that it's true? How do I know that anything is true? I've found out long ago that the faiths of my childhood were lies. What warrant is there that my later faiths—so far as I have any, are not? They all broke down before I got your letter. Why shouldn't they break down again? The very utmost that we can be sure of, is what *has* happened. How can we be sure of what is going to happen? We mites of men can't know all the influences at work around us. How do I know that my legs won't break if I try to walk, that the house won't fall on me, that you won't lie to me, that even— No! I can't think *that!* But surely no man can be certain of his next step. We're all stumbling along—no guide but blind unfeeling Chance. No man goes safely by his own wisdom. I've as much sense as most fellows: yes, more, if I do say it; and where am I? —while most of the fools of my acquaintance are happy!

"Now because you didn't admit all this squarely, I seem to lack confidence in you. Lots of things in your letter did seem true enough. But it soon got mighty plain that they only *had been* true, and might change at any moment. The queer thing is that you hadn't sense enough to see that, or honesty enough to acknowledge it.

"Oct. 19th.

"There seemed something wrong about it all again yesterday: so I stopped. But I'll be hanged if I can see to-day *what's* wrong, except that there doesn't seem much sense in questioning your gumption or your honesty.

"*What* is wrong?

"And why don't I blow my damned brains out?"

Legrand Calmire to Muriel Calmire.

"Oct. 20th, 18—.

"To begin at the end: the reason you don't blow your damned brains out, is that it's not a family habit. Some men in your fix, with your sort of brains (though they're not an altogether 'damned' sort by any means), would have done it before this; but there are some conserving elements in your make-up.

"'*What* is wrong?' is a question that has puzzled your sort of brains for several thousand years, but the way out seems simple enough now.

It was obscured by people claiming too much—claiming a warrant for truth—especially mathematical and logical truth, superior to experience. That blunder has been corrected by the discovery that even our recognition of those truths depends on ancestral experience—that the Hottentot can't be taught to count ten, while the Englishman writes the Principia. So when we own up squarely that *all* our knowledge is, like our capacities, limited—that our certainty is only approximate, we're in condition to realize that the approximation is close enough for a working basis. You haven't certainty, but you don't need it. Despite the tricks your present frame of mind plays you, you're not really afraid to get up and walk, or enter a house—or to trust me, as far as my capacities go. But I'm awfully sorry for you. I know all about it.

"Of your last letter, I only answered what moved me most. Now I'll take what's left, *seriatim.*

"'*Are* men's punishments in any way proportioned to the evil they intend to do?' No, not very closely. We've touched on that before. Even the churches, you know, don't teach an equitable distribution of rewards and punishments in this life; and one of their arguments for a future life is, that it will afford an opportunity to compensate the injustices of this.

"So far as the consequences of man's acts are regulated by Nature,—outside of man's will,—there is no room for justice. It is a purely anthropomorphic conception; we read it from ourselves into Nature. Thousands of men do just as you did and go scot-free. If Nature is just to them, she is unjust to you; if she is just to you, she is unjust to them. The fact is: she is neither just nor unjust. Justice regards motives, but Nature outside of man knows nothing of them: she is as merciless to ignorance as to crime. Our only safe guide, then, is the absolute hard experience that the race has had of Nature's ways, and that is embraced in the standard morality—in the religions or out. Yet never forget that Nature, in the social sanctions, in conscience, and in the hopes and fears of the religions, has evolved agencies which do reward and punish motive. But outside of man, Nature has simply her laws and forces. Anything we do sets them all in motion, and our littlest acts sometimes release the greatest of them, as a child touching an electric button blew up Hell Gate. Yet unless we absolutely know that they're in position to crush us, we start them on some slight temptation, hoping they will miss us just that once: and all the time we know (or would know, if it were not for our pestilent anthropomorphism) that Nature has no intelligence, no pity, no justice, to turn her forces to the right or left. Those qualities are man's, and make him ineffably Nature's superior, except as you think of Nature including him. Pascal puts it well: 'It is not necessary for the whole universe to arm itself to crush a man: a mist, a drop of water is enough to kill him. But though the universe crushes him, the man is still more noble than that which kills him, because man knows that he dies: and of the advantage which the universe has over him, the universe knows nothing.'

"Well! your difficulty about the water deceiving and drowning you, or the hills falling upon and crushing you, is answered. In fact, you answered it yourself when you said that *if* it were not for your superior intelligence and will, the water would deceive and drown you. Think of this in connection with the cause of all your suffering—you are overwhelmed in a sea of woe, simply because you did not use the superior intelligence and will. You were not 'deceived' at all: you knew your risk and ignored it. Nature can seldom be said to deceive, though she often refuses to communicate.

"But even suppose she were 'just,' how, after all, could the motives or punishments of any two men be the same? No two men are the same. In face of a given temptation, your realizations of consequence, and your resulting obligations, are very different from those of most men; and to offset that, most men, in your situation, would not be suffering much: they'd simply content themselves in repudiating the whole affair. So I have sometimes been led to wonder if there is not, after all, in Nature's way of distributing the apparently disproportionate punishments, a closer correspondence with our ideas of justice than we realize.

"I hope it's proved clearly enough by this time, that it's not 'all a damned farce.' And now let's see whether the fact that 'in a little while it's all over,' really does 'take all the meaning out of it.' Is a star not beautiful, because sometime its light is going to fade away? Is our Sun not warm, because sometime it is going to burn out? Are there no lovely things on earth because æons hence there will be none? Are there no duties plain to-day, because æons hence there will be no duties on earth? To make to-day's fruits sweet, to-day's love blissful, to-day's duties inspiring or even binding, is it necessary that we should be sure that the same soul which responds to them to-day will respond, say, the ten-millionth day from to-day? If so, to make them good that day, is it necessary that the soul should then be sure that it will respond the ten-millionth day from then? And so on to another ten-millionth day, and another and another *ad infinitum?*: All of which, you simply can't conceive.

"The argument from time, applies just as well to sensation. If nothing is good for a moment, because it is not good for an æon, so nothing is good to any eye or any palate, because it might not be good to a better eye or a better palate. So you can imagine no good that will not be declared bad by a sense finer than the one which declares it good. This is the trouble in your Glumdalclitch argument. What is the alternative? Simply that, as I answered before, where senses are balanced to objects, as they are when any organism is in health, *there is good*, and *that* good *is* good. We made the word for that kind of good, for we know no other kind. To deny this, and try to imagine an immortality to make room for a good nearer perfect than we know here, is simply to remove the difficulty a step farther off, and to land us amid the follies of the ascetics who avoid the plain good before them, because they can imagine a greater good farther off. Thus they ignore most of the very appetites which make good, so far as we know good, possible. In health, Nature gives us a certain amount of power to feel the good, and be unconscious of the bad. It's a fact that we can't escape, and we're fools (and ungrateful fools, if you want to be anthropomorphic) if we don't take the benefit of it.

"Good is found in the reactions between man and Nature. I don't deny that a man sometimes gets pinched in the machinery; and I don't deny that, *so far as I can see*, all men are ultimately destroyed in that same machinery. But don't let us take the fact that we *can't see* what becomes of the man's mind and consciousness, as final proof that they too are destroyed; and, as I indicated in my last letter, don't let's forget that not many men at once are pinched to death, or even to pain. Look at a Coney Island Sunday—its vast aggregate of happiness—more happy people in that one spot, than there are sufferers in the whole nation.

"But the beginning of wisdom, is to learn that there are things we've got to stand, and not to have our judgment upset by them. As to what is vulgarly considered the worst thing of all—death, a healthy man seldom thinks of it. That life is to end, detracts nothing from its value to him. Is each day in a month less valuable than each day in a year? each day in a year less valuable than each day in a lifetime? each day in a lifetime less valuable than each day in an eternity? Can't a man work just as hard if he knows his time is short, as if he knows that he has any amount of it to waste? If it requires an eternity to make life significant, aren't you in the midst of one now? Would its significance be gone if your single life were taken out of it? Can't the suns swing without your help? and don't you know that they swing? *It's eternity now!* Haven't you all you can do in it?

"It may be urged that some men are better for believing in immortality. Probably some persecuting bigots would have been better if they had not believed in it, and many men are good without believing in it. But I'm not quarreling with the belief, but only with the claim that life has no meaning without it. You can't know that you're immortal, but this you can know—that if you sit with folded hands, whining for more life, while more than you can handle is already within reach on every side, you don't deserve to be immortal."

"Instead of finding fault with modern religionists for not torturing for their faith, rejoice in their progress over their ancestors. Spencer's demonstration of evolution in mind, morals, and social institutions, is a *proof* of what all the ages have been longing to know—that man does progress, and that the grounds of hope are facts. Civilizations do fall as well as rise, but each inherits from its predecessors; and if evolution stops in one solar system, it must, *ipso facto*, if the latest hypotheses are correct, begin in another. So while you're wretched because the Universe is out of joint, be consistent and take the other side equally in the large: don't fret because occasionally a man dies, or a civilization crumbles, or a sun burns out; but reflect that the Universe as a whole, moves on. Rejoice, too, that if, so far as we can see, we are not to participate in much of the progress ourselves, many of us are at least evolved into enough altruism to be glad that others are.

"I hope I haven't bored you, and have helped you some. Probably in your state of mind, you may as well have been reading this, as doing anything else.

"I have no more news. Our friends return to town in three days. I go the day after.

"I sometimes suspect that the younger *knows*, though neither of us has said anything.

"I have reached two distinct conclusions as to what you had better do: I. That until what you dread, is an accomplished fact, and the future beyond any reasonable peradventure, you are to do nothing. II. That the best place to do it in, is where you are, or at all events away from here. You can do no earthly good here, and you might get yourself committed to something awkward and superfluous. Whatever can be done, especially in the way of making the burden easy for those who bear it, I shall do. Questions of what you shall do, can be met when they legitimately come. I need no better evidence that you would be the worst man to handle them before you have to, than myself realizing now, that the emotional side of the case so obscured my own vision that the fact that there's nothing for you to do for months to come, was not perfectly obvious at the outset. It is as simple as Columbus's egg.

"You know my love for you: try to trust my discretion."

CHAPTER L.

CAIN.

CALMIRE'S letters brought Muriel great relief. While he read them, and went over each a second time and a third, he felt (as he had felt more than once since he fell into his morbid state) that his doubts were banished, and could trouble him no more. He was still far from realizing that recovery from those emotional phases, like recovery from any abnormal condition, is not accomplished suddenly or with uniform progress, but settles down by oscillations in both directions, like a pendulum, in conformity with the universal law which Spencer has formulated as the Rhythm of Motion.

He felt better, however, for a time, and the night after he got the last letter, which had been delayed some days in the country post-offices, he started out for a walk beyond the village in the moonlight. He strode along more like himself than he had done since he left Fleuvemont. He felt strong in a certain sense of growth. All his earlier conceptions of man and law and duty, seemed to him like child's toys beside those that he had been getting glimpses of during the past few weeks. Before, he had been a boy, merely sentimentalizing over the necessities in life, as he did over its romance: now he was a man, strong for anything—for renunciation, self-sacrifice—those great virtues of which he had read so often, and professed, at a safe distance, to respect so much. But he had really thought them rather slow—of the same class of merits with those for which good marks were given in his school-days, in which the stupid boys generally excelled. Never before having essayed the practice of any virtues of that class, he had not realized how hard they were, nor had he realized how essential they were to the equilibrium of life. But now he saw that they were great things, not merely easy for boys born too poor and stupid to have anything to renounce, but tests of strength worthy of such splendid creatures as himself; and he was rather thankful to things-in-general for giving him the opportunity to make the creditable exhibition of himself for which he now felt prepared. Two or three times he had almost congratulated himself on his miseries,—perhaps because they were so big and majestic, or, lately, perhaps because they held out to him such great opportunities for the exercise, and even the display, of very impressive and melodramatic virtues. He was indeed rather disposed to congratulate the universe upon the opportunity to look at him. Faint realizations of all this had begun to dawn upon him; but his instinct was to banish such realizations, because they were uncomfortable. Yet lately, this old instinct had, a few times, been opposed by a new feeling which had peeped into being; he had already once or twice wished that there were no temptation to right-doing, as well as to wrong-doing, and he had even doubted whether there could be any merit in his readiness to immolate himself, so long as he was conscious of there being any; and—all the worse, so long as he thought of any admiration which it might compel. Then the virus of skepticism which was running its course in his blood, found its way to this virgin spot, and he began to be skeptical of his own sincerity and singleness of purpose; and, next, even of his tenacity of purpose; and then, of course, of the real existence of such qualities anywhere.

He had no God to dread or consult, and, as yet, no realization that the only thing to depend upon in such crises is one's self—self made worthy of reliance and accustomed to exact it. Therefore, the big man with the white robe and white beard having long since disappeared, and Self not yet having taken the awful form of the Undeceivable and Unavoidable Judge; and the most august object within sight during this evening walk being the full moon, of course the thing natural to our distracted young gentleman, who had so often professed his freedom from superstition, was to fall into a habit of his ancestors, and turn in a spirit of reverence to said moon and swear by it that, whatever might come, he would follow his duty, and find his way out of his maze of troubles in any direction where duty might lead.

This after-thought of finding his way out, coming in so quietly that he hardly recognized its advent, suddenly loomed up before him like some unexpected object when brooding eyes are raised from one's path. The conception that duty, blindly followed, sometimes leads the way out of trouble, he had before had a sort of unrealizing notion of; but he had not thought much about it one way or the other: he had not had any particular use for it, he had never been in any perplexity which he had not seen his way out of at a glance, and which his ingenuity and confidence in himself had not actually got him out of in twenty-four hours. True, he had had two or three hard and unexpected knocks; but they simply had to be endured, they had not, like this last one, brought with them any future to be dreaded or determined, and his conscience had not busied itself very much with any question of his own responsibility for them. But now he knew a misery beside which he felt, not without a sort of grim pride, that everything he had before endured was boyish. Here were the lives of, probably, three beings, his own among them, made miserable by his act and now to be shaped by his will. He could not spare himself the sweet agony of adding Nina's life, as a fourth, to those already involved. Yet, in his exaltation, he felt that it would be easy to take the course of self-sacrifice—to crush his own love and starve Nina's (which, of course, he calmly assumed to exist, as its complement had arisen in his lordly self), and to give the rest of his life to the two beings with whom a part of it was already incorporated. But would this obvious course be the best even for them? Calmire had doubted it, and Calmire was just, mercilessly just. But Muriel could not take Calmire's advice and let the question rest until the demands upon him should be matured and established beyond reasonable peradventure: he was too young, though he did not know that, and he did not even know that to postpone the question, was the part of wisdom—the part, even, of strength. He could not help some sort of realization that any present determination must be premature, and that any determination he could think of would be but the settling of one question by the raising of a host of others, some of them life-long. Yet he felt that it *must* be determined. And how? How?

And here, amid all this maze of perplexity, he had jumped at a true conception just as the earlier Greek thinkers so often did, without having any clear reasons for it. He hardly realized that because he was in an orderly universe with all its parts connected and ceaselessly moving, if he should find and conform himself to the true course of the motion, not attempting by mistaken will or desire to resist or divert it, it would bear him, if no exceptional disturbance should come, to where he had best go. But this process, so easy to describe, and so hard to execute, Muriel had begun, in a groping way, to associate with the old notion of Duty. Here it was, that old notion, which he had really regarded only as a good thing to versify and speechify about—here it was—no far-off star, but a real thing, to hold on by and yet to exert one's whole being by—like an oar when one rows. That it should help his boat over these dark and troubled waters, he was resolved; and he felt from it a sense of support akin, he realized, to that which many creeds had given to sufferers and martyrs.

He walked on, strengthened and reliant. In with the rhythm of his steps, began to fall an old tune which faintly ran in his mind, perhaps because he had thought of the waters. Soon he began to hum it, and after a few paces more, he was singing, at the height of his great voice, "Rocked in the Cradle of the Deep." By the time he reached the bridge, his burst of energy had taxed a little the frame already feeling the burdens of the past few weeks, and he paused and leaned on the parapet and contemplated the grand play of moonlight with waters, and clouds with shadows.

As he mused and sang of the troubled waves, again arose the question, "What will the port be? Shall I get over? *Can* there be any peace in reserve for me?"

Then he began to think again. What, after all, was this Duty which had made him sing, "Secure I rest upon the wave"? Was it not the very perplexing thing that he had been trying to determine? It would guide him to the end; but what would guide him to *it?* "The greatest good of the greatest number!" Well! Here on one side were Minerva and that other (possible) being, for whose life, it was true, the responsibility would be his, but whose life was unformed, whose requirements were uncertain, and whose possibilities would be the average of his and Minerva's: not, he bitterly told himself, the higher average of his and Nina's. Yet that was sophistical! Who could prophesy what it might be? Who would have foretold Shakspere from his parents? Yet Muriel, who loved children so dearly, could not even wish for this one, though it was his own! And on the other side were himself and Nina. On that side lay not only happiness, but, he felt, growth and usefulness — the happiness of many connected people whose usefulness was more important than that of the other side, and whose capacity for happiness and unhappiness was greater. Whose good, whose happiness, he should like to know, were to be consulted here? Which was the more important side?

But this sophistry could not hold him long. Whatever his feelings were, he had grown up primarily a creature of intellect, such as it was; and his intellect had been drilled beyond the possibility of any self-deception here. He saw the case plainly enough. It was not the apparent happiness of the people immediately interested that must determine the moral quality of an act. It was the effect that the general practice of such acts would have upon the general happiness; for obviously no one man had a right to do what not all would have a right to do. Human experience had fixed some things, and had fixed nothing more clearly than that the very existence of society, which includes the possibility of civilization, which makes man the creature he is, instead of a solitary beast—all this depends on parents taking care of their own children. That is the one safeguard of education and morality. "Ah, but this is only one case!" pleaded poor Muriel with himself; and promptly his just nature added: "Yes; and it is but one case if I kill that man riding up there on the hill against the sky, and take his horse, and ride away from the whole horrible business." No! Temptation could master him, at least it once could; but sophistry could not, at least not now. If Minerva Granzine should have a child, and that child should live, it was his business to take care of it—not merely to feed it and clothe it, but to make of it a creature that should do at least its share for the common welfare. That duty demanded this much, was clear; that it might demand more, was not impossible, especially when it was backed up by other sanctions,—some of them tender, the thought of which pained him,—some of them beautiful, the thought of which sickened him.

But broken though he was, painful and sickening things could not long possess his imagination, unless they taxed his intellect more than the almost routine rehearsal of the elements of morality which he had just gone through. The clouds were floating, a little portentously, over the moon; but when one passed, how doubly bright everything was, in the sky and over the river! Of course the well-worn image of a clouded life took possession of him, and soon our young gentleman, who, as has been remarked, had so freely proclaimed his superiority to superstition, relapsed into augury. There was that great black cloud marching up, its edge might obscure the moon, or it might not. The moon was the light of his life, the cloud was hurrying fate. If the cloud should long obscure the moon, fate would darken his life; if the cloud should pass by, leaving the moon uncovered, somehow these terrible threatenings would pass by him. The cloud passed leaving the moon clear. He turned away exultantly, then called himself a fool, then laughed, and walked briskly toward home.

During his absence, the late mail had been laid on his table. He picked up the morning paper, and after a time read, in the telegraphic columns:

"**Melancholy Suicide of a Student at —— College.**

"——, Oct. 25, 18—.—Soon after midnight, the students in —— Hall were startled by a pistol-shot in the building. It was found to have proceeded from a room on the fourth floor on the south entry. The occupant was discovered lying on the floor in a pool of blood coming from wounds in the breast and back. The ball from a derringer which lay beside him had gone through the whole body, perforating the heart in its passage. Death must have been instantaneous. No reason is assigned for the rash act. The young man was a hard student, though he had not studied hard enough to break down his mind. On his table were charred portions of a letter which appeared to have been held over the chimney of his lamp, but there are not enough fragments left to throw any light on the melancholy affair. The name of the unfortunate youth was John Granzeen. He was from Calmeer."

No "light on the melancholy affair"! Muriel needed no light upon it. "*I* did it," he said, holding the paper before him with a convulsive grasp and staring eyes. "*I* did it. So I'm a murderer, too!"

He fell into a chair and gazed out of the window. The night had become black. The poor boy had not even enough experience of distress, to light a cigar. After he had sat for ten minutes, he said aloud: "I must go to Uncle Grand."

A train left soon after midnight, and by ten o'clock next morning he was in his uncle's house in Washington Square.

CHAPTER LI.

TANTALUS.

THE man at the door told Muriel that Mr. Calmire had started down town half an hour before, and that Mrs. John was in the house, and had just gone up to dress to go out.

Muriel gave the man his overcoat and other traps, and went into the parlor and sat down before the fire. He felt deadened by the weight upon him. He was aroused from a profound revery by the rustle of a silk dress near him. He turned to greet Mrs. John, and found himself face to face with Nina Wahring. She had come to walk with Mrs. John.

"You here!" she exclaimed.

"Yes." In a voice with no more vibration than cork.

"This is not your place!" she said as if in remonstrance.

The untoward had become so much a matter of course to him that he did not even notice this confirmation of Calmire's suspicion that Nina knew.

She had a strong though vague conviction that Muriel had no right with her while that other was alone in the world. Meeting him brought up the feeling with double force, and, in her confusion, with the good woman's instinct to hold a man to his duty, especially if she loves him, made her propose to turn him out of a house where he had a better right than she had. And of course a young man like Muriel—imaginative, intense, dramatic, accepted such an extreme proposition unquestioningly, as a perfectly natural element of an extreme case.

"There is no place for me!" he answered in the same mechanical tone.

"There is one," she expostulated, "and you must go to it."

"So I sometimes think, but the time is not yet come. But I need not stay here to offend your sight." His dead voice might have come from a machine. He started to go. To reach the door he had to walk toward her. His resolution braced his whole frame and set his face. He was as she first saw him at Fleuvemont. The recollection kept her eyes unconsciously fixed upon him. His own were directed toward the door. Her head began to turn as he passed; the slight motion brought her to herself. She made a gesture, and said:

"This is your home. I have no right to turn you out."

"I have no right to stay—here or anywhere. I could not stay where I was yesterday. The curse of Cain is upon me. I must wander."

He still spoke mechanically, without looking at her. Then he turned and did look—from his deep black-rimmed eyes in his pale face, and in the same monotonous tone uttered:

"Good-bye."

"You shall not go!" she cried. "You are no Cain!"

"Yes! It makes no difference," continued the soulless tones. "I may as well go. Good-bye."

Oh, the misery of it! This dead creature—this thing that could not even seize kindness—this *humble* thing—*this*, Muriel Calmire! It was too horrible. Had he been Cain himself, it would have moved her.

"Stay! What harm can you do?"

"Me? Harm? None!"

Worse and worse! Was Samson shorn and blind?

"Then do stay and let me talk to you," she exclaimed, her face glowing with a yearning pity.

"No. Perhaps it would hurt you. Maybe I too can feel yet, though that doesn't matter."

"Then, in God's name, feel! Anything but this!"

"Well! What can you say to me? Don't stand."

She sank into a chair. He put his hands on the back of one opposite.

"Do sit down," she said.

"No! What can you tell me?"

"I can tell you to resist the misery you have; not to court more."

"Can there be any that I have not?"

"Yes! That which I have." She could not withstand the impulse, and hardly cared to.

"That which *you* have!" His voice at last was human. "You have done no wrong."

"Do only wrong-doers suffer?" she asked with a sad smile.

"Oh, if 'twere only they who did! if 'twere only they who did!" he cried. "Then he would not have killed himself." His heart was so full of his latest pain, that even its hunger for her failed to feel what her words had shown it.

"Who killed himself?" she asked.

"Johnny Granzine. I killed him."

"You did not kill him. His mother killed him," she cried, rising to her feet; and her energy flashed another thought through her mind. "And I doubt if he ever knew anything connected with you, to give him trouble."

"His mother killed him? How?"

"Oh, why must I talk to you of these terrible things?"

"Never mind! I will go," he said, with the little thrill all fallen out of his voice.

"No," she added in her old imperious way, "I told you to stay! Didn't you know that his mother had gone away?"

"No! So I made her go away!"

"Oh, don't talk in that dead way, and don't hold yourself responsible for every wicked thing that everybody else ever did! She went away because she's a bad woman. If she had been a good one, she would have felt it doubly her duty to stay at home."

"Why should Johnny kill himself because she went away?"

"She went away with a bad man."

"And Johnny knew nothing of me? But then perhaps his mother would not have gone away if it had not been for me. I was at the bottom of it."

"But you had nothing to do with her being bad. You cannot blame yourself for that."

"I set the ball rolling," he remonstrated. "True,

I could not see where it was going," he added as if meditating. "I could not know where all the precipices were." He paused and looked long in her face, and then said slowly in low tones, as if thinking aloud: "Oh, angel of purity and goodness, why should I defile your white soul with thought of my sins?"

At last he had spoken in Muriel Calmire's voice, and its vibration stirred the answering chords in her soul. They drove the tears to her eyes, and through them she looked up at him, sadly smiling, and said:

"Those thoughts cannot harm me. And oh! I pity you so! I pity you so!"

He fell on his knees before her and murmured:

"I have lost the right to love you, but I have still the right to worship you, and let me! Oh, let me!"

And without thought, yielding to the weariness of his overburdened soul, he buried his face, sobbing, in her lap.

How long they remained thus, neither of them cared to know. But at last he seized her two hands, kissed them, and arose.

"Now," said he, "I am ready for my duty, whatever it may be. When I falter, I will think of you!"

"Oh, Muriel, can that be right? What is right?"

"*Anything* I can think of you, is right and blessed. Oh! may you feel something of what you have done for me!"

He took her hands in both of his, kissed them long, and again, and was gone.

CHAPTER LII.

OUR ONLY GLIMPSE OF TOWN.

PERHAPS if life were not full of anticlimaxes, we should not be able to stand its strain. Nevertheless, after a period of great exaltation, nobody is quite satisfied to be in the commonplace position of not knowing what to do with himself. Few things make great moments seem, in retrospect, more unreal.

Mr. Muriel, being a youth of big impulses, of course put himself in this ridiculous position when he left his beloved, by rushing out of the house without the slightest idea where he was going. After his long legs had carried him ahead for some minutes, the absence of this idea occurred to him. The special motive to see his uncle had passed; and had it not, he would hardly have sought an interview at the office of the Calmire factories, in Wall Street. In fact, he had not turned in that direction, but, with no other impulse than habit, had turned up Fifth Avenue, not even finding room in his distracted mind for the notion that his face and apparel, after the experiences of the last twelve hours, were hardly such as he would wish to carry up that proper and populous thoroughfare.

When he concluded that he was not going to

Wall Street, it naturally occurred to him to look up and see where he was going. He was approaching Madison Square, and on all the great buildings before him, save the club-house (as it then was) beyond the monument, were flags flying at half-mast. Despite these profuse emblems of some heavy public sorrow, the scene was a pretty one,— the great white masses of building at his left running up into the clear blue sky (which, had it been known to literature earlier, and had it not become so befouled with soft-coal smoke in these later years, would be as proverbial as that of Italy); the contrasting large red building between Fifth Avenue and Broadway, the long avenue in front with its many spires piercing that ineffable blue; the great open mass of the same wondrous sky etched into by the naked branches of the trees in the square; and, most noticeable of all against the lovely high background, the contrasting colors of the waving flags. The prospect was beautiful and impressive —the nearest to a fine bit of purely urban scenery that any American city presents, though of course vastly inferior to much in Europe, and to some in America where more of Nature has been left to help.

As Muriel looked up at the half-masted flags, he mused: "Of course! Of course! Trouble everywhere! But in the misfortunes of a nation, what does any man feel that can at all compare with personal misery? If all the flags in the world meant mourning, no one outside of some bereaved family would be suffering as I suffer: and probably no one in that family would. What can Death bring, to equal what I have brought on myself?"

A policeman was on the corner Muriel was approaching, and he, being anxious, despite his own misery, to know what woe had fallen on the state, asked why the flags were at half-mast. The man answered:

"An old hotel-keeper down near Chatham Square, died this morning."

Muriel swore—really for the first time in two days and a half, then thanked the man and turned down the avenue.

In a few moments, he wondered why, after leaving Nina, he had not, instead of aimlessly rushing out into the street, quietly gone up-stairs to the room always known as his, and gone to sleep. Although the Calmires were good sleepers, no one of them, at least since their early "chivalric" Louisiana days, was sufficiently used to the impression that he had just killed a man, to be able to pass a restful night with it. But any one of them, after passing a restless night, was pretty sure soon to be persuaded by Nature to recruit the lost strength—all of which may be a rather long-winded way of saying that Mr. Muriel was sleepy. So, realizing that Miss Wahring was probably gone, he emulated the most famous of all the deeds of all the kings of France with all their armies, and took himself "back again."

He had a good nap on his lounge, and in the afternoon, invigorated by his sleep and a bath, he drove with his uncle, who had returned early from his office, and talked over the future. This he did with a certain grim calm, suggesting possibilities that made life worse than useless to him, as if they were simply the elements of a mathematical problem. This the men of the Calmire race were generally able to do—when they grew to be men.

Muriel tried hard to get from his uncle an opinion as to what he ought to do if everything should turn out as, in due course of Nature, was to be expected; but the utmost he could get was: "There are two things certain—first, that you would be a terribly sold man if you were to determine your whole life now with reference to an expected conjuncture, and then find the conjuncture failing to arise; and second, as you have time to await the conjuncture in, you have time (and you ought to be glad of it) to let a determination shape itself. Leaving your own will entirely out of account, there are a myriad ways in which a conclusion may be shaped for you. It's pitiful that youngsters never can rest in such a fact, but must torture themselves with curiosity and impatience."

"But waiting is the one thing I can't do," exclaimed Muriel.

"The ability to wait," said Calmire, "is one of the highest of all human powers. Don't throw away such a splendid chance to cultivate it."

"Yes! A splendid chance indeed!" gruesomely assented poor Muriel. "But in this case, so many people have got to wait! And I'd at least like to show that I have some sort of human sympathy for poor Minerva. I sometimes feel," he added after a moment, "as if it would be only decent in me to go and see her, or at least to write to her,"

"What sensible things could you say to her?"

"I hadn't got as far as that," said Muriel, with a half-sheepish look in his smile.

"I've said everything to her," rejoined Calmire, "that you ought to say, and a great deal more than it would be wise for *you* to say—or, possibly, than it was wise for me to," he added, with his candid habit (after the event) not exactly of self-mistrust, but of general mistrust of human wisdom.

"*If*," murmured Muriel, thinking aloud, "I ought to come up to the scratch, and marry her, to do it now would save her an awful lot. And if I've got to, I'd rather plunge and have it over with."

"'If' is a good pair of tongs to handle red-hot questions with, isn't it?" asked Calmire, and then exclaimed: "Marry one woman while loving another! The bravest man that ever did that, was a coward somewhere back in his soul—or a sentimentalist. Besides, it wouldn't be 'over with,' but just begun. I suppose," he continued, "that heretofore, you've thought of things that make a noise and kill, as the stuff to test heroes with. Probably tame little uncertainty never appeared to you dreadful enough for that. It doesn't make any more noise than bacteria do, but I've known men to do more cowardly things before it, than before cannons. Now keep up your pluck to wait. Besides, what did I tell you about the chance of your being sold?"

"But if my hara-kiri were done now," said Muriel, with that perverseness which always sends the tongue to an aching tooth, "all possibility of awkward conjecture could be nipped in the bud."

Well," said Calmire, "you must give me, and yourself too, credit for very little ingenuity if you think that can't be taken care of. For instance: when a man, after some years in Europe or far Cathay, returns with a wife and a child or two, does anybody bother over the exact ages of the children?"

"That's so!" exclaimed Muriel. "There doesn't seem much sense in worrying about that." But his exultant tone dropped as he added, "Yes, the sepulchre may be whited over; but within—! within—!"

Calmire's ingenuity was powerless before that problem, and for some moments both were silent. At length he said:

"Yes, Muriel, *all* our debts to Nature have got to be paid. But a wise man manages liabilities which bankrupt a fool. The main thing is not to be staggered by the debt, but to use hard experience to add to our resources in the rest of life."

"But I *am* bankrupt," declared Muriel.

"Bankrupts sometimes recover," said Calmire, "and you are young. True, the fact of having been bankrupt can't be obliterated, but it can be offset."

After another silence Muriel asked: "*Do* you see marriage looming up as a possible duty?"

"To my mind," answered Calmire, "when duty is the only motive, marriage and duty are contradictions in terms. I'm not wise enough, however, to consider all possible circumstances, and certainly not, at present, those of this case. Be glad of your spare time."

"Well, what's the next step at *this* end of it?" asked Muriel.

"None at all," answered Calmire, "or as near as you can get to it. Can't you go to work at something?"

"Perhaps I could if I knew my doom. But I wouldn't give much for any work I'll accomplish before I do."

"Well, you're young!" said Calmire, pityingly, "and haven't yet learned the worth of work as an anodyne. Perhaps some other would be best for your case."

"Oh, I don't deserve any anodyne," exclaimed Muriel. "I keep thinking about this thing all the time. If there's a right about it, I'll find it. I don't slip up in my duty there at least! The thing is never absent from my mind, except when I sleep."

"My poor boy!" exclaimed Calmire, turning towards him. "My poor boy! How in the world did I manage to forget that before? Why, do you know what you're doing?"

Muriel was astonished at his uncle's warmth, but simply said: "Why, that's the least I can do. I owe that to everybody concerned."

"You poor boy! Don't you know that you're simply doing all you can to drive yourself crazy? That's monomania—having one thing in mind all the time—that's the first step in insanity. And I'm such an old fool that I didn't think to warn you against it before! Yet I know perfectly well that in all distress, that's the first thing inexperienced people do. I've even heard a bereaved mother say that she owed it to her child's memory to blend it with every thought of her life. What earthly naturalness and sanity of thought can exist under such conditions—every natural sequence interrupted and clogged by a foreign element? People always begin that way when they go crazy. Now instead of keeping this thing in your mind, try every reasonable diversion to keep it out, as long as nothing can be settled about it. Why, haven't you found before now that many a day you've vainly puzzled yourself tired over something, when next morning the solution would come into your mind like a flash? Other things even, the mere fact that a question will stick in your mind to the exclusion of free attention to the other topics that naturally arise, is a reason why you should drive it out."

"Uncle Grand, how old must a man get, before he stops being a fool?"

"Ask some older man than I."

"But I mean," persisted Muriel, "that since I got into this trouble, there have been lots of things coming up like what you've just told me, that seem plain enough, but that I hadn't sense enough to think of. Now, how old must a fellow get, before he thinks of all the obvious things?"

"Ah! You can't count it by years!" said Calmire. "Count it by troubles, and then it depends on how big they are. You know that there's pretty good authority for saying that if a man happens to be a downright fool, even braying in a mortar can't cure him."

"Well, take a fool of about my grade?" Muriel inquired.

Our only Glimpse of Town.

"Is this really you?" Calmire exclaimed, turning toward him. "Your experience with the mortar has not been entirely without result. Well, to answer your question; your first long letter looked as if you'd had about enough for the first round, anyhow. But a man never gets so much that he can't get more. Yet when he gets knocked absolutely wrong-end-first, and has sense enough to begin to work around to natural bearings again, he'll have to take pretty much all the points in his individual horizon—he'll have to revise pretty much every belief he ever had—from that in his own existence out to that of the existence of a Law in Nature. And the queer thing is that nearly every time he thinks he's made a new point, it will simply be a new side of some one of his old commonplace ideas."

"Sometimes," said Muriel, "I feel so steady that I think I must have got around all right—that I needn't bother my head any more, but need simply wait until some new fact arises, and then *do*, and keep cool about it. And then a little later, I find myself in a perfect hell-caldron of questions and anxieties."

"That's all natural," said Calmire. "Your nerves *will* help themselves to a rest occasionally: if they didn't, you'd go crazy, and that's not our way. But just as soon as they have had a respite, they will want to get up and wrestle with the uncertainties again, as long as there are uncertainties before you. You can save yourself lots of trouble by diverting your nerves to other things, instead of encouraging them into this useless struggle, as I've been fool enough to let you do."

"Oh don't keep on scolding yourself so, Uncle Grand. Are you responsible for all my folly and inexperience?"

"I have a good deal of charity for a young fool, Muriel, but if there's anything I hate, it's an old one, and I sometimes fear that that's just what I'm getting to be."

And Muriel had the first hearty laugh, though a very short one, that he had had for many a day, as he looked at the splendid man, erect, alert, perfectly turned out, tooling his fiery horses along with the unconscious grace of young Phœbus Apollo.

Next they fell to talking about what Muriel had better do with himself for the immediate present. Solitude through the Winter in the monotonous country place where he had lately been immured, would not, his uncle was satisfied, be good for him. As for Muriel himself, he was indifferent on all points except that he did not want to remain in New York, subject, although he said nothing about that, to experiencing and inflicting such meetings as that of the morning. As it was, Muriel had led his uncle to drive outside of the park, in order to lessen the chance of imposing a sight of himself on Nina. He would himself have been glad enough of the sweet torture of seeing her again, but at last he had grown able to think of more sides than his own.

As, then, he wanted to avoid both New York and the country, and in fact everything that he had ever known, except his uncle, the obvious thing for him was to go to Europe with a friend who was soon to start for a saunter from Pau to Naples. This was not at first obvious to him, though, and he said some grim things about a man in his situation going on "a pleasure-trip." Calmire told him not to sentimentalize, though if it would relieve his inflamed conscience, he might regard the trip as a needed educational one. At last he decided to go, and to come back in time for his impending responsibilities. The existing ones, his uncle insisted on managing himself.

One thing surprised Calmire a little and pleased him immensely. Muriel had not once evinced the slightest inclination to shirk. His only desire had been to determine what his responsibilities might be; and while Calmire knew that this could not endure with absolute consistency, it made him realize more than anything else could have done, what the recent weeks had effected in Muriel.

Notwithstanding his usual unreserve, Muriel had not let his uncle know that he had even seen Nina that morning. Everything about that interview was too sacred for any soul that had not felt it. Down in the bottom of Muriel's, too deep even for his own thorough realization, the memory of it had already assumed some of the awful sacredness of death.

CHAPTER LIII.

WHERE MAN MAY GO.

It may well be supposed that the tender shoots of Nina's new convictions—shoots that, to most of the contemporary world, are hopelessly juiceless, had not yielded her during the few days since Calmire last tended them, all the tonics needed against her own harassing thoughts, not to speak of such a strain upon her as the interview with Muriel. Naturally the first fervor of what she might perhaps have been ready to call her conversion, had somewhat cooled, as such fervors always do, and her former habits of mind were assailing it, as such habits always do, and bringing her, if not intellectually, at least emotionally, back to the dark borders of her skepticism. The communion with the Infinite in which her soul had been immersed on that wondrous morning, had not since been so complete: for Nature—or what is behind Nature — had not since revealed itself to her with such inspiring unreserve. At moments, she had known something of the feeling which had so exalted and sustained her; but whatever be one's best affections—be he lover of a cult, or of man, or woman either, or of Nature, or of All, those moments of supreme exaltation are vouchsafed but seldom. Nina was not yet the matured creature who has outgrown the yearning for parental care. Though no girl of a loving disposition ever was naturally more independent, her independence was not yet fully developed; and moreover, she *was* of a loving disposition—to the extent that made a man's robuster intellect the natural complement of hers; and she had got into the habit of turning toward Calmire as most girls turn toward the ordinary modes of religious consolation. She now looked with positive dread for a communication from him postponing on some pretext but the real one—Muriel's presence in town, a chat she had hoped for on the next evening. It had been arranged that she and her mother were to run around and dine with Calmire and Mrs. John, who was staying with him.

No postponement was decreed, however; but Nina felt sure that Muriel would not be there, and she was glad to go. After dinner, Mrs. Wahring, who somehow, particularly hated smoke when the endurance of it would force any woman but Nina to keep Calmire company over his cigar, declined his invitation to that function of familiar friendship, dragged Mrs. John into the drawing-room with her, and left Calmire and Nina together before the library fire.

Calmire knew well enough that Nina would need her new lessons again and again before they could become part of her working fibre, and was only waiting to help her on. So he began:

"Well, how do our new philosophies progress?"

If he had studied for a good opening for her, as perhaps he had, he could not have done better. The question was almost impersonal.

"Well," she answered, "I get myself terribly mixed up. I think I must be very incapable of confining my mind to those hard certain truths you seem to content yours with, and keeping it away from the things you call imaginary, and hate so."

"It's awful for a poor old man to feel himself such a curmudgeon in the eyes of a nice girl," he said, laughing. "But seriously now: *do* you think my soul is filled only with 'hard' things?"

"It's the tenderest, gentlest soul a man ever had!" she exclaimed. "But your *mind* is so fearfully rigid beyond a certain point."

"You know," said he, "or perhaps you don't, that I think intellectual integrity, and even common every-day honesty, depend almost as much on the mind as upon the conscience—possibly more. I don't mean upon the range of mind, but upon its firmness in whatever principles its range includes. I suspect that most moral breakdowns are preceded by intellectual juggling—by the person convincing himself that the wrong course is right. No! in men cursed by 'the malady of thought,' strength depends largely upon judgment. Don't blame one for trying to keep his judgment firm."

"I didn't mean to blame you. But there's something awful in you: my mind seeks to roam up the pleasant valleys of my old beliefs, and you loom up before me like a great precipice."

Calmire laughed again, though with a certain serious satisfaction. After a little silence, he said:

"Do you want me to lecture some more?"

"I always like to hear you talk. What do you want to talk about now?"

"You're very kind," he answered. "I know that I must sometimes be an awful bore, because I'm so much interested in some things that are not generally found interesting. This isn't one of those cases, though," he said, smiling, "for I want to talk now because I'm interested in *you*. Well, if you care for it, I'd like to tell you something about the limits of real thought—where the precipices—more insurmountable ones than you make me to be, ought to stand, or rather where they do stand—all around the little circle of our capacities; and where we ought to realize that they stand, so that we may not blindly dash ourselves against them, but surmount them, or rather remove them, so far as we can, by the slow processes that Nature provides."

"Go on," she said, turning her chair a little more directly toward him. "You're very good!"

"Ah, you're the sort of pupil it's a pleasure to be good to!" he exclaimed, as he leaned forward and knocked the ashes of his cigar onto the hearth.

Often afterward, she thought of how noble he looked as he made that little commonplace motion—the fire throwing a certain radiance over his strong features, and glowing in the kind eyes, and his grand form seeming so powerful, outlined by the close-fitting evening suit, and emphasized by the white expanse over the chest.

"It's not an easy subject, and probably I'll have to show it to you in several ways. You'll tell me if I bore you?"

"Try me."

"Now among the nearest of those precipices," he

went on, "is one that you'll find it very hopeful to contemplate. It's the inscrutability of consciousness. We can't know anything about consciousness, except that it exists: so we can't have the slightest evidence that it ever dies. We know that the body with its nervous system—the apparatus that acts upon consciousness, and through which consciousness acts, does die—that the combination of ever-changing particles which make up that apparatus, is eventually resolved; but as we know nothing about consciousness, we have no evidence whatever that it may not survive independently of the apparatus of the body, or connected with new apparatus which our present senses are unable to recognize."

"That *sounds* pleasant," said Nina, "but I don't quite understand. *Why* can't we know anything about consciousness? I thought it was all we did know."

"So it is, in a sense," Calmire answered. "We know our thoughts and feelings, but what it is that knows them, we don't know and can't know. It is a law of our thought that there must be a something understanding and a something understood — a something experiencing and a something experienced—a subjective and an objective. Now on the subjective side we have our mass of sensations, thoughts and feelings, and they are subjective to the outside universe, and some of them are subjective to others of them—we understand and feel our own thoughts and feelings— some thoughts and feelings are a degree behind others, some a degree behind the second set, and so on in an indefinitely increasing series of degrees, but at the end of all the series, behind all thoughts and feelings, subjective to all the rest of our being, lies consciousness—in front of it is all feeling, all understanding. We can't get any feeling or understanding behind consciousness—in short: we can't make it objective to itself: for by the very nature of our thinking, it must be subjective to anything we can think of: so to understand consciousness, we would have to upset the very process by which alone we can understand anything."

"I'm so little used to the argument," said Nina, "that as yet it seems to me little more than a play on words."

"Keep it in mind, and it will become clearer," he assured her. "But," he went on, "if it's only a play on words, and really means nothing, it seems to make the case all the stronger: for it shows that with regard to consciousness, we have reached the place that we ultimately reach in exploring all other mysteries—time, space, matter, motion, force—the place where our faculties stop, and we begin to talk paradox."

"Then we have no truth!" mournfully exclaimed Nina. "Our beliefs rest on nothing."

"That's merely a metaphor," exclaimed Calmire, smiling, "but a very frequent one. Our beliefs rest on our experience, and so far as we are concerned—so far as any practical need for life or faith goes, experience is absolutely reliable—two and two have always made four, unsupported bodies have always fallen, fire has always burned."

"But how can we know that they always will?" asked the girl.

"We only know it as men: not as gods," Calmire admitted. "Absolute truth is not for us: for that matter, we don't know what we are talking about when we use the expression. For one thing, to hold any adequate conception of the absolute or infinite, our brains would have to be infinitely large: there could be no room for anything else in the universe. You see the notion lands us in impossibilities. But the truths that experience gives us, have never failed us; and it's very morbid to bother ourselves about whether they ever can. The only healthy thing is to use them as we have found them. The phenomena of the world without and the world within are enough for us to get along on, and more than we can ever master. But it's as impossible for us to get at the Verity behind thoughts, as I showed you some time ago, that it is to get at the Verity behind things. So it's as absurd to say that one dies as to say that the other dies."

"Why then," exclaimed Nina with a beaming face, "we *are* immortal!"

"Perhaps: but don't be too fast. I've only told you that there's not the slightest evidence against it. But I'm bound to tell you that there's no clear evidence for it. Yet there is a little evidence that in time *may* be clear: for there are some indications, which a few of the psychical-research men accept as evidence, of communication from consciousnesses that have survived death; and at worst, whether they are right or not, there is also something faintly visible that *may* mean that consciousness is at least independent of the body—that it can leave and return to the same body. I don't mean merely in fainting and sleep, when you might call consciousness latent, but in other circumstances, where two, or even three consciousnesses have alternated in the same body. There are several cases of people who have lost all recollection of their past, and all intellectual and moral resemblance to their former selves; and who have had to begin life over again with new minds, new characters, and new educations. The new consciousness sometimes has been an improvement, and sometimes the reverse—sometimes with more intelligence, and better dispositions; and sometimes with worse. It has been precisely as if there were a different soul in the same body. In many such cases, probably most, the first soul has returned after a while, at the same point in memory and faculty where it left; in some cases, the second has come a second time, and in some cases there has been even a third, each existing and coming and going independently of the others. Hypnotic suggestion has been able quite frequently to substitute the second soul, and sometimes the third."

"I don't understand," Nina interrupted. "How can that be?"

"Why," Calmire explained, "you know that a hypnotizer can make his subject fancy almost anything: why shouldn't he make him fancy himself somebody else? And by renewing such fancies with a good deal of completeness and uniformity, the subject can be made at will to take on virtually a new character, or even (as far as experiment has got) either of two new characters. In either of these ways—either by natural processes which we don't yet fully understand (though injuries and shocks help account for some of them), or by hypnotic suggestion, slow, stingy, timid people have been changed into quick, liberal, dashing ones, each either with no recollection of the other, or, if with a recollection, only as of another person. As, however, physical changes can produce these changes of soul, its identity with the body would seem to be indicated; but that is offset by the fact that hypnotic suggestion from another soul can produce them too, and perhaps by the other fact that a very slight change in body effects the total change in consciousness. But the subject is unending: you can find more about it in the books. The point I want to give you now is that there *is* something that may look a little like evidence for the soul existing independently of the body. Don't ignore it entirely, but don't attach much weight to it. There is also a faint possibility that that possible new hypnotic sense may yet get hold of more evidence. If it does, possibly there may then be more indication of the persistence of consciousness later than the apparatus, as well as for its independence of the apparatus. But this is getting too much like moonshine."

"But is there absolutely no such indication now?" she asked. "I'll give up what you would call the early fables, but how about what you said regarding the Society for Psychical Research?"

"There's not enough to satisfy my mind, but

there's enough to encourage suspense of judgment. We *may* be on the way toward something substantial: for already the evidence regarding the persistence of consciousness, seems at least even, while before the discovery of the persistence of force, I think the evidence was distinctly *against* the persistence of consciousness."

" How ?" asked Nina.

"Why, I don't see what there was to do then, when the force that moved a man's body and brain stopped moving them, but to believe that the force was annihilated."

"Why, isn't it ?" queried Nina. " What becomes of it ?"

"Weren't you lectured enough last Summer to know that *something* must become of it ? Why, it simply takes up other work. The share of force that the organism was constantly drawing from the air and food-supply is left free for other organisms; and that already contained in the body itself, goes to resolving the body into its elements —setting them free for new combinations; and in doing that, the force is turned into heat and absorbed into the universal heat ready, probably, to be converted into some new mode of force: though that's farther than we've yet been able to follow it. But thirty years ago, people didn't know that, and they had to believe, so far as I can see, that when a man died, what were called his 'vital forces' ceased to exist. And as they had to believe that, they had to believe, so far as I can see, that his consciousness ceased to exist too, unless they were simply going to believe against their senses under the inspiration of a few great geniuses;—and you find a myriad of great fools laying claim to the same inspirations. But, for that matter, it won't do to trust only to the geniuses: the hypnotic sense, if there's any such inspiration to be had through *it*, is by no means restricted to geniuses."

"Well, there's room to hope, anyhow," said Nina.

"Most certainly, if you'll keep your hopes within reason. But see how strongly Nature enjoins us to limit them—to regard them as conjectures—hypotheses; not to found faiths and practices upon them! Reflect how doing that, has led, probably, to more evils than any other blunder of the race. We're here to mind our business here. And now let's go on and find out a little more definitely what our business is, or at least what its limits are. Let's accept the inscrutability, with our present faculties and present evidence, of the question of consciousness continuing or ceasing, as we accept the inscrutability of its very existing. So, as we can't understand it in itself, let's go to its phenomena, as we have to go to the phenomena of that other Inscrutability behind the external world. I said a moment ago, that to understand a thing is to find a resemblance in it to something that we were previously familiar with. The degree of our understanding, of course, depends upon the number of such resemblances that we find. I showed you, too, that that's why we can't understand consciousness, and yet there's just one particular in which we *can* see that it resembles something else."

"I've caught it!" cried Nina, her bright face lighting up. "I've caught it! You just showed it! The verity behind the inner world is inscrutable, the verity behind the outer world is inscrutable: the soul is like God!"

"But that's merely in a negative particular," said Calmire. "There's a positive one."

"What is it?"

"I've told you. See if you can't think it up."

"When did you tell me?"

"A moment ago—as far as the soul's part goes."

Nina meditated and shook her head.

"I told you," said Calmire, "that consciousness, in a degree, originates the phenomena of the world within."

"Oh yes!" cried Nina. "Just as God originates those of the world without. So in our own little worlds, each of us is a God! We create! But I'm not so glad of the mere fact that we create, as I am that doing so makes us like the great God."

"Yet," said Calmire, smiling at her pretty enthusiasms, but more at her quick recoil from self-aggrandizement, "consciousness is nothing without the external world: the German didn't evolve much of a camel."

"No!" said Nina. "God's world outside of us must supply the sources of all right thoughts in our own worlds within us. We're absolutely dependent on God. I like that too. 'Our wills are ours to make them thine.'"
We're absolutely dependent on God. I like that too. 'Our wills are ours to make them thine.'"

"I don't know about 'absolutely dependent,' Nina. You know it seemed to us once—talking at Fleuvemont, that *some* power, and an increasing power, of controlling the universe, is possessed by man. But here we are in paradox again: paradox is the alarm-bell that always sounds when our reasoning is getting beyond our bounds. You see that as soon as we assert free-will, we assert an effect without a cause—which is something, you'll find if you try, that you can't think. One of the prettiest demonstrations of evolution is that our experience of it is so absolutely without exception, that our minds are actually incapable of thinking of anything as not an effect from a cause."

Nina reflected a moment and then said, "Yet you believe in free-will, Mr. Calmire?"

"Yes—as I believe in consciousness, and in the Ineffable Power that we apprehend as outside of our own consciousness, and that I suspect is inside of it too: I don't attempt to understand either. In one sense, by the way, believing in free-will is not believing in an effect without a cause: for we can refer it to consciousness as a cause; but that only puts our paradox a step farther back: for you can't refer consciousness to any cause intelligible to us. Even if you think of it as started by the Source of everything else, you can't help thinking of it as something now distinct and independent of its source.

"But we're getting a long way off from my attempt to indicate how our understanding is bounded. At Fleuvemont, we discussed what thought is—what the structure of our minds; and you just said, very properly, that the external world of God gives the sources of all right thoughts. Now all our talk has made it obvious that legitimate thinking is only thinking that can be, by sound logic, traced back to sensation—to experience, direct or ancestral. And so, beliefs which contradict experience, very seldom have any foundation: though, as experience is imperfect, a few may have had. Experience is, however, our only test, however imperfect it may be. It follows, then, that those precipices we were talking about, which surround human capacity, stand at the borders of experience; and the only way to move them farther away, is to enlarge the borders of experience. Or, to change the metaphor, the boundary of our little sphere of life is translucent but not transparent: it is penetrated by some of the light from the surrounding Infinity, but we cannot see what is outside, and all our speculations on it are vain until experience confirms them. Still we can enlarge the sphere, but only by learning the laws of its constitution, and following them."

"But what," asked Nina, "is meant by that phrase: 'the scientific uses of the imagination'?"

"Why of course the imagination can conjecture from the data of experience, as to the directions in which experience can be wisely enlarged. But our conjectures should be in the directions experience points out. The attempted short-cuts in other directions make up the great mass of the race's wasted effort, and have led to probably its greatest misfortunes."

"Yes," persisted Nina, "that may all be true in science and philosophy. But how can we be content to wait, with such terrible mysteries before us in life itself?"

"Nothing can be true in philosophy unless it s true 'in life itself,' and one great function of philosophy is to make us content before *all* mysteries—that is, content to wait and study them. But just what kind of mysteries do you mean?"

"Well, take that case of poor Charley Staller. He was a splendid fellow—good, capable, supporting his old mother finely, engaged to one of the nicest girls in town, respected by everybody, honorable, useful. Now why should he be cut off so suddenly and terribly, and lots of young men not worth their salt be left to grow old at somebody-else's expense and discomfort? Indeed, indeed, Mr. Calmire, much as I respect all your philosophy—much, perhaps I may say, as it has helped me, I'm afraid it can't help a great deal before a mystery like that."

"Why!" exclaimed Calmire, "I didn't know there was any mystery about it. The poor boy broke his neck, didn't he?"

"Yes."

"Chasing an anise-seed bag over a fence that was too high for his horse?"

"Yes."

"Doctor didn't find anything irregular about it, did he?"

"No."

"Then where's the mystery? Boys will jump fences, and even an old fool like me is known to sometimes. I can't see anything mysterious when we get our necks broken."

"Oh, you're teasing me again, Mr. Calmire! You know perfectly well what I mean."

"Well, I'd rather you'd put it to me in your own words."

"Why!" answered Nina, "it's so mysterious that God should permit such an awful thing to happen. Such a mystery is too terrible not to cry out against."

"I thought," said Calmire quietly, "that 'God' was liberal enough to let us have a good deal of our own way, and that it was the boy and his horse that made it happen. But of course if you want to put the responsibility back on the same God that sent your boat down on Courtenay, you can make it as mysterious as you please. But then it's you who are reading the mystery into Nature; it isn't really there. You make that sort of a God out of your imagination, and then think it strange that you haven't made him to fit the facts of the Universe. Of course you can put a God behind anything if you want to; but you'll find yourself no better off when you come to account for his ways. Your mind can't discover or construct a God consistent with the facts : nobody's mind ever did. You know lots of people, from the Greeks down to Stuart Mill, have tried to account for the way things get mixed up here, by the assumption that this planet, or this system, is governed by a viceroy of limited powers, with Almighty God behind him."

"Well!" said Nina, "if the god behind him is almighty, why doesn't he enable his viceroy to govern perfectly?"

"Good girl!" exclaimed Calmire. "There goes the alarm-bell again, you see! You're beginning to realize, aren't you?, that through all our talks (and always, for that matter,) whenever anything counter to experience is assumed, reasoning on it leads to paradox. Everybody who does that sort of thing gets into trouble, and it's well to watch out for the alarm. If only people would realize what it means, and stop!"

"But," said Nina, "those who have perfect faith don't get into trouble."

"'Perfect faith,'" answered Calmire, "is perfect confession that one knows nothing about it, and is willing to leave it alone. That's my position exactly."

"Yet," expostulated Nina, "you show me that there is a God, and a spiritual world. And when we began talking to-night, you showed me grounds for faith in immortality."

"Well, I haven't professed to know anything about any of the three, have I, except so far as they are *revealed* in Nature and humanity? And as to immortality, don't call that faith, Nina. It's not as clear as the other two. Call it hope if you want to; but better still, leave it alone if you can, and confine yourself to your life here. You'll find enough to do, and doing it is the best preparation we can conceive for more life. Beyond the precipices which surround us, no man has ever been, no instrument or formula has ever reached, and reasonable belief is impossible. The beliefs men have manufactured without evidence—like that in an anthropomorphic God, perfectly powerful, perfectly good and perfectly just, who is all the time conniving at evil and injustice—contradict themselves and, sooner or later, make trouble. Nature tells us, if she tells us anything, that we have no business with them."

CHAPTER LIV.

MAN'S RANGE ENOUGH FOR MAN.

NINA sat silent a good while and then said:

"I've got to get used to these thoughts. At times lately, I have realized more than I ever dreamed before, of the significance of the universe; but what you have been saying to-night makes me realize more than I ever dreamed before, of the littleness of our share in it."

"Yet you can't even think of our having an unlimited share in it; you can put in words some such idea, but all the same, it will be a false idea—what it's getting the fashion to call a pseud-idea. Place yourself, in imagination, beyond the farthest star you can see: there, you have every reason to believe, you would see others equally far: we have no reason to suppose that there is a limit."

"But, Mr. Calmire, I read the other day an argument showing that the space where there are stars is limited."

"Very likely: there have been many such arguments. What was that one?"

"Well, I can't give it exactly, but its conclusion was that unless the stars were limited, our nights would be bright."

Calmire laughed, and exclaimed: "Oh yes! The argument was that as there are many more stars of the second magnitude than of the first, more of the third than of the second, and so on, so we get more light from the many stars of second magnitude than we do from the few of first, more from those of third than from those of second, and so on down, until we get more light from the many very remote stars we see, than from the relatively few very near: therefore, the farther the stars extend, the more light we get, both relatively and absolutely, and if they extended indefinitely, we should be getting indefinitely increasing light. Was that it?"

"Yes, and it seems perfectly conclusive."

Calmire laughed again, and said: "We *are* getting indefinitely increasing light—and not in the physical sense alone; but, as I've often told you, there's a great deal more—of both kinds, that we haven't got yet; and your friend's argument, my child, is nonsense, as every human argument dealing with infinities must be. You won't find a prettier demonstration than this just here, of the inevitable limits to our faculties and to our perceived environment."

"Why, Mr. Calmire! The argument seems perfectly simple."

"Yes, dear, so simple that it leaves something out. You know, don't you, that the light of even many of the stars we see, has taken more time than we can conceive, to reach us?"

"Yes."

"Well, how then are we going to be conscious of the light of the stars far beyond even them?"

"I didn't think of that!" said Nina.

"Neither did your author. You see that we are

simply where our minds must stop. In the first place, we have no evidence that the medium which brings us light, can carry it an indefinite distance, any more than the medium which brings us sound can" (The aspects of this question have changed since Mr. Calmire held forth, but not so as to affect the argument); "and even if it could, the light of stars infinitely far off, would require infinite time to reach us: so we could never see it. Yet that expression really conveys nothing to the mind. It has the negative meaning of upsetting your author's equally meaningless hypothesis, though—in other words, of bringing the whole question into paradox —just where such questions always end. But suppose the 'fields of the stars' limited, we can't conceive space beyond them limited, and yet we can't conceive it limitless, though some comets come to our Sun in curves which seem to prove that after they leave it, they keep moving away forever."

"What a grand conception!" she exclaimed. "So would I have my soul go!"

"Paradox again, my child! It's simply no conception at all. Our minds can't really *conceive* it: we can't imagine the comets stopping, but we can't imagine their going forever, either. It would take infinite time to imagine infinite motion—which expression sounds as if it meant something; but really it doesn't, for reasons that you know by this time, Miss."

"Well, I want to know more than I can now, anyhow."

"An admirable desire, but, like every other one, needing proper regulation! If you had the answer to every question that tortures your soul now, each answer would raise a dozen new questions—you would find more questions, as you would find more stars, and so on to infinity; and knowledge itself, unless curiosity is tempered by reason, would tend to misery rather than to happiness. Those questions, rightly used, are new sources of interest and activity; but if we persist at looking at the subject in your mistaken way, the wider share in the Universe that we get, the more limited our share in it must appear. Looked at in the right way, the fields we have, and the privilege of widening them, give us more room for intellectual activity than we can hope to cover; and thought in those fields is useful and happy. If we keep within the bounds that Nature sets for us, we have plenty to do, and what's even more important, no need to occupy ourselves with chimerical speculations, or to cut each other's throats over them and burn each other at stakes."

"That's true! Perhaps if my faith about God and the spiritual world, were knowledge, I could rest content."

"Do even the orthodox claim much knowledge? Probably you know all of such subjects now that your intellect is capable of comprehending, except as you expand it by more study and more life. Plainly, if you could put your questions to a superhuman intelligence, the answers would require superhuman intelligence to comprehend; and the words we have yet made, could not frame them. You know that all through the talk of that great man Paul, runs the question: 'How shall the finite comprehend the infinite?' But yet we are not wholly restricted to our ignorance. There *is* an education of the human race, whatever may be the nature of the Power which instituted it: all evolution has been working toward intelligence and toward morality. But nothing is plainer than that we can only know the educating Power through the slow and salutary processes of the education. Remember that it is but by the patient use of those senses which you have been trained to despise, that we have learned that that Power is *one*—that the actual energy which swings the stars, blazes in their fires, warms the air and the plants, and vivifies the conscious creature, is the same force by which the human being thinks and feels, the same that glows from canvas, throbs through symphonies, and conquers Time and Death in poems."

His exaltation carried her with it for a moment. But soon her face fell listless again, and she said: "But Time and Death conquer in the end."

"And what if they do? Oh dear!" he added half wearily, but cheerfully. "How that always comes up to young people! How one has to go over it with them again and again! Well, perhaps it can't be gone over too often. In the first place, as we were saying a few minutes ago, we don't know that thoughts, or even memories, die. In old age, the memories of youth are said to be more vivid than in middle life; and certainly in dreams, things apparently long forgotten come up with all the vividness of reality; and the planchette boards and all sorts of automatic writing and talking are constantly showing a stock of memories and impulses beneath our consciousness."

"But," Nina objected, "the things themselves die, and the people, and everything that's lovely."

"Your faith of a few minutes ago was only in the gristle, wasn't it?" said Calmire. Then he went on, apparently regardless of the subject, to ask: "Can you make out that picture between the windows?"

"I seem to see the dome of St. Peter's in it."

"That's a *thing*, I suppose?" queried Calmire.

"Certainly!"

"Which?" pursued Calmire. "The picture there, or the stone dome in Rome?"

"Why both, I suppose."

"Which is St. Peter's—this, or the one in Rome?"

"Why, the one in Rome, of course."

"Well now," said Calmire, "suppose that an earthquake were to throw down the dome in Rome, and later, somebody taking the existing pictures and drawings were to reproduce it exactly. That would be essentially just as much Michelangelo's dome as the present one is, wouldn't it?"

"Certainly," Nina admitted.

"Yet," continued Calmire, "the thing you now call Michelangelo's dome would have yielded to 'time and death.' But there's something that endures nevertheless."

"Not the pictures and drawings and all that?" she asked.

"It's not inconceivable, is it," queried Calmire in return, "that without even them, a great architect could study the dome closely enough to reproduce it from memory?"

"No: I suppose one could."

"Well, then, there is a something that started with Michelangelo, and that outlasts granite. Now that something—the *thought*, is the essential *thing*. It accumulated paper and colors to itself, and expressed itself in Michelangelo's plans, or it accumulated stone to itself, and expressed itself in the dome by the Tiber; but what we call St. Peter's and go all the way to Rome to see, is not the real thing, but only one expression of it, like the other ten thousand expressions—pictures, models,—all are mere temporary accidents of it: the thing itself—the real St. Peter's, endures independently of them; it arose in the consciousness of Michelangelo and the other architects, it exists more or less completely in the consciousness of millions to-day, a dream can bring it up vividly in any one of them, and, as I have tried to make plain to you before, we have no conclusive evidence that it ever dies."

"Yes! How wonderful!" ejaculated Nina. Then after pondering a minute, she said sadly: "But that flower there, is not an expression of any man's enduring thought, and human beings are not, either."

"Some people," Calmire answered, "are fond of considering them expressions of God's thoughts; and some like to think of the human soul seizing carbon and oxygen and nitrogen and iron and lime and making a body to express itself withal, just as Michelangelo's soul seized charcoal and colors and stone, to partially express itself in his plans and pictures and statues and buildings. Of course so far as we know, this is all a mere metaphor regarding man and the flower, but there may be the deepest truth behind it. Certainly as long as the flower and the man can be reproduced, to a degree, on canvas or in memory—including the vivid memory of dreams, it's no more true of them than of the dome, that time and death conquer them; though to be fair, it *is* in one sense more nearly true of them than of the simpler things of man's voluntary production: for man's can all be expressed over and over again in the most perfect way, by human art; while Nature's cannot be reproduced by human art in any but most inadequate representation. Yet involuntarily, outside of art, in dreams, they are reproduced with strange completeness: immortality in the minds of those who love us, or hate us, or even are indifferent to us, means more than we ordinarily ascribe to mere waking memory. 'Time and Death' may 'conquer in the end': our minds simply can't conceive of the eternal existence of anything; but they don't conquer as promptly as, at first glance, they seem to! *Do they?*"

"No," admitted Nina. "They certainly do not. But this is all so new and strange! Give me some more sides of it, please."

"Well," said Calmire, with a little laugh, "you see, don't you, that when you say that Time and Death conquer, you are simply falling once more into the paradoxes that fringe our limited reason? We know just as well that they do *not* conquer, as that they do. That flower blooming near the window, *is* beautiful in spite of all that Time and Death can do; so is Hamlet; so is the Pastoral Symphony. Here our paradox relates to time, just as, when we were traveling off among the stars a moment ago, it related to space. You can't imagine the flower and the poetry and the music lasting forever, any more than you can imagine the stars and space extending without limit. Neither can you imagine the fact that the flower *is* beautiful, annihilated, any more than you can imagine space annihilated. Are you going to despise the flower because it does not last forever? Suppose that even your flower of a soul does not last forever, any more than your flower of a life does, are they not to be loved? We are not apt to think that being each of us limited in space, takes the significance out of life; why then should being limited in time? I confess that when I hear people say that life is worthless unless it is immortal, I am reminded of a creature of boundless greed, whose brief name is often a term of reproach, and seldom mentioned to ears polite."

Both were silent a little. Then he continued: "Now what's the moral of all this? It's not a speculative one: for it is proved every day in the lives that are happiest and most useful; it is the one that all rational thought leads to from every side: our talks always bring up at it; it is simply to use the faculties we have and the opportunities we have. No man ever found so little to do here that he really needed a bigger universe. Alexander's cheap yearning for more worlds to conquer, would have been superfluous if he'd had heart and brain enough to try a single world to improve. No man ever found in himself so much capacity to work or to enjoy, that average opportunities, discretion, and health, would not exercise it to the full, without giving him time to sigh for more opportunities. Of course there are many whose chances are below average: the world is not yet perfectly evolved, and may never be. But it's evolved far enough to give us our hands full, without our needing any more."

"Yes, but knowledge and work are not all," she sighed, thinking farther away than the subject of their talk.

"No," he answered, but still following his own thought, little divining hers. "There must be a faith beyond knowledge, as we felt it the other morning. But with you, the faith can't any longer be *contrary* to knowledge. Yet remember what I have said before, about the difficulty of changing old beliefs for new. You can't expect your new conceptions of the Infinite to fill your needs all at once: for that matter, what human needs ever are completely filled? All I claim is that they're generally filled far enough to get along on, if we take things rightly."

"But," Nina objected, "so many who have nothing here are sustained by hope of the hereafter."

"Well, certainly I don't object to their being, if they can, and can't find anything more substantial than that hope, to fill their minds with. But there are people whose minds seek demonstrable things. You're one: but you've got to get a new strength to pursue and hold the new conceptions. Even those who are satisfied with the old beliefs, have to do that before becoming really strong in them: you know the churches talk about getting a new heart, being born again, and the like. You have got to get a new heart, with which to rely on yourself and on the universe as you find it: not as, in your limited judgment, you would like it. Some maturer judgments prefer it as it is, rather than as you would have it. You remember Lessing's saying?"

"I'm afraid I never knew it. What was it?"

"What a delight to have a new generation to tell the old stories to!" Calmire exclaimed, laughing.

"Has this one anything to do with whiskey?" asked Nina, remembering when she had heard a story that did, and suddenly losing her bright expression.

"Not exactly. It's a beautiful allegory, and beautifully told. 'If God held truth in his right hand, and search-for-truth in his left, and were to say to me: "Choose!" I would bow reverently to the left hand and say: "Father, give! Pure truth is for thee alone!"'"

CHAPTER LV.

MAKING THE BEST OF A BAD CASE.

WHILE Nina and Muriel had been learning easy lessons in philosophy from Calmire, and Muriel, at least, hard lessons in morality from experience, poor Minerva, who, of course, was not capable of learning a very great deal of either, still was having her full share of that mysterious education which misery generally brings with it.

Whether, under all circumstances, "the prayer of the righteous availeth much," will probably long be an open question; and there may be a difference of opinion as to which side of the question is supported by the fact that Mrs. Granzine had given avail to Clint Russell's pious ejaculation when we last saw him with Calmire, by starting off in the direction it indicated with "Doctor" Leitoff.

It took a combination of many things to lead to a step so inconsistent with her years and her devotion to her children. But her maternal feeling has already been likened to that of the lower creatures, and among the points of resemblance, was its relatively evanescent character. A fortnight earlier, "Doctor" Leitoff, the same surgeon that Clint Russell had known in the army, had put out of joint the nose of the leading quack of the village, by appearing with a fine pair of horses constant black broadcloth, excessive blue-white shirt-front with a most impressive diamond in the midst thereof, and a great and suspiciously-black beard. All this glory had been preceded by flaring advertisements of his benevolent intention to cure all the ills of humanity, by various elements of a pharmacopœia whose uses were known only to himself, and which, in his one little life, he had raised into an efficacy superior to that of everything else provided by all the experience of all the ages. His remedies did not include "faith," for that function of that much-misused power had not then been revived from the desuetude into which it had fallen since the mighty claims made for it nearly twenty centuries earlier.

Mrs. Granzine was a strong woman—where there was anything to seek or anything to do. But where there was only something to endure—some loss to bear—she was of the weakest. And of all losses that she might be called upon to endure—the loss of love, or health, or fortune (as she knew it), or the deference of her neighbors, the last loss was to such a nature as hers, the greatest. Minerva's misfortunes constantly demanded from her mother a sympathy which it was not in the mother's nature to give, nor yet to suffer from her incapacity to give. But one thing the woman did suffer from, and that was an imagination. Despite Calmire's word that nothing should be spared to save untoward exposure, even to settling the family comfortably out of reach, she would picture herself the object, no longer of the deferential admiration of her ignorant circle, but of its gossip:

and that, she felt, would be doubly eager because of her "superiority." With the inconsistency of all dishonest natures, she found immeasurably terrible, the idea of the very exposure which she had herself threatened.

This picture pushed her, and Dr. Leitoff attracted her. The fires she had transmitted to Minerva were still far from burned out in her own veins. She still had power to inspire anew Leitoff's transcendental German dreaminess, and it produced on her the effect that a poetical nature, however cheap, can exercise on the sort of woman that she burlesqued. Small as her soul and his were, the ratio between them was the same that it would have been if he had been really a poet, and she really a woman. She had felt his magnetic charm in youth, and the long association with poor prosy Granzine into which prudence had led her, made her in her maturer years no less sensitive to Leitoff's fancies or to his pinchbeck imitations of what seemed to her, refinement. She never had much moral nature, and as is so frequently the case, it was at the expense of it, that she had cultivated her æsthetic nature. Here, too, within her reach, were what appeared to her, elegance and wealth: and she had never had an opportunity to test the emptiness of either. The result of it all was that she shuffled off the whole miserable responsibilities and dreads of home, leaped into the paradise of paint and tinsel constructed for her by Leitoff's imagination—and one evening started off with him behind his white horses, never, as she supposed, to return. Minerva was left alone with old Granzine, who might have been really her father: for so had some ancestral weak nature diluted in Minerva most of the forces but the dangerous ones, transmitted by her mother.

Now that Mrs. Granzine had gone where Clint wanted her to, though by no road of his selection, she was at least out of his way; and the gentle giant experienced toward Minerva a violent accession of that chivalrous tenderness and pity for everything weak and wronged, which made him as great a comfort to them, as he was a terror to oppressors.

Although he had no suspicion of how much Minerva needed her mother, he could not have been more profane (Or at least any other man could not) over Mrs. Granzine's desertion, if he had known all that she had deserted. As soon as he learned of that wretched woman's flight, he came to Minerva to swear, in his way of course, that he was going to do everything for her that he could, beginning by thrashing the whole town if it should by word or look make heavier the burden her mother's conduct had thrown upon her.

He was the first to bring her any consolation, and his rough kindness was peculiarly congenial to her. All that she was suffering made it easy for a stronger feeling than she had ever known before—a feeling of more character, to grow up toward Clint. Hers was not the nature to scotch such a feeling at the beginning, for the reasons that would have made it horrible to some women in her situation, or to lead her to prevent Clint coming again with more sympathy, and again and again with more and more.

In their earlier acquaintance, she had loved Clint, in his turn of course, as she had loved every man she knew who was worth it. One of the strange things about Minerva, as already intimated, was that, whatever her own shortcomings, her requirements in men—and her attainments, were generally high. If Clint had been persistent, if nobody else had too soon tempted her with variety, and if her mother had not corrupted her toward Muriel, she would have married Clint long before. That she could not do so now, was a fact painfully borne in upon her by the feeling that his assiduous kindness inspired.

Whether there was in Clint's own mind, any motive for that kindness, beyond his natural gentleness and chivalry, he had not time (for in such a matter he required more time than most men) to ask himself, before Minerva disappeared from the scene, and with her whatever germs there may have been in both of them for the development of an aborted idyl in misery and despair.

Minerva's disappearance came about naturally through Calmire. When she was deserted by her mother, he felt the necessity of some other woman in the case, and after carefully considering the situation, came to the conclusion that the arguments in favor of taking his sister-in-law Amelia into his confidence, were greater than the very obvious ones against it. That gentle lady's wisdom and loving care for all that concerned Muriel, would, Calmire knew, not only be of value now, but of inestimable worth in the probable future. She, as recognized helper of every woman within miles who needed help, could at once do for Minerva, without exciting comment, what nobody else could; and her unerring judgment, Calmire felt, would see the best courses for the future.

She was infinitely distressed, as Calmire knew she would be; but wasted no time in vainly wringing her hands or moralizing. She concluded to keep Minerva, for the present at least, within reach of herself. In driving, she had seen her with Huldah Cronin, touching whom she, and Mary Courtenay of course, knew more than anybody else in Calmire. The image of the pair together, came up in Amelia's imagination as it roamed over the neighboring country, seeking an asylum for Minerva. Huldah's house was singularly secluded. Many old residents did not know its existence. Winter was at hand, when it would be doubly secluded. A little discretion would enable Minerva to live there unobserved, at least until Spring. Should any complication arise, she could easily go away, and meanwhile the question of where to, could be considered.

After much deliberation, some talks with Minerva, and a final talk with Calmire, and the overcoming of a great repugnance, Amelia dispatched the following note to Huldah Cronin:

"Monday.

"You have been kind to Minerva Granzine. You know that her mother is gone. Your kindness has, I trust, been a happiness to yourself. I hope you will feel able to increase it by taking her to your house. If you do, you can depend upon me to supply money for everything that she needs. I shall be glad to do this, and to supply any counsel that I can which you may see fit to send for.

"I have not forgotten you in earlier and more hopeful days, and I know that in whatever you do, you deliberately wrong no one but yourself. If my good wishes for you and for poor Minerva could spare you both suffering, you would be spared much; if they could give you happiness, much would be added to you.

"AMELIA CALMIRE.
"*To Huldah Cronin.*"

When Huldah read this note, she shed the first tears that she had shed in a year. But she did nothing in the matter for two days, but write a letter (not to Mrs. John) and receive an answer. In the morning of the third day, when she was half dressed, she sat down and wrote to Mrs. John, and after a note or two more, regarding details, had been interchanged, she wrote as follows to Minerva:

"Thursday.

"DEAR MINERVA: You are to come and live with me. Tell your father what you please, and manage him. Mrs. John will help you. Probably he had better give up your house and go to live with his brother in Massachusetts. He is not to come to see you while you are with me. You can meet him where you please. I will meet you at the old place with my horse this day week at four. I am to see no one but yourself. Have your trunk and anything else you wish to bring, in your hall, with

your name on a tag tied to each article. I wil. send a man who will get them at six.
" Yours, HULDAH."

The change was effected as desired, but the weather was bad, and Minerva, weak and excited, caught a cold which sent her to bed with a raging fever and delirium. The doctor for whom, at Minerva's request, Huldah sent—a practitioner of some alleged "pathy" or other which had appealed to Mrs. Granzine's enlightened mind, told Dinah, Huldah's black factotum, that he was sorry that his engagements would prevent his attending a case so far from his office. He lied. Huldah wrote to Mrs. John, asking what she should do, but told Dinah to employ a boy to carry the note. Mrs. John went at once to Dr. Rossman, the leading physician in Calmire—one of the men not infrequent in country practice, who possess every element of greatness except ambition and experience of misery of their own; and when he bowed Mrs. John out, though she had told him nothing of her personal reasons for befriending the patient, their hands grasped close as they had often done, and tears were in the eyes of both; or, to be exact, there was one tear in the Doctor's right eye, which he had weakened over his microscope.

This good man kept Mrs. John informed regarding his patient, and was the medium to Minerva of many physical and moral comforts. Under his kindly ministrations, and some elements of a new moral atmosphere which began to surround her, Minerva soon was gaining strength in many ways.

Calmire showed his sympathy for her in a thousand things that affected her deeply. While his good taste, not to speak of his wisdom, would not lavish luxuries upon her, he managed, without attracting outside notice, to surround her with an atmosphere of care and kindly little attentions that might have surprised any forlorn banished princess in the land of the courtliest of sovereign hosts.

When in America, he always kept Fleuvemont in condition to receive him during the whole year, and now sometimes when he passed the night there, on his way home from the village in the dark evenings until Spring, he would ride over on Malzour to see Minerva. With infinite delicacy and tact, he had led her by degrees to open her poor heart to him almost as she would to a woman, or, say, to a sympathetic old family doctor. At the same time, without her half recognizing his agency, he had led her to realize that she was suffering the consequences of conduct that she herself was as responsible for as anybody, and so he had given her that most comfortable support in trouble: "It's my own fault." Yet he never shaded off his conviction of Muriel's responsibility, but rather proved his realization of it, by the responsibilities for Minerva's well-being that he took upon himself.

Mrs. John, too, sometimes managed to get to Minerva, and in some ways did more for her than Calmire. Between them, the two good people made her life much more than tolerable, and without encouraging any illusions, suggested enough cheerful possibilities in the future to prevent its appearing what, without them and the faith that Muriel would eventually carry on their work, it would have been,—black and desperate.

Under these influences, and especially under her personal causes for reflection, Minerva was becoming something like a serious, candid, and strong woman. Huldah, with whom she lived, was naturally all that, though her independence of judgment had led her to justify herself in things which probably, under a wider education, she would have disapproved. She was wiser than she once was, however, and her influence on Minerva was not only sustaining and cheering but, on the whole, expanding.

Moreover, Minerva's case had become one more to prove John Calmire's frequent assertion that there never was within five miles of the town, an instance of anything like blighted affections, that Mary Courtenay did not manage to find out and do something to help. She came near doing more harm than good in this one, but Minerva herself brought her to her bearings, and made her a valuable and helpful friend.

In short, Minerva's lines, despite of all, had fallen in such places that she said more than once, that she had not known, in her happier days, how much goodness and justice there was in the world.

So matters went on for some months.

CHAPTER LVI.

SOME TRAVEL AND SOME LETTERS.

MEANWHILE, Muriel had gone abroad. He and his companion proved such poor sailors that on the voyage their relation was one of mutual though ineffective sympathy. But they had not been on shore long before they found each other irksome. Muriel was too moody to be good company, and so unwilling to have his cogitations broken in upon, that he could not find his friend good company either. So, without any unpleasant explanations, they took a chance of separating which was offered in Paris by the happening along of a party that was going to Marseilles instead of to Pau, where Muriel's companion had to meet friends. The region between Pau and Marseilles being reported comparatively uninteresting, Muriel was glad enough to make that a reason for joining the party for the latter place, but with the unexpressed intention of leaving them before getting there.

When they neared Avignon, Muriel announced his desire of giving a few days to the old papal capital and the old Roman towns between it and the Mediterranean. His companions were not burdened with historical curiosity, but were more directly bent upon the delights of Monte Carlo and Mentone; and so Muriel found himself in the old city, for the first time alone in a strange land. He was not conscious of this fact during the bustle of getting fixed in his quarters at the quaint old hotel, and hardly conscious of it (though he did wish for somebody to enjoy with him) as he was looking at the time-worn bridge broken down perhaps by its great weight of tradition, the pretty little park, the inadequate little cathedral, and the old palace which seems a combination of fortress, church, and buttressed railway embankment. But when he sat down to dinner without anybody to talk all these things over with (For he was still timid in his French), he felt very solitary indeed—alone in a crowd and, what was infinitely worse, alone with a sorrow.

We seldom realize to what an extent our convictions are matters of environment—how much support they get from the soil in which they have grown, especially from that portion of their nutriment which comes from the corresponding opinions of friends. Mr. Muriel did not endure separation from all this—his loneliness and the inevitable introspection which, despite the novelties of foreign travel, it involved, without finding himself on the brink of the old agonizing skepticism which had vented itself in the letters to Calmire already given. This time, though, it did not take him long to recognize the noisome pool and to avoid it by the paths he had already learned. And as every nature sore and inflamed as his was, is open to every disease, of course the very opposite temptation assailed him too, through the appeal made to his imagination by the Church. At Avignon, with the aid of a book or two, he peopled the old scenes with their former dramas and pageantry, and while he was conscious of the weak and mean things that had been done there, the immensity of the power that did them, even when half bullied and half protected by other powers, impressed him as nothing human had impressed him before. He carried some of this state of mind to Rome, and posted off first thing, not to the relatively modern gauds of St. Peter's, but to the storied buildings by the Lateran, the famous triclinium, and the font where poor Rienzi took his mystic bath. For the first few days, Muriel was so absorbed in his historic enthusiasms that he felt the impulse, which of course he sardonically dismissed, to identify himself with the tremendous institution which is far the most picturesque and venerable of all that survive. Even to his keen vision, dimmed by repentant tears, warped by self-distrust, fagged by the need of rest, and enveloped in the haze of a fervid young imagination, the church's art and splendor could easily veil, for a time, its tawdriness and absurdity. But after the first few days of his enthusiasms, as he loafed about more leisurely on foot, he became aware of the fact that in no city where he had ever been, even in Italy, was the expression of the people's faces so low, and that he was among a race of beggars. While one priest in ten, perhaps, had a refined face, the rest were brutish to a degree that disgusted him; and when one of the latter assailed him at his hotel, clinking a money-box, he realized whence had come the example which had developed the race of beggars. Then the humbug pervading it all became obvious, and Muriel's disillusion began. Nevertheless, with all the moral enthusiasm of a penitent, and the susceptibility of a sufferer, his sympathies expanded to the tender imagery of the old religion, and filled him with the emotional exaltation that has responded to the same sentiments and many of the same symbols, through all human history.

He had bravely stuck to his resolution to leave Nina in peace, but these feelings and his terrible loneliness overpowered him, as of course something was sure to, and he wrote to her. Perhaps no other youngster would have done it, at least in his way: but our young man, as may have been already suspected, was very much of a law unto himself, and not always a very admirable law, at that; and he was half mad.

Muriel Calmire to Nina Wahring.

"ROME, December 10, 18—.

"May I not speak to you—not as Muriel to Nina, not even as man to woman, not even as human being to human being, but as penitent sinners speak to God—to the Holy Mother of God? So I see the poor and lowly doing here on every side: they may be foolish, but I am humble now, and their thought of their Madonna in the far-off Heaven is no holier than my thought of you.

"The thought may drive me mad, but if it is the only joy left me, let me at least be mad. In madness, I suppose, there is some oblivion.

"I am told that men are better and stronger for

their duty, if they think they work to honor some perfect being, remote, inaccessible, divine—such as now I picture you. If this is true of other men, why not of me? At last I find that I am not as different from other men as I had so arrogantly supposed. My ancestors are in me, and when I am weak with loneliness and despair, I turn, after all, toward what they turned to. I cannot fancy the laws of this vast Kosmos, which deal out our lives with less sympathy, less mercy, than even the laws of man—which sweep on with us and sweep on by us in a flood irresistible and inexorable—I cannot regard them as controlled by anything enough like our human selves to care for any cry sent forth from a human breast. And yet the old cry for sympathy—the old, old yearning to love and worship, spring out from my breast just the same. If you cannot be nearer, be far off like God, like the Madonna Mary, but hear me! Pity me, as these people say she pities even those viler than I, and redeem me, though I see you not, as they say she redeems them; and if I must not love you, let me worship, worship, worship you.

"In the old days, a man who sinned and ruined his life, as I have done, forsook his duties and turned monk, that he might do nothing but so worship. The old days still last here, and probably I see such men under their cowls almost every hour. But I am at least a child of our times. I can worship you always, and yet live in the world and face my duty as best I can see it. But Oh! Is there not in all this vast complexity of life, some trail of duty that leads to you? I am the only man—the only man near your years, at least, that I ever knew, who can fathom your soul and fill it. You are the only woman who can fill mine. Are our souls worthless, that they should be lost to each other? Is not their union our one final duty—above all other duties, comprehending all others? Should we not do that duty in any event, and then let the scope of other duties be determined by it?

"Of course I spin all sorts of webs of logic, and I build arguments that seem unbreakable and prove that you and I ought to be happy together, that we could be, and that haunting alien duty of mine still be done. But I mistrust all demonstration that points to happiness; and even if I did not, I would not wish—unless you bid me I would not dare, to show all my reasonings to you.

"See my faith in you, Madonna! I trust one wave of instinct in that pure soul of yours farther than I trust all my logic.

"Oh I love to humble myself before you! Upon the world, I have looked down, or thought myself looking down; to Uncle Grand, I have looked across, as from one peak to another (*I* fancying *my*self as on a peak! I don't believe that Uncle Grand fancies *him*self on one), but when I regard the thought of you, it is joy, or nearer joy than anything else I now know, to look up.

"What shall I do? Guide me, Pure One! You told me when I saw you in my uncle's house —my home, that it was not my place. What would you call my place? I know it must be where I can do my duty. But must it not be a demon's hand rather than an angel's, which bears the sword that would drive me from you, and perhaps would force me to vow to love where I cannot love, honor where I cannot honor, cherish where I can only tolerate—perhaps where I cannot be strong enough to do that—perhaps where thoughts even of murder, are more apt to crowd than thoughts of protection? Must I, who have been so weak, undertake a task in which I must be so strong that omnipotent Nature herself can have no control of me? Was duty ever the impossible? Is the impossible *my* duty? If not, what is my duty? Must I live a thing for which language has no word—a man with all the powers and passions of a man, forbidden to exercise the best of them—a man with a love—an adoration in his soul that would purify Gehenna, forbidden to let the good thing in him come forth to be blessed and (May I dare think?) to bless?

"Must you— But I will not dare.

"But what shall we do with our lives? They are of each other, even if we never meet again—inevitable parts of each other, unworthy as mine has been. But since yours has touched it, mine has been pure as Saint Anthony's. How *can* it be right, then, to sunder them?

"Perhaps it were a more manly part not to put questions before you, but to decide all myself, and then to try to lead you to my decision. But I have lost the right to do that—even a man's right to test my strength. You have purified me, but I have erred: whenever I try to conclude, up comes that thought, worse than the *memento mori*—

You have erred! Be not wise in your own conceit.' May I say it to you, pure soul?—I thought I had Nature's right to do wrong. How then can I decide in favor of any inclination now, lest I be the victim of some sophism again?

"But what inclination toward you can be aught but good? You have redeemed me, Madonna: take me into Heaven!"

Nina blushed two or three times at the boldness which the boy's agony had forced him into, and finally smiled through her tears, at seeing the mundane capture the transcendental with which he had begun his letter; and she was not sorry for it. At length she answered him.

Nina Wahring to Muriel Calmire.

"—— East 36th St.,
New York, Dec. 29, 18—.

"Muriel I have written you a dozen letters, and torn them up because they said too much or too little. This one I am going to send, and going to let it say all it will—probably both too much and too little. I have no hope of ever writing to you again, and for this once, I am going to write with my heart as open to you as I wish it could be always.

"I must not write again, because writing tends to draw us both from our duty. I write now mainly to tell you that. You ask if our first duty is not to marry, and let all other duties be determined by that. Exactly what your duty is, or may be, I do not pretend to judge. But whatever it may be, where it belongs was determined before you saw me, and therefore your relation to me cannot be first. Plainly my duty to you is not to interfere with that which claims you first, and I cannot marry you and leave you as free as you would otherwise be for whatever demands that first duty may impose.

"Those are the reasons why I cannot continue writing to you. It is not as if we could be mere friends. Therefore as we have no right to be more than friends, we must be less, except in our memories. Perhaps we can be to each other such memories as help. You tell me, and I love you more for it, if that were possible,—or would if it were right— that you are content, or at least determined, if duty demands, to hold me as such a memory—as one remote and inaccessible, who yet sympathizes and approves. If, despite all prudence, you *will* make me that being, I will at least try to be worthy. The thought that you so regard me will help and, I may say it now, console me.

"It is so pitiful to see you turn even to my ignorance for guidance in your perplexities! I wish I could give you some, but I am not wise, I cannot even be good: for I will turn toward you when perhaps I ought not; and some strange sense has come to me, that to be wise is to be good." ["Poor white dove!" thought Muriel as he kissed the paper, and tears came into his eyes. "But what she says is true for me. If I'd been better, I'd have been wiser. After all, it's best to begin at goodness, as the women do."] "I only know," continued the letter, "as I knew when I turned you out of your uncle's house, that I must not stand between you and some dark and undefined duty.

"But I did not turn you out, though, did I, Muriel? You may know, if you care to, that I am crying now. Yes, I want you to know it. I may indulge myself that far. Oh! If we but had the right— But it would be weak and not even kind, to say it: you are enduring enough already!

"Come, I will be cheerful. You should see what fun I have with the children at Mary's home, and sometimes at the school when Mary lets me teach them a little. I love them and they love me, or the things I bring them. Mary won't let me bring them much candy. For their sake, I have had to learn about digestion and lots of other horrid things that are perfectly delightful. Muriel, one *can't* be miserable all the while, and yet I believe that you are so nearly an impulsive poet, that you think it your duty to be. Don't you? Well, don't do it! Be just as cheerful as you can. I am. But Oh God! There, I'm mean and weak again! But this is the last letter I shall write you, and I'm going to be natural, or at least, after anything gets written, I won't cross it out. Oh I do so want to write something that will help you and do you good! All this seems so dry and cold. My heart won't go into it, because my conscience frightens my heart off.

"I think you are too hard on yourself in some ways. You say that you can't now know what is right, because you have done wrong. I don't feel sure that a person who had never known wrong, would have a clearer sense of right than a person who knew both sides. Surely one is more apt to be afraid of errors after suffering for them. But

your repentance, if that is the word for me to use,—
and surely you are filled with all the good feelings
that go with that word—your repentance seems to
me to go to extremes and to lead you to do yourself wrong. You are still strong and true, as I
have always known you—despising deceit and
loving the right, only now you are no longer careless about your duty to follow the right. Keep on
as you have been going lately, and you must make
your walk useful and noble, wherever it leads.
I catch some glimpse now of what is meant by
happiness being within, and not without. How
many happy lives, or at least peaceful and useful
ones, have none of the outer sources of happiness
—or what is infinitely worse, have lost them! I
learn much from being with Mary. She is generally perfect sunshine. I think the times of depression she often has, come from illness; and
something I heard the doctor say makes me think
that the fits of illness come from an early nervous
shock that I know she had, and think she has
never got over. But you are such a rock that
no strain on you is going to make you ill for
long. You need not long suffer from depression.
Think, if you will, of those same poor monks
you wrote me about. How many of them, after
having to give up everything that most men
care for, have led lives full of peace and usefulness!

"You say you will live in the world. Why not?
All ways to usefulness are open there. You can be
busy, and *I* know that to be busy is to be at peace.
I don't know whether it is best for you to travel any

more. Seeing things does not help one like doing things.

"Here I am, making myself a counselor to you! But as I cannot be everything to you, perhaps it would be wisest not to attempt to be anything. Yet if you were fainting, couldn't I give you a cup of water? And your letter makes me feel that writing to you, at least this once, is like that.

"Many people help me." [Here Muriel thought of Calmire and Courtenay and cursed himself for it. He was very young.] "You ought not to be off there alone. Perhaps it is because I sent you away! But I did not want you to go so far away, and alone, where there is nobody to love you. You poor great big Muriel, you need to be loved just as much as any child!" [Here poor Muriel's smile was like light reflected from a sword.] "It can't be wrong for me to love you," went on the letter, "if I only love you in the right way —as we ought to love truth and beauty and justice; and not as one loves a true and beautiful and just man. But I can't! Oh I can't! And so I must not love you at all! I don't love you for anything you are; but just because you are you. I'm afraid I would love you if you were bad. No I wouldn't, because then you wouldn't be you. So keep good, Muriel, keep good, though it takes you away from me. Perhaps it may be right to love you when you are away from me, and good; but I know it would be wrong to love you if you were near me; and I couldn't, either, because then you would not be good.

"Oh, my Love, my Love, my Love, Good-bye!"

CHAPTER LVII.

EXTRACTS ARRANGED FROM THE DIARY OF A PENITENT.

OF course the standard hero, on getting such a letter as Nina wrote Muriel, would start off by the next train, or as soon as he could get his armor on, and have his war-horse caparisoned and put on a box car, to take the lady by assault. But Muriel was not the standard hero. He had so far outgrown the "marriage-by-capture" notions of his ancestors, that he considered ladies who could be taken by assault, as not worth having. He did consider this lady worth having; and therefore it did not even enter his head that she could be taken by assault. When she trusted him so far as to drift into freely showing him her love, she honored him by knowing how implicitly he would honor her. Had anybody now suggested to Muriel, in one of his practical moods, anything lower than that, he would have answered to the effect that if all the vicissitudes of life held any chance of his marrying Nina, to assume her capable of marrying him at present, would be to destroy that chance; and deeper down in his soul, he would have found that his now entertaining such an assumption, or her tolerating it, would deprive such a chance of its value. This of course was all very inconsistent with his having lately tried to persuade Nina to marry him. But was he not young, and imaginative, and torn as not only the young are, between impulse and conscience?

So instead of getting out his lance, he got out his pen, and wrote to Nina:

"My Lady, Sovereign and Divine, I obey and bless you."

Then he girded up his loins and continued on his lonely way.

Here are some of his communings, earlier and later, with himself.

"This fitful old diary again!—Diaries seem to have been kept by two sorts of men—those that have nobody to talk to, and those that are always talking—those who are generally alone, and those who are seldom alone. Perhaps that means those who are generally miserable, and those who haven't time to be.

"Diary-keeping is another illustration of the way extremes meet. Perhaps all habits are shared by men who, in circumstances and nature, are diametrically opposite. And perhaps they're not! And perhaps everything is just what it isn't, and everything isn't just what it is. And perhaps Hegel wasn't a fool after all! But as he probably believed he wasn't, his own system would oblige him to admit that he was.

"Well! This may be at least a diversion from

loneliness, and even a nepenthe from despair. Communion of some sort I must have—I can't write letters all the time—and this, at least, is worth trying. The pen was always some sort of company to me, and it helps me straighten things out."

"I go out into the night, bearing my heavy question with me. I ask it of the earth and the sky and the stars. The only answer that comes is: 'We—the conditions of your life, are around you. We change not. We do not declare ourselves to him who merely asks, but does no labor to learn. What the best labor can know, is but little. That little you must *work* for, and by it you must guide your life as best you may.'

"It is very merciless! Never, indeed, outside of the heart of man, have I known any such thing as mercy.

"And yet I have not to learn it all for myself. Am I not 'the heir of all the ages'? Still I must labor even to learn the things they have bequeathed. Those things come not of themselves."

"What a humbug I've been! That seems the burden of my thought, first, last, and all the time. I've been such a humbug *to myself!*"

"From one little momentary act, months of agonized uncertainty, and probably two ruined lives and one stunted one! But putting a knife or a bullet into a man, is a little momentary act too!

"No, it isn't! Each act is the result of long development of character, even ancestral development. Then where's 'God's justice' that they prate so about? I never saw any sign of such a thing as justice outside of thinking man.

"Yet the biologists do say that the individual is but a link in a chain, and that all the generations are to be regarded as but one creature. There's some sort of justice, then, in visiting the sins of the fathers upon the children.

"But how about a God who says he does it because he's 'jealous'?"

"That notion *Justice!* There's that act of mine, done, fixed, its nature unalterable by a hair's breadth, and yet I can't tell if it's going to wreck my life, or if, after more of this suspense, there will appear some way out. But here's the rub: any possible way out now, is utterly independent of the moral nature of my act—is probably in some circumstance with which that had nothing whatever to do; and yet the consequences must be mine all the same! Where is 'justice' then? I don't think I've altogether deserved what has come upon me. Worse fellows than I have gone scot-free. Ah, I've often heard Uncle Grand say that there's no 'justice' in the operations of natural law. But I didn't know what it meant. I don't seem to have known what anything meant."

"Uncle Grand said that my act, if measured by its consequences, must be classed among the worst. Yet he did not definitely assert that it must be measured that way. (How few things he definitely asserts! And how definitely he asserts those few!) I don't think it fair to measure it that way. If a man amuses himself with a bonfire which, much to his regret, burns downs a house, he's not guilty of arson."

"Uncle Grand once said to me, 'Most young people's morality is a matter of sentiment. It takes the fires of suffering to harden it into practice.' I know what he meant now. It's one thing to imagine an ideal, but another to live up to it."

"I see it all now! I used to justify myself on the ground of Nature first: convention and even law might go hang. I see it! I see it! Why wouldn't I learn it from Uncle Grand that night he talked to me about love? What is natural to the lower creature, is not natural to the higher. Here the very Nature I thought I followed, has been working all the ages to evolve the possibility of this lofty love of one man for one woman. For a brief season it filled my soul with light, and I had yearned for it beyond all other yearnings, even when I let my passions follow 'Nature.' The 'Nature' I followed was simply 'Nature' in the beasts. Even the swan is said to be above it. The love of one creature for but one other creature was a great step. What a power has monogamy been in the evolution of man, society, poetry—soul!"

"Upon *my* soul, it strikes me that in being 'radical,' as I have liked to vaunt myself in being, I have indeed been grubbing around the roots, and kept my face turned away from the leaves and flowers!"

"Sometimes I lose my grip, when I think of things Nature might do for me, but doesn't. Well, at least she does what she gives me reason to expect. Perhaps the rest is none of my business."

"Perhaps she does the best for us that she can, after all! But what a poor fist she makes of it!"

"Nature is such a fool! She makes birds with beaks to catch worms, and gives worms colors to prevent birds from seeing them. She gives tigers claws and fangs to kill antelopes, and antelopes swiftness to escape tigers. And for each one of these four gifts, I've heard the 'goodness of God' descanted upon. No! There's only one way out —to take things as we find them."

"Nature deals us our cards. I've played my hand, and played it like a fool. What a hand it was! And here's the game lost!
"Yet I didn't know! I didn't know!
"I knew enough. If I'd known all, there would have been no merit in winning."

"There are more perplexities than we can master in the phenomena our present senses can respond to. It's lucky we've no more senses—at least before we get proportionally more brain. But if we could know all, there would be no such virtues as judgment and courage. The game of life would be a mean thing if played with loaded dice.

"Yet wouldn't more senses give us more solutions to present perplexities, and so more time and strength for the new ones?

"How I do keep finding shallowness in my brilliant-seeming generalizations now! Is it because I've grown more willing to find it? There can't be more there, after a fellow has been through what I have."

"'If one could know all, there would be no such virtues as judgment and courage'! An omniscient god can't have them, then. What utter asses they are to try to define a god, anyhow! Can't they see their contradictions at every step? Why don't they take what they can learn, and stop?"

"I'd be very sorry for a god who had to witness all this misery."

"It's been getting plain to me that if 'God' is an arbitrary power—uncertain, to be propitiated and influenced, man is but a slave. But if the universe is moved by unerring Law, man is a free citizen. The first notion will do for those who made even slavery itself a 'divine institution.'

"In our views of the Universe, as in Jurisprudence, progress has meant the substitution of Law for individual whim."

"As to gods in general, I never heard of one that left a fellow much room for self-respect."

"How I have always lived as if Nemesis were going to make exceptions in my favor! And how strange that *I* should be this broken wretch! Well, it widens my sympathies."

"One night, I remember, I preached to Her that man should be merciless with the weak and afflicted, because Nature is. How it expands a man's views to be one of the weak and afflicted himself!

"Once I thought Nature ought to kill that poor boy, because he was hopelessly maimed. Well, perhaps it's time for Nature to kill me. All right! I'm agreeable."

"How much power must have been wasted in despair and remorse over things that despair and remorse can't change! As the world grows wise enough to steer clear of that waste, how much more power will be left for work and sympathy!"

"What an ass I've been always to assume that 'the best will come'! The only sensible way is to expect the best, but to act so that you'll have nothing to reproach yourself with in case of the worst."

"If 'it's all right,' wouldn't a good God let us know it? And if it's *not* 'all right,' there's not a good God, or not much of a God.

"It's *not* all right. That's plain enough. It's just as right as we see it, and no more. What would be the use of its being any nearer right if we don't see that it is? Our very not-seeing it, prevents its being any righter than we see. 'It may come right'? But that doesn't make it right now. Well then, let's grin and bear it! There's where wisdom begins."

"'All for the best'? All for the best that is possible under our limitations, perhaps. But that's simply a truism."

"To be 'rational' and do without a human sort of God, is well enough for happy people. I don't find it good for much in misery. Perhaps I'm not rational *enough!*"

"A religion must be a handy thing in trouble. Its widest use, I suspect, is to make the afflicted believe against all the evidence, that life is less hard than it is—Nature less merciless. Yet I want none of it: let Truth hug me to her breast, though she be the iron virgin with the knives."

"A very easy thing to *write*—that up there! I've said it often, I suppose, and so have lots of others: it sounds too well not to have been said a great many times. But I do believe I have some realization of what I'm saying, this time."

"How far down into the little details of our lives—our characters, Law goes! I've felt it while this misery has been working in mine. Of course that close work is not so hard to realize regarding character, if every change in character can take place only with a change in matter: we're used to the idea of Law in nerve-cells, but that makes it very little easier to realize regarding events. The care of an all-seeing God over each footstep, if there were any signs of it, could be understood; but it's not easy to understand *Law* regulating circumstances down to such details. Yet, in a sense, Law must; but certainly not in a sense that averts evil. Law does not avert floods and earthquakes. No; the conclusion is unavoidable that it takes care of us to a certain point, and that from there we must take care of ourselves. 'De Lawd made me so high, and I growed de rest myself.' Well, if we were taken care of all the way through, where would liberty and character be?"

"And I thought that I could fill my mind with all sorts of images, and at will prevent their recurrence! I think I understand the myth of Saint Anthony."

"If one could only live in the higher air, where the steady currents blow!"

"How I've fooled myself with inconsequences! Our account with Nature is not like a merchant's, where any sort of asset will balance any sort of liability. Truthfulness won't balance profligacy; or kindness, laziness; or continence, the small-pox. Neither can profligacy entirely cancel truthfulness; or laziness, kindness. It's too late, though, for a robber to buy off by giving half his plunder to charity, or to save his soul by building a church.

An old Scotch Presbyterian woman Uncle Grand used to talk about, attributed the deaths of an acquaintance's large family of children, to the fact that the family amused itself by playing cards in the evening. That old woman simply believed in alchemy and astrology. Her own sons, by the way, grew up hale and strong, and two out of three became notorious swindlers. In the case of both families, of course those who respected the parents stood by and wondered 'that the good should be so afflicted.' The parents being 'good' had nothing to do with it. Heart-disease was hereditary in one family, and scoundrelism in the other—from the father's side, I suppose, as the mother was such a pattern of pharisaical virtue.

"We've pretty much outgrown that order of beliefs, but we haven't outgrown the involuntary intellectual habits they engendered, by a long shot: it has really been something of a surprise to me that being measurably truthful and honest, or trying to be, didn't protect me from my troubles. Ah! Why did I inherit so much superstition?"

"Shall I repeat, then, that all superstitions are debasing? That depends upon the mind you put them in."

"I'm beginning to try to amuse myself a little. As I look at life now, I suspect that anybody who wants it all sunbeams, must get most of them out of cucumbers."

"I got out my cornet to-day and played for the diversion of the boors, hoping that diverting them might divert me. It didn't. It was like food to a man with no sense of taste. So with everything."

" A good, simple, sympathetic soul—the clergyman of the village—met me as I was walking to-day. A flock of quail that I had started up had flown within sight of him, and so we got to talking. He's one of the new sort, and knows a dog and gun. One thing led to another, until all led right up to the fact that I am miserable, as all roads lead to Rome. I can't keep it entirely to myself. I told him I didn't care for shooting or anything else now—though I have shot a little. Truth is, though I didn't tell him, that I've grown too chicken-hearted, or possibly too sympathetic, to cause pain: know what it is myself, now! · Well, he said: 'Poor boy!' and I didn't get mad. Then he began very delicately, but at the same time with the old disgusting professional assurance, to inquire into the state of my soul. I told him flatly that I didn't believe much of what he thought most worth believing. Then he began to try and convert me, but in a very decent way. He said: 'Christianity offers you a loving God and immortality,' and the rest of it. I told him that I hadn't seen any evidence that it could deliver what it offers, and that its 'offers' reminded me of those of the architects who, I've heard Uncle Grand tell, have a fashion, in specifying even absurd extravagances which one is to pay for, of saying, 'I *give* you,' for instance, a mosaic hall or a lapis-lazuli chimney-piece. I hope I said it in such a way as not to hurt the good man's feelings. He seemed to take it in good part. It's a new sensation for me to care whether he did or not, but I'm glad to have the sensation.

"'Offers!' It might as well offer 'three acres and a cow.'"

"After all, humanity all along seems to have got its consolations and inspirations from pretty much the same ideas. The early fellows guess them vaguely, the later ones make the image clearer and more detailed.

"It's the same with me, too. Here I ponder, ponder, ponder, and at last think I've found some great truth, and behold! it phrases itself in some platitude that I've been impatient at having dinned into me from the nursery up. Experience is like the right light on a picture.

"Yet how *could* those old saws mean anything to me before I had experienced facts enough to understand the generalizations? There's a good reason for what I've heard Uncle Grand often say —that no experience but one's own, can be of much use."

"Here I am on the ocean—the 'vast' ocean that they talk about. It's simply the most oppressively circumscribed place I ever saw. The limits of our vision are distinctly presented on every side. Turn which way one will, he sees nothing else so marked as that limit where water and sky meet. On land, there are so many things in between, that one is hardly conscious of the boundary, even if it be much closer than here. Oh! I'm deadly sick of that constant ring of sea and sky! But I'm always reminded by it now, of that other limit against which we are always beating our wings, and beyond which we cannot fly. Why not settle down, though, and take our limitations peaceably, as the sailors take the sea?"

"At last I'm added to the millions who have felt that human lives are like these waves—merely shifting forms of a substance that precedes them and outlasts them."

"But when such a wave happens to bear on its crest, the Iliad, or Macbeth, or the Sistine Madonna, or the Pilgerchor!"

"I wonder if any of those poor old Infallibles that had such a tough time of it here at Avignon, ever was as miserable as I am! They at least always had enough to do—quarreling with the other Infallibles down in Rome, or wherever else men who were not infallible, infallibly elected one of themselves to be infallible.

"They didn't have as much chance as I to feel lonely, anyhow!

"I wonder if among the dozen or so that were here, there happened to be a decent man—a quiet man who 'walked with God'! Then he never could have been lonely, as I am! That's an idea! But haven't I God with me just as much as he had with him? What is this power that, independently of any effort of mine, keeps my heart beating? What is the Power that steadfastly conditions this Universe, so that the needle pointed my ship over here through the unmarked waters and through the dark? Ah, but those old chaps put a sympathetic soul behind it all, and when they were lonely and in trouble, consoled themselves by what they were pleased to term 'Communion with Him.'

"Well! Haven't I felt some such communion? Hasn't something which seems, after all, the best in me, responded, at times, to something beautiful and all-including outside of me? Yes, but that's not the human. Well! suppose it isn't: a good many fellows have managed to get along in deserts alone with it....And a nice, lazy, filthy lot they were! Much they've done to put food and clothing and clean water and healthy work and play within people's reach!

"I rather suspect that if a fellow is alone, and craves sympathy, the healthy thing for him to do, is to get it or go without it, and not interpret the reactions of his own mind as a response from the Power behind the Universe. That's a good deal too near to taking the images in his own brain for material ones outside—flat hallucination, the special test of insanity."

"How rare, after all, is an unmixed feeling, of either joy or sorrow—to suffer without distraction, or, for that matter, to enjoy without it; to hate without mercy; to love without criticism! Eternities ago, when I read novels, I took it for granted that life was full of such unmixed feelings, and used to think myself exceptional for not having more. Now when life is real, I begin to see how complex emotion is."

"How the poetry is gone out of the world! Here's another fact that wipes out a lot of it: there can't be any perfect love, because there can't be any perfect woman. There's no getting around heredity. Why didn't I realize its damnable implications when I was talking over the same thing with Uncle Grand last Summer? I don't seem to have realized the force of anything before I got into trouble."

"Yet there's more to say on that topic—first: that while writing yesterday, I 'realized' only the gloomy side of the case—that I really did not see the subject with new light, but with part of the old light obscured, as I find I've done more than once lately; and second that there can't be any perfect *man* either, and it needs a perfect being to feel perfect love, as well as to inspire it.

"And, too, come to think of it, I've read of other ideals of love than love for a perfect creature. A good many millions among the most advanced peoples have, it just occurs to me, been considerably influenced by an ideal of love for *im*perfect creatures, which they have exalted into something superhuman.

"I remember Uncle Grand told me the night after I first drove with Her, that I must suffer before I could love in the great way. His words were meaningless to me then. They certainly are not now. I wonder if I can love in the great way yet!"

"The instinct of worship is an old one and well ground in. When my soul expands at the sunset and the dawn and under the deep stars, and grows profound and beautiful with them, up comes that instinct of all the generations. But I do not crave an anthropomorphic god: yet I crave understanding, sympathy, response. Sometimes I feel them in the Immensity: yet even at those times, I most crave them from Her. Would it drive me mad if I were to indulge myself in grouping all those yearnings around her? She is now as far removed from me as any god in far Olympus or in Heaven. Yet wherever she is, she inspires me and holds me to my duty. Her soul reaches out to the measure of this Universe as no imagined god's has ever done. She is full of sweetest sympathies and completest responses, and, as when she saw me last, of unfathomable motherliness. Her grand and most lovely face tells things that Raphael's dreams could reach but once. With reverence greater than my forebears ever felt, I worship her! My Madonna! Oh my Madonna!"

"Why, from all her abounding loveliness, should my memory so often turn to that little blue vein just below the palm of her hand, in the soft depression of her white round wrist?"

"How often I recall that night when I asked her if she thought I'd been spoiled by the lack of a mother, and she said, 'Awfully near it!' I had not the slightest idea what she meant. Well, here I am!"

"She didn't mean *that*, though. No, but she meant a million possibilities which included that among them, though her pure soul never definitely reflected it."

"I wonder if Uncle Grand, either, had in mind anything definite, when he prophesied that she would do something colossal! He couldn't have had! There was something colossal, though, in what she did for me when I saw her last. Whenever I think of it, it makes me big."

"I have always admired greatness of soul, and so inferred that I had it. I've always admired the power to lift a ton, but never inferred that I had that! I'm stronger than I was, though."

"To live away from her, chained to my hard duty, and to feel that I am doing it to make me worthy of that minute when I saw her last! There's inspiration! But Heavens! Can I? Was ever man, man enough? I can and I will!"

"There's a great fascination in rhetoric! What's the use of my trying to make myself out heroic in staying away from her, when I know perfectly well that she would not take me to her if I left a single duty outside? Well! That's no reason I shouldn't do the duty. I do hope, though, that some day I'm going to get through cackling over doing a duty, like a hen over laying an egg.

"I prate of duty! What duty am I doing? Well, I'm at least resisting my old ways; and if a time comes for me to do more, I'm going to do it : that's all."

CHAPTER LVIII.

DE PROFUNDIS.

UNDER the conditions and influences already indicated, Minerva had passed a Winter not wholly devoid of peace or profit. A little discreet management had prevented her whereabouts being known to any person whom she was not willing should know it. She had come to rely upon Mrs. John as a beneficent Providence, and to feel that her unending kindness and wisdom would in some way provide that the future should be tolerable at least.

But now into the midst of this good handling of a bad situation, came a cataclysm. Mrs. John's heart had not been beating all these years for all the sorrows in the village, without being affected by its labors. She had known it long, and lately John had known it, and that tender gentleman's quiet solicitude for her was a poem, in spite of all his professed hatred of poetry.

While in her simple mind there was unbounded room for pity and forgiveness, there were none of the subtle allowances for temptation which make it cancel "sin," and Muriel's sin had been the heaviest of all the burdens which, up to that time, her patient heart had borne. But now the child was come, and the gentle lady was called upon to bear greater anxieties for the future than, with her other cares, she was equal to. Happily for Muriel, he did not know anything of this consequence of his act, or suspect anything of it until later, when he was better able to bear it, though also better capable of realizing it as an illustration of the unending ramifications of the risks assumed by one who disturbs the moral equilibrium of things.

So Mrs. John was dying. It was not from a gradual and unremitting failure of her powers, but from attacks increasing in frequency and intensity, which she now knew would soon be stronger than she was.

Not long after this conviction became established in her mind, she determined upon one thing that she could do for Muriel. It was a bold thing, such as gentle creatures, in extreme issues, dare to do. Early in May, she sent for Nina Wahring, and talked with her for three hours, bringing on herself, as she knew she would, utter prostration and the most alarming attack of her malady that she had yet experienced. The details of that interview, Nina never alluded to, except with one person, but its results were in time obvious to several.

The third morning after it took place, a boy sent by Dinah brought a letter for Mrs. John. Nina Wahring, who had not left John's house since the interview mentioned, took the letter, saying that Mrs. John, who was very ill, had instructed her to.

Five hours later, Calmire, who had ridden over in response to a telegram from John, was met at the door by his brother, who had awaited and recognized, far off, Malzour's trot free from the roll of wheels. With a set face, John opened the door and said, as they grasped hands: "She's dead! I'm glad you've come."

Calmire only pressed his brother's hand, and then took him by the arm and led him into the dining-room. There he said: "Light a cigar and let us go onto the back piazza."

John mechanically did as he was bid. He was a man of wonderful self-control and, despite his remote French ancestor, had enough Anglo-Saxon in him always to show less than he felt.

As the brothers silently seated themselves in the arm-chairs, Calmire left his right hand resting on his brother's arm for some minutes, neither of them speaking. These men had got beyond the need to "say something" when together. At length John spoke:

"Well! I suppose you're prepared to prove that the whole thing's not a humbug!"

"Oh, Amelia proved that, John!"

"Yes, so she did."

Another silence of a minute or two, and then John spoke again with a rough suddenness:

"Calmire, did any man ever succeed in not fooling with this immortality question?"

"I suspect not, John, when he was brought face to face with it."

"Well, did any man ever succeed in holding himself good and tight to a neutral position on it?"

"Not without *ifs*, I fancy: at least, when the man had any blood in him."

After another little silence, John said: "You

can't know how good she was, Calmire. Nobody can but me." And his voice faltered.

"Yes, John, I've been blessed by knowing how good a woman can be: so I do know how good Amelia was. And her life in this place gave such opportunities to develop the best that was in her!"

"Yes, she took care of everybody."

"Yes," echoed Calmire. Then after a moment he added: "Well, there are some things that I must take care of now. Have you any special wishes?"

"Only to be left alone by pretty much everybody but you. I suppose there must be some sort of a ceremony to satisfy her people. But I don't want to be tortured with it."

"Hadn't you better go back to Fleuvemont with me?"

"I guess so, but yet I do at times feel like lingering near—near what is left, even though Nature declares that I must leave it."

Poor John, during the dreads of recent months, had unconsciously got his opinions pretty well formulated. For the first time in their talk, his mouth was trembling.

And Calmire thought of the sympathy between this hard-headed brother of his who generally professed so much contempt for sentiment, and the creatures really no more faithful, but only less reasoning, who linger by clay they love even to their own death; and then there flashed through his mind the mortuary customs of many peoples. All that occurred to him to say, however, was: "You're wiser than the Egyptians, John."

"Yes. I don't intend to have my reason upset

by whatever vices of that kind may be in my blood. Whatever I feel, I know it's best that my association with her should, as nearly as possible, end where Nature ended it. It would be a relief if memory alone could be left. After all, anything more that can intervene, is simply horrible."

"You feel precisely as I should, precisely as I *have* felt; and I will do what I can to meet your feelings."

After a moment, Calmire added: "Will you take the children too? Will they be willing to go?"

"Entirely. I can trust the older ones to feel as I do. Of course the younger don't think much about it."

"Is anybody here besides the servants?"

"Yes. Nina, and Amelia's sister Agnes and her husband. Those two are disposed to all the necessary absurd conventions. Leave things to them. I suppose," he added bitterly, "that it's not essential to the dignity of the occasion, that our spirits should commune with tailors and sempstresses before we are permitted to face the light of Heaven."

"I'd leave that whole nuisance until it comes up of itself," said Calmire. "If you feel like it, there'll be time enough. We may as well go at once. I shall come back to-morrow. Any instructions about the traps?"

"You come in the T-cart," answered John. "I'll drive; and I want to take Genevieve on the seat with me. The other children and a maid or two can be piled into the wagonette. I'll go, and arrange it all right away. You stay here. Or, order the carriages, if you'll be so good. We shall be ready as soon as they are."

And they separated for their respective preparations.

When John told Genevieve of their plans, she said, after a moment's hesitation: "Papa, 'dear, Effie had better ride in the carriage with us. It makes no difference about the younger children, but when she's not with you, she wants to be all the time with me. I would like to sit by you; but if you sit with Uncle Grand, I shall do very well taking care of Effie."

"You're your mother's child, darling," said John, kissing her. And until they joined Calmire, he kept by the child's side as if he were some dependent creature.

When they started, Calmire saw John's face seek some upper windows with an expression that was pitiful to see, and his muscles convulsively contract until he almost stopped the horses. But in less time than it takes to tell it, he jerked his head square to the front, said: "Come," to the horses, as his way was; and, as his way was not at starting, picked up the whip and put them into a brisk trot. Then, instead of driving nearly half around the square and through the main street, as he usually did, he went up the side street near his house and kept through by-ways until they had gone quarter around the town and struck the main road outside of it. The moment John pulled the horses' heads in the unaccustomed direction, Calmire understood, and unconsciously threw his arm over the back of the seat so that it touched John.

Nobody had ever before seen him in that position in a vehicle.

They had not been in the country long, before John moderated the quick pace he had been driving. He seemed soothed by the great tender influences of the sky and earth.

For a mile or two, nobody spoke but the children. Genevieve, on the back seat with Effie, had got her much interested in the objects they were passing. While their attention was obviously absorbed, John broke silence, half-meditating, with:

"How about this immortality business?"

"Ah," answered Calmire. "The question won't down when it comes home to one's very self, will it?"

"No. It won't."

"I understand," said Calmire.

"Yet I can grin and bear it," said John, but he nearly bit his cigar in two. Then he went on: "Once while this was coming, Courtenay said to me, 'Let us pray that it may be averted!' and I had a queer feeling that seemed disloyal to Her, but I understand it now."

"What was it?"

For a moment John searched for expressions. Then he said: "I didn't want to feel that there are any uncertainties in life and death but those of our own ignorance and weakness. What has come to her cannot be worse, nor can even what has come to me, than it would be to live in a world ruled by fluctuating laws."

"John, you've struck bottom!" exclaimed Calmire.

"Yes," answered John, with a long breath, "I've struck bottom! God, how deep it is!"

After a moment Calmire said: "You're not the man to blink anything about it. Yet there's a good deal to be said without blinking anything. Do you care to talk, though?"

"Yes, it will do me good. I feel better out here. What a thing a river is!"

"Yes—it's even more soothing than a cigar. Well, now if you really care to talk, John: you remember Ted Bargwin from whom you couldn't live apart until you were seventeen or so? When did you see him last?"

"Some twenty years ago."

"You'd been separated twelve years?"

"Yes, and I found him simply a nuisance. I see what you're coming to. It's tough."

"It's not as tough as it looks at first sight. For if we imagine meeting those who, as some say, have 'gone before,' we may as well, while we're about it, imagine them freed from all the influences which made Ted disagreeable to you—free from the things that belittle us, so we may as well imagine them simply improved in every way."

"But," asked John, "how about our precious selves? Perhaps they might not regard us any more favorably than I regarded Ted."

"And *there's* a reason for doing our best!" responded Calmire, "and that *is* what I've been 'coming to.' There's a big inspiration in it!"

"But a fellow has so little chance to lead a big life!" John complained. "And those who've got out of this mess, may have so much chance."

"Suppose they do!" was Calmire's comment. "They may have a chance, withal, to learn how to be charitable and patient with us."

"True!" John exclaimed. "But here's another trouble. What satisfaction can they take all by themselves—out there in the cold?" and he shuddered—his terrible strain had weakened him. Then he went on. "In spite of everything, they must either be wretched or get absorbed in something— something that we know nothing about and can't be interested in. Just the same way, we in time must get absorbed in what they're not interested in. No! It's all nonsense to talk about our sympathies being kept up when there's no communication."

"John, haven't you pondered sometimes on what it is for a man to keep the course of his own life at one with the course of the universe.?"

"Some vague notions in this direction have crossed my mind once or twice."

"Now," resumed Calmire, "the course of the universe is definite and consistent. Two people who cannot communicate with each other, can walk as close to it as they may be able. If they do that, though they may not be very near each other, they will at least be on paths that do not diverge. Such notions become very clear and strong, when one feels that leading such a life is the only conceivable means of saving the dearest sympathy he has ever known. When a man gets his slavish allegiance to a fickle God, expanded into intelligent coöperation with steadfast Law, and then feels that in such coöperation he may be still living in sympathy with one whom he has loved with all his soul, and lost, he has the strongest incentive to right living that has yet been found out, so far as I know."

"It's a good deal of a notion," said John meditatively. " I wonder if they had any grip on it when they began to preach that one who lives according to God's law, will meet the loved ones gone before in Heaven?"

"Not a very clear grip, I suspect," answered Calmire. "But I'm more struck every day with the fact that pretty much all our ideas have been guessed at in some fashion before."

John pulled hard on his cigar for a few seconds and then said:

"Calmire, I'm half afraid of playing with this immortality question, even as far as you've been speaking of it: it unsettles a man. I'd get to going farther, and imagining and doing all sorts of things—praying to her, for all I know. Even now, I generally think of myself before her, as on my knees. It would drive me crazy to think much about her, except as in the past."

"That depends upon whether you let what you think run counter to what you know. To follow Nature, as we were talking of a moment ago, is to make no assumptions beyond the bounds Nature has set for our knowledge. Live as a wise man would live anyhow; you will have a new incentive now. My counsel really is to avoid the very extravagances you dread. You're in the situation of Orpheus over again—you must keep your eyes to the front."

"All right," said poor John, with a sickly attempt at a smile, "I'll keep my eyes on you."

"And yet," continued Calmire after a moment's pause, "there's another important thing that doesn't seem to have been dwelt upon as much as the immortality question: probably because there's no selfish side to it. That is, the influence of the memory of our dead, utterly independent of the question of joining them again. I don't know but what it's rooted in some notion of their survival and supervision of our acts. But in the best form I know of, it seems a very single desire to be worthy of what they have been to us. There's lots of imagination in the feeling, lots of exaltation, very likely lots of superstition: but whatever it is, I don't believe any man knows what lofty incentive is, until he has had to mourn."

"Pretty superstitious for you, Calmire!"

"Superstitious for me! I'm one of the most superstitious men alive—under some definitions. If anybody thinks oftener than I do of the myriad unknown forces at work around us, it's about time for his friends to shut him up, that's all!"

"You wouldn't have applied that definition to anybody but yourself," said John, beginning a sardonic little laugh which his sadness smothered at its first breath. "You think that being superstitious would add force, by contrast, to your unorthodoxy: but all the same you're *not* superstitious. Thinking about what's beyond us isn't superstition: it's believing about it, as you've often said yourself; and I'm going to think all I want to. But it tires me even to think. Couldn't a fellow just go off quietly and die?"

"How about those children chattering on the back seat," asked Calmire, "and those in the wagonette behind?"

"Oh, there's no decent way out of it all," exclaimed John mournfully; "no way out! I've just got to stick it through!" In a moment, he added: "That's just what I hate most of all about it—the cold fact which I can't help realizing from the experiences of other men, that I shall in a sense 'get over it.' Why, this misery is only her due as long as I draw breath!"

"Ah!" ejaculated Calmire, "that's the damnable way of looking at it that we've inherited from Puritanism and the older diseases like it. But you know all the same, John, that there's no sense in nursing misery: enough of it is inevitable. The only thing to nurse is happiness."

"And yet you wouldn't say that we should forget a human being like a dog!"

"You can't forget a dog—a good one. There's no danger that you'll forget Amelia in any way you ought not, even after the sharpness of this misery is past."

After a little musing, John said: "It's good to talk to you, Calmire. But the worst of it all is that I can't talk to *her*. If I could only go to her and tell her all about it!"

"Yes, that's the worst, old man, the very worst!"

After they got to Fleuvemont, Calmire, while apparently leaving John to himself, took pains to keep within a moment's reach of him. The children distributed themselves over the grounds, except Genevieve, who kept by her father, or rather, as Calmire realized, her father pitifully kept near her.

After dinner, as the brothers smoked on the piazza, John's talk was mostly monosyllabic, and before his cigar was finished, he said he was tired and would go to bed. Calmire took him to a room communicating with his own, and as he was about to bid him good-night, remembered himself and said:

"Shall I stay with you, John?"

"I wish you would."

So he sat, making a tremendous effort to divert John's mind until he was ready for bed. Then the elder brother said:

"I know you'll sleep. There's at least that advantage in being a Calmire. After you go to sleep, I shall read in my room there, as I often do, for an hour or two; and if you wake before I do, call me."

For a moment John grasped his hand as if it were a floating spar, and in a very few moments more was sleeping the deep recuperative slumber of exhaustion.

The next morning, Calmire, as he intended, awoke first, and as soon as he knew John's sleep was over, was beside him. When John saw him, he murmured:

"Oh God, Calmire, what a life to wake into! I knew nothing about it yesterday. And to think that I've got to wake into it every day! I dread sleep!"

Calmire sat down beside the bed and stroked his brother's hand.

"You can't wake into exactly it, another day, John, even if you try. To-day's facts will intervene, even if no more than as panes of glass, between you and yesterday; next day, to-morrow's facts will be as a few panes more; and so through the next day and the next, until by mere accumulation, they will render the view of yesterday dim. You can't help it, John. You may even think that loyalty requires you to keep all the misery clear and distinct before you, but you can't do it. Omnipotent and beneficent Nature is working against it. Living is changing: if you don't change, you die."

"That would suit me exactly," said John.

"But you can't have it," said Calmire, "and as you can't, every experience, every thought, every breath takes from you something old and substitutes something new. The one fact that includes all of life, is change. Change you must, and the bearings of this misery must change with you."

"Yes, if a man lives."

"Well, you've got to. The happiness of so many others depends upon you."

"Yes, I suppose so."

Calmire could say nothing, yet he found something infinitely pitiable in his matter-of-fact brother, who had always been mildly cynical regarding all expression of emotion, now wishing again and again for love and sorrow's sake, to lay down the life that had been so undemonstrative and strong.

After a minute or two of silence, John resumed: "I'm glad of what you said about all life being change. But here's a queer change in mine: I want to go back where she is."

"We don't know where she is, John."

"Oh well, you know what I mean," said John, half irritably, and then added with a sad smile: "I suspect that after all, I've enough of the instincts of a dog, to follow till the last."

When they met downstairs, John said:

"I've thought it over and put my own mind in command again. I'm not going."

"Do exactly as you feel when the moment comes," said Calmire. "So far as possible, do nothing and refrain from nothing that you'll regret hereafter."

"All right, I sha'n't go."

As the brothers had provided, the grief of John and his children was not made a show of to the whole population of the town. For the people's sake, and because he thought she would have wished it so, Calmire had decided on a memorial meeting, and had told Courtenay that, though he would not profane their benefactress's memory by placing the clay from which her loveliness had gone, for them to look upon, he would still like Courtenay to read before them as much of the venerable service of his church as would be fitting, and to speak whatever he might wish. He also told the choir and the men's singing society to do their own will about music.

The people gathered to pay their last tribute of gratitude at the library hall where Amelia had done so much for them. It could not contain all who came, but those who could not get in lingered outside till all was over. Within it was all very beautiful with the afternoon sunlight slanting through the windows. When Courtenay tried to talk to them of their sweet benefactress, he found it hard to begin, and when he said: "The mothers here know best what she was," he could not go on for the sobs among the people. He saw some of the men crying, and then he simply broke down and buried his head in his hands over the reading-desk. When after a minute he raised his eyes, and tried to falter on, he met the eyes of Nina Wahring, who sat with Calmire in one of the front seats. Tears were rolling down her cheeks, but her face was firm as marble, and in it was a strange gentle sternness and resolution, which came to him through her eyes. It was the manhood women give great sons. And she gave it to him, and afterward his voice was firm, and his words calm and wise, and he talked to the people with such strength and fitness and feeling that the dullest of them always remembered that hour, and referred back to it many a repression of brutal impulse, and many a leading to gentleness and charity.

Calmire, feeling that funeral pageants are but survivals of barbarism, took upon himself to perform simply the sad offices which he had spared his brother. Amelia's sister was ill, and Calmire welcomed an intimation from her that an emergency at home was clamoring for her husband, and sent him away. Nina he sent to Fleuvemont to the children, and it was not with reluctance that, at twilight, he found himself alone, save for the laboring men, by a grave on the hillside at the edge of a wood, where one sees far. Before him was a long covered basket of the sweet white withes of the weeping willow. Flowers with their stems woven into its meshes covered the sides, and the top was heaped with them.

As Calmire stood looking beyond what was at his feet, into the yellow afterglow over the far blue hills, and upon the yellow gleams of the river here and there between them, he felt, among many wide and deep thoughts, that sure dependence on Nature's courses which, under many names, has been sung through all the ages. His lips almost uttered some words that came to him: "This order and this beauty endure—will endure somewhere, if not here, longer than any hope or dream of mine can measure. What am I, that I should think lightly of it if I respond to it but for a little while more? I feel it now, and could not feel it better if I knew that the emotion would last beyond all the æons I can conceive. I feel the higher moral order which, to me, it always symbolizes. Joy that I do so, is the emotion to fill my soul with: not questioning discontent lest I may not do so long."

The first earth fell softly on the thick mass of flowers, and he felt:

"She knew it too, and probably more sweetly than I: for she knew wider love. Pelion and Ossa piled over her coffin, would do nothing to shut out that fact." And a smile of half-amused scorn turned his proud kind lips, as there came up in his mind the old question: "Grave, where is thy victory?"

Then came the antecedent question: "O Death, where is thy sting?" His lips became set and he frowned, and said to himself: "How long will they amuse themselves with fictions? If one is a man, it does sting! Death is death! It does sting! Oh, my sweet sister!"

And he sat down on a rock beside him and rested his face in his hands, and looked through wet eyes long and wistfully into the beckoning mystery of the twilight.

He did not notice footsteps over the cracking branches in the woods behind. Somebody came down and over the noiseless turf, and sat unheard beside him. In time his emotion spread its waves to the borders of his strong will, and was checked. As he lowered his hand, another hand was laid upon it. He turned and put his arm around Muriel's neck.

The two sat thus without a word, looking beyond into the deepening sky, until the grave was filled with earth, and the sky with night.

"It is over," said Calmire.

"And it begins," said Muriel.

"So always!" responded Calmire.

CHAPTER LIX.

FACING IT.

"Let's walk," said Muriel. "You're going to Fleuvemont? Tell the carriage to keep within call."

"Hm!" said Calmire to himself. "So you run the situation your way, do you, even with me? My poor boy, what you must have had to handle, to make this grip spontaneous!" But he assented, and they walked on together to Benstock, the station next below Calmire, where the track was crossed by the road which went past Huldah's.

"How does Uncle John take it?" said Muriel after a while—the first time he had alluded to John as "Uncle," since he was a boy.

"Like a man," answered Calmire, "and what's rarer, like a reasoning man."

"He's another person to whom I never did justice," said Muriel.

"Very likely. He's not your style."

"No, but I've learned that there are other styles than mine. I'm so sorry for Uncle John! *Is* it worthwhile to love any mortal thing? Hadn't a man better bury himself in the verities that are sure to outlast him?"

"No; the best in us lives on things that perish quickly. We may in time be evolved beyond that; but when we are, down goes the charm of sex, down goes procreation, down goes the race, and dissolution takes the place of evolution. No, let's take all the life we can get, pain and all. That's living."

"Yes. Pain fertilizes, at least," responded Muriel. "I see now that life probably never is what a young man has imagined it to be. But I begin to get a dim glimmer of an idea that the ordinary materials of happiness may not be its essentials, or at least may not be essential to peace." After a pause he went on—apparently finding it a relief to unburden his mind after so much solitude: "And I've got another new notion—that by a man with any claims to decency, even peace can't be had with duty shirked. I've often imagined myself building happiness that did not rest on duty, and every time, after a day or two, I've found my structure full of cracks that let in the glare of Hell."

"There's some of the old Muriel left in you yet!" said Calmire, half thinking aloud.

"It's queer, isn't it," continued Muriel, "how things won't hold together, and how they will?"

"Yes," said Calmire, "it takes a long while to realize that moral forces act under the same laws as physical ones. An engineer will look at a plan and say: 'That looks well, but it won't stand,' while at the same time he's just as apt as the rest of us, to build into his own life little weaknesses that will make his happiness shaky all his days."

"A man can't often avoid the consequences,' Muriel assented.

"He has some choice among them, though," Calmire rejoined.

"Yes, I've worked that out too," responded Muriel, and continued unbosoming himself: "The choice between carrying a perfidy like a snake in his bosom, chilling his conscience, and deadening his comradeship with all honest things—a choice between that and candidly owning his fault, that he may work with that comradeship restored—with sunlight and heat and frost and air and gravity—he and they all friends working honestly together in the same evolution—and," he added after a moment, "it's better still to get the feeling that even if he cannot grasp what he loves, any more than he can grasp the sunset, he has an honest man's right to love it apart, and is better for it."

"You've thought out a good deal, for the amount of living you've done!" said Calmire.

"I've done an enormous amount of living for my years, and I've *had* to think it out. It was the boy and the woodchuck!" and Muriel laughed almost like his old self.

"Well," commented Calmire, "we'd both have been dead if there hadn't been some humor in us. But, my boy, mind this thing well. Don't cultivate the power of seeing the ludicrous side of serious things. Perhaps it's worth more to see the serious side of ludicrous things, if it doesn't make a prig of one."

"Why are people without humor generally such small potatoes, anyhow?" asked Muriel.

"Why, didn't you know that, as far as we've got, a sense of humor is among the very latest things evolved? It's later than even many of the moral sentiments. All the higher animals have sympathies and antipathies; some of them have occasional notions of right and wrong; lots of them are playful, of course, but very few have anything like a sense of humor."

"It is interesting! Shakspere knew a thing or two! Would you believe that during all the horrible torture of the past half-year, I've sometimes had spasms of fun or bursts of music come to me in the most painful moments? At first I thought that I must be very depraved to make them possible; but by and by I came to regard them as narcotics."

"They're more healthful than that," said Calmire. "You wouldn't have mistrusted them if you hadn't had the vices of puritanism in your blood. The first need in trouble is to take what comes, naturally: trouble always tempts to self-mortification."

"I wish that I'd realized all that when I was young," said Muriel.

"'*When* you were young'? How long ago was that?"

"Not a year," said Muriel, "but you don't measure experience by time, do you? For my part, I think a fellow ceases to be young when he has it well burned into him that pleasure may destroy happiness, and that duty's the real thing, after all! —It has a queer power to brace a fellow, and even gives him now and then a gleam of something like triumph."

"Ah, yes!" exclaimed Calmire, sadly. "But while I hate to croak, there's no unkindness in telling you that you'll find humdrum daily life something very different from a triumphal procession of good resolutions. So far, you've resolved nobly, though—at least in generalities : but what are you going to do?"

"Proclaim it and stand the consequences! What

else is there for a man to do? I don't want the credit of being any better than I am."

"So you propose to proclaim your son a bastard, and to destroy that much of what chance there may be for him and his mother during the rest of their lives!"

"What chance is any one of us three entitled to?" cried Muriel, bitterly.

"*He* is entitled to the chance of the innocent; and you, and Minerva too, I trust, to the chance of the repentant."

"Hm!" muttered Muriel. "I suspect I'm an ass!"

"Well, the ass's head faced the brave way, at least," laughed Calmire. "But plainly the relief of open confession is denied you."

"Well," said Muriel, "confession or no confession, I've got to take care of the child and its mother."

"Certainly!" assented Calmire. "Do you mean marriage?"

"No. The matter is not one on that plane. Do you think I ought to try to lift it there?"

"You know I never did—at least immediately. You'd get no farther than a sham and a desecration; and no *rights* can be claimed unless they were claimed and promised *before*. But with the suicidal enthusiasm you showed a moment ago, I didn't know what you had come to."

"I had simply determined to take care of them and take the consequences. But to make marriage one, would, as you say, be to desecrate it. Its only legitimate place is as an antecedent."

"You're right. But you're undertaking a hard task."

"Yes, harder than it seemed before you showed me the need of concealment. And if it were only all working! But it's enduring, that I can't stand. Oh! can't there be any way out of it all?" cried the boy who a moment before had been exulting in his resolution to stay in.

"Not for a good while, if ever," said Calmire. "The tangle is too complex for me to see any unravelment yet. There's nothing visible but patience."

"If I could only end it all by dying for them!" murmured Muriel.

"Dying! Any fool can do that! To live and suppress one's self, is the thing that tests a man!"

"If there were only something to *do!*" cried Muriel. "But merely waiting, when one doesn't know what one is waiting for, is about as dead as death."

"Nevertheless, it's sometimes the strongest and wisest thing a man can do," said Calmire, "though sometimes it's the weakest and stupidest. But waiting should not mean idleness. That's full of dry-rot. I thought of you the other day when I had to get a carpenter to make some repairs. We build a house to rest in, and after a little while, Nature has attacked it with storm, and rust, and decay, and shrinkage, and gravity, so that we've got to get up and repair it. It's just so with our bodies and minds: the environment is constantly acting upon them, and unless they healthily react, they're rotted out. Queer how everything is a corollary of the Persistence of Force, isn't it?—even the fact that you've got to go to work to keep yourself together!   Now what is to be your first step? You'll attract attention if you're all at any one place long. Her history will be pried into, and then you'll have to move on. That will at least keep you active, though!"

"Again, the curse of Cain! A wanderer on the face of the earth!" exclaimed Muriel.

"Oh, don't indulge in that sort of thing. You've done nothing as bad as that. Stick to the subject!"

Calmire put his arm in Muriel's while chiding him.

"Well," said Muriel, "possibly I can fix myself somewhere at the centre of a circle, so to speak, and have the others make their moves on the circumference, within reach of me. All of which opens the interesting question of how much lying I've got to do. Why, when a fellow gets down, does everything conspire to push him farther?"

"Say rather," commented Calmire, "'Why, when a man runs counter to one law, does he find himself at war with the whole system?'"

"Yes, the system seems to hang together pretty well," Muriel agreed. "You pull a thread in any direction, and the first you know, the strain has got around to your own heart-strings. But Heavens and Earth! I can't go on lying and wandering all my life. What can I do? *Anything* I can do is absurd."

"Yes," responded Calmire, "that's the worst of the worst situations. The only way is to plan as little as possible. First try what seems least absurd, and then follow the indications."

"Uncle Grand, the thought has crossed my mind a thousand times that it's mere mawkishness not to reduce this to a simple question of money, pay up, and clear it off."

"Well," asked Calmire, "what do you think of that thought?"

"That it's the thought of a brute," Muriel responded promptly.

"Anything else?" queried Calmire.

"Yes. That it's the thought of a fool. The thing wouldn't stay cleared off."

"It would if you were brute enough."

"But I'm not."

"That's just where the trouble comes in," observed Calmire. "What did I write you last Fall about men's punishments not being alike? Make the best of yours, and leave the rest to the infinite possibilities of Nature. Try to ignore it," and his voice fell to a tone that had something awful in it, "and no matter what your external life may be, it will crush the soul out of you as sure as gravitation!"

Muriel pondered a moment, and then said: "Whatever externals may be, there will always—always—always be something abnormal in my life. Oh, the misery of it—the unending misery of it!"

Calmire's face was a strange study. His wider experience made him realize ramifications to the wretchedness, that the boy's imagination had not yet reached; but yet he felt that skepticism regarding *any* definite expectations for the future, which becomes habitual to men who have seen and thought much. This and a certain amused pity for the wholesale way in which the young expect either sorrow or joy, united to interfuse a faint gleam of a smile among the deep shadows of his grand features. After a minute, he said, very slowly:

"Muriel, there are very few lives—very few, if any—that reach their climax without *something* abnormal and irreparable in them. Don't get demoralized because you can never be perfectly happy. Do you know anybody who is?"

Muriel reflected a little, and then answered:

"Uncle Grand, under ordinary circumstances you're the happiest man I know."

"The nearest to happy, you mean. Well, do you want to know the secret?"

"Always behaving yourself, I suppose."

"No; that would be but half of it, even if it were true—at least as your phrase is ordinarily understood. Always *occupying* myself does much of it—always, on being attacked by painful thoughts, finding something to do, and so leaving no room in the mind for irremediable trouble."

"And yet," remonstrated Muriel, "you've told me that we ought to get growth from our troubles."

"Certainly, and perhaps the most important growth we can get, is just that power of ignoring them. Only the remediable ones should be thought about. Enough means of growth will be found in *them:* in fact, they give us the very 'something to do' that we need."

"Shouldn't we think of Aunt Amelia?"

"Yes—that we had her: not that we've lost her."

"But my one fixed trouble?" urged Muriel. "It seems irremediable: shall I give it no thought?"

"None to its irremediable features. You'll find enough remediable ones; and they'll pound your conscience hard enough, too, to keep it tender."

"Well, that seems rational," Muriel admitted.

"But you told me that work is only part of your secret of happiness. What's the rest?"

"Constantly realizing one little truth—that it's absurd to expect perfect happiness without perfect evolution—that for us, the conditions of perfect happiness don't exist. Plainly, then, the moral is to make the best of what happiness the conditions permit. No matter what Fate sends, I take all the happiness I can get (Of course selfishly trying not to forget that the most is to be got from giving it), and in spite of Fate's hard blows to us both, I do mightily enjoy my life."

He stretched out his great arms and expanded his deep chest and looked over to Muriel with a smile that made him think of Browning's Hercules —so full was it of the joy and pity of the gods.

"'*Fate's* hard blows' is a kind way of putting it—at least my part of it," said Muriel. "No! I've spoiled my life myself; and after all, there's some grim comfort in not being anybody-else's victim."

"That's honest!" exclaimed Calmire. "But this thing need not spoil your life. You've told me that you're even now able to lose yourself in what interests you. Lose yourself, then."

"What shall I do?"

"Anything that adds to the aggregate happiness."

"I may as well amuse myself, then. Thank you: I've lost all taste for that."

"Then amuse others, if you will. I should be sorry to see you become an intelligent being wholly devoted to selfish pleasure; for such a creature has always seemed to me the saddest incongruity in nature, and one of the most disgusting: I hardly know which is the worse—the pettiness of the object, or the stupidity of the way of seeking it. But it's all right if you add to the pleasure of others at the same time. Why, even yachtsmen and turfmen who advance their arts are useful; and so," he said with a smile, "is a cornet-player who delights many people."

"But why do you talk about playthings, Uncle Grand? I'm past them."

"Now stop right there, Muriel! I never knew a really big man who had no playthings, even if they were live soldiers."

"Probably I've got to put up with the cheap inspirations of ambition anyhow," Muriel muttered: "But lacking love, I lack even ambition."

"But don't despise ambition, Muriel," urged Calmire. "Surely there are noble ones. And whether you succeed or not, the work is the main thing for you. Can't you lay out something definite?"

"The country's greatest need is in politics," answered Muriel. "But I can't make myself an object of public investigation just now: so I've simply closed that career for myself!" Muriel said it bitterly, but added with a sneer: "I never had much taste for it, though. I don't like to shake hands that are seldom washed, and that's politics."

"That depends," said Calmire, "upon whether you take the cheap notion of 'a career.' It might be hard for you to get office, but lots of men have done the greatest good in politics—in the art as well as in the science, without holding office."

CHAPTER LX.

WHERE ALL ROADS MEET.

THEY stepped upon the platform at Benstock. Calmire looked at his watch and said: "We've over half an hour: let's drive to the next station." He told his men to throw back the top of the landau. Despite Calmire's attitude regarding mourning conventions, he had sent to New York for a big close carriage that he had never before used in the country, in which, alone, to follow his sister's body to the grave.

After they were seated, Muriel resumed: "Do you know, I've sometimes really thought I'd like to preach?—for the sake of teaching some other poor devils what has cost me so much to learn."

"Certainly!" responded Calmire. "Every youngster with any seriousness in him gets taken that way sometime."

"Well!" exclaimed Muriel, "at least I've made up my mind that I'm not going to pitch into the churches any more."

"You've found at last that they have their uses, have you?—even outside of charity and police?"

"Yes. Why, will you believe that I've wandered into them for help more than once of late?"

"Of course! Of course! So did I in my early time of trouble. A young man has all sorts of impulses then—grasps at every straw. But did you get any comfort?"

"Hardly, except in occasionally having the cockles of my heart warmed by a little sense of human sympathy. But I did get another thing," he added after a moment,—"a realization that a good deal of what I've struggled to through all this sweat and fire, the churches have been quietly preaching all the while."

"Yes, a good deal of it," said Calmire. "I tried to get that into your head long ago, but of course you wouldn't take it. The sort of man who needs it has to learn it for himself—as he has most things. But after a while, you'll begin to criticise the churches again. When that time comes, don't forget what seems very simple, but what, like many other simple things, it will take you a good while to really feel—I mean that, speaking broadly, to do any good, the churches have got to take pretty much the lines they do. The idea of giving most people the direct truth is simply comical. Suppose that instead of giving them the cosmogony of Moses, you were to try to make them understand evolution; suppose that instead of the power and wisdom of God, you were to try to make them understand the persistence of force and the universality of law; suppose that for the jealous God who visits the sins of the fathers upon the children, you try to expound to them the law of heredity; suppose that instead of the hope of Heaven and the dread of Hell, you tried to substitute the Utilitarian basis of morals; suppose that for the mysteries of religion (and there's great stimulus to all our higher faculties in the contemplation of mystery) you try to give them a grip on the relativity of our knowledge—on the fact that both the external universe and the universe of consciousness too, float on an Infinite Mystery."

"Yes," said Muriel. "I've thought that all out. I'm not going to quarrel about the symbols any more: the moralities are about the same."

"Yes," assented Calmire, "fruits from the same experience. It's in the sanctions, that the difference comes: the Hell you've been through, couldn't be understood by a fire-and-brimstone congregation."

"No, nor my Heaven either, if it were attainable. And yet," he mused after a moment, "I don't know that I know much more about my Heaven than they do. When a fellow's in such a fix as I am, a purely philosophical Heaven won't fill the bill: when he's alone as I've been, all his ancestors cry out in his heart for God, and when his life is broken as mine is, they all cry out for another life."

"Well," said Calmire, "there's no necessity of your altogether drowning the ancestral voices: you can't escape a great deal that they assert regarding God; and as to immortality, you've no more right to deny it than they to assert it."

"I know that's the accepted lingo," responded Muriel, "but I *will* speculate, speculate, speculate: and if a fellow keeps speculating after he's broken with Christianity and all that, what's he going to do when he's all alone in the dark?"

"He'd better stop speculating and mind his business and keep out of the dark. Thinking is all very well as far as it goes : when a man first gets into deep trouble he's got to think (unless he lets somebody else do it for him), until he has a lasting sense—direct, or symbolic like Paul's, of at least four things—the enduring Verity behind all the shifting phenomena we call life, the inscrutability of consciousness, the sanctions of morality in the very structure of the universe, and the hopefulness of evolution. He'll be more comfortable, too, if he will realize the relatively limited pain in dissolution—cosmic as well as personal, I mean : that's a big subject that hasn't been gone into much. But all the same, when those foundations are once in good and firm, it's best to cover them up and leave them alone, and busy one's self in the daylight. Digging among the fundamental verities, is like mining —work for short hours. It's not as healthy as any sort of 'active work,' as they call it,—politics, hygiene, charity, education, or even business routine if a man is condemned to it. Why the churches themselves, as they improve, pay less attention to that sort of questions—less to dogma and more to morals, less to 'doctrine' and more to practice. Under our eyes they are differentiating from institutions given wholly to 'services' and preaching, into clubs where people have good times and disseminate good times among the less fortunate. Why, sects which when I was a youngster thought that cards, dancing, billiard-playing, and the theatre all came from the devil, now have annexes to their churches where all those things are used, and used *ad majorem dei gloriam*, too. On the other hand, social clubs are changing in the direction of the churches

—they enforce many moralities—they'd expel a man now for publicly making such bets as they once registered in their books ; they are getting libraries, and even annexing lecture-halls where they discuss many themes that the pulpit *now* does. Apparently both religious and social organizations are approaching some plane where they will hardly be distinguishable from each other—where religion will be what its most intelligent supporters have all along wanted it to be—a part of common life, and where common life will be imbued with religion."

"And then," exclaimed Muriel, "the churches will be out of the way!"

"That's hard to prognosticate," Calmire answered. "Yet they don't even now stand out as the mediæval cathedrals do: the modern churches are already more on the general level, partly because the level has risen. The universities are looming up with wonderful rapidity. But try to realize what the religions have done to raise the whole. And, as I intimated before, the faster they raise it, the less they occupy themselves with speculation on what is beyond our knowledge. That always was an element of weakness in them, and is in anybody. It won't do to get so engrossed in the questions underlying life, as to lessen one's usefulness in life itself : you know that nine tenths of the half-philosophical half-religious speculation is the work of weaklings and cranks."

"Why, Uncle Grand, I took it for granted that you held philosophy to be the highest possible pursuit: then it ought to be the healthiest."

"So it is, if it heeds the very principle I've mentioned, and busies itself with real things—with the relations between the laws actually discovered in matter and motion and life and mind and morals and society. A man working on actual phenomena is constantly getting his Antæan strength: but if he keeps too long away from mother Earth, in the mists of old-fashioned speculation, his power is going to ooze out fast."

"But," objected Muriel, "there have been some very strong men given to that sort of speculation."

"Yes, men strong enough to be strong in spite of it, but few of them for all their days: the best philosophers, from Aristotle through Descartes down, have devoted a large part of their time to verification too—to science. And what steadied the best of those not given to science, was their big human interest: if Socrates (who, by the way, although one of the world's most precious moral inspirations, is hardly to be called a philosopher, though he may have been something better)—if he hadn't been going around boring all sorts of people with his questions, and if Christ hadn't been going around blessing them with his sympathy, I doubt if we'd have heard much of either Socrates or Christ."

"But, Uncle Grand, why won't you call Socrates a philosopher? Surely he was a lover of wisdom."

"Bless you, boy, haven't you outgrown etymologies yet? Don't you see words getting past them every day, as knowledge changes; and only the ignorant holding on to the old meanings? Nobody who reflects what philosophy means to-day, would think of calling Socrates or Emerson a philosopher, though they were two of the greatest and most useful men that ever lived."

"Well, how did the meanings get so mixed?" asked Muriel.

"Because they were so vague. Before Evolution was discovered, Philosophy was largely a jumble of guesswork: the old 'systems' did not confine themselves to laws actually found in Nature, as Evolution is, but were to a great extent mere structures of words for pseud-ideas. They were the parents, too, of half the dogmas of the churches."

"Yes," responded Muriel, "I've often wondered why most of the teachers of philosophy are parsons." (A marked change is visible even in the few years since Muriel spoke.)

"That's plain enough," Calmire answered him. "Philosophy is, at bottom, the attempt to explain man's relations to the universe, and to deduce the correct principles of conducting them—of conduct, in short,—Phi Beta Kappa and that sort of thing, you know. Theology professes to do the same thing: and so philosophy has got all mixed up with theology, as you find them in the old-fashioned schools even to-day. But after all, the guesswork philosophy has been only a male parent of dogmas: unregulated emotions were the female ones."

"And that's why the women run the churches," Muriel commented.

"Of course—so far as they do! And for the same reason, the studious women are more apt to take to the alleged philosophies than to the real one: they give more play for fancy and the cheaper sort of feeling, and call for less real thinking-power. But don't let all that shut your eyes to the good side of the women, or the churches either. The churches seek what philosophy seeks, and they're better adapted than philosophy to the average needs."

"Well, there's something in all that," Muriel admitted. Then after a little silence he added: "But after all you've said about wasting time in speculation, you know that you let your own mind run a great deal on the same subjects that the early philosophers did."

"Yes: but only in the modern way, I hope; and not to an abnormal degree unless under abnormal circumstances. Under normal circumstances, one ought to take those subjects only subconsciously, as one does light and gravitation. I don't mean to say, though, that it's not well at times for one's consciousness to be as full as it can of the Infinite Mystery on whose surface we live. But we don't get the most and best of such moments by dropping our work for the sake of them."

"That's so: we don't! But *in* such moments, we do want more, more, both in space and time."

"You haven't yet known the best moments," responded Calmire, "if you say that in them we most long for more : for they are the nearest to complete and satisfying. In them, we feel that we are part of the All. It is in moments a degree lower, that the longing is strongest; and the same rule holds with that lofty longing as with our very lowest— temperate indulgence is wisest."

"But you *do* sometimes long for immortality, then!" exclaimed Muriel, partly with the eagerness of one who has gained a point in argument.

"I certainly do long for wider life," Calmire answered. "Did you ever turn over in your mind the inevitable narrowness of any one man's? Why, many a savage has experiences that you or I would be glad of. Probably neither of us will ever know how it feels to kill a lion as he is springing on a child. What does a man feel that a woman does? I doubt if he ever touches an ecstasy at all like that of a mother nursing her babe, though he may have some others as strong. No two people ever saw the same rainbow, no matter how close their heads were together, or the same thing, for that matter: for the identical vibrations never entered more than one eye—each sees his own little aspect, especially of general truths: each philosophy or religion has its own view of the same truths the others look at, and all philosophies and religions are vastly nearer alike than is generally realized. But as to our narrowness: think of the future in the light of the past thirty years: I would give a year of my life now, for a day five hundred years hence! Or take what the inhabitant of that planet nearest the sun must experience—what the inhabitant of the planet most remote (though probably we shouldn't want much of that)—what the myriad creatures in the myriad systems' experience, have experienced, are to experience! Yes, I do want an hour under the archéd glory in Saturn's sky, and I would like to know by what name the inhabitants of Uranus call the planet we live on. I want to know it all—to feel it all!"

"A very modern sort of a Heaven, you want!" commented Muriel, "but I don't see why it can't hold its own with the earlier varieties."

"Hold its own with the earlier varieties! Why, as far as mere imagery is concerned, the earlier people had not the knowledge to make much of a heaven. We know that there are a *myriad* heavens where 'there is no night'—in each of which a myriad suns revolve so clustered that to our paltry vision they seem but a single star. On the other hand, were our vision fine enough, it would see the molecules in a partial vacuum no bigger than your thumb, performing a dance more wondrous than that of all those suns. One wants to know it all: but the very idea of 'all' becomes more absurd with each step outward, and the circle of what was known before shrinks to nothing. The telescope comes: the heaven of our ancestors dwindles like a dying flame; the spectroscope comes, and of *its* heaven, the telescope's is but a little fraction. The microscope comes, and man marvels at a second universe: along come the electric spark and the exhausted tube, and the universe of the microscope becomes a trifle."

They were silent for a while, contemplating the sky, which was exceptionally beautiful that night, when Muriel said:

"But don't you think that, independently of the question of a future life, we may sometime establish communication up there?"

"It's not inconceivable, even now," answered Calmire, "*if* hypnotic susceptibility is telepathic. Mind, I say *if—if* you can read a mind a hemisphere off, why not read one an orbit off?"

"But we haven't the same language."

"That makes little difference. Hypnotic reading is as much by visions—sights and sounds in general, as by words. The sensitive often simply experiences fragments of what the person being read has experienced. Why, then, shouldn't we see or hear what the inhabitants of Mars, or even of the dark companion of Algol, see and hear?"

"Provided they see and hear at all," commented Muriel.

"Well!" Calmire answered, "if there are any such folk, they are probably subjected to some such vibrations as have evolved our sense of hearing, and unquestionably to influences akin to those which have evolved our senses of sight and feeling. Of course their phenomena must differ widely from ours, but probably many of them would be within the range of our appreciation.

"It *is* hard," he added in a moment, "to feel that our faculties only touch such a little film of the Infinite; and it makes it harder, to realize that in all probability other sets of faculties no better, are touching other films which our minds might be able to touch too. Our apparatus couldn't stand the other fellows' conditions, though. That needn't interfere with mutual mind-reading, however," he added, laughing.

"Yes," that's very consoling," said Muriel, laughing too. "And it seems rather simpler than the immortality method."

"Not so protracted, however," Calmire responded. "We'd have to stop reading minds when we stop other things; and at best, reading finite minds is not quite what we're after."

"Yes," said Muriel. "If we're going to dream, we may as well dream something bigger."

"Yes, only we can't dream an infinite," Calmire objected. "But mind-reading isn't exactly a dream: there's something to start on, and it hardly seems to contradict anything now. But for that matter, the dream of immortality itself doesn't necessarily contradict anything. There's no *self*-contradiction about it—like parallel lines meeting, or things equaling the same thing and not equaling each other. Neither is there any evidence against it: for there's no clear evidence in. But it's different from the other great conceptions—evolution, the Universe beyond revealed Nature, the inscrutability of consciousness, and the universality of the moral Law. They're *facts:* the evidence for them *is* in, while immortality is hardly more than a speculation. Yet while I should be glad of something better than our present evolution, and can't think much of any soul that wouldn't, nevertheless as our share in the present evolution is the best we're sure of, I think still less of any soul not ready to take its share cheerfully and make the best of it. A man hasn't learned anything until he has learned that. But Lord, how long-winded I'm getting! But we've got back to business now, and I really think you need a word or two more about these speculations—if you can put up with me?"

"If I can put up with you!" His tone was sufficient, and Calmire went on:

"Well! So far as any speculation tends to interfere with a man's hearty interest in his life here, he'd better, as a rule, leave it alone, except as implications from positive knowledge force it upon him. I see evidence written all over life and history that if Nature means anything, It means (and mark this well, there's nothing in practical philosophy more important) that this life is best treated as sufficient unto itself. There never was an honest, invigorating duty predicated on the hypothesis of another life, that .does not stand out boldly as a duty if this life is all; while upon the assumption of another life, there have been more swindles and enervations imposed on men—and especially on women—than upon any other assumption ever devised. For my part"—he paused a moment, and then continued in a lower voice with a strange vibration in it : "if I, for one, were to play with the emotional aspects of the immortality question as some people do, my intellect would simply go—where I have found a large proportion of the intellects I happen to have come across, that do play with those aspects. But," he added in his usual cheery way, "I don't want to make a dogma of the non-committal attitude. Some day, something—perhaps a trifling increase in some little vein or artery—perhaps death, may turn the shield, and we be amazed at the simplicity of all our puzzles. But probably you're in no hurry for the latter solution: few folks are as eager for Heaven as they profess to be."

"I don't care!" answered Muriel, gloomily. But then, influenced a little by the contagion of his uncle, he brightened up and said: "But don't you really play with the question of a longer life, as you've just been doing with the question of a broader one?"

"Yes, perhaps I've even more than played with it."

"Well, give us some of your notions, Uncle Grand: I'll promise not to be foolish over them."

"*My* notions? Few men have any notions to speak of that are not made out of the common stock. We simply string them together our own way. Well, here's one of my strings if you want it. Plenty of others have had strings like it. But mind! I don't say that there's any probability about them. We can only get up hypotheses at best, but there may be no harm in hanging on to them provisionally, if you're sure to hang on *only* provisionally, and don't insist upon sending to Coventry anybody who won't hang on with you. Well: it seems pretty reasonable to think that the conditions of imperfect evolution are reducible, in the last analysis, to the limitations we group as time and space. You really intimated that yourself a minute ago. Now, take away those limitations (as we get hints when the body seems to go toward death—in dreams and some somnambulistic and hypnotic conditions); and evolution as we know it, must go with the limitations; and with it, go its painful conditions. Then let consciousness survive unlimited by time and space; and let it retain (as it does not in the dreamy states) its coherent relations to the environment, and its correlating powers within itself. Then—time and space surmounted—the whole past, the whole future, the whole scale of being—of knowledge, thought, and feeling, would be open to us—all that had been—all that may be—Shakspere, Socrates, Job—Rome, Greece, Egypt—Saturn, Sirius, Aldebaran—and all not in the evanescent jumble of dreams, but systematically as in our thinking life, and real and intense as, you know, are some dreams which are more powerful, even over our physical functions, than are the more complex and disturbed emotions of our waking hours. Such a state of consciousness would seem to satisfy all the noble curiosities, and the nobler and deeper and more terrible questions of the affections."

Muriel paused a little to take it in, and then exclaimed gayly: "Quite a comfortable little scheme for immortality! Any patent on it?" His comparatively untouched young life left him responsive only to the cheerful side: not to the pathetic suggestions behind Calmire's last words and his earlier kindred ones. Even the recent death of her who had filled to Muriel his mother's place was not to him the sort of loss which made Calmire's strong soul shrink before those terrible problems.

"In some shape or other, the notion is as old as history," responded the elder man to the younger's light question. "Therefore it's not patentable. But let's look into its corollaries a little seriously."

"Uncle Grand," Muriel interrupted, "I may have seemed flippant; but I'll apologize if you say so."

"Never mind, Muriel! I'm ready, at last, to assume seriousness underneath, whenever you appear flippant. Now here's what it all leads up to—assuming such a future, what sort of an interpretation does it give to our present life? The universe is full of possibilities of growth and happiness. There's a 'call,' so to speak, for souls to enjoy them. The souls appear (probably in a myriad more ways than we know), and get started in some school, or hot-bed, or whatever you see fit to call a planet; but they appear, so far as we can conceive, under limited conditions. It seems a pity that the conditions are limited, but the wherefore seems none of our business, and we can't even conceive unlimited ones: limited they are, and it's only our business to make the best of them. Now *any* limited conditions must pall in time, and death be welcome: that's not saying that, so far, death doesn't much too often come prematurely. But it's simply mathematics that, to a being continuing to live under limited conditions, a time must eventually come when death would be welcome: therefore the only way to keep up what enjoyment the limited conditions hold, is to keep presenting them to new lives. Well! the new soul gets started under them, and the tired old one is released—but released to free swing of the Universe—free," and his tone changed, "for unlimited association with all those who have preceded us" —here he laid his hand on Muriel's, adding—"and with all those who are to follow us."

Muriel placed his other hand on his uncle's, and they were silent for a little time. At last Muriel said, but not in his former careless voice: "Uncle Grand, does that scheme hold water?"

"I never said it did! In fact, I'm not prepared to say that it's anything more than a form of words."

"How about the deterioration of the faculties in disease and old age?" asked Muriel.

"Perhaps the deterioration is only of the apparatus they work through: there are many things—

vivid dreams and memories of youth, for instance, that look as if the faculties themselves might be latent, and only the machine out of order. But," he added after a moment, "there's one more thing which, much as I avoid the questions ordinarily, each death that comes close to me makes clearer. Very likely it has been clearer to other men than it is yet to me; but I've thought much over it since I've talked with John. It's a little foreign to his habits of mind, though, and our language is so miserably inadequate that I've never tried to express it to him."

"Try to get it into me, Uncle Grand: I feel to-night as if I could catch on to anything."

"Very likely it has crossed your mind in some shape before. You know the old, old notion that our souls are but rills from the infinite soul: well, there seems growing reason to believe it— you know about different individualities existing at different times in the same body, sometimes under hypnotic suggestion, and all that. Now if, after separation from the body, the rills flow to their source, it is conceivable that they can blend there in closer union than love's fondest dreams ever imagined here. An obvious objection to such a merging in the All, is the destruction of identity: but perhaps we'd better agree on what identity is, before we begin to fear for its destruction. No one of us knows anything more about his identity than that there is an element of memory in each moment's group of thoughts and feelings, connecting it with those that have gone before; and it's a good deal to assume that either consciousness of a wider group, or participation of other consciousness in that wider group, is going to destroy anything in 'identity' that we need care for. In fact, isn't the one thing that wise people prize most—sympathy itself, a sort of blending of individualities—the participation of other souls, in one's psychical experiences; and one's own participation in those of other souls? But aside from that doubtful 'identity' difficulty, there's the other objection that in the interval between the deaths of two people who love each other, their souls may change beyond sympathy, or even beyond what we know as recognition. Now against both of those objections, we have the virtually demonstrable fact that the human forms we love, and to a great extent—perhaps entirely, the human characters we love, are but temporary and varying manifestations of the Infinite Source of all experiences. It is not inconceivable, then, that such manifestations may be accessible at will in the infinite experience independent of time and space, into which we all may become blended —that we may take up any broken thread—that we may know each other as we knew each other at any moment here, and infinitely better, and that, in knowing each other, we may know All."

"I think I get a glimmer of the conception," said Muriel, "and it's the greatest conception I ever did get a glimmer of."

"Well," responded Calmire, "don't put too much faith in glimmers. But don't ignore them either: for everything we know, was a glimmer once."

"And you believe we're going to know more about this?" asked Muriel.

"Perhaps! But all the same, you'll notice that

this scheme seems to oppose some contradictions to the one I sketched before: for the very essence of that was individuality, while this one seems to attack individuality. And so we can go on sketching schemes forever, and find each not quite consistent with the rest. It's of doubtful profit; and yet I confess that while, at your age and for a good many years later, I used to flout all idea of immortality, and think myself very bright and bold for doing it, the older I grow, the more irrational flouting it seems, and the apparent contradictions involved in it, become less significant."

"Is any of that because life seems of more value?" asked Muriel.

"No! I don't think the clinging to life increases: perhaps the contrary. It's simply because immortality seems less unreasonable. I long thought it absolutely unreasonable. The men who had charge of what they were pleased to term my education, mixed up the doctrine of immortality with so many absurd ideas, and with so many repellent views of life, that I got to despise and hate that doctrine because of such associations, and to think the denial of it a mark of a strong soul." He paused a moment, and continued: "Then the heaviest possible loss came, and changed my emotional attitude toward the doctrine, which minor losses could not do. It took me some time, however, to realize that the denial of immortality is as unphilosophic as the assertion of it; and of late years, there have come some little glimmers that may be indications in its favor."

"Such as?" queried Muriel.

"Well!" his uncle answered, "of course the subject is at the very edge of our knowledge, and therefore not easy to apprehend clearly—much less put in words. But I'll try: The question of course regards consciousness surviving the body. Now consciousness is certainly more independent of the body than we ordinarily realize. In sleep, it experiences many sensations, and quite probably all ordinary sensations, entirely independently of bodily function; and what's more, it causes bodily functions, in the entire absence of the outside physical agencies needed to cause them in our waking hours. You can think of actions of various organs, from the muscles to the viscera, in response to purely subjective impressions during sleep. Now doesn't the fact that the soul can control the body in this way, go far to support the notion that the soul makes the body, rather than the body, the soul—and that the soul uses the body, and finally relinquishes it? What's more: our worthiest and dearest impressions ordinarily come to us from those we love, through bodily organs—the eye, the ear, the pressure of hand, or lips. Now we get such experiences, apparently all kinds of them, in sleep, without the bodily organs being influenced from the outside at all. Why, then, shouldn't the disembodied soul give and receive them?"

"But," objected Muriel, "the dearest thing about them is that they come from the beloved person. As mere illusions, they would be of no value."

"Ah, now we're getting into the fog that limits all our knowledge. One might say: 'What difference if they are illusions, if we don't know them to be?' or even: 'What essential difference is there between an illusion and a reality? At the moment, the illusion is as good as the reality: it is only afterward, that the illusion fails: it may lead to subsequent conduct which will not be attended with the result that can be counted upon in what we consider the real order of Nature. But I don't see that mental impressions *need* be incoherent between themselves, or with whatever environment there may be, unless they are accompanied by a flesh-and-bone body. Neither do I see why those impressions in one consciousness whether so embodied or not, may not be produced by another consciousness no longer so embodied."

"The cold loves of wraiths—of the classic underworld!" exclaimed Muriel.

"That's all ignorant prejudice," answered his uncle, "ignorant, we'll agree; and we'll also agree that it's judgment in advance of knowledge— which I believe is the long name for prejudice. And so, for that matter, you might call much of what I've had to say on my side; but mind you, I say it all hypothetically, and I contradict no facts, while you do. It's not 'the cold loves of wraiths': you've pressed hands as warm, and lips as warm, in your dreams, as when you were awake—at least I have. Your body hasn't done it: your soul alone has done it: so why shouldn't your soul, when it has got through with your body?"

Then Calmire was silent for a full minute, at the end of which he put a hand on Muriel's arm, and said: "I'll tell you something. I've not told it to anybody yet, not even to John: for now it would upset his judgment; but I may in time. The new light on the subliminal consciousness has changed my views of dreaming."

"But," interrupted Muriel, "before you go on, tell me why they give the thing that frightful name."

"Why, they had to give it some new name because it was a new thing—newly discovered, at least. If they'd called it subconsciousness, for instance, that would have referred merely to part of the ordinary consciousness, in a quiescent condition. But the subliminal is not the ordinary consciousness: on the contrary, it's a consciousness so far 'under the threshold'—as it was named by Myers, who is something of a poet—that ordinary people are not aware of possessing it at all."

"Are those with it most in evidence, extraordinary people?" Muriel asked.

"No: in no other way, apparently, than in this susceptibility to telepathy."

"You account for all the performances of the mediums, then, by telepathy?"

"Provisionally, yes. But some people claim what I'm not yet prepared to,—that the telepathy includes communications from minds beyond the body, as well as those in it."

"And that's what you were going to tell me about? Pardon my interrupting you."

"Glad you did. Well, as I was saying to you: the discovery of the subliminal throws some very interesting (and perhaps misleading) light on dreams. I don't believe we've taken dreams seriously enough. It looks as if the part of us that dreams, were the same part that takes hypnotic suggestion and telepathic communication, and as if they might come from what we may assume to be the general consciousness at times showing itself at one with our individual consciousness. Well! The capacity for telepathic communication seems, so far, to be evolved only in limited degree, and in exceptional organisms; and to be dependent upon exceptionally favorable conditions, just like communication in the early stages of the telegraph or telephone. Supposing it to exist between us and souls that have passed beyond life as we know it, in the very nature of the case, it would probably be vague and fragmentary. From this point of view, the argument against the genuineness of the so-called "spiritual" communications, because of their insignificance, incoherence, stupidity if you please, is rather an argument *for* it.

"Foster told me that his communications were, as far as he could explain, waking visions. That he did have correct visions of things that he could not independently have known anything of in the ordinary way, I believe from my own observation, as firmly as I believe anything. At the time, I believed he got them from my own mind. I don't feel so sure regarding all of them now. Well! Another great 'medium,' still living, 'conveyed' to me a 'message' that I am a 'medium'; but I have not tried to develop the power, whatever it may be. Yet I do have very remarkable dreams—not waking ones, but in ordinary sleep, and apparently more remarkable than those of any person with whom I ever compared notes. For instance: as a child I dreamed architecture beyond any I have seen, and long before I had seen *any* to speak of; and in recent years, though when awake I have very little decorative faculty, and even though my interests are much stronger in other things than in 'objects of bigotry and virtue', I have had dreams of decorative art, beside which all the collections and color schemes I have seen, are mere nothings. Now I can't conceive that I, who am no artist, ever *created* those visions. If I must frame a phrase to explain how they got there, the best I can do is to attribute them to the same source that 'inspires' all artists—not only architects and decorators, but musicians and poets as well. 'The Muse' outside of the poet's self, is not a mere figment. I'm inclined to believe (as far as one can believe without very full verification) in 'inspiration' from what I've called 'the general consciousness.'

"Well!" he said after an almost imperceptible pause, "I hardly expected to go any farther, but talking to you sometimes is a little like talking to myself. Among my strange dreams have been three *very* strange and very personal ones that could not have been created by me, as I know myself: and therefore seem to have been created by some agency outside. Probably I shall never tell them, at least in this stage of existence, which is not saying there is any other. But if I were to assume the hypotheses I have been pouring on you, I should deduce from those dreams that conscious individuality does survive death; that, though many people have told me that they never have seen the faces of their lost ones in dreams, communications just as vivid in all respects as those of ordinary life, *can* take place with the departed in dreams, but apparently, in our present stage of evolution at least, only in very fragmentary ways, and under very exceptional conditions; that the life beyond is one of great cheerfulness and naturalness—none of the fabled austerity and strange imagery—no robes and harps and halos; but just our familiar old friends, yet relieved from some—perhaps all—of the weaknesses—the petty stupidities, anxieties and jealousies, which prevented our relations from being perfect here. Then, too, the faint indications tend to show (but tend very little, I'm bound to say) that the subliminal consciousness, whether tied to the body or freed from it, holds all that the ordinary consciousness holds, but is free from many of its limitations, including those of time and space."

"Does your experience," asked Muriel, "enable you to hazard a guess as to how those who are gone are affected by the sight of our errors and sufferings?"

"The 'guess' need relate only to the genuineness of the communications. Assuming that, the rest is legitimate deduction—that to their larger vision, our shortcomings appear so trivial and temporary as to be of no account—perhaps they have the wide charity of full knowledge—'*Savoir, c'est pardonner,*' you know. And as for themselves, they would even seem to live in a world where the false relations that constitute our evil do not exist."

After a little silence, he continued: "I had to overcome some reluctance to say anything about those experiences, but since I've overcome it, I feel like saying more. Yet I probably shall not give you details enough to prevent my talking in riddles."

"I shall be very glad if you will give me what you can."

"Well! In the first of those dreams I saw my father for the only time I can remember during the fifty years since he died. The circumstances were the very ones of all during the fifty years when I should least have expected to see him, and his mien and manner (he did not speak) were, of all possible under the circumstances, the last I should have expected: so it would seem to look as if that dream were more of his making than of mine.

"The same verdict attaches to the second dream. A hidden person whose identity I couldn't make out, seemed to be trying, against another voice's expostulations, to talk to me from another room. I asked: 'Who is it? Who is it?' and then, though I did not see anybody come in, for the first time since we parted, suddenly stood before me, as if on a low pedestal, statuesque but human and sympathetic, a familiar friend long since dead, and was gone in a flash as I awoke.

"The latest dream seemed as little of my making, and was much more remarkable. When it began, the same person was with me in the dark, touching me, but unrecognized. When I wondered who it was, the identity was revealed in a most unexpected word known to us alone, and, strange to say, in a voice that I at once felt had grown older in the many years since I had heard it last; and when light came later, the person appeared to have grown older in aspect too. Then I was told, hurriedly, things which of themselves meant little or nothing without an interpretation of one of the words— determining what noun belonged to a pronoun. Taking the only noun which, so far as I can see, can make the utterances of any consequence, they at once become enormously significant, *but* directly counter to my former convictions. Yet on reflection, I have been forced to admit that my former convictions omitted important truth, and that the utterances, interpreted as I have said, contain the truth which I had overlooked, and (this is of immense importance) a truth which I needed sadly, and which, since I obtained it, has had a fundamental and most salutary influence on my life. Another most important fact is that the speaker seemed (as did my father in the first dream, though he did not speak) entirely free from certain passions, and unconscious of certain evils, all of which, in this life, would have colored everything that could have been said on the topic spoken of in the last dream. It would seem, then, that assuming a present life of those persons, it is emancipated from many—perhaps all—of the evil conditions of this one."

"You say, Uncle Grand, that the person was present in the last two cases before you knew who it was?"

"Yes: in the first of them, in an adjoining room; and in the second, touching me in the dark. And in each case, I was greatly surprised when I found out who it was."

"It doesn't look, then, as if any of the persons had been evolved out of *your* consciousness?"

"No: such a supposition would appear very gratuitous."

"But," continued Muriel, "it was natural for you to allow for the growing old."

"No," objected his uncle, "it distinctly was not: for such vague notions as I had of the possible future life, were distinctly counter to any growing old in it."

"And what was told you was still more counter to your ideas?" again asked Muriel.

"Yes. But it required interpretation. Now *if* we have communications from another life, I need hardly repeat that they are very limited, and appear to be made with difficulty; and I wonder, of course, whether the conditions limiting them, made it impossible that that important word I have alluded to, could have been replaced by the more definite alternate which I have had to assume. But the slight uncertainty of that single word, you see, really reduces the whole matter to the basis where all our ideas of the other life rest —a basis of pure hypothesis. As far as we are yet evolved, natural law seems to confine us to that limit: apparently we can *know* nothing. But, to answer your question: under what *seems* the obvious interpretation, the communication was clearly opposed, not to mere vague notions of mine, but to clear verdicts of experience, and that communication, interpreted rightly or wrongly, has led me to realize that my very experience was largely mistaken. The dream was not only truth-telling —veridical, in the new slang — but more truth-telling than my every-day experience. And yet, don't forget, its apparent extraordinary truth is based on a hypothesis—*but* the truth I got from it is true, even if the hypothesis is mistaken. I won, even if I made a wrong play. But doesn't the result of such a play go to prove that under the circumstances it was a right one?"

"Well, Uncle Grand, it would appear simply ridiculous to claim that you made those dreams yourself."

"The impressions were made through my organism," Calmire admitted, "but whoever or whatever made them, it certainly does not seem reasonable to suppose that I made them on myself: however they should be interpreted, I cannot but believe that they contain a wisdom, a freedom from our mortal failings, and an adaptability to certain great needs of mine which could hardly have come from merely mortal intelligence." After a little silence, he went on, almost as if talking to himself: "That dream was made by some power greater than I. I certainly never had wisdom enough to make it, and it was opposite to anything I would have made. To take the credit to myself would be absurd. Years ago, the combined powers of 'Nature' as we call it, and of the person who appeared to me in that dream, created the aggregate of phenomena known to me as intercourse with that person." Then he turned to Muriel: "Doesn't it look as if the same powers made that dream—, or, to put it in everyday language, as if I received a communication from that person, and as if the person had been lifted above the limited intelligence and the passions and evils of this life?"

"I give it up, Uncle Grand: it's too new and strange for me to form conclusions about: I can only provisionally accept yours."

"Well, Muriel, of course my conclusions must be vitiated by my inclinations. I've tried to keep them as unbiased as I can, and I'm not a novice in that art, but if I must form any conclusions at all, I can form no others."

"But," objected Muriel, "one sees many people in dreams. Do you suppose they actually make the impressions?"

"It would be hard to prove that they don't," answered Calmire. Then his earnest expression, perfectly visible in the moonlight, broke up into a broad smile, as he said: "I mustn't forget to tell you that there wasn't in any of those experiences of mine, any of the austere character that our dear Puritans, and pretty much everybody else, have led us to associate with a future life. All were agreeable, and the last one, despite the deep and reliable meanings I have extracted from it, had elements that were humorous—indeed, nothing short of jolly."

"Why, Uncle Grand, at this rate some of us will be wanting to go to heaven."

"Well, it doesn't look as if we'd have to go very far—or as if we couldn't come back if we didn't like it. It would be amusing, wouldn't it, if people in another life had as good a time over us as mothers do over unrealizing babies—and did as much for us?"

"Yes, but mothers can't cure all the colics," answered Muriel grimly.

"No," Calmire assented.

Muriel pondered a while and then asked: "Do you really *believe* it was supernatural, Uncle Grand?"

"'Believe' is a pretty big word, Muriel, and often carelessly and dangerously used, and 'supernatural' merely means beyond previous knowledge. All that is or can be, must be natural, though we usually apply the term only to the little part that we're familiar with. The psychical-research men are beginning to say they believe some such communications to be real, and I don't know that the belief has hurt them any; but I don't propose to risk my sanity by holding any *belief* that can't be abundantly proved. The utmost faith that I have in such ideas, is that they *may* be true. But despite what I have often said to you from old habit, the new evidence seems to me perhaps stronger for, than the lack of better evidence is against, though my estimate varies from time to time. That's not the sort of evidence to 'believe' on. It's a hope rather than a belief, but despite the caution with which I entertain it, it has strongly and favorably influenced my life, and it makes for happiness. But if it were not for the caution, it might make for misery."

"Not much 'Help Thou mine unbelief!' in yours, is there?" exclaimed Muriel.

"No: truth must be best. Help to find that, may well be prayed for; but prayer for help to believe any particular thing, may be prayer for mental destruction."

After a little silence he continued: "I suppose it's a standard old commonplace that if we really do get glimpses of immortality now, it's probably best that they are so faint and uncertain: for great absorption in the subject of a future life might take the significance out of the present one."

"So as to get a better start in the new one!" commented Muriel.

"Certainly," responded Calmire, "and in face of the strong presumption that the best way to get a start there, is to exercise the soul in the best activities here. But," he added cheerfully, after a moment, "if there's anything to know, we'll know it when the time comes; and it's wisest all around to leave it to take care of itself till then, and, as you've probably heard me say before, go about our business."

"Especially mine," exclaimed Muriel, "as it's so attractive."

"Fortunately," said his uncle, "the attractiveness of our business is none of our business. I hear the whistle. Write me as often as you can, and keep a brave heart. You've reached the point,

I think, where a life can't be altogether spoiled. Few happy men are happy in their own way : you may yet be as happy as most: in fact, you have conquered the things that make the unhappiness of most. Take care of your health, so that your appetites—spiritual and physical, will respond to every natural stimulus; keep yourself occupied; don't wait for something to turn up, but turn something up—find something worth doing, and do it hard, and you'll not often stop to think whether you're happy or not. When you get settled somewhere, I can come to see you; and what's more to the point, as I'm getting old, by that time there will be nothing here to prevent your coming back to see me. Good-bye!"

And Muriel jumped on to the car and was whirled back into his loneliness, while Calmire drove through the eloquent night, to take sympathy and comfort to others that he loved, thinking much and suffering much, but with the steadfast stars mirrored in his deep soul.

But one thing disturbed his calm. After he had said that there would be nothing to prevent Muriel's coming back, he thought, with a start, of Nina at Fleuvemont. How much would she be there? And, generous, honorable gentleman though he was, he could not help at least wondering whence might come the strong guidance that her strong young nature with its new independence of traditions, now so sorely needed.

CHAPTER LXI.

NOBLESSE OBLIGE.

THAT young lady, however, did not seem in any immediate need of guidance: for she had enough of it—not in the shape of religion or philosophy, but in a shape even more effective—that of plenty to do. She had made up her mind that for the present at least, until some suitable relative should be freed from the tangles that tended to hold them all away, she was going to do what she could for Amelia's children.

She decided, too, that, before coming home, John had got to go to some place where he would not be reminded of his loss at every turn, and to take Genevieve with him; but Nina had got so much tamed down from her habit of deciding for herself and everybody about her, that she opened her idea to Calmire, and begged him, if he approved, to manage John. He did approve, and John required no managing. He was used to controlling himself and to scorning attempts at compromise with the irremediable. He simply said:

"I'd better be within reach of you, Calmire. Things are in such shape that they won't smash up if we're both away for a few weeks. You come too."

So Calmire made some arrangements at the

factories, and, with Nina's help, at John's; and in four days the brothers and Genevieve started for the mountains, and Nina took the children home to John's.

Since the early Fall, she had wondered at the relief brought to her own sorrows by interesting herself in those of others, and during frequent long visits, she had become Amelia's effective helper in her work among the sick and needy. She had also grown very intimate with Mary Courtenay, and not only helped her in the administration of "The Home," but had herself become quite a nurse, and was very fond of exercising the art. She had got such control over the sick boy that she had seen with Muriel, that he generally recognized his illusions as illusions, and when, as was becoming more frequently the case, they were not attended with pain, he was amused by them. He had gained in spirits and strength, and Doctor Rossman was hoping for a cure.

Probably Nina would have gone to that house nearly as often as she did, even if Mrs. Walters had not talked so much about Muriel: for though she liked most of what Mrs. Walters told her, the thought of him was generally pain. Yet she would encourage the woman to run on, and then go home and be miserable over it.

The relief that Nina got from the benevolent work into which she had thrown herself, might perhaps have been greater if it had not brought her into such frequent contact with Courtenay. They had had to work together in more than one charitable scheme, and sometimes had had their sympathies drawn to some common object in ways sure to draw them toward each other. His attitude toward her was never aggressive, and he never distressed her by any exhibition of his own distress at their relations. She had even begun to wonder whether his calmness was based on the confidence in their future that he had already professed; and this was so uncomplimentary to both her judgment and her consistency, that the thought of it was a little irritating. And, too, in presence of the bravery he often showed before contagion or self-sacrifice, she had begun to wonder how, in intellectual matters, he could avoid strenuous problems, and accept for true, simply that which seemed most good and beautiful—how, where the paths that lead to the broadest views reach up rugged heights and must be followed blindly into many clouds, such a man as he should note only the level ways among the lilies—how, in short, he *would* find the universe as beneficent as he was himself. Her own enthusiasm had begun to crystallize around the realization that no mistaken belief, however beautiful it might appear, could be so precious as the homeliest truth. She had come to know the enormous difficulty and rarity of intellectual integrity—intellectual honesty, she had come to call it, and this was not complimentary to Courtenay.

In his presence, the play of so many opposing feelings was apt to keep her nature tremulous. Combinations so unstable, of course contained the elements of an explosion, and as soon as the conditions were supplied, one very naturally came.

Nina, like the rest of the people we are telling about, was not one of those creatures of romance who never break down. One morning after a night that had been restless, partly because of one of John's children being a little unwell, and before Nina got the morning nap she had intended to take after breakfasting with the children, she had been sent for to soothe young Walters. It was one of those prematurely warm days of early Spring when all the electrical tone is lowered, which are particularly hard on sensitive or diseased nerves. At such times, despite the boy's improvement, he was sure to have relapses, and as the day was specially bad, all will to reason against his illusions seemed to be relaxed by the dead air, and when Nina got to him, he was almost raving. His mother's morale was pretty well gone before she was willing to disturb Nina, and the latter found the poor woman helplessly wringing her hands, and praying to the Virgin and all the saints in a fashion which proved that her American accent was not more than a generation old, if as much. The boy, too, was moaning, and sometimes shrieking. Into this little pandemonium, Nina went with a resolute gentleness that calmed the woman as soon as she saw Nina's face, and that soon had the boy diverted and amused, and in half an hour sleeping the deep sleep of exhaustion. To interest him, she had for the first time in many months herself introduced the subject of Muriel. Six years before, when Muriel was a strapping boy and young Walters but a little chap, Muriel had flung him a pair of outgrown skates, and these had been kept when not in use, Winter and Summer, hanging, brightly polished, by the fireplace near the boy's accustomed seat. Nina, although she knew their history, seized them as one of the best things to rivet the boy's attention, and even made him put them on her feet, whose tiny proportions those of both the owners of the skates had years before grown past. She got the boy busy and diverted, but it cost her dear.

Going home at a pace doubly brisk because of her nervous excitement, she was overtaken by still quicker footsteps, whose haste jarred on her overstrained nerves. It was Courtenay.

He, too, was out of sorts, not only from the conditions which that day affected all living things, but because he had very lately undergone one of those annoyances from the over-appreciation of a female member of his congregation, to which all clergymen are subject. Through some inherent circumstances, the matter had come to the knowledge of one of his deacons—a bluff kindly old gentleman, living at his ease in Calmire, and he had half an hour before said, "I tell you what, Courtenay, you've got to get married. It'll be a great protection to you and to the congregation. A man like you will find it easy. Go ahead!" Courtenay had gone out, the half-hour before, "to walk the thing off," as his custom was, and had got his spirit again at peace with all mankind—and womankind, and was in rather a hopeful state, when he caught sight of Nina in front of him. Without asking himself why, he very naturally started to catch up with her. He found it a little harder than he had counted on, so when he was beside her, he abruptly exclaimed:

"Why, you're running away from me, Miss Wahring!"

She was in just the mood to make his speech go wrong—not only overstrained to the verge of hysteria, but, as it unfortunately happened, thinking, with justifiable satisfaction, of her success with the half-mad boy, and of a thing bolder still which had lately crossed her mind more than once. Her answer was:

"I run away from nothing."

The general drift of his recent half-formed thoughts made it natural for him to answer:

"And yet you avoid me, who bring you nothing but devotion. Oh, why," turning his beautiful pleading eyes directly to hers, "why must you?"

"Because you're not an honest man."

Children and fools tell the truth. Nina had undergone a strain that for the moment was too much for her wisdom, and she told the truth as it was in her.

There was no indignation in his gentle face, but surprise and sorrow unutterable. Its quick change brought her to herself, but the realization of what she had said, added to what she had lately undergone, was too much for her self-control. She shrieked out hysterically:

"What have I done? What have I done? Oh, my friend, forgive me, forgive me! You can! You're so noble! You're so noble!"

His heart gave a great bound, and he tried to calm her. Fortunately they were in a sequestered part of the town, where the few houses stood well back in the lots, and where the people were of a kind to be busy with their domestic affairs in the rear of the houses: so nobody but Courtenay heard her rave on:

"You don't understand! You can't understand! But let me atone! Let me atone! I know you are good and noble, and that what you think I meant, is vile and untrue! Let me atone!"

He had taken her hands, which she let him do, and was looking down kindly and soothingly into her face. He managed to make her listen to him say:

"Do calm yourself, dear friend. I know you never meant any wrong."

"Oh, but it *was* wrong—cruelly, vilely wrong!"

The shock had spent itself, she was calmer, and she started to walk, without taking from Courtenay the hand that was next him. He put it on his arm with the unconscious feeling that she was not herself, and needed support.

After a moment, her face brightened with an impulse, and she said:

"See here! I'll prove to you that I believe in you. Ask me anything: I shall assent—I am at your disposal."

"You don't love me?"

"No."

"And yet I am to presume," he asked, "that despite what you said at first (which I'll not attempt to understand now—or ever, if you prefer), you believe the kind things you said later, so fully as to be willing to trust your life to me?"

"I shall if you ask it."

He pondered a moment, and then made one of the master-strokes of his life:

"You put the greatest prize you could before me, to prove your faith that I would not take it selfishly?"

"Yes, that was my feeling—the prize *you* had thought great."

He was silent a moment, and then exclaimed: "How you have honored me! No man could ever deserve it. But I can at least act as if I did." And he gently lowered the arm on which her hand was still resting, so as to release it. Then he said: "But may I not hope yet to obtain the blessing for reasons that would make it right to have it?"

Nina was now very much herself:

"You have just proved how you can be trusted. Now I am going to trust you to believe, whether you understand it or not—for you have a genius for believing things you don't understand"—she said it with a smile which seemed to crown him —"to believe that it is a deep, deep grief to me, to have to tell you that only such reasons as influenced me just now, could ever influence me in that way. As you are too noble to avail yourself of them, I can now say that, in declining, you have acted wisely, as well as nobly. I could never make you happy; and perhaps I owe you the confidence of saying that I could not have made that strange offer, if there were anything to make *me* happy. But oh!" she added a moment later, taking his hand, "I do respect you so, though we are so different! Let me be the best friend to you that woman ever was to man; I half believe I can be, and I should consider the right to be, an honor through all my life."

For many moments he gave no answer. Then he turned to her with the expression on his face that deplored the death of what was dear—the expression he wore at the memorial meeting when he faltered in speaking of Amelia, and when Nina gave him strength to go on. This time, as his eyes met hers, she strengthened him again, and he said:

"I had a beautiful dream. I understand it now. There is something strange in the reality you offer me—something that seems to me (though the dream did too) to come from God—it is so strong and true. I feel it now for the second time. It is better than what most men call love. I am grateful, and I will try to be worthy."

"You will not have to try, my dear friend."

They walked in silence a few minutes, when she said:

"We're so different that I don't believe I can ever make you understand what it was that led me to say that vile thing to you. Yet I feel a little as if I wanted to try."

"You think an honest man believes only what he knows?"

"No: but he shouldn't try to believe in spite of what he knows. But I had no right to use that word in speaking to you, because to you it means something I did not mean. To you it means only moral honesty, to me it means both."

"You don't think I'm intellectually honest!"

"I think you intend to be. But I don't think we could ever understand each other. You know Mr. Calmire: now I'm not sure that you're not a better man than he is, but you're not as honest, in the sense I mean."

"Now I'm getting some idea of what you mean," he answered. "That man is so honest that every time I come near him, I feel weak and ashamed."

"My friend John Courtenay has no right to feel weak and ashamed before any man that ever lived, and I won't have it!" said the Nina of other days, playfully seizing his arm and stamping her foot.

A breeze soon came, and they walked on more rapidly, but in congenial silence, until they reached his corner, when he said: "May I go on with you? I want to tell you something—to prove that I welcome your friendship, by taxing it for a little sympathy, and perhaps advice."

"You make me very happy. What is it?"

"I *am* going to set up as an honest man!"

"Mr. Courtenay! What do you mean?" looking up at him.

"I mean that you've pulled the last scale from my eyes. There's been something going on in me since I knew you that I haven't told you or anybody. It began when you first told me that you could not be my wife. (It seems to me that every great growth has its root in some great suffering.) This was the way of it: I had felt, you know, that God had destined us for each other. I wanted to feel it, and it seemed good to feel it: so I did feel it. Well: your kindness and truthfulness that time

—your divine sweetness and goodness (since you've given me a friend's right to say as enthusiastic things to you as I please) got through my dense head some sense that there was a divine in you which contradicted what I had assumed to be the divine in me, and in time I came to see that it wasn't very modest to set mine up against yours."

"But, Mr. Courtenay—"

"Let me go on, please: I owe you something—very much, and it will do me good to tell you of it, and," he looked down smiling, "you're going to be the means of all the good to me you can now, aren't you?"

She reached out and took his hand and held it for an instant.

"Well," he continued, "all that set me thinking: and I realized that I believed many other things merely because I wanted to—even things at first unreasonable and repugnant to me, simply because I wanted to believe the whole system of my church. I had been taught that the harder to believe, I found anything, the more I must try to believe it. Many a night of strife and agony have I passed to crowd somewhere into my faith, things which, in the last few months, other nights of strife and agony have taken out. But I don't want to trouble you with my struggles. Perhaps you know a little of how I was brought up. My poor old father was a splendid man—a man of New England granite (we were from there originally, you know), but he had its faults as well as its virtues. Yet I honored him so! And of late years—since I have been old enough to appreciate a great sorrow brought on by his stony virtues, I have loved him so! But though I left his church for one of a more merciful faith, when I was very young, that wasn't much of a strain, and I couldn't really reason much against him while he lived. But soon after you set me thinking, he died, and among the last things he said to me was: "John, I haven't felt the *love* of God enough. Our fathers handed us down a terrible faith. I'm old now, and I see so many good men disbelieving those terrible things. Learn of Love, John.' I was learning of it!—as the poor old man little suspected," said Courtenay with the nearest approach to bitterness in his tone, that Nina had ever heard.

"Oh John!" exclaimed Nina, simply. "I'm so sorry!" She had echoed his Christian name not quite unconsciously, but with a little feeling of sympathetic spontaneity.

"Don't you be sorry a bit, dear. You've been everything to me without meaning to be."

"Not without wanting to be—in such ways," said Nina.

"Well!" exclaimed Courtenay, "I believe God did send you to me after all!—though I don't profess to know as much about His ways as I did once. Well, as I was going to say, my poor old father's last words set me thinking a great deal more, so that the next Sunday in church, I did not like the people all calling themselves 'miserable sinners'— among them my dear old mother who, I verily believe, never committed a sin in her life. Then there was the cry through the litany, of 'Spare us, spare us, good Lord!' as if God were a vengeful tyrant to be propitiated by complimentary address.

So all these things led me to ponder on the views of the men who got up our liturgy, and at last I've come to see that my views are not their views at all, or those of anybody who got up a church in the gray cold morning before our present knowledge rose. They were narrow and slavish, and they even cramped the grand image of our Master down to fit their feudal notions. I love God more, since I've got rid of so much of the foolishness that men have talked about Him. No! I can't believe as they did. And I've been reading earlier too—not in the books that left out everything that did not support the current notions, and I find that almost all the things in Christianity which anybody can call unreasonable, were simply the extravagances with which the world was filled while Christianity was taking shape, and are not peculiarly Christian at all. Those who tried to record the traditions of Christ, simply colored them with the phases of thought prevalent throughout their world, and represented Christ as saying and doing many things that he could never have said or done. And I've come to see, too, that men at different grades of knowledge must put different constructions on whatever Christ did say: and so each age hands down doctrines which later ages find absurd. Well, through all this, I've come to sympathize with the men whom, God forgive me, I've helped to persecute—the men who are making our church a church for to-day, and not for two hundred, or two thousand, years ago."

"How are you going to manage about the liturgy of two hundred years ago?" Nina thought to herself, but wisely said nothing, and Courtenay went on:

"And now, the long and short of it is, that, going back to that time when you made me—when I made myself, suffer so because of you, I owe you my intellectual emancipation, and that word means a great deal—a very great deal," he added in a tone of pathetic earnestness, "and I'm proud and happy to owe it to you."

"You're not as proud and happy as you're making me—if I could only believe myself to deserve it all, but there are too many other things working in the same direction in these days."

"Yes, and until you came, didn't they glance from me as if I'd inherited all my father's granite? No, lady fair! your magic softened the stone."

She touched his hand again.

After a minute's silence, he said : "And now to keep up my new character of an honest man, I've got to tell you something more :—that pestilent old way of believing things because I wanted to, has blinded me about you and me."

"Ah! you didn't want me so much, after all!" exclaimed Nina, still nervous enough to push a little banter between herself and the painful subject.

"Yes, I think I did, but it has all grown clear since we began talking. It's as you made me suspect long ago—I never could have made you happy, even though I'm now getting to look at things more as you do; and the consciousness of not making you happy would have made me miserable all my life—if anybody could be miserable near you. You have more thoughts than I have, and our thoughts come from different sides of things. Between us lies the old gulf that will separate Aristotelians from Platonists to the end of time—Although," he added with a laugh, "they did try to bridge it at the same time they were infusing the absurdities into the traditions of Christ: but I've done with thaumaturgies now. There *are* those two different ways of looking at things, and people born with the opposite ways can't live together as one person. I've known at least one couple to do that, and I never saw such happiness: and you must have no happiness but the best."

His single-minded devotion brought the tears to Nina's eyes, but in a moment she turned to him smiling through them, and said: "So must you have the best, John. Now that you see you have made a mistake regarding me (though some of your reasons are more complimentary than I deserve), your life is not going to be maimed, and I feel sure that it will yet be full in every respect."

"I should have to change a great deal first," he said.

"It seems to me you're learning how, and that it's far from doing you harm."

"Perhaps!" he said rather sadly, and then continued in a cheerful tone: "But I'll tell you something you can do for me. You can continue keeping me from running to extremes, as you've lately been doing: for, you know, people of those opposite kinds of mind we were talking about, make the best possible friends, if they're only broad-minded, and I'm going to be very broad-minded now!"

And Courtenay straightened himself up and

squared out his broad shoulders all in a humorous way that was almost the first healthy attempt in that direction which Nina had known him to make.

In a moment, she said, almost as if meditating: "And yet I said you were not an honest man, and you admitted it! Heaven forgive us both!" Then she looked up at his beautiful face, strengthened by his recent struggles and his new resolution, and her mind was crossed by a thought that enraged her: "How would it have been, if he had been like this a few months earlier?"

And any calm student of human nature might wonder how it might be a few years later.

CHAPTER LXII.

A HUNTER'S FIND.

SINCE Minerva had been well enough to read, she had had three letters from Muriel. In the first two he had poured out all the enthusiasm of self-sacrifice whose excesses Calmire had gently rebuked, but he had had an unconscious deference to Minerva's weak condition that prevented his burdening her with details; and the general effect on her was reassuring and sustaining.

It was a fortnight after Calmire and Muriel had separated, when Minerva received the third letter:

"I'm coming on Thursday afternoon to see you and talk with you about going away. It seems best that you should be where neither of us is known.

"What will be best next, we must wait to see; but if such happiness as is possible to yourself, and all the good that is possible for the child, do not come, it shall not be because I do not devote myself to securing them.

"Trust me.

"M. C."

"May 29, 18—."

Muriel had directed it to Huldah, writing in the corner: "For M. G."

On Wednesday afternoon, which was bright and balmy, Minerva ventured, as she had done once or twice before, to take her baby, which was now over a month old, a little way back of the house to a pretty secluded spot beside a brook. She found the infant a very amusing toy, but she was her mother's daughter, and her mother had deserted *her*.

She was sitting on a log, singing low to the child, whom she had nursed and put to sleep, when she saw a man with a rifle over his shoulder coming through the woods on the other side of the brook. She rose to conceal herself, but it was too late: the man had the far sight of one who had spent many youthful days in the fields, and four years in war. He recognized her and called out:

"Why, Minervy!"

She flushed and trembled, but sat still until he had crossed the brook on the stones, and stopped on the bank a little way from her, and stood there leaning on his gun, and smiling at her. He was a tender-souled gentleman, though rugged in speech and garb; and after his first ejaculation of surprise, and the reception by his rather slow but wonderfully sure wits of the fact that perhaps he was not wanted, he felt shy about intruding upon her.

With a tremendous effort, she spoke first:

"Well, Clint, where in the world did you come from?"

"Been up the maountain. There's been some sort of a beast up there comin' down among the sheep, and none of the folks could git him, and Jim Bellows wrote down to me, and so I went for him."

"Did you get him?"

"*Git* him? God a'mighty! He got me! My gun hung fire, so I only hurt him a little, and he got madder'n blazes and dropped down on top o' me. So I had to choke him to death."

"You choked him to death?" cried Minerva, with big staring eyes.

"Sure! He got me so that it was my throat or hisn, and I nat'r'lly preferred it to be hisn."

"Great God! Didn't he hurt you?" The idea of Clint with the beast at his throat made her almost sick.

"Scratch or two! And tore my coat considerbul," and Clint held up a sleeve that hung in strips. So did the flannel shirt under it, and there was blood on both. "Does look kind o' mussed, don't it?" he added, with a grim smile.

"Poor dear old Clint!" murmured Minerva, and he drew nearer.

Minerva hung her head and felt as if she wanted to sink into the earth.

"Why, what you got there?" said Clint, softly. "Blest if 'tain't a baby!"

Despite Clint's cautious tones, the baby had woke up, and was looking very quietly at Clint with its great serious eyes.

"Purty little thing!" said Clint, holding out a great finger to it. "May I take it? Always liked 'em."

Minerva let Clint take it, which he did with surprising skill and a tenderness that, in him, was not surprising at all.

He looked at it with great interest. "Purty little thing!" he repeated. "Where'd you git it? Hain't been married all this time and not let anybody know about it?" and he laughed pleasantly at his bovine joke.

"I'm not married;" and she hid her scarlet face in her hands. Then an idea struck her. "You shouldn't make such jokes, Clint, and make me hide my face. Of course the baby belongs where I'm staying."

Clint laughed again, and said, "Didn't mean no offence, Minervy." Then, still holding the baby, he sat down on the log beside her.

"What made you go 'way without sayin' anything or even biddin' a feller good-bye?"

"Oh, I was so miserable, Clint. Hardly anybody but you, at least among our people, was kind to me, and I got a sudden chance to come away and stay with some people near here, and just felt like slinking out of sight and hiding myself. I couldn't bear to say good-bye to you," she said, turning her great swimming brown eyes toward him, "for you'd been so good to me."

"Sho! 'Twarn't nothin'!" said Clint, putting his big right forefinger into the corner of his right eye, while the baby reposed comfortably on his left arm. "But now I've caught you," he continued, "mayn't I come to see you again?"

"You're always so good, Clint, but it's very far."

"Sakes alive! Ain't I just been further'n this to see a catamaount? And I'd a sight rather see you." And he laughed heartily again, and she managed to laugh a little with him.

She reflected that she was going away in a day or two, and that he would not be at all likely to take a second consecutive day from the mill; so there was no need of opposing him farther.

"Guess I'll have to come and glimpse at you," he persisted. "Where you stayin'?"

Her old instinct of coquetry stood her in good stead now. Turning toward him in her old saucy way, she said:

"I thought you said you'd caught me, and yet you don't know where I live. Now you've got to find that out too." Her natural impulses were strong enough to carry it out lightly, but her heart felt terribly heavy over the prospect that she was never to see this faithful friend again, and not a little over the deception she was practising upon him.

"Well," laughed Clint, feeling all the fascination of her way, "I guess you won't be harder to find than the catamaount. But here I am, losin' the train! I've got to git back to start the night-gang, and I feel a bit tuckered and don't want to have to walk the hull way. This arm with the baby hurts a little too. Good-bye! I'll find you."

He rose and kissed the baby and handed it to her. Then as he looked down on her, he almost unconsciously exclaimed, "I'd like to kiss you too!" but added in a bashful exculpatory way, "It's so long since I've seen you!"

It was a strange fact that Clint never had kissed her, or tried to: and probably he would not have thought of doing it now, if something in her attitude and expression as she took the child had not made him feel toward her exactly as he had felt when he kissed the child.

She rose, the child in her arms, and looked at him with a face that he never forgot—it was awful,—and she said, "You may if you want to, Clint," and he bent over and kissed her forehead and was gone.

He thought of that face late into the night, until he was driven to sleep by the fatigue of his morning's struggle.

When he awoke the next day, refreshed and buoyant, that face came up again and sobered him. Then with the activity of wit that a healthy man always feels while dressing in the morning, he thought over the details of his interview with Minerva—most prominent, of course, the baby; and then again came up her strengthened and saddened face. That was strange! Then, by the law of contrast, he saw her face brightened as she bantered him about finding her out. That was natural enough! But she had told him absolutely nothing. In just the same way, she had told absolutely nothing when she left the town. At the time, that too seemed strange. True, the people whom she could talk with about it, had not treated her in a way to lead her to say anything to them; but why in the world shouldn't she have said something to him? He had seen her the very night before she went; and two or three days later, he learned that the house was locked up, and a little later still, Bevans the furniture man had packed up everything and sent it to old Granzine in Massachusetts, where he had gone to live with his brother. Why had not Minerva gone there too? Clint had supposed that she had, but now that she was near, her not having spoken appeared doubly unaccountable. Then came again that face of hers when she let him kiss her the day before.

"Damned if I like it!" he said aloud—a strange thing for him. Then, after a little more fitful cogitation, he mumbled—a still stranger thing in him: "Must have had to go to livin' out and doin' nussin'. Maybe she's stuck up about lettin' me come to see her—don't want nobody to know about it—can't see her company in the parlor, maybe. That's the reason, too, that she looked so kinder ashamed and serious. But she hadn't oughter feel that way, leastways with me: ain't I her friend?"

And Clint performed the operation which more introspective people call dismissing a subject from their minds. At least he flattered himself he had, but he hadn't.

It seems almost incredible that Calmire had managed his interview with Clint the day after Muriel went away, some half year before, with such consummate tact that not even yet had Clint imagined the real situation. But Calmire's experiences in diplomacy had not weakened his natural powers; and he *had* performed just that marvelous feat.

Probably Clint could not have very readily described the feelings which, a little later, made him say again half aloud: "Poor thing! she hain't got no brother now, and her father never was worth a continental, and he ain't worth half a continental now."

A Hunter's Find.

By the time he had walked meditatively to the mill, he had come around to a repetition of substantially the same phrase with the addition: "And she ain't married! Guess I've got to look arter her myself!"

But this: "She ain't married," now insisted on coming up again, and the vision of the baby was presenting itself at intervals all along. But Clint's was not a soul to which suspicion of evil was natural; rather it was one to which it was natural when suspicion approached, to ward it off. The word "gentleman" is open to several definitions.

He had got away from the mill the day before, because of some repairs needed in the machinery. They were found to be more serious than at first supposed. The night-gang he had come home to start, had not gone on, and he found no chance that the day-gang could work. So, after fussing around a little, looking for odd jobs to make himself useful, he felt justified in turning homeward, and he walked slowly and meditatively. Before he got to his boarding-house, he had said to himself: "Here's a good chance to go out and look into this thing, and see if there's anything to be done about it."

When he got into his little sitting-room, he felt like dressing up a little more than he had to go to the mill: Clint was a spruce fellow when off duty. When he went to a closet for his clothes, his eye fell upon his gun. He seldom went to walk in the country without it. Even at this season, he could get a shot at a rabbit, and rabbits were getting to be a nuisance. Yet this time, he said to himself, without half realizing what he was saying: "Like's not another catamaount's got another lamb!" Then he turned scarlet, half with rage at the idea, and half with shame at entertaining it, and burst out: "If one has, he's too damned dirty to choke, and I guess I'd better take that thing along."

He went back from the closet and sat down, and leaned both his elbows on the table, his chin in his hands, and for some minutes looked across out of the window. His was one of those natures which move gradually, like the elemental forces, but irresistibly too, toward tremendous climaxes of love or hate. At last he arose and, with movements unnaturally slow for him, went to the closet. He paid no attention to the clothes he had first gone there for, but took the gun and started out in his work-a-day garb to find Minerva Granzine, with a grim purpose, though half defined, to succor or avenge her.

CHAPTER LXIII.

THE FINDER'S HUNT.

CLINT tried in vain to find Minerva at two houses within an easy walk of their meeting-place of the day before. As he turned away from the second place, he groaned, for Huldah Cronin's was the only house left, and Clint did not know any satisfactory method of accounting for a baby there. He had heard, too, that Huldah never would see anybody. It was not his way to turn back, though.

The negress came to the door.

"Is the lady of the house to home?" asked Clint.

"No, sah, she ain't. She done gone away."

Clint thought this was a ruse, though the woman's good-natured expression did not look like it.

"Now see here, Queen o' Night," said he, "I want to see that lady, to find out if she can put me on the track o' Miss Minervy Granzine. I've somethin' very partickler to say to Miss Granzine, and somethin' I hope she'll be very glad to hear," and by way of emphasis he unconsciously raised his gun from the floor and banged it down again.

"Isn't gwine to say it wid yo gun, is yo?" said the woman, laughing.

"No, not without she wants me to go shootin' for her," and there was a look in his blue eyes that made the woman feel timid.

"Well, 'deed, sir," she said, "Miss Huldy ain't here. She don't live here no moh."

"When did she go 'way?" asked Clint.

"A week ago, sah."

One more hopeful hypothesis about the baby excluded!

"Don't you know nothin' yerself about Miss Granzine?" said Clint, with eyes like blue steel probes. "I've got somethin' to do for her!"

"Well, sah—" began the woman in a tremor.

"Come in, Clint," rang Minerva's clear voice from upstairs. She had heard the whole colloquy through the little spaces of the cottage, had realized that Huldah's absence did not necessarily exclude the hypothesis regarding the baby which Clint had just excluded, knew that Clint would learn her own presence in some way, looked at the clock and saw that it would be five hours before Muriel was due, and decided that it was not worthwhile to make the negress fight a losing battle for concealment. She came downstairs and gave Clint her hand, and went into the parlor with him. He closed the door as he went in, which added to her nervousness.

"I didn't think you'd try to catch me so soon, and to shut me up too," were her first words.

"No more did I, but we've had to stop work to-day too, so I thought I'd come and see if I could do anything for you."

"Thank you, Clint, but you see I'm very well taken care of."

"Yes, you an' the baby."

Then he relapsed into a deliberative silence.

His sympathies generally carried him so well to the right point, that it was not his way to anticipate situations by preparation. After a brief moment, he said, with face and voice full of kindness:

"Minervy, somethin's not right. I never seen a miserabler face 'n yourn when you bid me good-bye yesterday evenin'. I know it wasn't my goin' that made you so miserable (though I wouldn't have minded if it had been), so it must be somethin' else. Now I want to know if I can't make it lighter for you somehow."

"Why, Clint," she responded, "we all have our troubles. Many women have more of them than I have. I have kindness and plenty. There's no use in my wanting anything more."

He did not like the way in which she said: "There's no use." He answered:

"You've kindness and plenty—and misery, Minervy! A good many women have all three of them things, and sometimes because they haven't any brothers or fathers to help 'em from the misery. Now ain't there nothin' I could do for you if I was your brother, Minervy?"

"Why no, Clint."

"I don't want you to tell me nothin' without you want to, and without I can do you some good. But I'd give my life for you, Minervy. Maybe I would for any woman in great trouble, or I'd take any other man's if he deserved it."

Minerva, though an adept in many dangerous things, was not an adept in deceit, or even in concealment. Her nature habitually flowed outward—flowed outward too much. She answered:

"Upon my soul I believe you would, Clint, but I don't need anybody to champion me."

"Be you in love, Minervy?"

She looked up at him with some of her old banter.

"Oh, I'm old enough to see the folly of all that, Clint."

"Mighty sorry you've had to see the folly of it!" said Clint simply.

"Oh, we all do as we grow older," Minerva forced herself to say.

"I never did," said Clint, "'n' I'm a good deal older'n you be. Sometimes a feller does the right thing the wrong way 'n' calls it foolishness, and so, I suppose, does a gal: but it's the right thing all the same." After a pause he continued slowly and more slowly until he closed his sentence with a pathetic intonation of appeal: "There's a power o' things I ought to be doin' to-day, and if I can't do nothin' for you, I'll jog along 'n' come 'n' see you again sometime, 'n' perhaps you'll let me do somethin' for you then," and, with disappointment in every motion, he reluctantly rose to go.

It was not strange that often during Minerva's wakeful nights since this kind champion had presented himself after her mother left her, the prospect of going off to live at arm's length from Muriel, had been interspersed with visions of living less remotely from Clint. She had suppressed these right loyally—with loyalty to Clint; but the exercise of that loyalty had made her none the less ready now to be affected by the tender generosity he had shown. She did not see how it could really help her situation; but nevertheless she felt a rest and tremulous joy in it, and was greatly moved by the idea that she was never to feel it again. This feeling was strong enough to overflow into an impulse—an impulse ridiculous perhaps, but one characteristic of such women, and one that could never have carried away a woman who was very mean.

"Clint," said she, "you're as good as God himself, and a great deal better for all I can see; and it makes me feel mean to part with you trying to deceive you. I know that if you suspect any secret of mine, you'll keep it, and you're so true and generous that if it could do any good, I'd trust you with the whole of it."

"I don't want it, Minervy, if it can't do you no good." But he had got it now, all the same.

"I know that, Clint."

Clint sat down again, and after some hesitation queried, "You said you wasn't married, Minervy. Wouldn't you like to be?"

"That depends," she answered.

"If any man ought to marry you, by God I'll make him!"

"Clint: marrying is for life. It wouldn't be well to force it in a moment and have to stand it always. There are things better than that."

"That's so, Minervy. You talk as if you'd been doin' a devil of a thinkin'."

"I have, Clint; and besides—"

"Besides what?"

"Never mind!"

There had been a good deal of sub-conscious speculation going on in Clint's mind during the talk. Minerva seemed to admit the fact which he had tried not to suspect, and her speaking of "kindness and plenty" turned his thoughts to the source of most of the kindness and plenty in those parts. He thought of Muriel with the rest of his family, and suddenly reflected that he had lost sight of him about the time he had lost sight of Minerva. Then he remembered his own mysterious talk with Calmire, a little before Mrs. Granzine's disappearance, and his thought was scarcely framed before he turned deadly pale and almost wailed:

"But my God! I can't kill *him!*" Then his expression changed, and he turned to her and said: "God help you, Minervy!" and he passed his hand over his forehead as if trying to rub something away.

Minerva understood and buried her face in the sofa-cushion. This was too much for Clint. He sprang to his feet and ground out between his teeth:

"But I *will* kill him!"

Minerva too sprang up, and stood before him erect and resolute as her mother:

"No you won't! He's not to blame!"

Clint had loved Minerva before, in his big protecting way, but now, for the first time, he respected her. For the first time, too, without realizing it, he felt jealous regarding her.

"You love him!"

"No I don't, and I never did, not as I love—" And she rushed back and buried her face in the sofa-cushions again.

Clint's simple mind did not change direction quickly. He was under-way in the direction of serving her, and he had momentum enough, despite her disclaimer, to reach the next natural stage in his own course :

"I'll make him marry you!"

"And make me more miserable still! We're not fit to live together. He would be terrible, terrible, terrible!" She sat up again. "He wouldn't mean to be, but he would be.—Besides—" and still again, her face went into the cushion.

And as Clint looked over at her, despite what he was suffering he became conscious, as she lay, of the rich and beautiful lines she made, of her little feet peeping out below her loose gown, and of that very atmosphere which seemed to surround her, that it would take Courtenay's purity or Calmire's philosophy to resist.

"You could make any man love you!" said Clint.

"Not him! I haven't seen him for more than six months, though he has everything done for me, and means to be good to me always. But I know now he could never love me. Oh, there are great deep places in him that I can't even see into, much less go into, and he would hate me because they would be empty. No, I wouldn't, if he would. I'm afraid of him. Besides—"

"Then by God I'll marry you myself!"

Clint's deliberate emotions had at last not only felt her power as she lay there, and reinforced his chivalry; but he had come to interpret her reiterated "besides."

"No you won't, Clint. You're too good for me, and—and I love you too much to let you."

Clint went and picked her up like a child, and sat and held her in his arms.

"Yes I will," he said. "I ain't a bit better 'n you be. Women get into trouble when men don't, that's all the difference; and your trouble has made you better 'n ever I was, but not better 'n I'm goin' to be. And I'm goin' to take you away from all this. My brother's got rich out there 'n Afriky, and I'll go out there 'n' get rich too—get as rich for you as anybody is. Guess I can handle niggers! Saw enough of 'em when I was in the army. Hello! what's that comin'?"

"It's only the pony-carriage," said Minerva, looking out over his shoulder. "The boy brings it for me to drive. But he can wait," and she turned to put her head on Clint's shoulder again, when all the reasons against putting it there rushed anew upon her, and she cried, "No, I'm not fit! You'll despise me yet," and struggled to get away. But if the heavy oak chair had suddenly grown up and held her, she could have produced just as much impression upon it.

"Keep still, Minervy," said Clint, "you hurt my sore arm. Besides, you needn't make such a fuss, for me to believe that you're brave and honest. I wouldn't have picked you up and set you here if you hadn't proved that you've come to be a bang-up square woman—And my God, what a purty one you be!" he exclaimed, as he held her off and looked into her glowing face. "That's all there is of it, 'n' I'm goin' to marry you: so put your head down an' keep still. May as well kiss me first, though," and she did kiss him, and said: "Oh Clint, I'll love you as good women love God," and probably her misery had strengthened her to do it. She kissed him again and put her head down as he had told her, and quietly wept happy tears.

Soon he said: "Now, Minervy, I'll tell you what I'm goin' to do. You're not to stay here another day. I'm goin' to drive into town with that boy. In two hours I'll be back here with Mr. Courtenay. In four hours, Mr. and Mrs. Clint Russell an' the kid 'll start for New York. So you be ready. I can come back here and straighten up things next week."

And in less than four hours, they had left the house with all she cared to take with her, and drove in a big carriage that Clint had brought, to the station beyond Benstock. Courtenay went back to town in the pony-carriage, and blushed at recalling that when, country-fashion, he kissed Minerva, he felt that he had wanted to before.

CHAPTER LXIV.

THE BEGINNING.

An hour after Courtenay had left the cottage, Muriel reached it on foot from Benstock. The day was glorious. It marked one of the first timid steps of Summer, wnich in those climes are doubly beautiful from the contrast with the cold that they banish. The air was warm and balmy, the trees were green, the birds were singing, and here and there a daisy had already peeped out.

The door stood open, and Muriel had to take a step into the hall to ring the bell placed, as the way is in those parts, in the centre of the door between the panels. The negress came.

"Where's Miss Huldah?"

"Done gone down Souf wid her husband a week ago, sah."

"Her husband! She isn't married."

"Yessah! Married just befoh she went."

"To Mr. Redfield?"

"Yessah, to Mars' Redfield!"

"Well, I'm glad to hear it!"

"Yessah!"

"Well, let me see Miss—Mrs. Granzine."

"She done gone wid *her* husband too, sah!"

"What?"

"Yessah. Wid a gemman as swears."

"Impossible!"

"Yessah. If yo's young Mars' Calmire, dis

yar letter's for yo, sah. Walk right in de parlor, sah, and hab a seat."

Muriel took the letter into the little room and read,

"Before you get this, I shall be gone where you will never hear of me again, with the only man I ever loved. I am married to Clint Russell. He offered to take the child, and I don't doubt that he would be good and kind to it always, but I love Clint too much to burden him, and you can do better for the child than we can, and he has a right to that.

"Good-bye. I hope your life will be happy. I know mine will be, and I hope you are glad of it. You never wished any harm to me, I know. And I didn't to you. Good-bye. M.

"P.S.—Clint says good-bye too."

The letter simply numbed Muriel. It took him a minute to realize it. But there was no mistake about it. Here he was—a free man, with his child upon his hands. He sat some minutes more pondering and speculating; then, to do it better, he took a few minutes more to walk up and down the room. By that time, having slept poorly the night before and having already, to avoid attention, walked from Benstock, he felt exhausted and sat down again. Since reading the letter, he had run through the whole gamut of feeling from a suggested desire to murder the child, (which suggestion, he had learned enough to laugh at,) to a pretty good imitation of parental interest in it. Yet what was to be done with it? His duties to it were the same that he had always acknowledged, and with them before him, all that he cared for most, was as far off as ever. At last, he gave up meditating from sheer incapacity to keep his tired brain working, said: "I may as well face my music," and went into the hall and rang the door-bell again. The negress appeared.

"Where's the baby?" he asked.

"Gone out wid de lady, sah!"

"What lady?"

"De lubly lady I'se sometimes seed down by de 'Home.'"

"Dear old Mary!" thought Muriel. "She's always on hand when there's trouble. Well, I'd rather have her know about it than anybody else. No Aunt Amelia now! And some woman's got to help me." Then he asked the negress:

"How in the world did she get here?"

"She rid up wid de nuss and tole de carriage to come back for her at six o'clock."

"But what made her come?"

"She 'lowed dat Miss Minervy tole her de baby was here, and she must send a nuss from de 'Home.' So she com'd herself wid de nuss to look 'round arter tings."

"Where is she?"

"Gone out wid de baby, sah, to gib it a little walk, jus' as I done tole ye. She be back soon."

"Thank you! I'll wait." And he sat down exhausted, on the platform at the foot of the stairs. The woman went to the back of the house. He leaned his overburdened head against the newel-post, thought how beautiful the coming Summer appeared through the open door, and in a minute was asleep.

The Beginning.

After a little time of oblivion, he awoke confused and as if dreaming. Before him, backed by the sunlight of the doorway, stood a figure in white, with radiant hair; on its arm, a child. It all seemed very natural, as Muriel's eyes opened upon it, and with a feeling of reverent admiration, he raised them, partly dazzled by his sleep and the glory of the Summer air, and dwelt upon the face.

When he could think for a moment, and realize who it was, and what she had done, he gave a low cry that was half a groan, and unconsciously sank forward from the steps to his knees, looking up to her as men look from thirsting death to the nearing palms. Then he put his arms around her robes and buried his face.

"Not there, Muriel!" she said, passing her free hand tenderly over his head, while, for a little, to them Time stopped.

At last he moved and took the caressing hand in both of his, and pressed it to his lips, and murmured:

"If I were but worthy! If I were but worthy!"

She answered: "You have expiated, my Love, you have expiated. Come!"

And when she raised him, while one arm held his child, she put the other around his neck and kissed him. For a moment, he held both woman and child in his embrace. Then Nina called the nurse and gave her the boy, and went out into the sunlight with Muriel.

THE END.

www.ingramcontent.com/pod-product-compliance
Lightning Source LLC
Chambersburg PA
CBHW031956220426
43664CB00005B/43